Beginning WordPress 3

Stephanie Leary

Apress®

Beginning WordPress 3

ISBN-13 (pbk): 978-1-4302-2895-0

ISBN-13 (electronic): 978-1-4302-2896-7

Printed and bound in the United States of America (POD)

President and Publisher: Paul Manning
Lead Editor: Ben Renow-Clarke
Technical Reviewer: Shelley Keith
Editorial Board: Clay Andres, Steve Anglin, Mark Beckner, Ewan Buckingham, Gary Cornell, Jonathan Gennick, Jonathan Hassell, Michelle Lowman, Matthew Moodie, Duncan Parkes, Jeffrey Pepper, Frank Pohlmann, Douglas Pundick, Ben Renow-Clarke, Dominic Shakeshaft, Matt Wade, Tom Welsh
Coordinating Editor: Laurin Becker, Fran Parnell
Copy Editor: Mary Behr
Compositor: Bytheway Publishing Services
Indexer: Toma Mulligan
Artist: April Milne
Cover Designer: Anna Ishchenko

Distributed to the book trade worldwide by Springer Science+Business Media, LLC., 233 Spring Street, 6th Floor, New York, NY 10013. Phone 1-800-SPRINGER, fax (201) 348-4505, e-mail orders-ny@springer-sbm.com, or visit www.springeronline.com.

For information on translations, please e-mail rights@apress.com, or visit www.apress.com.

Apress and friends of ED books may be purchased in bulk for academic, corporate, or promotional use. eBook versions and licenses are also available for most titles. For more information, reference our Special Bulk Sales–eBook Licensing web page at www.apress.com/info/bulksales.

The source code for this book is available to readers at www.apress.com. You will need to answer questions pertaining to this book in order to successfully download the code.

Contents at a Glance

Contents

About the Author

Stephanie Leary began designing websites out of boredom in high school. After earning a B.A. in English literature, she discovered that her skill with HTML had saved her from a career in the food services industry. In 2002, she became the web designer for the Texas A&M University Health Science Center, where she established accessibility and web standards. She also pioneered the use of blogs to manage press releases, columns, and newsletters. While at the HSC, she teamed up with web designers from the main University campus to offer free workshops in standards-based design and CSS. Eventually, this core group founded Uweb, a grassroots organization for web education and advocacy at Texas A&M. Stephanie now works for the University Writing Center and manages several campus departments' websites in WordPress.

After winning one of the coveted red staplers at HighEdWeb in 2005, Stephanie joined the conference's programming committee and has since overseen the tracks in Usability/Accessibility/Design and Social Media.

In 2006, Stephanie and Sarah Schroeder combined their interests in writing and web design to opened Paged Media, a freelance business catering to authors and other publishing professionals.

About the Technical Reviewer

 In ecommerce Web development since 1994, **Shelley Keith** changed gears in 2005 to become the sole Web professional on a 100-year-old public university campus with more than 3000 undergraduate students, a thriving graduate studies program, and 400 faculty and staff. Her primary focus is managing a variety of content providers and juggling the site needs of several dozen departments while also supporting recruiting and retention initiatives campuswide. She also handles all social networking and outgoing e-mail marketing communication for the entire University and has been honored with district CASE awards yearly since 2006 for her work.

Shelley is entering her fourth year on the Program Committee for the Higher Education Web Professionals (HighEdWeb) conference, is actively involved with the higher education and WordPress communities online, displays all the symptoms of Twitter addiction (@shelleykeith) and may have actually launched the first University Facebook page. Currently in the midst of a campus-wide WPMU implementation, she's incredibly happy the days of 16,000 static pages and duplicated template files are behind her.

Acknowledgments

I owe a huge debt of thanks to Andrew Nacin, Andrea Rennick, Matt Mertz, Brad Williams, Dion Hulse, Ptah Dunbar, and Jared Atchison for hanging out in IRC and on Twitter, providing lots of help and encouragement.

Thanks also go to Sarah Schroeder for early feedback on the manuscript, and to Fletcher Comstock for asking great questions that led to better answers.

I'm enormously grateful to my technical reviewer, Shelley Keith, and to my editors at Apress, Ben Renow-Clark, Fran Parnell, Steve Anglin, and Laurin Becker, for for catching all sorts of errors, large and small.

And I can't thank my husband, Michael, enough for doing the dishes, bringing me chocolate, and reminding me to get some sleep now and then. Best husband *ever*.

Introduction

This book is for people who want to use WordPress. It's for web designers who'd like to get to know WordPress a little better—or a lot better. It's for writers who have been asked to contribute content to a WordPress site, but haven't been shown how to use the software. It's for server administrators who'd like to know more about this little CMS that users are always asking them to install. It's for Drupal developers who suddenly need to write a WordPress plugin for a client this week.

If you're familiar with PHP or MySQL, or if you've used another open source content management system in the past, great! This book will take you from novice to professional. By the end, you'll know not only how to manage and customize your own site, but how to contribute your innovations back to the community by submitting plugins and themes to the central repository at wordpress.org.

If you've never touched PHP before, that's OK. Understanding arrays, for example, might be necessary if you want to write your own plugin, but not if you want to install the software and configure your site with plugins and themes. And if you do want to learn more about code, WordPress is a great place to start.

Resources

Of course, if you have questions for me, you can contact me via my own website, sillybean.net. However, WordPress is a vast, sprawling project, and there are many other places to find help.

The Forum (wordpress.org/support) is the best place to tap the collected knowledge of the entire WordPress community. If you have questions about installing WordPress with your server's configuration, or you need to know why you're seeing a particular error message, or you want to report a problem with a plugin, the Forum is the place to go.

For real-time help, you can jump in to the WordPress IRC channel, #wordpress on the irc.freenode.net server. There's usually at least one person who can answer your question or direct you to the appropriate page in the Codex.

The Codex (codex.wordpress.org) is the central source of documentation. It's a wiki, so it's a work that's perpetually in progress. If you find something missing, feel free to contribute! The Codex is huge, but there are a few pages I return to over and over again, and you'll see them referenced throughout this book.

Because the Codex is written by WordPress users and developers, it's a little haphazard, and like all open source documentation, it's not as complete as it could be. When you run across a function that isn't documented in the Codex, you can refer to the documentation in the source code itself. The code can be intimidating at first, but if you have any experience with programming references (like php.net), the inline documentation in the WordPress source code can be incredibly helpful. WordPress developer Joost de Valk has created a wonderful search tool, located at xref.yoast.com, where you can enter a function, class, variable, or constant, and go right to its origin—and documentation—in the code.

If you have an idea for improving WordPress, post it in the Ideas forum (wordpress.org/extend/ideas/). If others like your idea, it might find its way into a future version of the software!

There are thousands of plugins and themes you can use to extend WordPress. You'll find them in the central repository, wordpress.org/extend/. Throughout this book, I'll provide the specific URL for a plugin only if it can't be found easily here. If you don't see a URL, just type the name into the search box and look for an exact match.

Getting Involved in Development

If you need to report a bug in WordPress or you'd like to offer up an improvement to the core code, Trac (`core.trac.wordpress.org/`) is the place to go. You can sign in with the same account you use elsewhere on wordpress.org to search the existing tickets or open a new one.

For discussion of particular topics, there are several mailing lists (`codex.wordpress.org/Mailing_Lists`). There are lists for discussion of documentation, accessibility, plugin and/or core development (`wp-hackers`), user interface design, XML-RPC, and alpha/beta testers.

To track the day-to-day development of WordPress, you can follow the weekly developer IRC chats. You can listen in if you like—they take place in `#wordpress-dev` on the `irc.freenode.net` server—but keep in mind that the meetings follow a strict agenda and the topic is limited to development of the WordPress core code, so general support questions and discussion of themes and plugins should be taken to the #wordpress channel instead. The chat agendas and minutes are archived on the development blog (`wpdevel.wordpress.com`), where you'll also find discussion threads for topics that come up between meetings.

A word of caution

The WordPress developers are constantly improving the software. The code samples in this book were tested against the beta version 3.0, but the book is going to press just as the first release candidate comes out. Things might change! In fact, the copy of WordPress you download will look a little different than the screenshots in this book, because the developers introduced a lighter color scheme late in the game.

Check my website (`sillybean.net`) for updates and errata.

CHAPTER 1

■ ■ ■

About WordPress

WordPress has, according to the *Open Source CMS Market Share Report 2009* (www.cmswire.com/downloads/cms-market-share), become the most popular blog—and content management—system in the world. It is a flexible system that can be used to create sites for businesses, project collaborations, university departments, artist portfolios, and (of course!) personal or group blogs. It requires only PHP and a MySQL database, and it can run on Apache or IIS web servers.

But what is it, and why would you use it?

Why WordPress?

WordPress is one of many PHP/MySQL content management systems that allow content editors to use a web interface to maintain their sites instead of editing and uploading HTML files to a server. Some systems, like Movable Type and Textpattern, have reputations as good blogging platforms. Others such as Joomla, Drupal, and Expression Engine are more commonly associated with commercial or community sites.

WordPress began as a blogging tool, but early on the developers added pages as a separate content type. This opened the door for people who didn't want a blog, but did want an easy, web-based interface to create and manage web content. (And if they later decided they needed a blog after all, the world's best was just one menu click away!) Since then, the page features have evolved. Whether WordPress acts a blogging tool or a true content management system, then, depends on which content you choose to emphasize in your site.

Despite its flexibility as a simple content management system, and despite winning the Overall Best Open Source CMS Award at the 2009 Open Source CMS Awards, WordPress is still widely considered to be a blogging tool. So why would you choose WordPress over a more traditional CMS?

Easy to Set Up

WordPress is famous for its five-minute installation. In fact, if you have your database connection details in hand before you begin, it might not even take you that long! The system requirements for WordPress (discussed in more detail in the next chapter) are modest, allowing it to run on most commercial shared hosting plans that include PHP and MySQL.

WordPress comes with everything you need to set up a basic website. The core system includes:

- *Posts and pages.* In the most traditional use of WordPress, a blog (composed of posts) will feature a few "static" (but still database-driven) pages, such as "About." However, as you'll see throughout this book, you can use these two primary content types in a number of other ways.

- *Media files.* The post and page editing screens allow you to upload images, audio, video, Office documents, PDFs, and more.

- *Links.* WordPress includes a link directory, often referred to as the *blogroll.*

- *Categories and tags.* WordPress includes both hierarchical and free-form taxonomies for posts. There is a separate set of categories for links.

- *User roles and profiles.* WordPress users have five possible roles with escalating capabilities (Subscriber, Contributor, Author, Editor, and Administrator) and a very basic workflow for editorial approval. User profiles include a description, avatar, and several forms of contact information.

- *RSS, Atom, and OPML feeds.* There are RSS and Atom feeds available for just about everything in WordPress. The main feeds include recent posts and comments, but there are also feeds for individual categories, tags, authors, and comment threads. An OPML feed for links is also built in.

- *Clean URLs.* With the included .htaccess file, WordPress supports search engine-friendly URLs (or permalinks) on both Apache and IIS servers, with a system of tags that allow you to customize the link structure and several built-in configurations.

- *Spam protection.* The WordPress download package includes the Akismet plugin, which provides industrial-strength filtering of spam comments. Because it uses a central web service, it constantly learns and improves.

- *Automatic upgrades.* WordPress displays an alert when a new version is available for the core system as well as any themes or plugins you have installed. You can update any of these with the click of a button (although it's always a good idea to back up your database first).

As of version 3.0, you can easily expand your WordPress installation into a network of connected sites. The setup process is just a little more involved than the basic installation, and your host has to meet a few additional requirements, which I'll go over in chapter 13.

Easy to Use

WordPress has an amazingly user-friendly administration interface. In 2008, the WordPress team worked with designers at Happy Cog, a web design firm famous for its user-oriented approach, to streamline the interface for WordPress 2.5. Later, for version 2.7, the WordPress team incorporated suggestions from a large-scale user survey and worked with Happy Cog's Liz Danzico to refine the interface even further. The result is an intuitive system that even web novices can use with very little training. Features include:

- *Rich text editing.* WordPress includes the popular TinyMCE editor that provides you with an interface similar to Microsoft Office products. TinyMCE is not perfect, but WordPress provides a basic HTML view as an alternative. The editor includes tools to import content and remove embedded styles from Office documents.

- *Media uploads and embeds.* The content editing screens include a media uploader. You'll be prompted to provide titles, captions, or other metadata based on the file type, and you can easily link to the media files or insert them directly into the document. WordPress also includes a basic image editor that allows you to rotate or resize the image. Furthermore, WordPress generates thumbnails automatically, and these can be used in place of the full-size image. Images can be aligned left, right, or center, and can include captions as well as alt text. It's easy to embed audio and video files from other sites into your content: just paste the URL as you edit, and when your post or page is published, the address will be replaced with the appropriate media player.

- *Menu Management.* You can create navigation menus as easily as you create sidebars. You can choose items from your pages, categories, and link manager; you can also add links to external content.

Easy to Extend

WordPress offers a robust template system as well as an extensive API. Anyone with experience in PHP can change a site's appearance or even modify WordPress's behavior. At www.wordpress.org/extend, you can download thousands of themes and plugins to do just this.

- *Themes* determine how content is displayed. Theme files are simply HTML documents containing some WordPress-specific PHP functions. A theme can be as simple as a single index.php file, or it might contain separate templates for posts, pages, archives, search results, and so on, with a number of included images and JavaScript files.

- *Widgets* are drag-and-drop components that can be added to your site's sidebars. For example, there are widgets to display polls, Flickr photos, and Twitter streams. You can use widgets to list pages, posts, and links; provide a search box; add arbitrary HTML; or display an RSS feed. Some themes come with their own widgets; other widgets can be installed as separate plugins.

- *Plugins* can add functions, template tags, or widgets; modify existing functions; and filter content. A plugin could add administration screens, or it might just provide a new tag you can insert into your theme files.

Advanced users can even extend the basic types of content in WordPress. Posts and pages include custom fields in addition to the basic title, content, and excerpt. The custom field user interface is not ideal for novice users, but a number of plugins exist to improve and expand it. The More Fields, Flutter, and Pods plugins all make custom fields easier to use. WordPress also supports custom content types and taxonomies. The core system does not yet include a user interface for these features, but they are available for developers to use in custom theme functions and plugins.

If the built-in category and tag system for posts isn't flexible enough for you, you can create custom taxonomies for posts, pages, or media files. In version 3.0, you can go even further and create whole new content types. I'll go over custom taxonomies and content types in Chapter 14.

To see just how far you can go using themes and plugins, visit www.buddypress.org. BuddyPress is a set of themes and plugins for WordPress that turns a basic site into a complete social network with member profiles, friends, private messages, forums, and activity streams. The transformation is amazing!

The Business Benefits of WordPress

Because WordPress has built-in support for clean URLs, canonical URLs, microformats, categories and tags, and standards-based themes, it does a stellar job of optimizing sites for search engines. At the 2009 WordCamp in San Francisco, Google's Matt Cutts explained to the audience that WordPress is the best blogging platform for search engine optimization purposes, and that choosing WordPress would be a good first step for any small business seeking to build an online presence.

Sites Built with WordPress

These are just a few examples of WordPress sites. For more, visit the Showcase at www.wordpress.org.

Personal Blogs

Many of the web's most famous designers have adopted WordPress: Jeffrey Zeldman, Eric Meyer, Jason Santa Maria, Douglas Bowman, Dan Cederholm, and Aarron Walter are a few. Famous geeks Robert Scoble, Chris Pirillo, and Leo Laporte use WordPress, too.

Celebrities using WordPress for their personal sites include Felicia Day, Kevin Smith, Stephen Fry, Martha Stewart, Emeril Lagasse, and Andy Roddick.

Figure 1-1. Author Jennifer Crusie's site

Figure 1-2. Actor Stephen Fry's site

Blog Networks

The New York Times, Edublogs, and wordpress.com are large sites with anywhere from a few dozen to hundreds of thousands of individual blogs. These sites use the Network feature in WordPress 3.0, formerly a separate product known as WordPress MU (Multi-User).

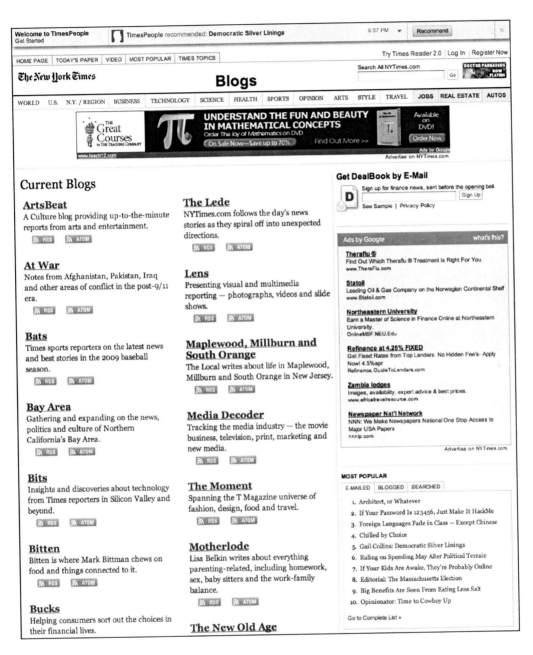

Figure 1-3. The New York Times blog network

Social Networks

Using the BuddyPress suite of plugins, a WordPress site can be turned into a complete social network in just a few minutes. Niche networks built on BuddyPress include Vivanista, Nourish Networks, Hello Eco Living, Gameserfs, and Huckjive.

Figure 1-4. Nourish Networks

Colleges and Universities

Bates College, the University of Arkansas at Little Rock, Texas Tech University, and Queens College at the University of Melbourne all use WordPress to maintain their schools' websites. A number of schools use WordPress for individual departments, such as the Yale School of Drama, Vanderbilt University Alumni Relations, University of Virginia Department of Environmental Sciences, Cornell Department of Music, Duke University, and Texas A&M University—just to name a few.

Figure 1-5. Bates College

Universities using WordPress MU to create a unified presence for their main sites and departments include the University of Maine, Southern Arkansas University, Wesleyan University, Wheaton College, and Missouri State University. Many universities also use MU to provide blog networks for students and/or faculty.

WordPress is also a popular choice among teachers, both in secondary and higher education, for providing students with blogs for their classroom writing projects.

Small Businesses

Wandering Goat Coffee and IconDock are among the many small businesses using WordPress to run their main business sites.

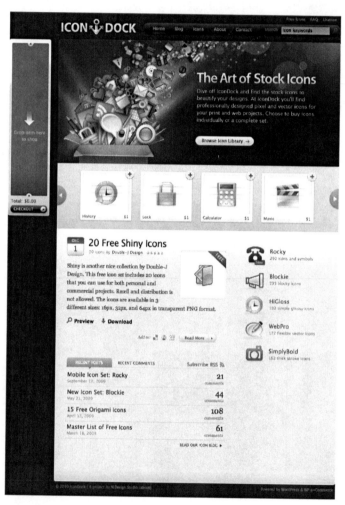

Figure 1-6. The IconDock site

WordPress Tour

When you install WordPress for the first time (see Chapter 2), you'll have a simple site dressed in the lovely new 2010 default theme. (If this theme is not your cup of tea, don't worry. In Chapter 2, I'll show you how to install other themes, and in Chapters 6 and 7, I'll show you how to create your own.)

Figure 1-7. A simple WordPress home page using the Twenty Ten default theme

Let's break down this page and see how WordPress put it together.

At the top of the page, above the image, you'll see the site title you chose when you installed WordPress. Off to the right is the tagline ("Just another WordPress blog"), which you can specify on the General Settings page (see Chapter 3).

The black area just under the image is a navigation menu. You can specify which links appear in your menu, and you can create additional menus to use elsewhere on your site, but this example shows a simple list of the pages that have been written in this WordPress site.

Below the header and the menu, there are two columns: the content area and the sidebar. This content area shows the most recent blog posts. In later chapters, I'll discuss a number of ways you can change what appears here.

This site's sidebar contains four widgets: search, calendar, blogroll, and meta. You can add and remove widgets by dragging them into the sidebars on the Widgets administration screen in the Appearances section. These four widgets are part of WordPress's built-in set. Some of the themes and plugins you install will come with additional widgets; in Chapter 8, I'll show you how to create your own.

Anatomy of a post

Take another look at the content area, and compare it to the post editing screen:

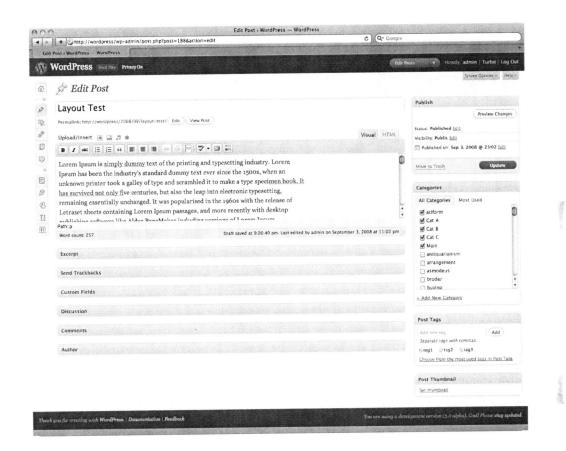

Figure 1-8. The post editing screen

Here you can see how each post is built behind the scenes. Theme files are made up of standard HTML interspersed with WordPress template tags corresponding to the post's component parts: `the_title()`, `the_content()`, `the_author()`, and so forth. On this site, the post's categories were shown ("Filed under...") but the post tags were not. If you wanted to change this, you'd locate the appropriate theme file and add `the_tags()` where you wanted the tags to appear. Template tags are formatted exactly like PHP functions—in fact, they *are* PHP functions—so if you're familiar with PHP syntax, you'll have no trouble learning to modify WordPress themes. Even if you've never used PHP before, you can begin modifying your site by copying template tags from the Codex or a tutorial. As you grow more comfortable with the language, you'll find yourself making bigger changes with confidence.

Now that you've seen how easy it is to put together a basic WordPress site, let's get started with yours!

Summary

In this chapter, I've introduced you to WordPress. I've shown you how WordPress is easy for to install, easy to customize, and easy for you (and your content authors) to use. I've discussed the accolades WordPress has won, and I've shown you just a few examples of the wide variety of sites that can be built with WordPress. I've gone over the components of a basic WordPress site and explained some of the terminology (like template tags, sidebars, and widgets) you'll see often throughout this book.

In the next chapter, I'll show you the famous five-minute installation process. I'll look at the extra configuration steps needed to expand your WordPress installation into a network of sites. I'll show you how to upgrade your site when new versions of WordPress are released, and how to install and upgrade themes and plugins. Finally, I'll go over some common installation problems and troubleshooting tips.

CHAPTER 2

■ ■ ■

Installing and Upgrading

WordPress is famous for its five-minute installation. Many commercial web hosts offer one-click installation from their account control panels. If your host does not, you can upload the WordPress files to your web directory. You can complete the installation using the web interface, or you can create a configuration file based on the sample included in the WordPress download.

System Requirements

WordPress's requirements are modest. At minimum, your server should support:

- PHP version 4.3 or greater

- MySQL version 4.0 or greater

- For clean URLs, a URL rewriting module that understands .htaccess directives, such as mod_rewrite on Apache or URL Rewrite on IIS 7

Your host should list these features and version numbers in the description of hosting plans or the support area (or both). Note that PHP 4 reached its end of life in 2008 and is no longer supported by its developers. While WordPress will run on these older versions, I highly recommend using a web host that supports PHP 5.

One-click Installation

A number of web hosts offer one-click installation of WordPress via the control panel, usually using the Fantastico application installer. In actuality, it really takes about half a dozen clicks, so I'll walk you through it. (If your host doesn't offer Fantastico or another one-click option, you'll need to see the "Installation using the Web Interface" section of this chapter.)

First, locate the Fantastico icon in your host's control panel. You'll see a list of applications that Fantastico can install for you; WordPress is in the blogs category. Once you've chosen WordPress, you'll see an informational screen letting you know how much disk space is required and that one of your MySQL databases will be used.

On the following screen, you'll be asked to fill in some information. Fantastico will create a database and user for you, but you still need to specify which of your domains (if you have more than one) you want WordPress to be installed on. You also need to specify the administrator account username, email address, and password you want to use for WordPress. Finally, you'll be asked to give your new site a name and a description. All of these things can be changed later in the WordPress settings, so it's OK if you aren't sure yet. Just make up something!

When you're ready, press Install WordPress, and in a moment you'll see a confirmation screen. Make sure you know the password (or copy it to your clipboard), then proceed to the Logging In section later in this chapter.

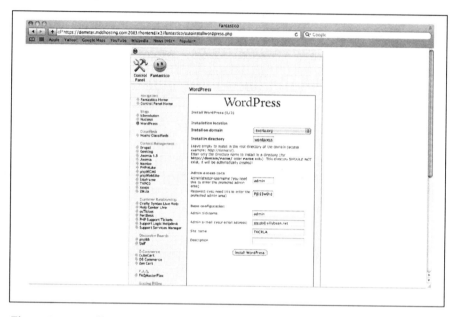

Figure 2-1. Installing WordPress with Fantastico

Installation Using the Web Interface

To install WordPress without a one-click installer like Fantastico, you'll need to create a database, upload the files, and run the installer. I'll walk through the most common ways to accomplish these tasks. First, you'll need to set up a database for WordPress to use. If your host has already created one for you, simply locate the database name, username, password, and host you were provided (usually in the welcome e-mail you received when you signed up). Otherwise, create a new database according to your host's instructions. Figure 2-2 shows how to do this in PHPMyAdmin (the MySQL web interface most commonly used by commercial hosting companies). If you are asked to specify a character set, choose UTF-8, which will support any language. If you are asked to specify a collation, choose utf8-general-ci. These are the language and character settings WordPress expects, but some older MySQL installations use more restrictive character sets. If you'll be importing content, see Chapter 5 for more detail on these settings.

If you have the option to create a new database user, you should do so. Be sure to grant the new user all permissions on your database, as shown in Figure 2-3.

Once you have your database credentials in hand, you're ready to install WordPress.

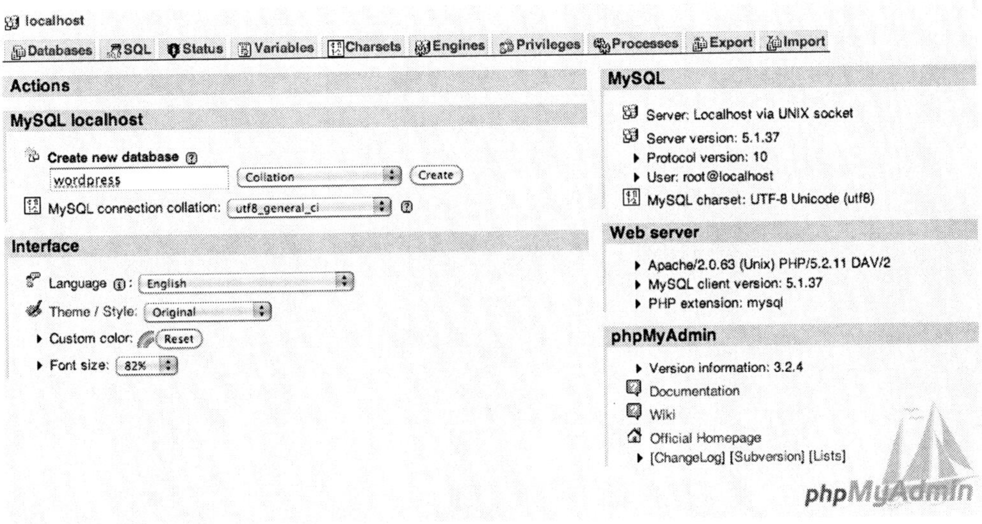

Figure 2-2. Creating a database in PHPMyAdmin

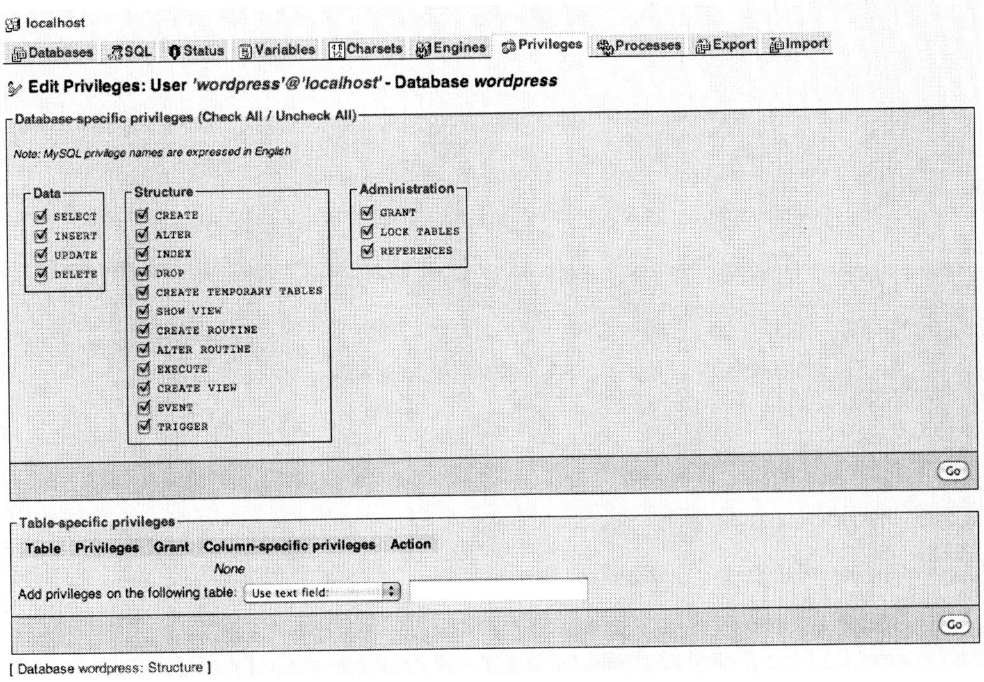

Figure 2-3. Granting user privileges on the new database in PHPMyAdmin

Download the installation package from wordpress.org and upload the files to your web host using FTP client software. Simply place the files where you want your WordPress site to be located; that is, if you want the site to be located at mysite.com, upload the files to your web root folder. If you want the site to be located at mysite.com/blog, create a folder called blog and upload the WordPress files to that folder instead.

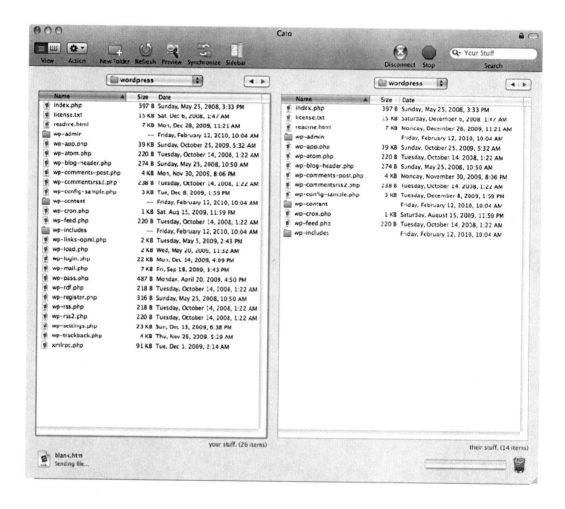

Figure 2-4. Uploading files via FTP in Transmit

Once you have uploaded the files, visit the site in a web browser. You will immediately be presented with an install screen. Fill in the requested information as shown in Figure 2-5 and press Submit to complete the installation.

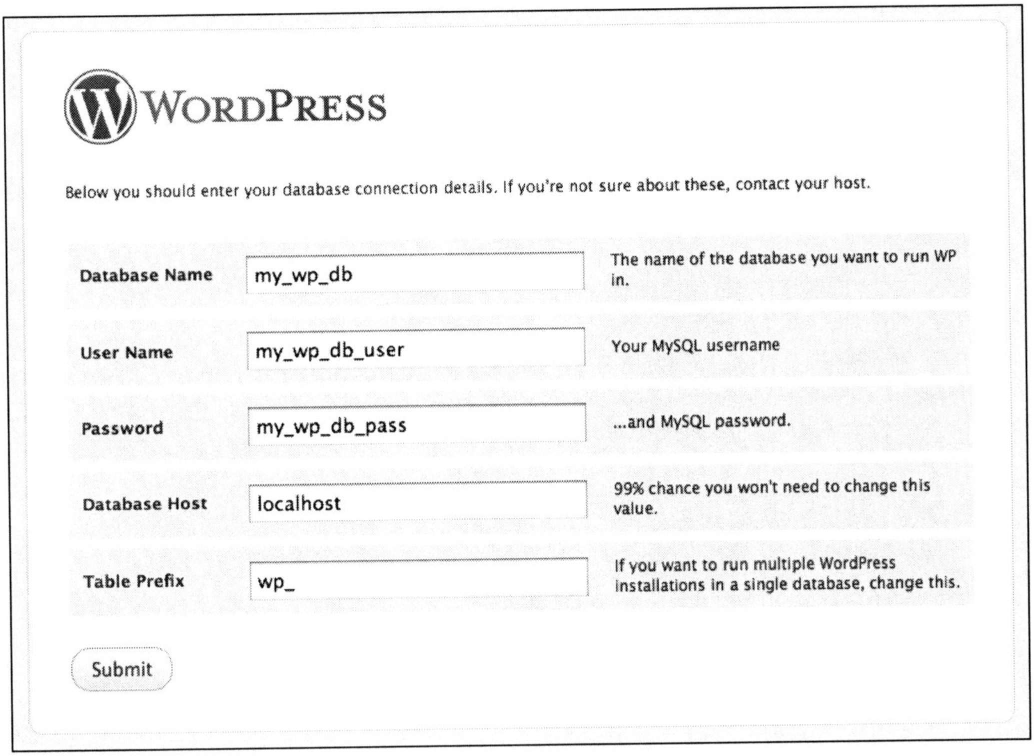

Figure 2-5. Filling in the database connection information

■ **Note** While localhost is the most common setting for the database host, your web host might use something different—even if the host was not included in the database settings you were given. GoDaddy and Dreamhost, for example, do not use localhost. Check your web host's documentation.

Logging In

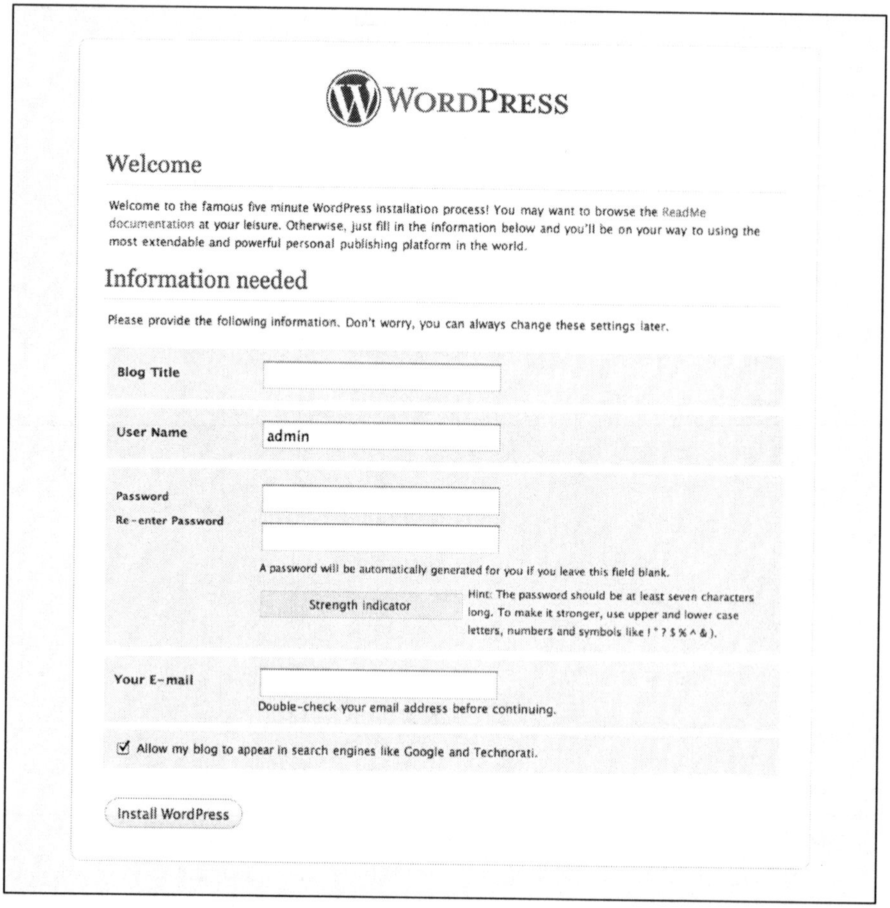

Figure 2-6. Creating the admin account

Once the installation is complete, you'll have the opportunity to create your account, as shown in Figure 2-6. In previous versions, the first user was always called 'admin,' but as of version 3.0, you can choose your own username for this account.

Log in using the password you just created (Figure 2-7). You should see your Dashboard with a message at the top prompting you to choose a more easily remembered password (Figure 2-8). We'll go over the Dashboard and the rest of the WordPress settings in the next chapter.

Figure 2-7. The WordPress login screen

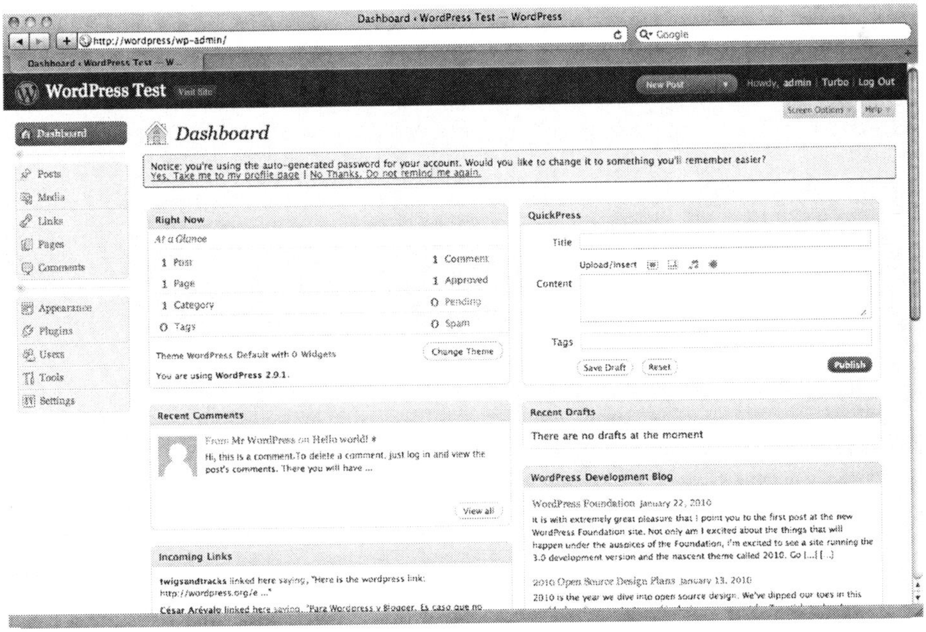

Figure 2-8. Logging in to the Dashboard for the first time

Editing and Uploading wp-config.php

If you prefer to edit configuration files rather than rely on the web-based installer, or if you need to use some of the extra configuration options (a default language other than English, for example), you can create the configuration file by hand. Download the installation package from wordpress.org. Unzip it and rename wp-config-sample.php to wp-config.php. Open wp-config.php in a text editor. The sample file contains comments instructing you how to fill in the necessary values. See Listing 2-1 for a completed example. You should fill in:

- The name of your database

- Your database user name

- Your database password

- The database host name

If you were given a port number as well as a host name, you should include the port in the host definition, separated by a colon, like so: define('DB_HOST', 'localhost:3303');

If your WordPress database will be shared with other installations or applications, you might need to change the default table prefix from 'wp_' to something less generic. For example, if your web hosting plan allows you just one MySQL database, but you need to create two independent WordPress sites on that account, you'll need to choose another table prefix for one or both of those installations.

There are many translations available for WordPress. You can change the language setting by entering a language code in the WPLANG line. However, you'll also need to download the corresponding language file. For a complete list of available languages and instructions on installing the files, see http://codex.wordpress.org/Installing_WordPress_in_Your_Language.,

Once you have filled in all the required values, your completed file should look something like Listing 2-1.

Listing 2-1: The completed wp-config.php

```
// ** MySQL settings - You can get this info from your web host ** //
/** The name of the database for WordPress */
define('DB_NAME', 'my_wp_db');

/** MySQL database username */
define('DB_USER', 'my_wp_db_user');

/** MySQL database password */
define('DB_PASSWORD', 'my_wp_db_pass');

/** MySQL hostname */
define('DB_HOST', 'localhost');

/** Database Charset to use in creating database tables. */
define('DB_CHARSET', 'utf8');

/** The Database Collate type. Don't change this if in doubt. */
define('DB_COLLATE', '');
```

```
/**#@+
 * Authentication Unique Keys.
 *
 * Change these to different unique phrases!
 * You can generate these using the {@link https://api.wordpress.org/secret-key/1.1/
WordPress.org secret-key service}
 * You can change these at any point in time to invalidate all existing cookies. This will
force all users to have to log in again.
 *
 * @since 2.6.0
 */
define('AUTH_KEY', '%DX<OoKh8Docq=$l6k&+Fy2`J-@qELUUr(U-2BvjS|xu}n=bf;9aPkt5&.FDP@,y');
define('SECURE_AUTH_KEY', '[3Y7|1jK8?iUyK_VSr5W+!xl_OOv8vG|V1+[^E4I+Ealw@<T@S?:AWK?3m#zT)bD');
define('LOGGED_IN_KEY', '4q-TS=Y+}hgM9j(bw.[C!j1!zcj{3M8:u@:STF(N R.7E6u1]Ouci FYr.$0~FJK');
define('NONCE_KEY', 'UdXil[`WffO[|+Hh*+RR&{z4l4U!T_HS/8oH{SpKe#m!Z6;I2Y,% @mW4ucSfuIQ');
/**#@-*/

/**
 * WordPress Database Table prefix.
 *
 * You can have multiple installations in one database if you give each a unique
 * prefix. Only numbers, letters, and underscores please!
 */
$table_prefix  = 'wp_';

/**
 * WordPress Localized Language, defaults to English.
 *
 * Change this to localize WordPress.  A corresponding MO file for the chosen
 * language must be installed to wp-content/languages. For example, install
 * de.mo to wp-content/languages and set WPLANG to 'de' to enable German
 * language support.
 */
define ('WPLANG', '');
/* That's all, stop editing! Happy blogging. */

/** WordPress absolute path to the Wordpress directory. */
if ( !defined('ABSPATH') )
        define('ABSPATH', dirname(__FILE__) . '/');

/** Sets up WordPress vars and included files. */
require_once(ABSPATH . 'wp-settings.php');
```

Troubleshooting

On most web hosts, PHP errors are logged rather than printed to the screen. This is good security; it prevents you from accidentally exposing your database password or other sensitive information if you mess up your code. However, this feature also prevents you from seeing what's gone wrong if there was a problem during your installation. Instead of a login screen, you'll just see a blank white page.

If you know where your PHP error log is, you can check it to see what the problem was. If you don't know where the log is, you can check your web host's documentation to find out, or you can simply turn on the error display until you resolve the problem. WordPress will not display your database connection information even if there is an error.

To display errors, add the WP_DEBUG constant to your wp-config.php file, as shown in Listing 2-2. You can put it anywhere, but I like to keep it at the top.

Listing 2-2. Debugging with wp-config.php (partial)

```
define('WP_DEBUG', true);

// ** MySQL settings - You can get this info from your web host ** //
/** The name of the database for WordPress */
define('DB_NAME', 'my_wp_db');

/** MySQL database username */
define('DB_USER', 'my_wp_db_user');
```

Visit your site again, and you should see the problem. Ignore any warnings and notices, and look for fatal errors. Is there an unknown function? Look for a missing file, or simply re-upload the entire WordPress package. Figure 2-9 shows the error messages you would see if one of the files from wp-includes were missing–in this case, capabilities.php. The first message, a warning, could be safely ignored, but in this case it provides us with a clue as to why the second error occurred. The fatal error is the showstopper. Resolve that problem, and WordPress should work correctly.

When you've solved the problem, switch the value of WP_DEBUG to false, as shown in Listing 2-3.

Listing 2-3. Turn off debugging in wp-config.php (partial)

```
define('WP_DEBUG', false);
```

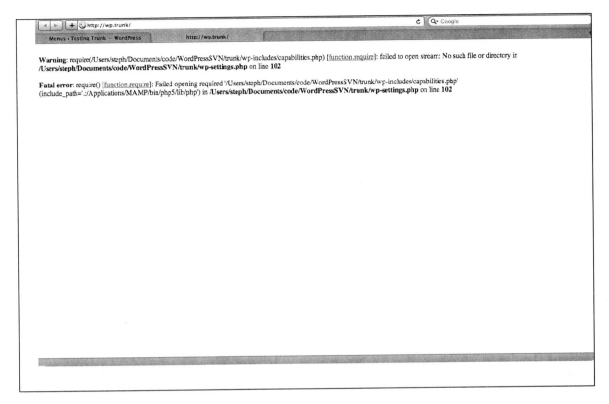

Figure 2-9. Error messages

Installing Themes

Once you have WordPress installed, you'll want to make it look good! You can change themes at any time. The new 2010 default theme in WordPress 3.0 is excellent. However, if you want something different, visit www.wordpress.org/extend/themes.

Figure 2-10. *The theme repository*

You can download the theme files and upload them to your wp-content/themes folder if you wish, or you can use the automatic theme installer. From your Dashboard, visit Appearance → Themes. On this screen, you'll see two tabs, Manage Themes and Install Themes. Under Manage Themes, you'll see all the currently installed themes. Click Install Themes, and you'll see a search screen. Here, you can search for themes by name, or you can check off a list of the features you want (color, number of columns, etc.) as shown in Figure 2-11. You'll get a list of results with links allowing you to preview and install the themes (Figure 2-12).

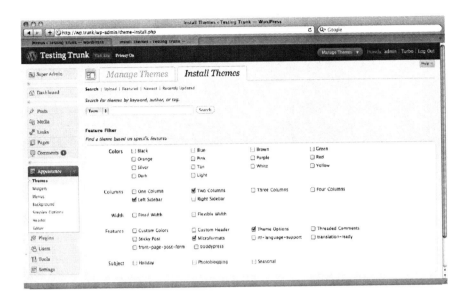

Figure 2-11. Choosing themes

Figure 2-12. Installing and previewing themes

Once the themes have been installed, they'll appear in your list of themes under Appearance. Click the theme's thumbnail image to see a preview of the theme on your site. If you like it, you can activate the theme by clicking Activate in the upper right corner (Figure 2-13).

Click Visit Site (next to your site's title at the top of the screen) to see how the theme looks.

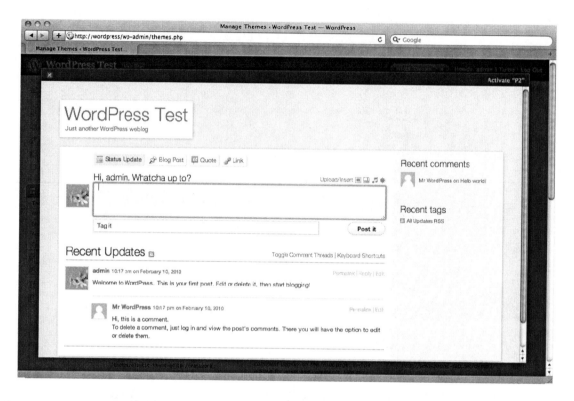

Figure 2-13. Previewing and activating a theme

Installing Plugins

While WordPress includes most of the features you would want in a basic site, sooner or later you'll probably find that you want something more. Visit www.wordpress.org/extend/plugins to see all the things–over 9,000!–you can add to your site.

Figure 2-14. The plugin repository

You can download the plugin files and upload them to your wp-content/plugins folder, just as you did with themes. However, there is also an automatic plugin installer. From your Dashboard, visit Plugins → Add New. On this screen (Figure 2-15), you can search for plugins by keyword or author name.

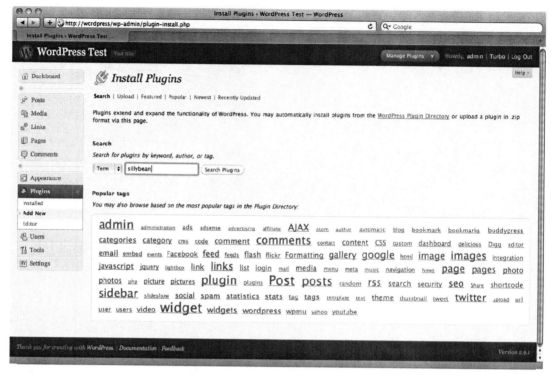

Figure 2-15. *Searching for plugins.*

Once a plugin has been installed, it will appear in your plugin list. You'll see a brief description of what the plugin does, a link to its home page, and a link to activate it.

Try activating Hello Dolly, the sample plugin that comes with WordPress. When the plugin list reloads, you'll get a message confirming the activation. You should also see a lyric from "Hello, Dolly" in the upper right corner of your screen, as shown in Figure 2-16.

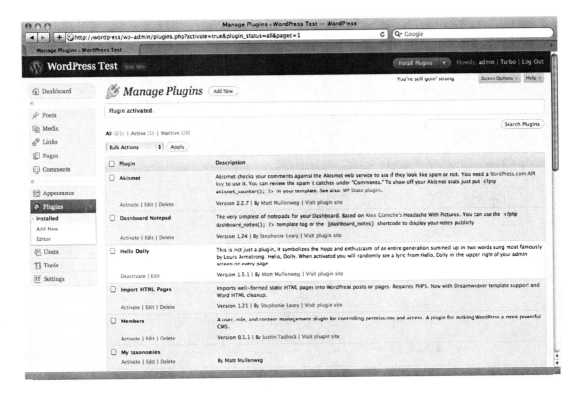

Figure 2-16. Plugin list after activating Hello Dolly

Some plugins will not activate. They might contain coding errors, or they might conflict with something else you've installed, or they might not run properly with your version of PHP. When a plugin will not activate, you'll see a message containing the PHP error that caused the problem, as shown in Figure 2-17.

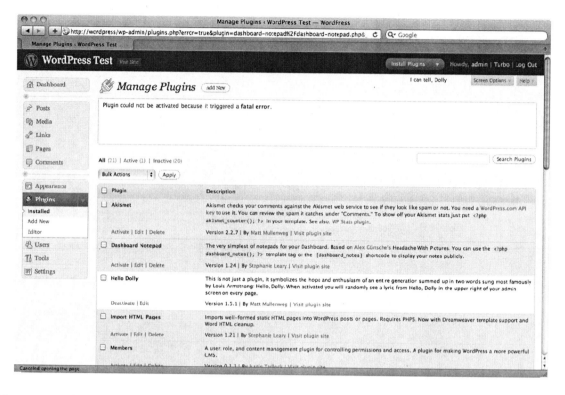

Figure 2-17. *Plugin activation error*

Plugging the gaps: Essential Plugins

There are some things every WordPress site should have:

> **DB Backup** provides a button to quickly back up specified database tables and can be scheduled to back up to a specified directory. I recommend that you create a backup of your database before importing content or upgrading WordPress to a new version.

> **Maintenance Mode** displays a simple maintenance message to everyone except administrators. At times throughout this book, I'll recommend that you put your site into maintenance mode while performing operations on the database or filesystem. While it's possible to do so without a plugin, this plugin gives you a simple button to turn maintenance mode on and off.

> **Search & Replace** allows you to replace text in chosen database fields. This plugin is especially useful after importing content (see Chapter 5).

> **Google XML Sitemaps** generates XML sitemaps (optionally gzipped) according to the sitemaps.org specification.

If you use another traffic monitoring service, chances are there's a WordPress plugin for it. **Google Analytics for WordPress** (http://yoast.com/wordpress/google-analytics/) includes the Google Analytics code in your footer and provides checkboxes for advanced Analytics options, such as tracking file downloads and outbound links. It also shows a basic traffic graph on your Dashboard. **Wordpress.com Stats** provides a graph of visitors and search queries as a Dashboard graph.

Akismet provides spam filtering for your comments. The plugin comes with WordPress but requires a key to use. You can get a free key at wordpress.com.

Contact Form 7 allows you to create e-mail contact forms with Akismet spam protection.

▓ **Note:** All the plugins mentioned in this book are listed in Appendix 1, Plugin Directory. Plugins hosted in the official plugin repository at wordpress.org/extend/plugins are referenced by name only, and you can find them by searching the repository for the plugin name. URLs are provided for any plugins that are not part of the repository or have names too generic to search.

Upgrading Plugins

New versions of plugins are released often. They'll contain new features, security improvements, or compatibility with newer versions of WordPress. When newer versions of your plugins are available, you'll see a number next to the plugin menu item on every administration screen and automatic upgrade links in your plugin list, as shown in Figure 2-18.

You can upgrade the plugins one at a time, or you can use the bulk upgrade feature to do them all at once.

Figure 2-18. *Plugin upgrades available*

Bulk Upgrades

If you have several plugins that need to be upgraded, you can process them all at once. Put a checkmark next to the plugins' names, then choose Upgrade from the Bulk Actions dropdown at the top of the plugin list (Figure 2-19). WordPress will place your site into maintenance mode automatically, then upgrade each plugin in turn. You'll see a running status report as each plugin is upgraded, and when they're all finished, WordPress will take your site out of maintenance mode.

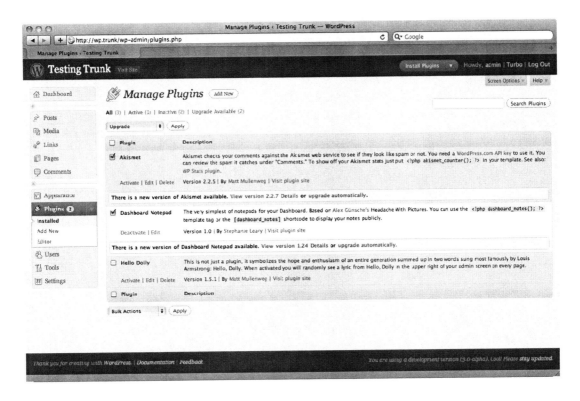

Figure 2-19. Bulk plugin upgrades

Upgrading WordPress

It's important to stay current with the new releases. In addition to providing you with new features, the updated version often includes corrections for newly discovered security problems. Keeping your installation up to date is the most important thing you can do to prevent your site from being hacked.

When a new version of WordPress is available, you'll see a banner message on every administration screen. You'll also see an announcement in the WordPress blog, which appears in one of the Dashboard widgets.

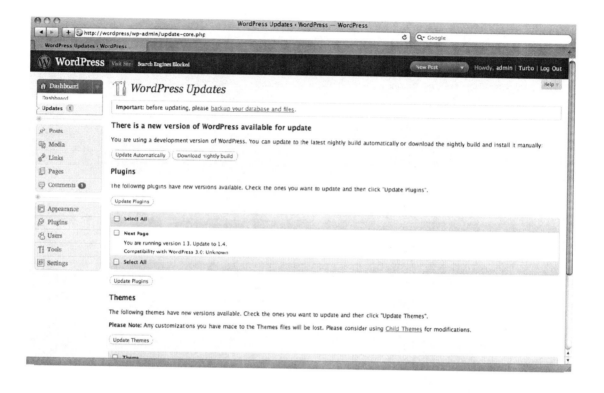

Figure 2-20. *The Update screen*

If you don't log in to your WordPress site very often, you might want to subscribe to the RSS feed or the e-mail announcement list for new releases. You can find both at wordpress.org/development/. The WordPress blog includes general news as well as release announcements. If you want alerts about new versions only, subscribe to the Releases category instead, at wordpress.org/development/category/releases/feed/.

WordPress can upgrade itself automatically, or you can download the files and upload them to your web server.

Automatic Upgrades

Automatic upgrades couldn't be simpler. The banner announcement includes a link to upgrade automatically. Follow it, and you'll be taken to the core upgrade screen (also available under Dashboard ITRA Update). Here, you'll be reminded to make a backup of your database and files before upgrading. If you have installed WP-DB-Backup, you should use it now (Figure 2-21). Otherwise, use your web host's database administration tool (such as PHPMyAdmin) to make a complete dump (structure and data) of your MySQL database. To back up your files, you'll need to use your favorite FTP client. You can back up your entire WordPress installation if you wish, or you can just copy the files that are unique to your site: wp-config.php and the wp-content directory.

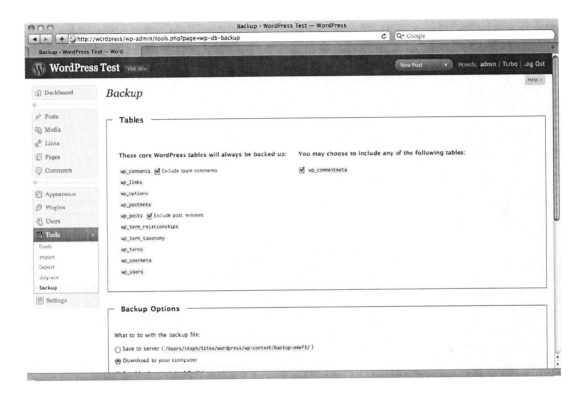

Figure 2-21. Backing up the database with the DB Backup plugin

Automatic Upgrades via FTP or SSH

In order for the automatic upgrades to work, all the files in your WordPress installation must be owned by the same user Apache runs under. If you're prompted to enter connection information when you try to upgrade, you can enter the information and let WordPress upgrade through an FTP or SSH connection, or you can change the file owner.

Changing the owner might not be the best choice if you're on a shared server, and it will be a hassle: you'll have to create a group that includes you and the Apache user so you can still write to the directory, and you'll have to make sure to change the owner again on any new files you upload.

However, if you simply fill in the requested information on the upgrade screen, it won't be saved, and you'll have to enter it again every time you upgrade the WordPress core, a theme, or a plugin.

A far better option is to save your connection information in your wp-config.php file, as shown in Listing 2-4. With your connection settings saved, WordPress won't have to prompt you every time you upgrade. You'll need to fill in the full path to your WordPress installation as well as your wp-content and plugins directories.

Listing 2-4. FTP connection settings in wp-config.php

```
define('FTP_BASE', '/home/user/wordpress/');
define('FTP_CONTENT_DIR', '/home/username/wordpress/wp-content/');
define('FTP_PLUGIN_DIR', '/home/username/wordpress/wp-content/plugins/');
define('FTP_USER', 'username');
define('FTP_PASS', 'password');
define('FTP_HOST', 'ftp.example.com:21');
define('FTP_SSL', false);
```

If your files are no longer visible to the public after you upgrade using FTP, ask your host if default permissions are set on newly uploaded files when using FTP. On many servers, a umask setting is in place. This is a way of adjusting permissions on newly uploaded files. If this is the case on your server, you'll need to ask the host to change this setting for you, or you'll need to upgrade WordPress through some other method.

If the SSH library for PHP is available on your server, the upgrade screen will give you an option to use SSH instead of FTP. To use SSH, leave the password field blank. Instead, generate a pair of keys: one public, one private. Place both files on your server, and fill in their locations to your configuration file, as shown in Listing 2-5. See www.firesidemedia.net/dev/wordpress-install-upgrade-ssh/ for more details on generating SSH keys for use in WordPress.

Listing 2-5. SSH connection settings

```
define('FTP_BASE', '/home/user/wordpress/');
define('FTP_CONTENT_DIR', '/home/username/wordpress/wp-content/');
define('FTP_PLUGIN_DIR', '/home/username/wordpress/wp-content/plugins/');
define('FTP_USER', 'username');
define('FTP_PUBKEY', '/home/username/.ssh/id_rsa.pub');
define('FTP_PRIKEY', '/home/username/.ssh/id_rsa');
define('FTP_HOST', 'ftp.example.com:21');
define('FTP_SSL', false);
```

■ **Tip:** Pass phrase protected keys do not work properly in WordPress. You should generate your SSH keys without a pass phrase.

Manual Upgrades

If you can't get automatic upgrades to work, or if you're uncomfortable letting WordPress doctor its own innards, you can always upgrade your files manually. Simply download the new version, unzip it, and transfer the files to your host, just as you did when you first installed WordPress.

To make sure I don't accidentally overwrite my themes, plugins, and uploaded media files, I always delete the wp-content directory from the downloaded package before I upload the files to my web server.

Even though it's faster to use my FTP client's synchronize feature to upload only the files that have changed, I usually delete all the standard WordPress files from the server–everything except wp-config.php and the wp-content directory–before uploading the new copies. Otherwise, strange errors can occur due to duplicated functions, as files are sometimes eliminated and functions deprecated between versions. If a function has been deprecated (and therefore moved to `wp-includes/deprecated.php`) but you still have the original function in an old copy of its original file, you'll get fatal errors when you visit the site because the function has been declared twice within WordPress.

▧ **Tip:** Make sure the `wp-includes` and `wp-admin/includes` directories are completely uploaded. When things don't work correctly in the administration screens (menus don't appear, widgets can't be moved, Quick Edit doesn't work) after an upgrade, the problems are almost always caused by missing or corrupted files in these two directories.

Moving a WordPress Site

If you ever need to move your WordPress installation from one server to another, start by reversing the installation process.

Step 1: Download the WordPress files from your server. Make sure you have a complete copy of your `wp-config.php` and `.htaccess` files and your wp-content directory.

Step 2: Export your database. If you have installed any plugins that create new tables, be sure to include them in your backup. They will share the prefix (e.g. 'wp_') you specified during the installation. You can install Austin Matzko's WP-DB-Backup plugin or use your host's control panel (e.g. PHPMyAdmin) to export your WordPress database.

Step 3: Put your old site into maintenance mode so your visitors can't continue to submit comments and trackbacks to your old database. Michael Wöhrer's Maintenance Mode plugin works well.

Step 4: Edit your `wp-config.php` file. Change the database connection settings to correspond with the values on your new server. You should also define your site and blog URLs in the configuration file, as shown in Listing 2-4. This will override the settings in your database so you can log in on your new server. (Otherwise, WordPress would constantly redirect you to your old site!) See `codex.wordpress.org/Editing_wp-config.php` for details on these and other advanced configuration settings.

Listing 2-4: Overriding database values for your site URLs in wp-config.php

```
define('WP_SITEURL', 'http://example.com);
define('WP_HOME', 'http://example.com');
```

Step 5: Upload your files, including the modified `wp-config.php`, to your new web server.

Step 6: Import the database backup you made in Step 2 to your database on your new server using your new web host's control panel tools.

Step 7: Log in to your WordPress site at its new location (e.g. `example.com/wp-admin`).

Step 8: If you changed your site's URL, your posts and pages probably contain many hardcoded paths to your uploaded media files. Use the Search and Replace plugin to change these to your new URL, as shown in Figure 2-22.

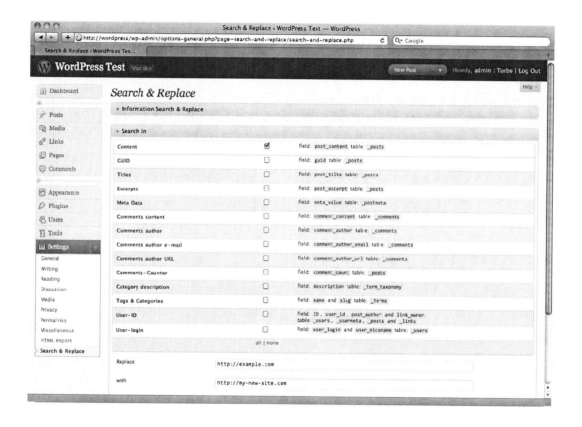

Figure 2-22. Replacing URLs with the Search & Replace plugin.

Summary

In this chapter, you've learned how to install and upgrade WordPress. I've talked about things that can go wrong and how you can correct the problems, and I've shown you a few ways to make your WordPress site more secure. You've also learned how to install themes and plugins. Lastly, I've shown you how to move a WordPress installation from one site to another.

You're ready to begin building your site! In the next chapter, I'll go over the options that will determine how your site will work.

■ ■ ■

CHAPTER 3

Dashboard and Settings

Once you've logged in and changed your password, it's time to go exploring. You've probably noticed the navigation menu along the left side of your screen. Did you notice that it has two formats? By default, each menu option displays an icon and text (as shown in Figure 3-1), and you can click each option to expand the submenu below. Once you learn your way around, though, you might find that you recognize the icons alone and it's faster to hover over the main menu options to reach the submenus. You can switch to the icons-only, hover-style menu using the small arrow dividers between sections.

Figure 3-1. The two menu styles

I'll go through the whole menu by the end of this book, but for now I'm going to focus on the first and last options: the Dashboard and Settings.

The Dashboard

Most of the time, the Dashboard is the first thing you see when you log in. It shows you a snapshot of statistical information about your site and some updates about WordPress development and plugins (see Figure 3-2).

Each box on the Dashboard (Right Now, Quickpress, Recent Comments, etc.) is a widget. If you've just installed WordPress, you'll see the widgets displayed in two columns. Click the Screen Options tab (to the top right of your Dashboard), and you'll see that you can specify the number of columns, from one to four. You can also turn off widgets altogether by unchecking them here.

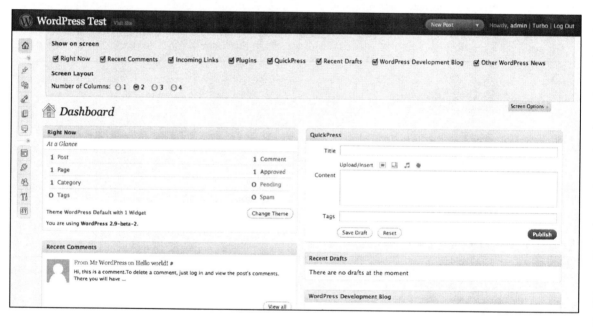

Figure 3-2. The Dashboard widgets and screen options

You can drag widgets around to rearrange them (Figure 3-3). You can also collapse them so only the titles are displayed using the down arrow that appears to the right of the title when you hover your mouse over the title area. Some of the widgets, like Incoming Links and Development News, have configurable options. You'll see a Configure link next to the arrow if you hover over these widgets' titles. Let's take a look at what some of these widgets do.

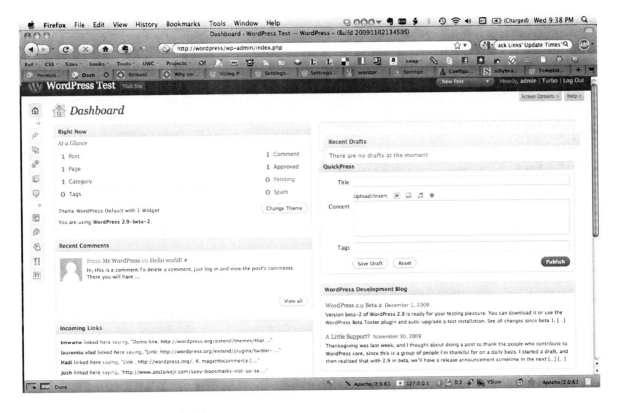

Figure 3-3. Moving Dashboard widgets

QuickPress

The QuickPress widget lets you write a blog post right from the Dashboard. It's handy but limited; you can use tags but not categories, media uploads but not the rich text editor, and you can't change the post's publication date or status. Still, if you need to dash off a quick missive to your readers, QuickPress can save you a step.

Incoming Links

The Incoming Links widget is set up to show you Google Blog Search results for your site's URL. The widget is configurable (Figure 3-4), so if you'd rather see results from some other service (like Technorati) or if you want to change the number of search results displayed, click Configure in the widget's title bar and edit the settings.

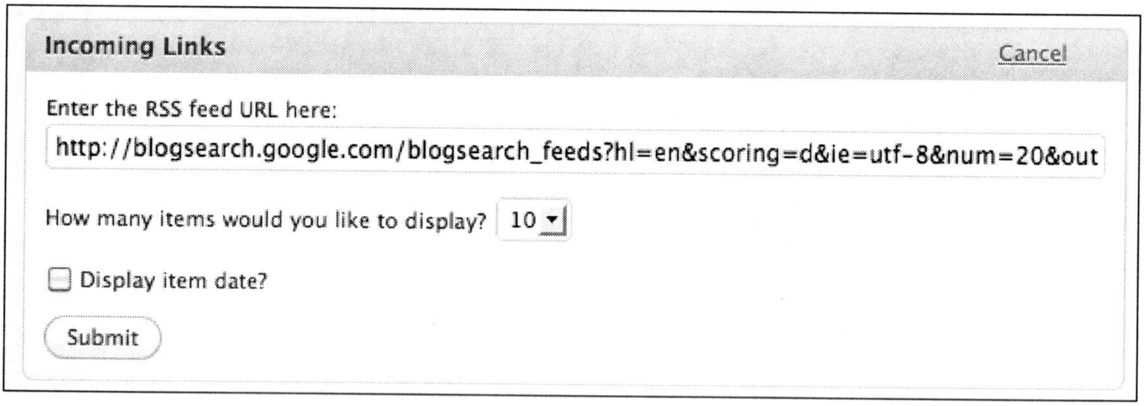

Incoming Links   Cancel

Enter the RSS feed URL here:

http://blogsearch.google.com/blogsearch_feeds?hl=en&scoring=d&ie=utf-8&num=20&out

How many items would you like to display?   10 ▾

☐ Display item date?

(Submit)

Figure 3-4. Configuring the Incoming Links Dashboard widget

■ **Tip:** Incoming Links, the WordPress Development Blog, and Other WordPress News are all just RSS readers with some preconfigured options. If you want to show other RSS feeds instead of these three, click "Configure" and replace each widget's RSS feed URL with your own.

WordPress Development Blog

This widget displays headlines from the blog at http://wordpress.org/development. New releases, including security updates, will be announced here. If you decide to configure this widget to use another feed, you should subscribe to the development blog feed (http://wordpress.org/development/feed) in your RSS reader or sign up for email notifications at http://wordpress.org/download.

Plugin dashboard widgets

Some of the plugins you will install (see Chapter 2) might add more widgets to your Dashboard. One of the most popular plugins available for download, WordPress.com Stats, displays a graph of the traffic to your site as a Dashboard widget. These widgets behave exactly like the built-in Dashboard widgets; you can drag them around, configure them, or turn them off altogether using the Screen Options.

Dashboard Widgets and Users

Screen Options are personal settings; that is, while you might turn off some Dashboard widgets, they'll still be visible to all other users. If you're managing a site for users who might be confused by the developer-specific information, particularly the Development Blog, the Plugins, and the Other WordPress News, you might want to turn off these widgets for all users. You can do so using the Clean WP Dashboard plugin (Figure 3-5).

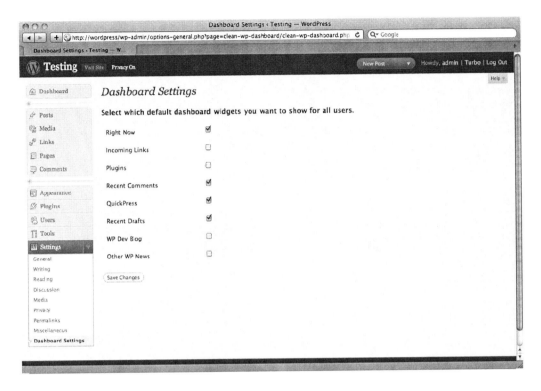

Figure 3-5. The Clean WP Dashboard plugin options

Settings

The Settings panels give you control over almost every aspect of your site. In addition to the options below, many plugins will add settings panels with even more options. There's a lot to cover in the Settings panels, so let's dig in.

General

The General Settings are shown in Figure 3-6. You've already seen the first few options. The blog title and URLs shown here are the ones you chose during the installation process. The tagline is new; this is a brief description of your site that might be displayed near your blog title, depending on the theme you choose.

The Membership and Default Role options are useful if you want to start a group blog. If you allow visitors to sign up as users, you can allow them to contribute posts to your blog. I'll discuss WordPress user roles in depth in Chapter 10, but for now, here's a quick overview:

> **Subscribers** can edit their own profiles and not much else.

> **Contributors** can submit posts for editors' approval, but can't publish anything.

Authors can write and publish posts.

Editors can write and publish posts and pages. They can also publish posts and pages submitted by other users.

Administrators can do everything.

General visitors to your blog have no role at all. These five roles apply only to registered users. No matter what you choose as the default new user role, you can promote users later in the Users panel.

The rest of the settings on this page deal with date and time formats. You can set your local time zone and choose the date format you prefer. WordPress dates are formatted with the same strings that PHP's date() function uses; see http://php.net/date for all your options.

The Week Starts On setting changes the way calendar grids are displayed. If you use a calendar archive widget in your sidebar, this setting determines which day begins the week.

Figure 3-6. The General Settings screen

Writing

The first three options you'll see on the Writing Settings screen (Figure 3-7) have to do with the editor you'll see on the Post and Page Edit screens. WordPress uses the popular TinyMCE editor for its rich text option. The HTML view uses normal markup, but line breaks are converted automatically: one becomes a `<br />` tag; two denotes a break between paragraphs. In either view, the size of the post box is determined by the number of lines specified on this screen. The next two options determine how the editor will handle emoticons (a complete set of smilies is included in WordPress) and any XHTML you enter.

▨ **Tip:** TinyMCE doesn't always handle advanced markup well. If the visual editor drives you crazy, look on your user profile page (Users > Your Profile) for a checkbox that allows you to turn it off altogether.

WordPress requires posts and links to be assigned to at least one category. Here, you can specify which categories should be checked by default when you create new posts and links. You probably haven't set up any categories yet, but you can always return to this page later.

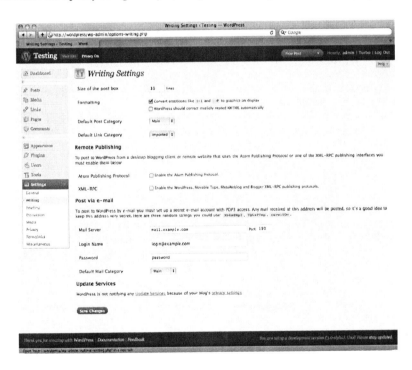

Figure 3-7. The Writing Settings screen

Remote Publishing and Posting by E-mail

If you prefer to compose your posts in a desktop client, or if you plan to blog from your phone, you'll need to enable either the Atom or the XML-RPC protocol. Your client should let you know which one to use. If you don't plan to post remotely, you should leave these protocols disabled; occasionally, hackers discover vulnerabilities in them. While security updates are always released quickly when this happens, it's no fun to realize that you've left yourself open to attack for the sake of a feature you never use!

Popular desktop clients include MarsEdit and the BlogMate plugin for TextMate on the Mac, and BlogDesk, Windows Live Writer, and Word 2007 for Windows. Desktop clients allow you to write while offline and post when you are connected to the internet. Before autosaving and spell checking were available in the WordPress edit screens, desktop clients were essential for many bloggers.

Posting by e-mail is possible, but somewhat limited. HTML tags will be stripped from e-mail messages. Attachments are not converted to media uploads, but are instead included as raw data. The post will be assigned to the default category specified in this section, if different from the usual default category, unless your e-mail subject begins with [n], where n is the ID of another category.

In addition to filling in the e-mail account details listed on this screen, you'll also need to set up a way for WordPress to check that mailbox periodically. You can use cron, the WP-Cron plugin, Procmail, or .qmail. Check `http://codex.wordpress.org/Post_to_your_blog_using_email` for detailed instructions.

Update Services

There are a number of ping services that aggregate information about recently updated blogs. In other words, they let people know that you've posted something new. WordPress uses the XML-RPC protocol to ping these sites every time you publish a post. If you've just installed WordPress, you'll see one service listed here, Ping-o-matic. It's a central site that feeds into lots of other services.

If you want to go beyond Ping-o-matic, take a look at the list of ping services maintained by Vladimir Prelovac at `www.prelovac.com/vladimir/wordpress-ping-list`. If you use Feedburner, you can also add their Pingshot service to your list.

Reading

The Reading settings (Figure 3-8) determine how your posts appear to your visitors. This is where you can determine whether your site works like a blog, with the most recent posts on the home page, or displays something else. (There are more advanced ways of doing this, which I'll cover in Chapter 8.)

If you select a page as your home page, you'll have the option to display your blog posts on another page. Anything you've entered into the body of that page will not be shown; instead, it will be replaced with your most recent posts.

The next setting, Blog pages show at most, determines how many posts per page appear on the blog home page, archive pages, and search results. You can choose a different number of posts to appear in your Atom and RSS feeds, if you wish.

If you want to make your feed subscribers click through to your site to read your complete posts, you may choose to show them only a summary of each post. Keep in mind, however, that the feed summaries strip the HTML formatting from your posts, including things like lists and images. If your unformatted posts wouldn't make sense, consider leaving this setting on Full text.

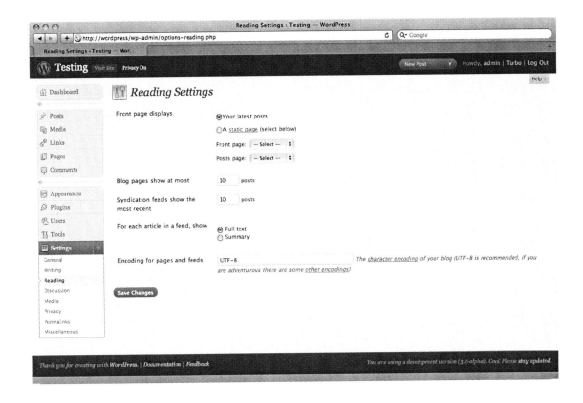

Figure 3-8. The Reading Settings screen

Discussion

The Discussion settings (Figure 3-9) allow you to control how your site handles comments and trackbacks: whether comments and/or trackbacks are allowed, how they're moderated, who's allowed to comment, how you get notified of new comments, and whether commenters' avatars are displayed. This is a dense screen with a lot of settings. I'll go through each section in detail.

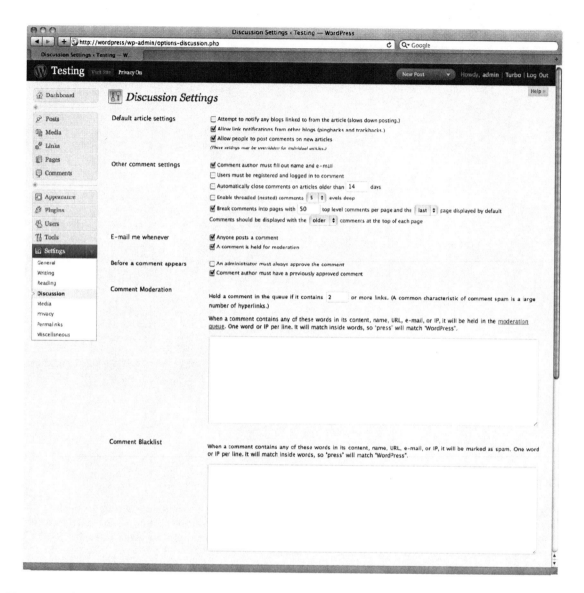

Figure 3-9. The Discussion Settings screen

Default Article Settings

You've probably noticed by now that posts and pages in WordPress are usually labeled as such, so the word "article" here is a tip that these settings apply to both posts *and* pages. These three options will be the default settings for any new posts or pages you write, but all of them can be changed on individual posts or pages if you need to deviate from the norm.

If Attempt to notify any blogs linked to from the article is checked, WordPress will scan your post or page for links to other blogs. If it finds any, it will ping them in addition to the Update Services you selected in the Writing settings. The next option is the inverse: it allows you to decide whether to allow other bloggers to ping your articles when they link to them.

The third option determines whether comments are open by default on new posts and pages. Changing this option will not affect the comment status of any posts and pages you've already published; you'll have to change those from the Post or Page Edit screens.

Other Comment Settings

The first three settings in this section are designed to help you eliminate unwanted comments. First, you'll have to decide how much information a commenter must provide. By default, they have to leave a name and an e-mail address. If you uncheck this option, only the commenter's IP address will be recorded.

If you are planning a community site, you might choose to allow comments only from registered users. This option is not on by default, and it overrides the previous one.

You can have WordPress automatically close the comment threads on older posts. This is a useful anti-spam feature, since spambots are indiscriminate about which posts they target, but most of the real discussion on a blog post generally takes place in the first few days after it's published. You can adjust the number of days to suit your readership; if you notice that comments are lively for two months before dropping off, turn this setting on and change the number of days to 60. Note, however, that the word *article* appears again here: this setting applies to pages as well as posts. If you want to allow comments on your pages indefinitely, you'll want to leave this setting off.

The next three settings determine how comments are displayed on your site: threaded or linear, nested or flat, and chronological or reversed. Not all themes take advantage of these features; only themes that have been updated to use the `wp_list_comments()` feature introduced in version 2.7 support these options.

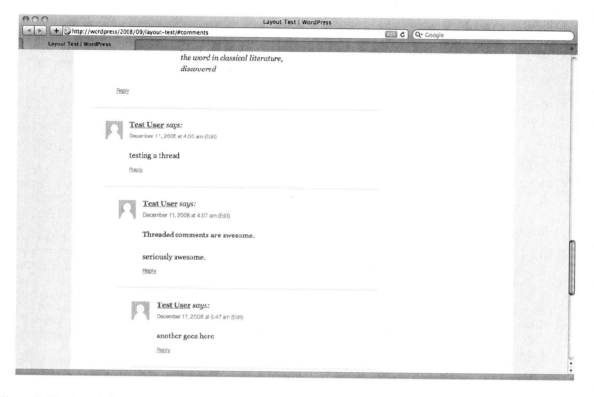

Figure 3-10. *Threaded comments*

If comments are threaded, your visitors have the option of responding to individual comments as well as your post. Each comment will have its own Reply link, as shown in Figure 3-10.

In a nested comment list, replies to individual comments are shown indented underneath, as shown in Figure 3-10. In a flat list (and in all versions of WordPress prior to 2.7), comments are simply listed chronologically, no matter whether they are responding to the post or another comment.

WordPress also supports paging for very long lists of comments. If your post or page contains many comments, you can choose how many you'd like to display at one time. Once the number of comments exceeds your per-page setting, visitors will see navigation links allowing them to browse through the additional pages of comments.

Most sites show comments in their original chronological order. However, if you have a post or page with many comments, you might want the newest comments to appear first. Choose Older or Newer from the dropdown box in this last setting as needed, and if you have chosen to split your long comment lists into pages, decide whether the first page will show the newest or oldest comments.

Comment E-mail Notifications

The two settings in this section are checked by default. Unless you turn them off, the author of a post or page will receive an e-mail for every comment posted. Every comment that's held for moderation will generate a notification to the e-mail address you specified in the General Settings panel (Figure 3-6).

Comment Moderation

The next three sections determine which comments are held for moderation. This means that they will not appear on your site as soon as the comment author submits them; instead, they'll go into a queue in the administration area, and you'll have to approve them before they're published.

You can require that all comments be held for moderation. This is not the default behavior, and for a typical blog, it would slow the pace of the discussion while inundating you with notification e-mails. A less restrictive choice would be to require that comment authors have at least one previously approved comment. This setting lets your trusted repeat readers comment without your intervention, so you need only worry about the first-time commenters.

You can moderate comments based on their content as well as their author. Since spam comments typically contain long lists of links, by default WordPress will hold a comment for moderation if it contains more than two links. You can adjust the number here if you find that your legitimate comments often contain more links than you have allowed.

In addition to the number of links, you can specify a list of words, names, e-mails, and IP addresses that will be held for moderation. This lets you throttle known spammers, but it's also useful for keeping your discussions on track. If you know that certain topics tend to spark flame wars, list the relevant keywords here, and comment authors will quickly find that they can't discuss those subjects without your explicit approval.

Avatars

Avatars— those little user images on Twitter, Facebook, instant messenger clients, etc.—are all over the internet. They're on your blog, too, unless you turn them off in this section (Figure 3-11). Keep in mind that your choice of theme also has a lot to do with avatar display; some themes don't support them at all, regardless of the setting here. Most themes that do support avatars display them only in comments, not for post or page authors.

If you allow avatars, you have some control over the kinds of avatars that appear on your site. WordPress uses Gravatars (`gravatars.com`), a central service where people can choose avatars to be associated with their e-mail addresses. Gravatars include content ratings loosely based on the MPAA system for movie ratings: G for child-friendly images, PG for audiences over 13, R for audiences over 17, and X for explicit images. By default, only G-rated Gravatars are allowed on your site.

You can also choose the image that's used for comment authors who don't have a Gravatar. The options include several generic settings (blank, Mystery Man) and three randomized selections: Identicon, Wavatar, and MonsterID.

Identicons are computer-generated geometric patterns. A unique pattern will be assigned to each commenter's e-mail address, so the same pattern will be used every time they comment. MonsterID uses the same concept, but draws images of monsters instead of geometric designs. Wavatar assembles avatar images from a pool of pieces (faces, eyes, noses, hair), rather like assembling a Mr. Potato Head toy.

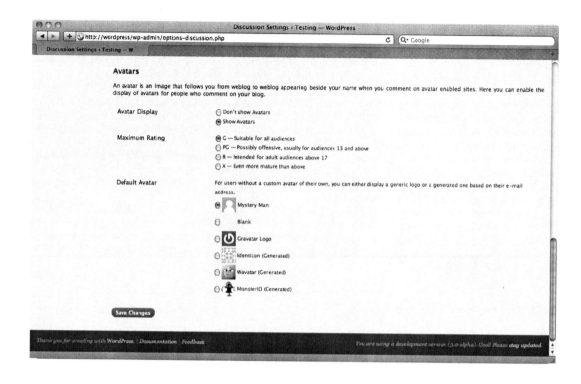

Figure 3-11. The Avatars section of the Discussion Settings screen

Media

The media Settings screen (Figure 3-12) allows you to determine the maximum dimensions of your uploaded images and videos. When you upload images to be embedded in your posts and pages, WordPress generates several copies of the image at different sizes: thumbnail, medium, and large, in addition to the original size. You'll be able to include the smaller sizes in your post and link to the original if your image would otherwise be too large to fit in your layout, or if you don't want to make your visitors download the full size until they've seen a preview. Set your default image dimensions based on your site's layout: if you're using a fixed-width layout, and your post area will be 600 pixels wide, use 600 as the max width for your large size. If your image is small to begin with, only those sizes smaller than the original will be generated.

Note that the default settings for thumbnails result in a 150-pixel square, even though (as the screen says) "normally thumbnails are proportional." Square thumbnails are ideal for magazine-style themes, but you might find that your photos are badly cropped using these settings. If you decide later that square thumbnails are not ideal, you can change this setting. If you need to, you can then use the Regenerate Thumbnails plugin to correct the thumbnails for images you've already uploaded.

Like images, movie dimensions can be limited using the maximum sizes specified on this page. In addition, you can choose to turn off WordPress's media auto-discovery, which will attempt to embed videos based on URLs found in your post or page content.

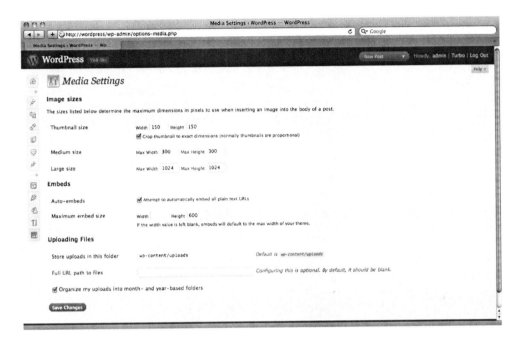

Figure 3-12. The Media Settings screen

Directory for file uploads

At the bottom of the Media Settings screen, you can change the location of your uploaded files. If you'd like the path to be something other than wp-content/uploads, you can specify it here. Why would you want to? Perhaps you anticipate that your visitors will link directly to your uploaded files, and you'd like the URLs to be shorter (e.g. img) or more descriptive (e.g. reports). Maybe you're migrating a site from another CMS and you want to store your new files alongside the old ones.

You should enter a path relative to your WordPress installation. You also need to specify the full URL in the next field. If this directory does not exist, WordPress will try to create it the first time you (or one of your content authors) use the media uploader. Of course, you can simply create the directory and make it writeable.

You can also choose whether WordPress creates date-based subdirectories for your upload files. By default, WordPress will create subdirectories for each year, and within those, for each month. Your files will be stored according to the dates they were uploaded. For example, if you upload a file called image.gif in December of 2010, it would be stored as wp-content/uploads/2010/12/image.gif. If you uncheck this option, all of your uploaded files will be stored in your specified upload directory. Our example file would be stored as wp-content/uploads/image.gif whether you uploaded it in December or June.

Privacy

There are just two options under Privacy (Figure 3-13), and you've seen them before: they appeared during the installation process, when you were asked if you wanted your blog to be visible to search engines.

If you choose I would like to block search engines, but allow normal visitors, WordPress does the following:

- Adds `<meta name='robots' content='noindex,nofollow' />` to your `<head>` content

- Responds to requests for a `robots.txt` file with one that disallows all user agents—but only if a `robots.txt` file doesn't already exist *and* WordPress is installed in your site root directory.

- Prevents you from pinging linked blogs or blog update services when writing a post.

- Hides the *Update Services* section on the Writing settings panel.

These privacy options apply only to search engine crawlers and other machines. They do not prevent human visitors from seeing your site. When you write posts and pages, you'll have the option to make them private or password-protected on an individual basis. If you want to make your whole WordPress site private, you'll need to install a plugin such as Members Only.

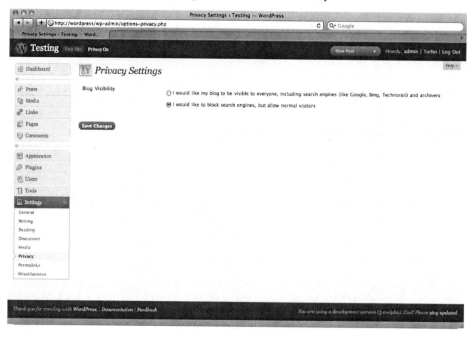

Figure 3-13. *The Privacy Settings screen*

Permalinks

By default, WordPress uses post and page IDs in query strings in its URLs: example.com/?p=123. On the Permalinks Settings screen (Figure 3-14), you can choose a custom URL structure (also known as clean URLs) if you have installed WordPress on one of the following servers:

- Apache or LiteSpeed, with the mod_rewrite module installed

- Microsoft IIS 7, with the URL Rewrite 1.1 module installed and PHP 5 running as FastCGI

- Microsoft IIS 6, using a 404 handler or a third-party rewrite module

- Lighttpd, using a 404 handler, mod_rewrite, or mod_magnet

If your server meets these conditions, you can switch to one of the other URL structures shown in Figure 3-14, or create your own using the available tags.

If your server uses .htaccess files to manage URL rewrites, WordPress will attempt to create or modify your .htaccess file when you save your Permalink options. If WordPress can't write to the file, you'll see the necessary rewrite rules displayed, and you'll be asked to edit the file yourself.

If you're using IIS 7, you'll need to add a rule to your web.config file after saving your Permalink structure. See codex.wordpress.org/Using_Permalinks for detailed information.

▪ **Security Tip:** Once you've chosen your permalink structure, you should adjust your file permissions so that WordPress can no longer write to .htaccess. A number of common exploits involve altering your .htaccess file to redirect your visitors to other sites or append unwanted links to your WordPress pages. If changes to .htaccess are needed, they'll be displayed and you'll be asked to edit the file yourself.

If you are using any permalink structure other than the default for your posts, your pages will use pretty permalinks as well. The permalink structures use the page name (no matter what structure you've chosen for posts), and they form a directory-like chain based on the page hierarchy. Parent pages appear in the URL as if they were parent directories of static files. Table 3-1 shows a sample category structure and the resulting category archive URLs.

Table 3-1. Parent and child category permalinks.

WordPress		http://example.com/category/wordpress/
	Plugins	http://example.com/category/wordpress/plugins/
	Themes	http://example.com/category/wordpress/themes/
Books		http://example.com/category/books/
	Fiction	http://example.com/category/books/fiction/
	Mystery	http://example.com/category/books/fiction/mystery/

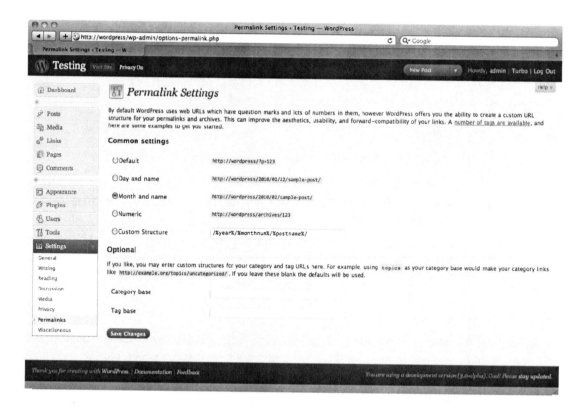

Figure 3-14. The Permalinks Settings screen

You can change your permalink structure at any time. WordPress will store your previous permalink structure and will automatically redirect visitors from the old location to the new one using HTTP's 301 redirect protocol. However, it stores only one previous structure, so if you've changed it a few times, your visitors (and any search engines that indexed your site) might get lost.

■ **Tip:** URLs that contain a page's keywords tend to rank higher on most search engines. If you are interested in optimizing your site for search engine results, choose a permalink structure that includes the post name: Day and Name, Month and Name, or something like the Custom Structure shown in Figure 3-14. However, permalinks beginning with the post name or category can cause performance problems, which I will discuss in Chapter 11.

Short URLs

If you have included your post name in your permalink structure, or if you have deeply nested pages with long titles, your permalinks can get very long. Sometimes you'll want shorter URLs to paste into an email or Twitter message. A number of URL shortening plugins are available; Short URL is one of the most popular.

However, you don't need a plugin to get a shorter URL. No matter what permalink structure you have chosen, the default ("ugly") structure will always work. To use it, just find the ID of your post or page—it's in the URL in the Edit Post/Page screen, among other places.

Category Base

Category and tag archive pages contain a permalink "base," which by default will be "category" for categories and "tag" for tags (http://example.com/tag/humor/). It's possible to remove the category base—for search engine optimization purposes, to keep your URLs short, or just because you don't like the way it looks—using a plugin such as No Category Base. However, be aware of the following drawbacks to this approach:

1. Conflicts with page names. You'll need to be careful to avoid using identical names for categories and pages. Without a category base, categories and pages with the same titles will have identical URLs. Visitors trying to reach your category archive will end up on the page instead.

2. Slower performance. Because WordPress will have to compare the requested category URL to all of the page URLs stored in the database, removing the category base can result in significantly slower response times for your visitors.See Chapter 11 for more information.

Summary

Once you've combed through all these settings, you should have a pretty good idea of how your blog is going to work. You've decided how you want the editor to behave when you write new posts and pages, and you've determined how visitors will see your posts displayed. You've set up your comments, decided how they will be moderated, and chosen a set of avatars for your commenters. You're all set to begin adding content to your site!

■ ■ ■

CHAPTER 4

Working with Content

WordPress comes with several basic content types: posts, pages, links, and media files. In addition, you can create your own content types, which I'll talk more about in Chapter 12.

Posts and pages make up the heart of your site. You'll probably add images, audio, video, or other documents like Office files to augment your posts and pages, and WordPress makes it easy to upload and link to these files. WordPress also includes a robust link manager, which you can use to maintain a blogroll or other link directory.

WordPress automatically generates a number of different feeds to syndicate your content. I'll talk about the four feed formats, the common feeds, and the hidden ones that even experienced WordPress users might not know about.

Since WordPress is known for its exceptional blogging capabilities, I'll talk about posts first, and then discuss how pages differ from posts—and how you can modify them to be more alike.

Posts

Collectively, posts make up the blog (or news) section of your site. Posts are generally listed according to date, but can also be tagged or filed into categories.

At its most basic, a post consists of a title and some content. In addition, WordPress will add some required metadata to every post: an ID number, an author, a publication date, a category, the publication status, and a visibility setting. There are a number of other things that may be added to posts, but the aforementioned are the essentials. Figure 4-1 shows the basic post editing screen.

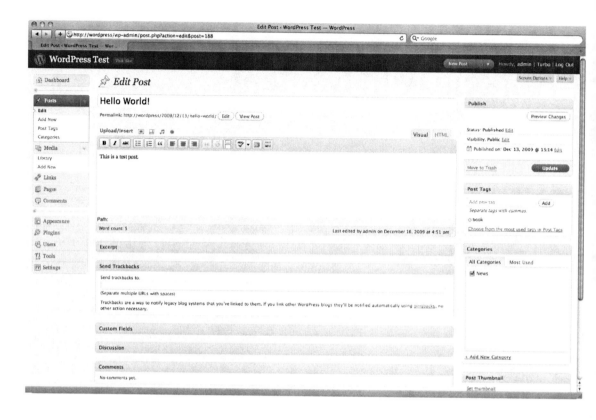

Figure 4-1. *The post editing screen, using the Visual editor*

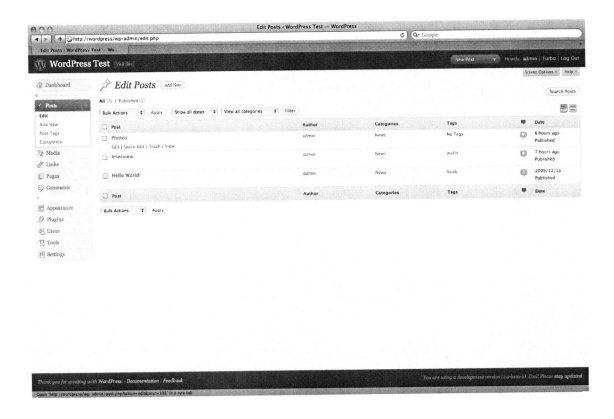

Figure 4-2. To find a post's ID, look at your browser's status bar while you hover over the title.

You'll occasionally need to locate the ID of a post or page, but it isn't visible on any of the Edit screens. To find it, take a look at your URL while you're editing a post or page or while you hover over a post on the Edit screen (Figure 4-2). The ID is the number at the end of the URL. In this case, the URL is example.com/wp-admin/post.php?action=edit&post=12 which means the ID is 12. If you prefer, you can install a plugin like Simply Show IDs, which will display the IDs next to the post titles on the Edit Posts screen.

Content

The content box lets you edit your content in a rich text editor (the Visual tab, on by default) or work with the underlying source code (the HTML tab). Most people are comfortable writing in the Visual editor. It behaves more or less like familiar desktop word processors, allowing you to add formatting (bold, italic, lists, links) without having to write HTML. Of course, if you know HTML, you can check the Visual editor's work by switching to HTML view. In either view, the editor automatically converts single line breaks to <br /> tags and double line breaks to properly nested paragraphs. If you include <p> and <br /> tags in the HTML view, they'll be removed unless they include attributes. For example, <p> would be removed, but <p class="caption"> would not.

The last button in the Visual editor's toolbar is labeled Show/Hide the Kitchen Sink. Press this button and a second row of tools will be revealed, including a dropdown that lets you create headings, addresses, and preformatted text using the appropriate HTML tags.

The Visual editor does not include tools for working with tables, subscripts, superscripts, and other relatively unusual formats. If you need these tools, use the TinyMCE Advanced plugin to add them to your toolbar. Install the plugin as described in Chapter 2, then go to Settings → TinyMCE Advanced to configure your toolbars. You'll be able to create up to four rows of buttons (Figure 4-3). Simply drag the buttons you don't want out of the toolbar areas and drop in the ones you do want to use.

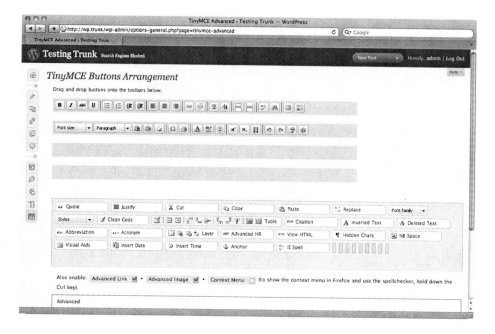

Figure 4-3. Configuring the TinyMCE Advanced plugin

If you often include code samples in your posts, you might find that the Visual editor mangles your formatting and changes some of your code to HTML entities. If this drives you crazy (or if you just hate the Visual editor!), you can turn it off entirely by checking the Disable the Visual editor when writing box in your user profile.

Dealing with Content from Microsoft Office

Even those who have been using WordPress for a while might have overlooked the handy Paste from Word button on the second row of the Visual editor's toolbar. If your Visual editor's toolbar has just one row of buttons, press the one labeled Show/Hide Kitchen Sink. In the second row, you'll see a clipboard with the Word logo on it. Press this button, and you'll get a pop-up screen where you can paste the contents of your Word file (see Figure 4-4). It works well with Excel tables, too, and even does a decent job with text copied from Adobe PDF documents.

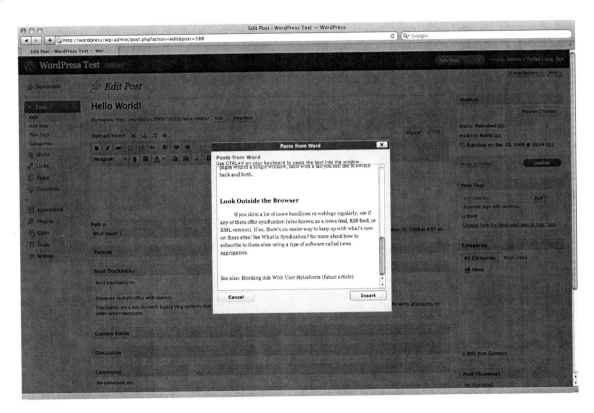

Figure 4-4. The Paste from Word tool

Press Insert, and your post now contains the cleaned-up contents of your Word file. The editor will attempt to retain your formatting, and it will translate headings from Word's style menu into proper HTML headings. It will also remove the Word-specific markup that will clutter your document if you paste it into the editor without using this tool, such as extraneous `<div>` tags, `MsoNormal` classes, inline styles, and smart tags.

■ **Tip:** If Paste from Word is not as thorough as you'd like, save your Word document as HTML, then run the resulting source code through the cleanup tool at wordoff.org before pasting it into your post's HTML view.

Shortcodes

WordPress allows developers to define shortcodes—bracketed words that are replaced with content when the post is displayed to visitors. Shortcodes work like text macros in Microsoft Word. WordPress itself uses shortcodes to insert some forms of media (photos with captions, image galleries). A typical image caption shortcode is shown in Figure 4-5, and the resulting image display (in the Twenty Ten theme) is shown in Figure 4-6.

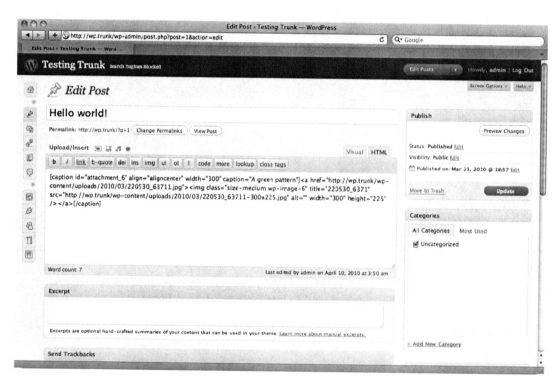

Figure 4-5. An image caption shortcode

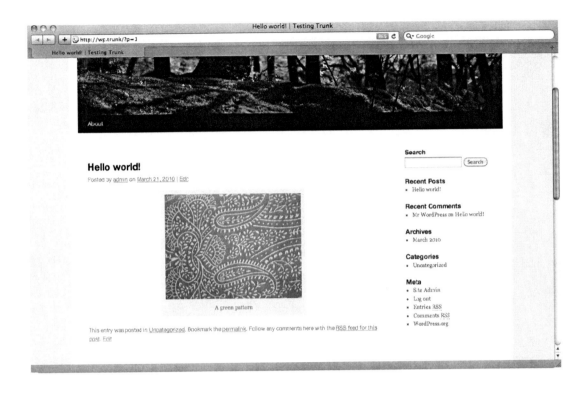

Figure 4-6. The image display resulting from the caption shortcode

You might install plugins that provide more shortcodes. For example, if you have pieces of content that you'd like to write once and reuse throughout your site, you could define your own shortcodes using a plugin like Post Snippets (Figure 4-7) or Reusables.

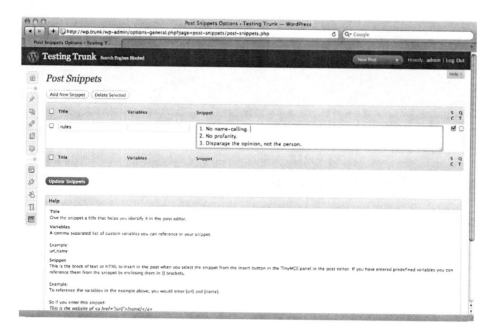

Figure 4-7. *Post Snippets lets you define new shortcodes. It gives you the option to place corresponding buttons on the editors' toolbars.*

To create a snippet, enter the shortcode you'd like to use into the Title field, as shown in Figure 4-7. Then enter the expanded version in the Snippet field. You'll see the shortcode while editing the post, as shown in Figure 4-8, but when a visitor views the post, she'll see the expanded version, as shown in Figure 4-9.

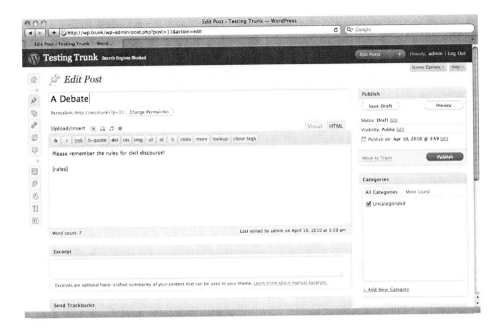

Figure 4-8. The post snippet in the post editor

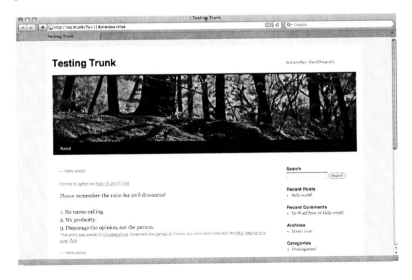

Figure 4-9. The expanded snippet

Permalinks

If you enabled permalinks in your Settings, you'll see a Permalink field on each post and page. The portion highlighted in yellow is derived from the title, with spaces replaced by dashes and other punctuation removed. This is called the slug. (Posts, pages, categories, and tags all have slugs.) If you don't like the generated slug or if it's too long, you can edit it using the Edit button to the right (Figure 4-10). Note that you can't edit the rest of the URL; it's constructed based on the pattern you chose on the Permalink Settings panel.

If you edited your permalink and later decided you'd like to get the generated slug back, you can just delete everything in the slug field and press the Save button. WordPress will fill in the blank.

Figure 4-10. Editing the post slug

Publish Settings

In the Visibility section, you can choose who's allowed to see your post. The default setting is public, which means that anyone can read it. Just below this option, you'll see a checkbox labeled Stick this post to the front page. Making a post "sticky" means that it always appears at the top of lists, including archives, as well as your home page.

The other two Visibility settings are not as intuitive as they appear to be. A private post is one that only registered users of your site can read, *if* they have permission (in WordPress parlance, the *capability*) to read private posts. By default, only editors and administrators have this capability. You can change that fairly easily, but it requires a few lines of code in your theme files. You can also use a plugin like Role Manager or my own Private Suite.

A password protected post is not public, but visitors don't have to be registered users in order to read it. When you choose the Password protected option in the Visibility box, you'll be asked to provide a password for the post. You can then give that password to anyone you like (in an e-mail, let's say). When they visit your site, they'll see the title of the post but not the content. In place of the content, there will be a password field. When your visitors enter the correct password, they'll see the post content.

The Status setting provides a rudimentary workflow for your posts. When you begin a new post, it remains in Draft status until you press the blue Publish button. At that point, the status changes to Published and the post becomes visible to your visitors. A contributor, who doesn't have the ability to publish posts, would see a Submit for Review button instead of Publish. The contributor's post status would then change to Pending Review, and an Editor would have to approve and publish the post.

You can leave posts in Draft mode indefinitely. If you need to close the editing screen before you've finished writing, press the Save Draft button rather than Publish.

■ **Note:** While the Permalink, Visibility, Status, and Publication Date fields have their own OK buttons, none of your changes to these settings will take effect until you press the blue Publish (or Update) Post button.

Publication Date and Scheduling Posts

When you press Publish, the post becomes visible to the public and its publication date is set to the current date and time. However, you can easily change the date if you need to backdate a post or schedule it to appear in the future.

To change the date, press Edit next to Publish immediately in the Publish Settings box. An extra set of form fields will appear, as shown in Figure 4-11. Enter your desired publication date and press OK. If the date is in the past, the post's publication date will be adjusted, and it will appear in the archives according to the new date. If you chose a date in the future, the post will be scheduled to publish at that time. The Publish button will change to Schedule, and the post will not be visible on your site (or in your feeds) until the time you specified.

Figure 4-11. Scheduling a future post

Categories

Categories can be a powerful tool for organizing your posts. Many magazine-style themes for WordPress rely on categories to break articles into divisions, much like a magazine's departments or a newspaper's sections. You can also get a feed for each of your categories (see the Feeds section of this chapter). By styling your categories differently and publicizing the otherwise hidden feeds for individual categories, you can create the illusion of multiple blogs for your visitors, even though behind the scenes you're maintaining just one. I'll look at this more closely in Chapter 7.

To manage categories, go to Categories under Posts in the main menu. You'll be able to add, edit, or delete categories. You'll also be able to add descriptions, change slugs, or even convert categories to free-form tags (Figure 4-12).

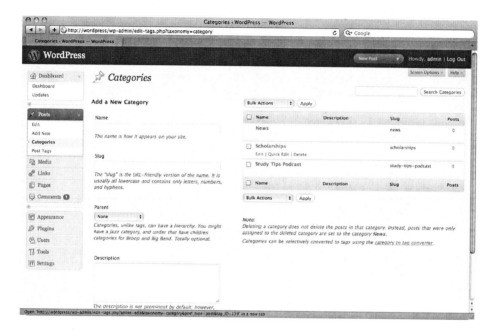

Figure 4-12. Managing categories

Categories can be arranged into hierarchies. When you create a new category, you'll have the option to make it a child of an existing one. There is no limit to the depth of your categories.

Categories must have distinct slugs. Even if two categories have different parents and would therefore have different permalinks, you can't assign them the same slug. If you choose a slug that's already in use, WordPress will discard your new category and highlight the existing one that uses that slug.

When you're editing an individual post, the Categories box shows a hierarchical list of all your categories. If you don't check one, the default category you chose in your Writing Settings will be checked for you when you save the post. All posts in WordPress must have at least one category selected. However, you can select as many as you like. Once you've selected categories, they'll be moved to the top of the list—outside the normal hierarchy—the next time you edit the post. If your hierarchy is important and you'd like to preserve the normal, indented view, use the Category Checklist Tree plugin.

Tags

If you're familiar with the concept of tagging from social media sites like Flickr, YouTube, or Delicious, the tag feature in WordPress holds no surprises for you. Tags are subject keywords, just like categories, but where categories must be set up ahead of time by an editor or administrator, authors are free to create new tags simply by typing them into the Tag box while writing a post (Figure 4-13).

Note that after you've added new tags, you must press Add in order to apply them. Then, you still have to press the blue Publish/Update button before your changes take effect.

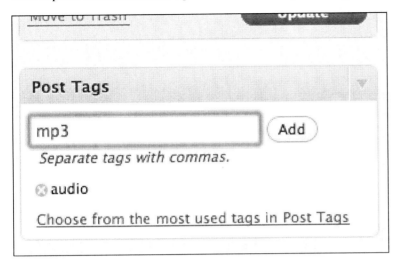

Figure 4-13. Editing tags on a post

To manage your tags, go to Post Tags in the main menu. Here, you can add or delete tags, edit slugs, add descriptions, or convert tags to categories (Figure 4-14). Like categories, tag slugs must be unique—and since categories and tags share the same pool of slugs (they're both considered taxonomies), a category and a tag can't share a slug, even if they have the same name.

You can get feeds for each of your tags, as you'll see in the Feeds section of this chapter.

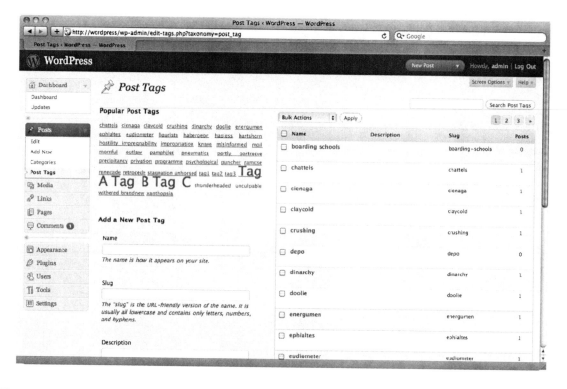

Figure 4-14. Managing post tags

Featured Images

The featured image (formerly known as the post thumbnail) is an image that represents your post. It might be shown by itself, or alongside the post content or excerpt, depending on how your theme displays posts.

I talk about uploading images in the Media Files section of this chapter.

Figure 4-15. Setting a featured image

If you don't see a Featured Image box on your Edit Posts screen (Figure 4-15), your theme probably doesn't support them. You can enable them by adding a line to your theme's `functions.php` file. See Chapter 6 for details.

Excerpts

An excerpt is, as the box says, a summary of your post. Some themes show excerpts rather than the full content when posts are listed, either on the home page or in archives. If a theme calls for an excerpt and none is specified, it will be generated automatically from the post content. However, any HTML formatting will be removed. If your content contains lists or tables, the results might be very odd. You can preserve HTML formatting in excerpts using the Advanced Excerpt or the_excerpt Reloaded plugin.

Excerpts are shown with a continuation string. By default, '[...]' is appended to your excerpt text. As of version 2.9, this can be modified via plugins.

Also new in 2.9 is the option to modify the length of your excerpts. By default, they are 55 words long.

Comments and Trackbacks

In Chapter 3, you set your preferences regarding comments and trackbacks. Here, you can override those settings for the current post. If you're editing an existing post that has comments, you'll see the comments listed, and you can edit them right from this screen.

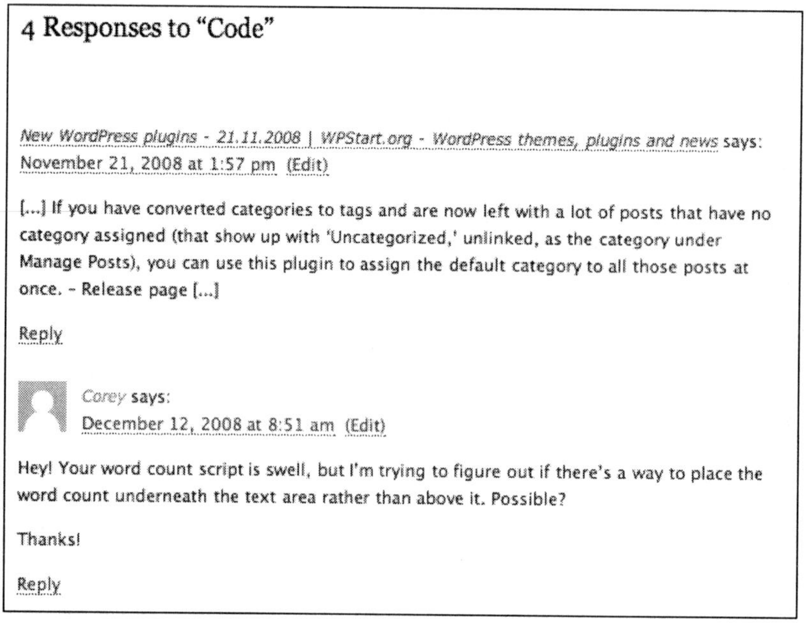

> ## 4 Responses to "Code"
>
> *New WordPress plugins - 21.11.2008 | WPStart.org - WordPress themes, plugins and news* says:
> November 21, 2008 at 1:57 pm (Edit)
>
> [...] If you have converted categories to tags and are now left with a lot of posts that have no category assigned (that show up with 'Uncategorized,' unlinked, as the category under Manage Posts), you can use this plugin to assign the default category to all those posts at once. – Release page [...]
>
> Reply
>
> *Corey* says:
> December 12, 2008 at 8:51 am (Edit)
>
> Hey! Your word count script is swell, but I'm trying to figure out if there's a way to place the word count underneath the text area rather than above it. Possible?
>
> Thanks!
>
> Reply

Figure 4-16. A trackback and a comment on a post

Trackbacks are automated notifications (pings) from other sites that have mentioned your post. They let you (and your readers) know that there are conversations taking place elsewhere about something you wrote. Trackbacks are usually displayed alongside comments on a post (see Figure 4-16). Here on the Edit screen, you'll see a list of any trackbacks your post has received.

In the Trackbacks box, you'll be able to ping sites about your post. Keep in mind the list of sites you chose to ping for all your posts in the Update Services section of your Writing Settings. Also, if you chose on that screen to ping linked sites, any links included in your post will be pinged automatically. If you want to ping any sites in addition to your Update Services list and the sites linked in your post, you can add the URL in the Trackback section, as shown in Figure 4-17. If your post has already been published, this box will display a list of the sites that have already been pinged.

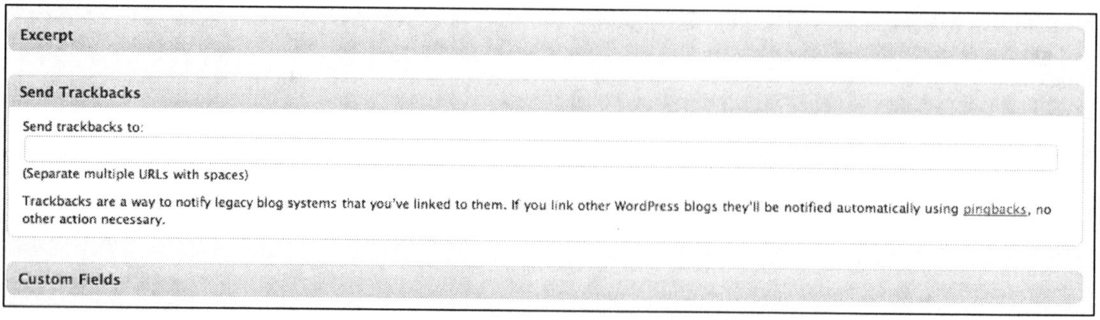

> **Excerpt**
>
> **Send Trackbacks**
>
> Send trackbacks to:
>
> (Separate multiple URLs with spaces)
>
> Trackbacks are a way to notify legacy blog systems that you've linked to them. If you link other WordPress blogs they'll be notified automatically using pingbacks, no other action necessary.
>
> **Custom Fields**

Figure 4-17. Sending additional trackbacks from the Edit Post screen

Revisions

WordPress saves every revision of your posts and pages, including the most recent autosave, if there is one. If you messed something up and need to revert to a previous version, scroll down the editing screen to the Revisions box. There you'll see a list of all the revisions. Click one to view it. The title, content (as source code), and excerpt (for posts) will be shown (Figure 4-18). These fields, along with the author, are the only ones stored for each revision. At the bottom of this screen, there's another list of all the revisions, but this time you'll see radio buttons allowing you to select two revisions for comparison. Each revision also has a restore link on this page.

Restoring a post or page actually creates *another* revision. WordPress copies the revision you chose, saves it as a new version, marks it as the current revision. In other words, if you revert a post and later realize that you really do need the newer copy, it's still there. Just look in the revision list for the corresponding date.

As you might imagine, storing all these revisions can inflate the size of your WordPress database. If you're concerned about storage space, you can limit the number of revisions WordPress stores by adding the following line to your wp-config.php file:

```
define('WP_POST_REVISIONS', 3);
```

To turn off revisions altogether, set the number to zero:

```
define('WP_POST_REVISIONS', 0);
```

There are also several plugins that will handle this setting for you. They provide a Settings screen where you can make changes without having to edit your config file. Revision Control is a good one.

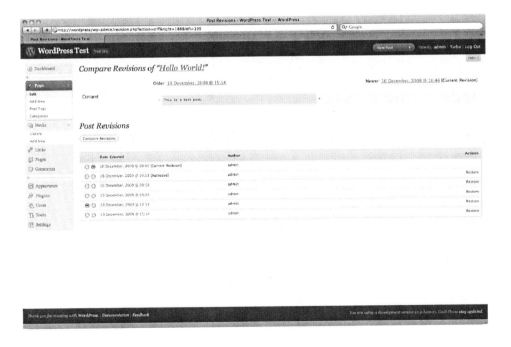

Figure 4-18. Comparing revisions

Custom Fields

Custom fields allow you to create new attributes for your posts and pages. Some common uses for custom fields include adding a mood to each blog post, providing custom CSS for posts or pages, listing what music you're currently listening to or the books you're reading, or setting an expiration date for posts. Many themes and plugins have been built around the idea of using custom fields to store an image to represent each post, but as of WordPress 2.9, that can be accomplished using the field instead.

Pages

Pages in WordPress are for all the things that are not part of a blog. You'll notice that your first page, About, was created for you during installation.

Simple pages are much like posts: you need a title and some content, and that's about all. The ID, author, date, publication status, and visibility will be set for you when you publish the page. However, there are some important differences. The publication date is not displayed for pages in most themes, and pages are not organized by date. Also, you probably noticed that categories and tags are not available for pages. Pages can be organized into a hierarchy, but since they exist outside the collection of posts, they don't share the same metadata.

Page Attributes: Parents, Templates, and Order

You can arrange your pages into filesystem-like hierarchies by making them children of parent pages (Figure 4-19). In the Attributes box on any single page's Edit screen, you'll be able to select another existing page as the parent. That page could, in turn, have another parent, and so on.

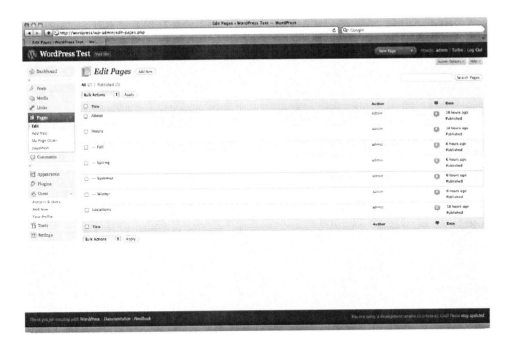

Figure 4-19. *Pages arranged in a parent/child hierarchy.*

If you've turned on permalinks, your page's URL will be built by adding its slug to that of its parent and any other page ancestors, as shown in Figure 4-20.

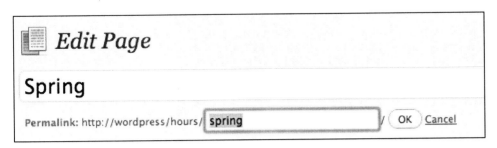

Figure 4-20. *The slug of a page with a parent*

As you'll see in Chapter 6, WordPress themes can have multiple templates for pages. When you create a new page template, it becomes available as an option in the parent dropdown portion of the Page Attributes box (Figure 4-21). To use your new template instead of the default page template, select it here and update the page.

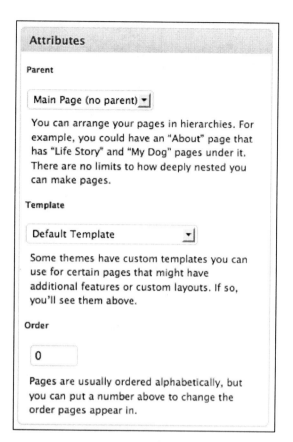

Figure 4-21. Page Attributes

The page order determines how your pages are listed in navigation menus. Numbering them using this field is a bit like programming in BASIC; inevitably, you'll find that you need to insert a new page between two existing ones, and then you'll have to redo the numbering for all the pages. To avoid the problem, you can use a numbering scheme that leaves you plenty of room between pages (111, 222, 333, etc.). If you prefer, there are plugins that provide a drag-and-drop screen where you can rearrange your pages without having to count. My Page Order (Figure 4-22) and pageMash (Figure 4-23) are two of the best.

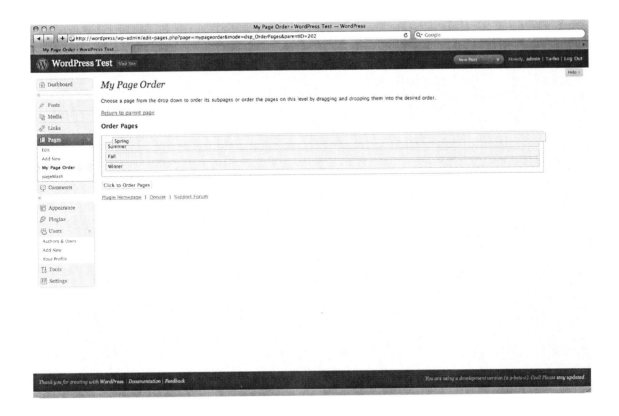

Figure 4-22. *My Page Order*

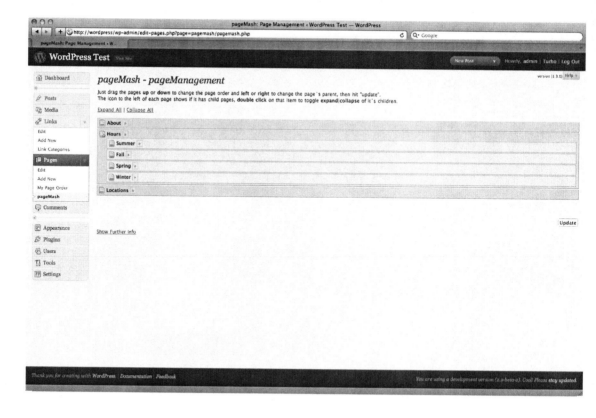

Figure 4-23. PageMash

Posts vs. Pages: Same, but Different

Sometimes it's not immediately clear whether your content would work best as a post or a page. On the surface, they are much the same in WordPress: they share a similar editing screen and both can accept comments and trackbacks. How do you decide which to use?

In general, posts are ideal for date-based content: blogs, podcasts, columns, newsletters, journals, or a press release archive. In short, for news of any kind, you should definitely use posts for that section. Putting the rest of your content into pages will provide a logical division for both your visitors and your content authors.

Posts are shown in a chronological sequence (usually newest to oldest) on a single page, such as your home page or an archive of posts from a particular month or category. Once your visitors select a post to view by itself, they'll be able to read the comments as well as your content. Pages are generally not grouped in chronological order. Each page will appear on its own screen. You can create a list of pages using a widget or a menu (see Chapter 6).

If your site consists mainly of articles that will not often change and need to be arranged in a simple hierarchy, like files in folders, then pages will probably work well for you. In this case, you could ignore the post screens altogether or create a basic "What's New?" blog as an adjunct to the main site.

If no such clear division exists in your content, think about your content taxonomy and your subscribers' needs. Pages do not have tags or categories. They can be arranged in a parent/child hierarchy, but if you need a more complex or flexible taxonomy, posts would probably work better. Also, pages are not included in feeds. Will your readers want to be notified every time you add a document? If so, your content should go into posts.

Posts are Pages; Pages are Posts

Posts and pages in WordPress are essentially the same thing. They share the same table in the WordPress database (wp_posts), with one field to distinguish them: type, which could be "post" or "page." (In fact, media files also share this table, as you'll see later.) Posts and pages use most of the same fields in that table. The big difference is in the way they're presented to you. Even though all the database fields are available to each type of content, only some of those fields appear in the Edit panels.

As with nearly everything in WordPress, this default behavior can be changed using plugins. For example, you can add excerpts, categories, and tags to pages.

Pages do not have excerpts, even though they have a database field for them. Since pages never appear in archive lists, excerpts would never be used for pages in a typical WordPress site. However, excerpts can be useful for pages as well as posts. For example, you might tweak your search results theme file to display excerpts rather than the full post content. Also, some heavily customized themes do list pages in archive-like lists. You can use a plugin such as PJW Page Excerpt or Excerpt Editor to add excerpts to your pages.

In version 3.0, you can create content types of your own in addition to the built-in posts and pages. In Chapter 12, you'll see some examples of custom content types.

Editing Posts and Pages

You can filter the list of posts by category or date using the dropdown menus at the top of the list. You can also search your posts and pages using the box at the top right side of the Edit screens, but beware: it searches not only the titles but the complete content of posts and pages.

Autosave

WordPress does save your posts automatically, once per minute, as you write. However, if you try to publish or update a post while the autosave is running, you'll get nowhere: the button is deactivated while autosaving. So how can you tell when it's safe to hit the button? The button's colors will fade out, but the effect is subtle: the button loses its three-dimensional, shadowed look and becomes a flat shade of blue. The button text becomes light blue instead of white (Figures 4-24 and 4-25) and a small donut-shaped progress indicator appears next to it.

When in doubt, check your browser's status bar. Is the page reloading? If so, wait for the yellow Post updated message to appear at the top of the editing screen. If you pressed the button but the page isn't reloading, try again.

Figure 4-24. The Update button while Autosaving

Figure 4-25. The normal Update button

By default, WordPress autosaves every sixty seconds if you've made changes in the content editor. You can adjust this timing by adding this line to your wp-config.php file:

```
define('AUTOSAVE_INTERVAL', 120 );  // autosave every two minutes
```

Screen Options

Like the Dashboard, the Edit Posts and Pages panels have Screen Options available. You can choose which columns you want to see; the post/page title will always display, but the author, categories, tags, comments, and date columns are optional. You can also choose how many posts or pages you'd like to see per page (Figure 4-26). Twenty is the default, but you can increase it if you have lots of content and you'd like to scroll through it faster. Keep in mind that the more posts or pages you put on each screen, the longer it will take WordPress to generate the screens.

Screen options are also available when editing individual posts and pages (Figure 4-27). If you're working on a small screen or a monitor with a low resolution, you might want to switch your editing layout to a single column. You can also choose to disable boxes you don't intend to use. For example, if your site doesn't use custom fields, you might turn off that box so you don't have to scroll past it to see the post revisions.

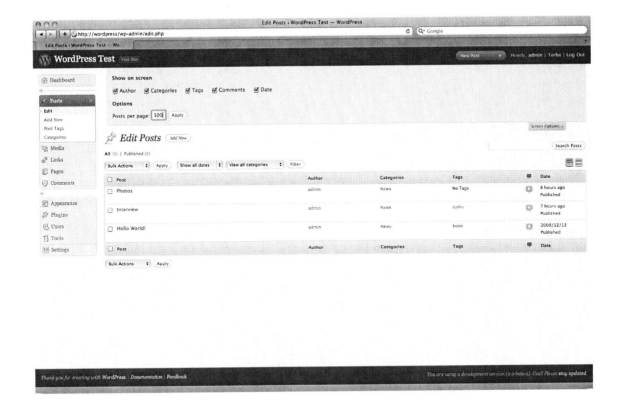

Figure 4-26. *Screen options for the Edit Posts screen*

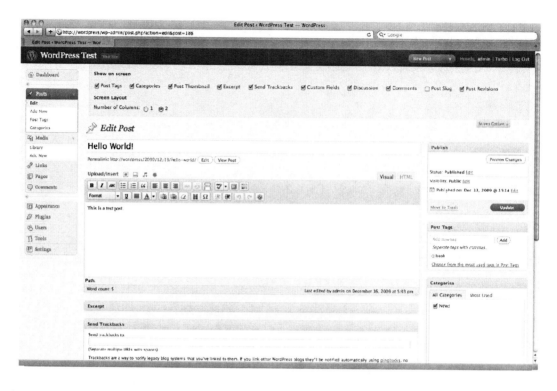

Figure 4-27. *Screen options for an individual post*

Quick Edit

If you need to change the attributes of a post or page without editing the content, you can do so quickly using the Quick Edit feature. Go to Edit Posts (or Pages) and hover your mouse over the post you want to modify. A row of links will appear below the title: Edit, Quick Edit, Delete, and View. Choose Quick Edit, and the table row will transform into a miniature editing form (Figure 4-28) that lets you change nearly everything about the page except the content, excerpt, and custom fields.

Figure 4-28. The Quick Edit feature

Bulk Edit

What do you do when you need to change the attributes of many posts or pages at once? Again, go to Edit Posts (or Pages). Select the checkboxes next to the posts you want to edit, then choose Edit from the Bulk Actions dropdown above the list of posts and press Apply. (If you want to select all the posts on the page, just use the checkbox in the gray table header.)

The Bulk Edit form (Figure 4-29) offers fewer options than Quick Edit. Things that would be illogical to change for multiple posts, like titles and publication dates, are not available. You can edit the categories and tags (for posts), parent and template (for pages), and the comment, trackback, visibility, and publication status settings.

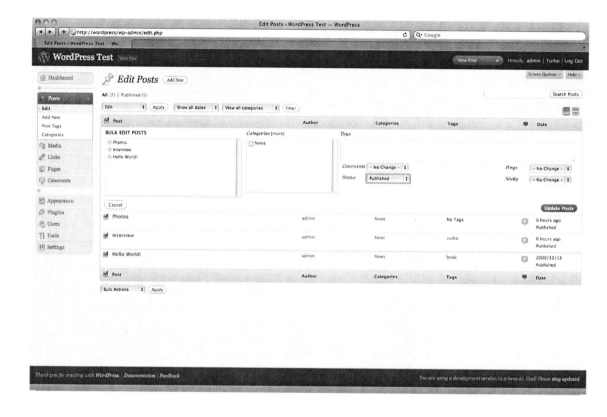

Figure 4-29. Bulk editing posts

Media Files

WordPress allows you to upload virtually any kind of file and attach it to your post or page. You can add files using the uploader found on the individual post/page editing screens and in the Media Library section. Files are stored in the location you specified on the Media Settings panel.

WordPress offers specific upload dialogs for various file types. In order, the icons represent images, videos, audio files, and all other file types. While the upload interface looks more or less the same no matter what kind of file you're working with, the settings you choose will vary depending on the file type. Let's take the four categories one at a time.

Images and Galleries

Edit any individual post or page, and you'll see that there's a group of four icons labeled Add Media above the content box. Click the first icon (Add an image) and a pop-up box should appear with three tabs: From Computer, From URL, and Media Library. Once you've uploaded at least one file to this post, you'll see a fourth tab, Gallery.

Uploading an Image from Your Computer

The media uploader comes in two forms. By default, if you have Flash installed, you'll see the Flash-based uploader. This allows you to upload multiple files at once. However, if you don't have Flash installed, or if the Flash uploader doesn't work correctly, you can switch to the browser uploader. This gives you a basic Browse button that allows you to upload one file at a time.

Using either version of the uploader, go ahead and choose an image to add to your post. Once WordPress has processed the image, you'll see a dialog (Figure 4-30) where you can fill in details about the image: a title, a caption, a description, a link URL, and some alignment and size options.

Title: This is for internal use only. When you're browsing your media library, you'll see this title next to a tiny thumbnail of the image. If you don't fill in a title, the file name will be used.

Caption: This will be shown beneath the image in your post. The exact formatting will depend on your theme's stylesheet.

Alternate Text: The text that will be displayed if the image is missing. It will be read aloud to visually impaired users browsing your site with a screen reader.

Description: This will be displayed in your media library. It will also be displayed on the image's attachment page, if you're using the "[gallery]" shortcode.

Link URL: This lets you specify whether your image is linked, and if so, where it leads. Linking to the file URL is a great way to let your visitors see the full-size image if you're inserting a smaller version. If your post discusses another site, you might choose to paste that URL here instead.

Alignment: Choose whether the image should be aligned to the left, the right, in the center, or not at all. If you choose left or right alignment, your post text will wrap around the image. If you choose center, your image will appear on its own line.

Size: You can insert the full-size image into your post. WordPress will generate up to three smaller sizes (based on the dimensions you choose in your Media Settings), and you can choose any of these if one will fit better in your post content.

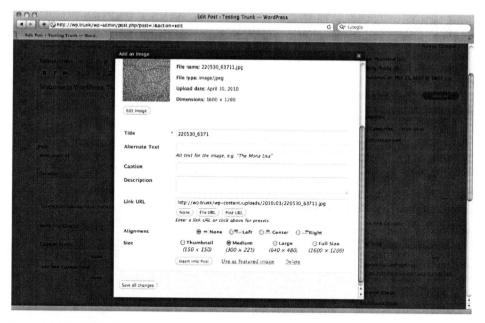

Figure 4-30. Uploading an image from your computer

Some themes do not support image alignment. If your images are not aligned correctly, add the lines in Listing 4-1 to your theme's `styles.css` file. These CSS rules correspond to the classes WordPress inserts into image tags; with these styles in place, your images will be aligned according to the settings you choose in the upload screen.

Listing 4-1. Image alignment styles

```
img.alignright, a img.alignright { float:right; margin: 0 0 1em 1em}
img.alignleft, a img.alignleft { float:left; margin:0 1em 1em 0}
img.aligncenter, a img.aligncenter { display: block; margin: 1em auto; }
```

Below these fields, you'll see a button that lets you insert the image into your post. If you've enabled post thumbnails, you'll see a link that will set the current image as the thumbnail. Off to the right, you'll see a link to move this image to the trash.

If you chose multiple files, you'll see all these options for only the first file. Below the form, you'll see a collapsed row for each additional file. To edit the details for these, you'll need to click the Show links off to the right. The first image's form will collapse, and the one you chose will expand (Figure 4-31).

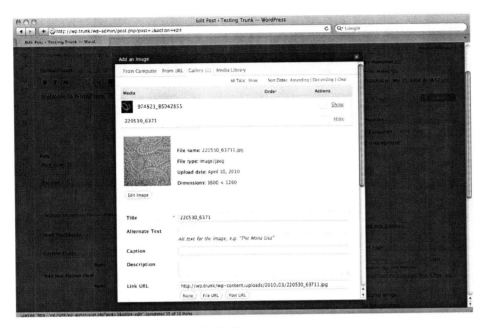

Figure 4-31. Adding an image from the Gallery

Inserting an Image from a URL

You can use images hosted on another site without downloading them to your computer and uploading them into WordPress. Instead of selecting files to upload, click the From URL tab. You'll be asked for the source URL in addition to all the usual image fields (Figure 4-32). However, WordPress won't generate other sizes; you have to use the image as-is.

Keep in mind that images inserted this way are not copied to your server. If the owner of the original file moves or deletes it, it will no longer appear in your post.

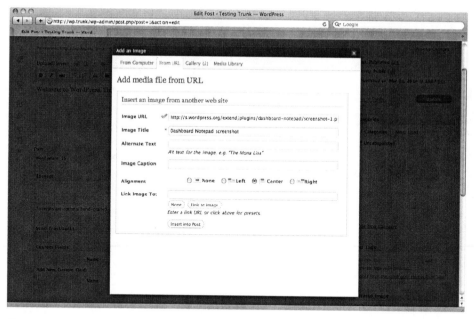

Figure 4-32. Adding an image from a URL

Editing Images

The WordPress media uploader includes a basic image editor. You can crop, resize, and rotate the images you've uploaded. To begin, click the Edit Image button beneath the thumbnail shown in the image details (you can see this button in Figure 4-31). A simple editing interface will appear (Figure 4-33). Click the image once, then drag your cursor to choose an area to crop. If you want to scale or crop the image to a precise number of pixels, use the numeric scaling and cropping forms to the right of the image.

Figure 4-33. Cropping an uploaded image

Galleries

If you have several images to add, you can do them all at once and insert them as a gallery rather than working with them one at a time. Instead of Insert into post, click Save all changes at the very bottom of the window. When you're finished uploading files, choose the Gallery tab. This is where WordPress groups all the photos that have been uploaded for this post. If you want to edit the title (or other details) of a photo, click Show (to the right). When you're done, you can insert all the post's photos at once by clicking Insert gallery into post at the bottom of the pop-up. You'll see that [gallery] has been added to the post's text. Just leave that shortcode on its own line and type whatever else you'd like to say. When you publish the post, a thumbnail-sized copy of each photo appears in the post, as shown in Figure 4-34. The thumbnails will be linked to a new page, where the full-size copy of the photo will appear along with the title and description you entered.

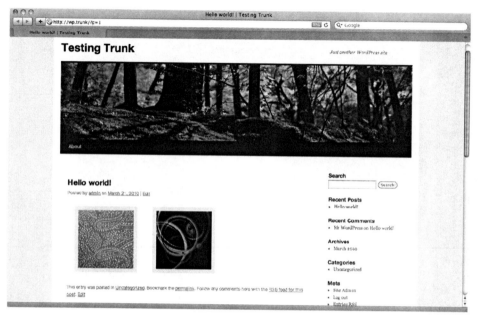

Figure 4-34. An image gallery as shown in the default theme

Video

Uploading videos is much like uploading audio. You'll be asked to fill in the four basic attributes: title, description, caption, and link URL. Inserting the file into the post results in a plain link to the video file. For most site owners, that will not be satisfactory. As a result, there are a number of plugins available that will replace your video file links with video player interfaces (usually Flash-based). My favorite is XHTML Video Embed, but you'll find dozens in the Extend section of wordpress.org.

oEmbed

Embedding video from other sites is quite easy. As of version 2.9, WordPress supports the oEmbed standard. What this means is that you don't have to paste the complicated HTML provided by sites such as YouTube. Instead, you can simply paste the URL of the video page into your post as plain text. If you turned on the oEmbed options in your Media Settings, try it out now! Grab a URL from YouTube, save your post (Figure 4-35), and view it. If everything is working as expected, your plain text URL should have been replaced with a video player, as shown in Figure 4-36.

Figure 4-35. Embedding a YouTube video is as easy as pasting the URL into your post.

OEmbed works with a number of video providers. See codex.wordpress.org/Embeds#oEmbed for a complete list. This page also contains instructions on adding other video providers, if your favorite is not already included.

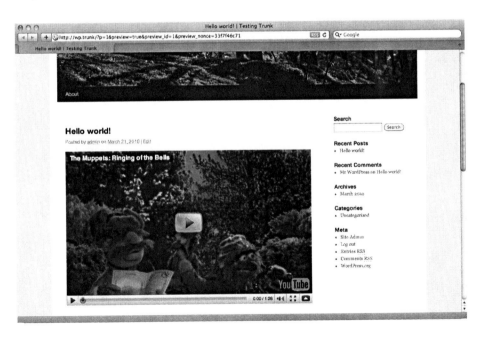

Figure 4-36. The YouTube video embedded from the URL

Audio

Uploading audio is fairly straightforward, too: choose the file, and you'll be asked to fill in the title, description, caption, and link URL. When you press Insert into post, a link to your audio file will appear. If you're not thrilled with this low-tech approach, take a look at the popular Audio Player plugin, which replaces links to MP3 files with a simple Flash player interface.

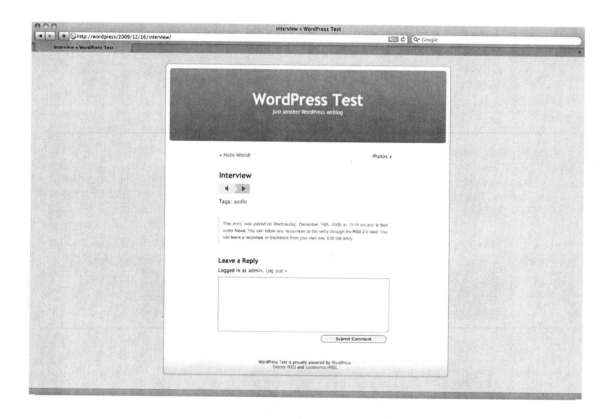

Figure 4-37. Audio Player replaces links to .mp3 files with a Flash-based player.

Podcasting

Podcasting with WordPress is relatively easy. If you've inserted your audio file into your post (even as a simple link), WordPress will automatically add the proper enclosures to your feeds. However, if you want to include your podcast in the iTunes podcast directory, you'll need a plugin to configure some additional fields for your feed. PodPress reigned supreme among podcasting plugins for quite some time, but was abandoned by its developers and doesn't work with recent versions of WordPress.

Podcasting and PowerPress are the best plugin currently available. If you'd like to manage more than one podcast using categories, the Podcast Channels plugin will configure the additional feeds necessary.

▨ **Tip:** The various podcasting plugins work for both audio and video podcasts.

Other File Types

For all other kinds of files, you can use the fourth icon, the one shaped like a starburst. For these files, you'll have just a few attributes: title, caption, description, and link URL. As with audio and video files, inserting another file type will result in a simple link to the original file.

Unfortunately, there is no easy way to list all the files attached to a post, unless they're images. The [gallery] shortcode doesn't work with Word documents or PDFs. You can use the List Child Attachments plugin, which provides both a template tag and a shortcode to list all attached files.

File Sizes and Upload Permissions

If you are working with other users, occasionally your content authors might get an error message when uploading unusual file types. While the error might mention the file size as a potential problem, more likely the real issue is the unfiltered upload capability in WordPress user roles. You'll quickly find, for example, that only administrators can upload Flash videos (.flv). To get around the problem, you can use Role Manager to allow unfiltered uploads for other user roles, or you can use a plugin (like PJW Mime Config) that allows you to specify individual MIME types that will be allowed.

Of course, it's possible that the file size really is the problem. If you have access to your server's php.ini file, increase the `file_uploads`, `upload_max_filesize`, and `post_max_size` values. If you can't modify php.ini, check with your server administrator.

The Media Library

You can see and edit the details for all the media files currently on the site (Figure 4-38) by choosing the Media Library option in the main navigation menu. You can add files to the library directly. They won't be associated with any posts or pages and won't be included in galleries, but individually they can be inserted into posts and pages from the Media Library tab in the upload dialog box.

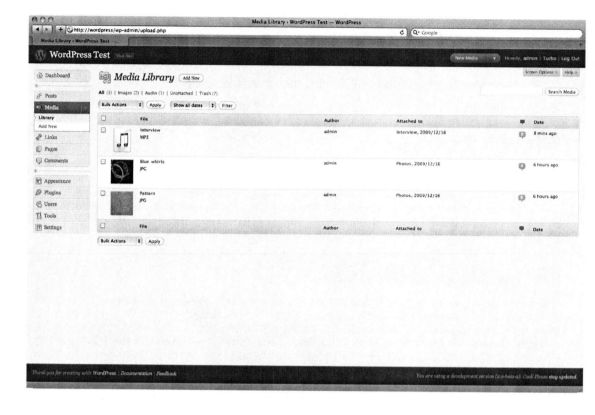

Figure 4-38. All media types are shown in the Media Library.

Links

WordPress comes with a handful of links to resources on wordpress.org. These are all useful sites, and you should bookmark them for your own reference, but they're probably not the sort of thing you want to promote to your visitors. Let's delete them! In the main navigation bar, choose Edit under Links. At the top of the list, in the gray table header next to Name, you'll see a checkbox. Select it and all the prepackaged links will also be selected. In the Bulk Actions dropdown, choose Delete and hit Apply. Now you're ready to add some links of your own. Click the Add New button at the top of the page.

Basic Link Attributes

The Name you specify here (Figure 4-39) will be used as the linked text. Copy the link URL into the web address field. If you'd like to stop there, you can! All the other fields are optional.

Depending on how your theme handles links, the description might be shown as text or as a title attribute on the link tag, which will be shown when you hover over the link.

Links do not use the same group of categories that posts do. If you've just installed WordPress, you'll have one link category, Blogroll. You can manage your link categories by choosing Categories in the Link section of the main navigation menu. If you don't choose a category when adding a link, the default you specified in your Writing settings will be used.

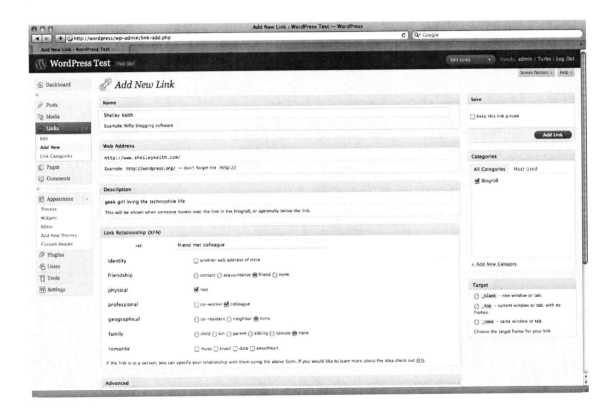

Figure 4-39. Adding a link

Link Relationships: XFN™

XFN™ (XHTML Friends Network) is a microformat; that is, it's a way of adding classes and IDs to basic tags in order to turn plain HTML into a richer source of data. XFN lets you indicate how you know the people whose sites you're adding to your blogroll. XFN data is not visible to visitors. It's used by search engines and social networking sites to determine your relationship to the people listed in your outbound links.

If you've defined your relationship with the owner of a link, WordPress will add the rel attribute to your <a> tag. For example, if you and your brother live in the same household and you're linking to his site, you would choose co-resident in the geographical settings and sibling in the family group, and WordPress would generate the link like so:

```
<a href="http://example.com" rel="co-resident sibling">…</a>
```

The various relationship options should be relatively self-explanatory, but you can read the full explanation of each at the WordPress Codex page at codex.wordpress.org/Defining_Relationships_with_XFN.

Do not fill in the rel text box. It will be filled in automatically as you check off the options in the XFN area, so you can preview your rel attribute before saving your link.

All XFN fields are optional. If you don't care to specify how you know someone, simply leave this section blank.

Figure 4-40. *Advanced link attributes*

Advanced Link Attributes

The image address (Figure 4-40) is the URL of any image you want to represent your link. You could use something small, like a favicon that could be displayed next to the link text in a typical blogroll list. At the other extreme, you could choose a large image, and customize your theme so that the images are shown and the titles appear only as `alt` or `title` attributes. Using this technique, you could turn your link manager into an image gallery—and, by adding a little Javascript into the mix, you could even transform it into a featured content carousel.

Justin Tadlock has written an excellent tutorial on using link images to create a gallery. See `justintadlock.com/archives/2009/01/09/creating-an-image-gallery-with-wordpress-bookmarks` for more information.

■ **Tip:** To use images from your own site as link images, upload them in the Media Library, then copy the file URL to use in this field.

The RSS address field is intended to store the feed (which could be Atom or RDF, not just RSS) of the site you're linking to. However, this field is seldom used in themes. The notes field is also not generally used in themes; you can use it to store private notes for yourself (and any other users of your site who might edit links).

While few themes take advantage of the rating field, it could be essential if you were building a link directory with the links manager.

Finally, you can make the entire link private if you wish. All the link information will be stored in your link manager, but none of it will appear when link lists are displayed on your site.

Link Feed

WordPress generates a feed of your links. The OPML format is commonly used to share lists of links (like bookmark files and blogrolls) on the web, so WordPress generates a basic OPML 1.0 feed, located at `example.com/wp-links-opml.php`.

Feeds

WordPress generates RSS 2.0 and Atom 1.0 feeds automatically for your posts. Links to these feeds are available in your site's footer if you're using the default theme, and can be added to other themes using the Meta widget. If you're using a browser (like Firefox) that discovers feeds automatically, you'll see that both feeds are available on every page of your site. Both feeds display your most recent posts, as determined by the number you chose on the Reading Settings panel. If you've set up permalinks, you can find your feeds by adding `/feed` (for RSS) or `/feed/atom` to your site's URL. If you haven't set up permalinks, you can use the query string URL format instead: `/?feed=rss2` or `/?feed=atom`.

WordPress also includes feeds for the most recent comments on your post. The number of comments displayed, like the number of posts, is based on the number you chose in the Readings Settings panel.

However, WordPress generates a number of other feeds in addition to those for posts and comments (see Table 4-1). There's a feed for each of your categories and tags. You can get feeds of the posts written by an individual author. You can even get feeds for search results!

Since WordPress doesn't advertise these hidden feeds, you'll have to do a little URL manipulation to find them. Of course, once you've located them, you can place the links somewhere in your theme so your visitors can find them too.

Table 4-1. Hidden feeds in WordPress

Feed Type	Default URL	Clean URL
Posts RSS 2.0 (default)	/?feed=rss2	/feed or /feed/rss2
Posts Atom 1.0	/?feed=atom	/feed/atom
Posts RSS 0.92	/?feed=rss	/feed/rss
Posts RDF	/?feed=rdf	/feed/rdf
Comments	/?feed=comments-rss2 /?feed=comments-atom	/comments/feed /comments/feed/atom
Category (ID: 1 slug: news)	/?feed=rss2&cat=1 /?feed=atom&cat=1	/category/news/feed /category/news/feed/atom
Tag (slug: book)	/?feed=rss2&tag=book /?feed=atom&tag=book	/tag/book/feed /tag/book/feed/atom
Multiple Tags (slugs: book, apress)	/?feed=rss2&tag=book+apress /?feed=atom&tag=book+apress	/tag/book+apress/feed /tag/book+apress/feed/atom
Taxonomy Term (genre: mystery)	/?feed=rss2&genre=mystery /?feed=atom&genre=mystery	/genre/mystery/feed /genre/mystery/feed/atom
Author (ID: 2 nickname: Joe)	/?feed=rss2&author=2 /?feed=atom&author=2	/author/joe/feed /author/joe/feed/atom
Search Term (apress)	/?feed=rss2&s=apress /?feed=atom&s=apress	/feed/?s=apress /feed/atom/?s=apress

Content Types (page, course)	/?feed=rss2&post_type=page /?feed=atom&post_type=course	/feed/?post_type=page /feed/atom/?post_type=course
Links OPML 1.0	/wp-links-opml.php	n/a

Summary

If you've been playing along at home, your new WordPress site is now chock-full of delicious content. In Chapters 6 and 7, I'll talk about how to make that content look good by creating your own theme.

Things to keep in mind:

- When choosing between posts vs. pages, any content that's organized by date or anything that belongs in a feed should be stored as a post.

- Stored revisions can drastically increase the size of your database. Limit the number of revisions WordPress keeps if you're concerned about storage space.

- Use your screen options, bulk edit, and quick edit features when you need to make fast changes to groups of posts or pages.

- Audio and video uploads will be treated as links. Install a plugin if you want to provide your visitors with a player interface instead.

- While WordPress generates lots of feeds for you, most of them aren't visible to your users. Create links in your theme files or a text widget if you want to make them available.

■ ■ ■

CHAPTER 5

Importing Content

WordPress comes with tools to import content from a number of other blogging systems. In addition, its API makes it relatively easy to import content from MySQL-based content management systems. If you already have a site, you can probably import its content into WordPress. If you don't have another site, you can skip to the next chapter!

I'll look at the built-in import tools for Blogger and wordpress.com, two of the most commonly used sites. These tools can import blog posts, pages, comments, images, categories, and tags. I'll also show you lesser-known, more complicated import scripts for Joomla (and Mambo), Drupal, and a general script template that can be modified to suit other MySQL databases. Finally, I'll walk you through my own HTML Import plugin, which can be used to import static files as posts or pages. These scripts are not as easy to use as the built-in import tools, but even a complicated import process is better than copying and pasting thousands of entries by hand!

Before Importing

Importing can be tricky, and it doesn't always go well the first time. Therefore, it's important to install the DB Backup and Mass Page Remover plugins in case you need to start over. (Despite the name, Mass Page Remover works just as well on posts.) If you aren't using one of the built-in importers, you'll probably need to do a little bit of cleanup work afterward, so you'll need to install the Search & Replace plugin as well.

If you're importing content into a WordPress site that already contains content, back up your database and put the site into maintenance mode before you begin importing, just as you would if you were upgrading (see Chapter 2).

If you've installed a plugin that crossposts your content to another site (like Facebook or LiveJournal) or automatically notifies another site of your new posts (like Twitter), be sure to deactivate those plugins before you begin; otherwise, you'll flood your social network with your imported posts.

Importing Blogs

Some of the built-in importers will import only the most basic content from your old blog: posts and perhaps comments. Others will import categories, links, and even users. The list on the Tools → Import panel specifies what can be imported from each type of blog. The list of available importers (Figure 5-1) is:

- Blogger

- Blogware

- DotClear

- Graymatter

- LiveJournal (and all sites based on the underlying software, such as DeadJournal)

- MovableType/Typepad

- Textpattern

- WordPress

You can also import posts from an RSS feed or a blogroll from an OPML file. The list of import tools also includes the tools for importing or converting categories and tags.

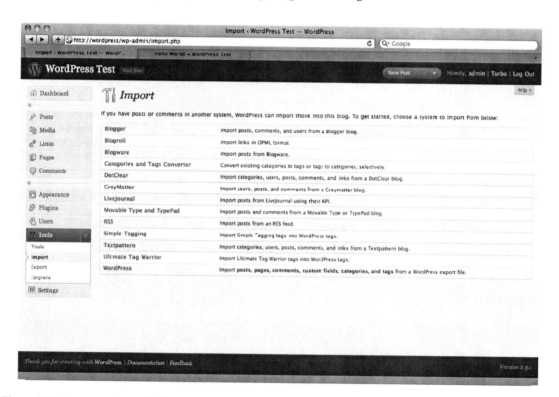

Figure 5-1. Import tools available in WordPress

Importing from WordPress.com

To import content from a wordpress.com blog, first you need to export it. Log in to your wordpress.com account and go to the Dashboard of the site you want to move. Under the Tools menu, choose Export. If your blog has multiple authors, you'll have the option to export just one person's posts. You'll be prompted to save the XML file containing your posts, as shown in Figure 5-2.

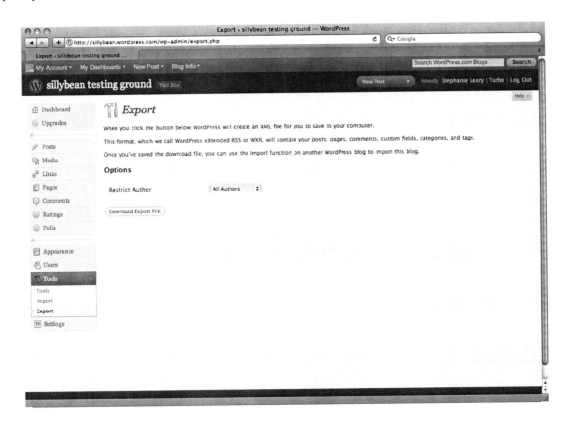

Figure 5-2. *Exporting from wordpress.com*

Once you have the XML file, log in to your new WordPress site and go to Tools → Import. Choose WordPress from the list of importers. On the following screen (Figure 5-3), upload the XML file you saved from wordpress.com. Here, it's also referred to as a WXR file. WXR is a WordPress-specific variant of XML.

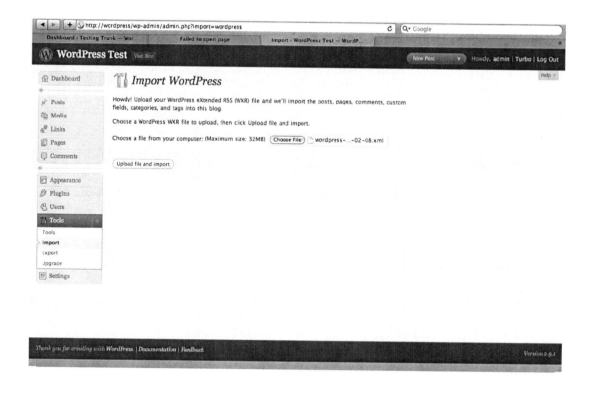

Figure 5-3. Importing from wordpress.com

WordPress will then ask you to map the authors of the wordpress.com posts to the users in your new site or to create a new user for the imported posts (Figure 5-4). You'll also need to choose whether or not to import the media files uploaded to your old posts.

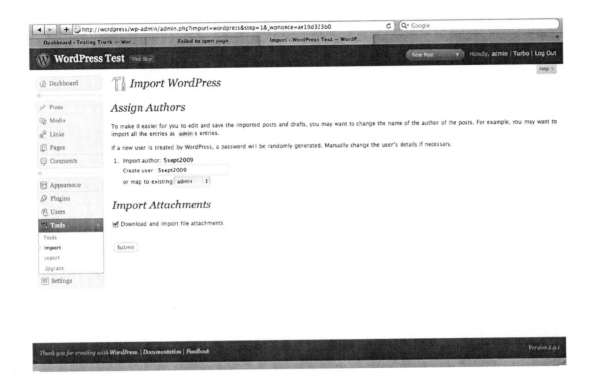

Figure 5-4. Author and attachment choices

Once you've made those decisions, press Submit. WordPress will process the files and present you with a log when it's finished (Figure 5-5).

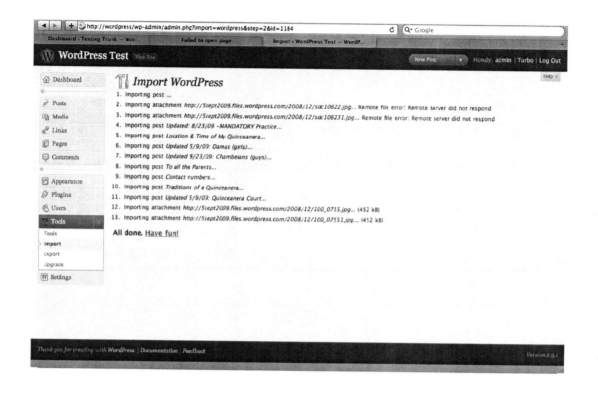

Figure 5-5. Import log and status

Importing from Blogger

To import posts and comments from Blogger, you'll need to authorize your WordPress site to access your Blogger account. Under Tools → Import, choose Blogger from the list, and you'll see the authorization request shown in Figure 5-6 and 5-7.

Figure 5-6. WordPress asks for authorization

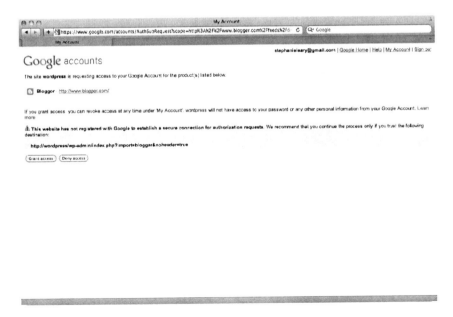

Figure 5-7. Granting access in your Google Account

Once you give it permission, WordPress will show you a list of your Blogger blogs. Press the Import button to the right of the progress bar to begin the import, as shown in Figure 5-8.

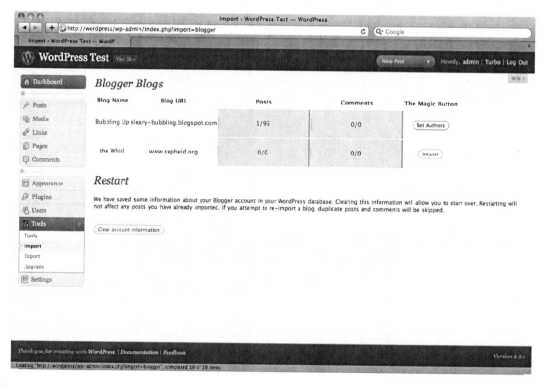

Figure 5-8. Import progress screen

After WordPress has imported your posts, click the Set Authors button. You'll be able to choose which user should be the author of your imported posts (Figure 5-9).

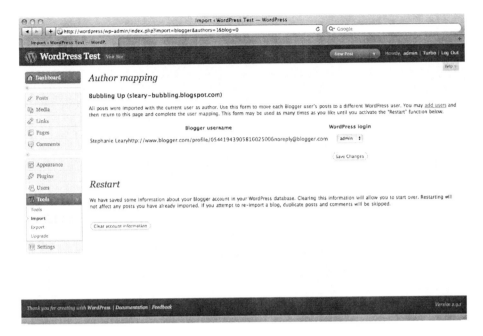

Figure 5-9. Set authors for imported posts

Once you've chosen the author, press the Save Changes button. You'll be whisked back to the Edit Posts screen, where you should see all your imported posts.

If you need to change any attributes other than the author, you'll need to go to Posts → Edit once the import is complete, select all the imported posts, and use the Bulk Edit functions to make your changes. Remember that you can use the Screen Options to change the number of posts per page if you have a lot to go through.

Importing Joomla or Mambo Sites

The unofficial importer for Joomla and Mambo (`azeemkhan.info/2008/joomla2wordpress-import-wizard-v3/`) by Azeem Khan does a lovely job of importing content and static content from versions 1.x and 1.5x. It does not import users or anything added by modules, like forms and comments. While it was written for WordPress 2.7, in my testing it worked with 2.9 as well.

Before you begin importing, you need to create WordPress categories corresponding to the sections and categories in your Joomla or Mambo site. You'll be able to import whole sections at a time or individual categories. You can also import links, one link category at a time.

Download the importer and fill in the database fields for both databases. Copy all the files in the zip package to a directory called `export` in your WordPress directory (Figure 5-10) and visit the URL in your browser.

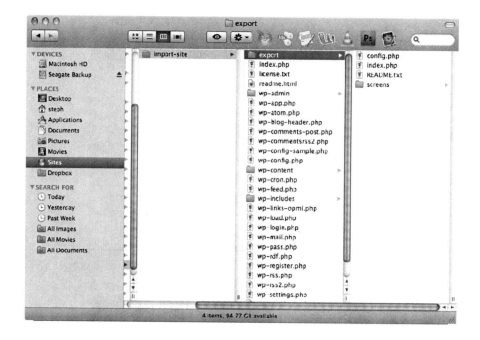

Figure 5-10. *The Joomla/Mambo export files in the WordPress directory*

Step One is to select the section or category of your Joomla/Mambo site, as shown in Figure 5-11. In Step Two, you need to select the corresponding category you created in WordPress. Select that, and MySQL queries will begin scrolling down the page as the importer processes your posts, as shown in Step Three (Figure 5-12). Don't worry if your content is littered with \n and \r characters; those are whitespace characters (mostly line breaks), and they appear in the importer's report. They'll be replaced by the appropriate spacing in your WordPress posts and pages.

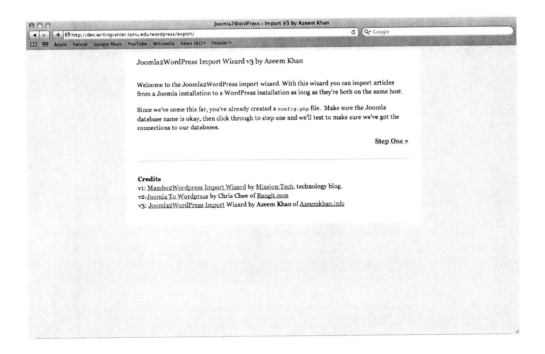

Figure 5-11. *Mambo/Joomla import, Step One*

You can repeat the process for all the categories in your old site. Be sure to remove the export directory when you're finished.

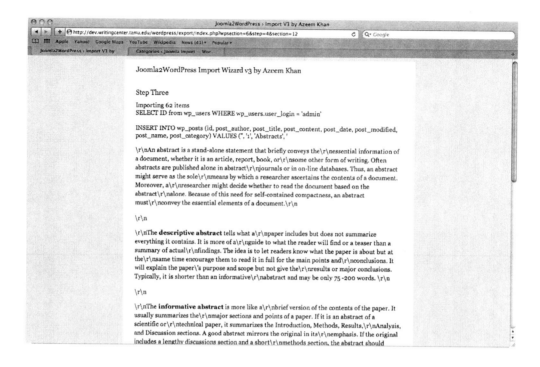

Figure 5-12. Mambo/Joomla import, Step Three

Importing Other MySQL-based Sites

To import content from a MySQL-based site that isn't represented on the official importer list, be prepared to get your hands dirty. There are no friendly web interfaces for this; it's a matter of filling in database values in a script. You might also need to set up a second, temporary database for the migration process.

Developer Joost de Valk has written a tutorial on importing content from another MySQL database into WordPress. The article (`yoast.com/importing-from-another-mysql-into-wordpress`) contains a PHP script (broken into sections) that you can adapt to your own situation. The Codex article on the `wp_insert_post` function, at `codex.wordpress.org/Function_Reference/wp_insert_post`, lists all the possible fields you can insert into the database.

Drupal

There are scripts for importing Drupal sites, but they are somewhat dated. They were written for previous versions of WordPress and will not work correctly on modern installations. If you already have your WordPress site set up, but you need to import from Drupal, I recommend that you install a second WordPress site using the older version required by the importer. You can download old versions of WordPress from the Release Archive at `wordpress.org/download/release-archive/`. Once you've completed the Drupal import, you can then use the WordPress export format to get the data into your current site. If you do not already have your WordPress site set up, you can begin with one of the older versions, import from Drupal, then use the automatic upgrade process to reach the current version.

All that might sound daunting, and indeed, importing a Drupal site into WordPress is tricky if you've set up a lot of custom content types, views, or content blocks. However, if you just need to get the basic content (pages, stories, comments, and taxonomy) into WordPress, these import guides will help you get the job done.

To import a Drupal 6 site into WordPress 2.7, use the SQL queries described at the Social Media Buzz website, socialcmsbuzz.com/convert-import-a-drupal-6-based-website-to-wordpress-v27-20052009/. You'll need to use PHPMyAdmin or a similar MySQL administration interface, unless you're comfortable running queries from the command line. Figure 5-13 shows how to run the necessary queries through PHPMyAdmin.

To import a Drupal 5 site into WordPress 2.3, use the script provided by D'Arcy Norman at http://www.darcynorman.net/?p=1632.

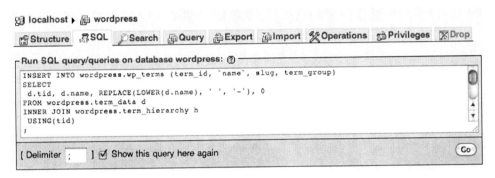

Figure 5-13. Running SQL queries through PHPMyAdmin

Importing HTML Files

I created the HTML Import plugin because the most common scenario, both in my day job and my freelance work, is moving a site from Dreamweaver templates into WordPress. I got very tired of copying and pasting!

The plugin works by reading in HTML as XML and copying the specified tags' contents into various WordPress fields. It therefore works best on well-formed HTML. Your files don't necessarily have to validate according to the W3C specification, but they should at least contain tags that are properly nested. They should also reside on the same server as your WordPress installation.

To begin, download the plugin from the repository at wordpress.org and activate it. You'll find the import options page under the Settings menu. The first thing you'll be asked to fill in is the path to the directory of files you want to import. Find the absolute path—not a site- or file-relative one—to this directory. On a Windows machine, that path will begin with a drive letter (e.g. C:\sites\import). On a UNIX-based server (including Macs), the path will begin with a slash (e.g. /users/username/home/public_html or /Library/WebServer/mysite). Enter the path into the first field on the importer's options page, as shown in Figure 5-14.

Then, identify the types of files you want to import and list the file extensions, separated by commas. If there are any directories the importer should skip, like image or script directories, specify those as well.

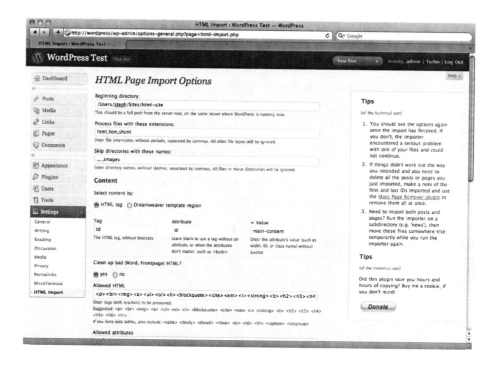

***Figure 5-14.** HTML Import: specifying directories, file types, and the content area*

To select the part of the file that contains the main content—what will become the post or page content in WordPress—you can specify an HTML tag or a Dreamweaver template region. If your pages are based on Dreamweaver templates, select the Dreamweaver option and enter the name of the content area (e.g. "Main Content") into the template region field. If you're using a tag without attributes, or where the attributes don't matter, simply enter the tag (without brackets) in the tag field, and leave the attribute and value fields blank. If your tag does have an attribute that makes it unique, enter the attribute name (like `class` or `id`) in the attribute field and the value in the value field. For example, if your content is contained in the `<td id="main-content">` tag, your import setting would look like Figure 5-15.

You can also have the importer clean up any unneeded HTML, if you wish. For example, if your files came from Microsoft Word or Frontpage, they're probably littered with extraneous `div` tags, smart tags, and `class` attributes. To clean them up, choose Yes under the Clean up bad (Word, Frontpage) HTML heading, then specify the HTML tags and attributes that should be allowed. Any tags and attributes not in these lists will be removed. A list of suggested tags and attributes is provided, along with an extra set that you should include if your content contains data tables.

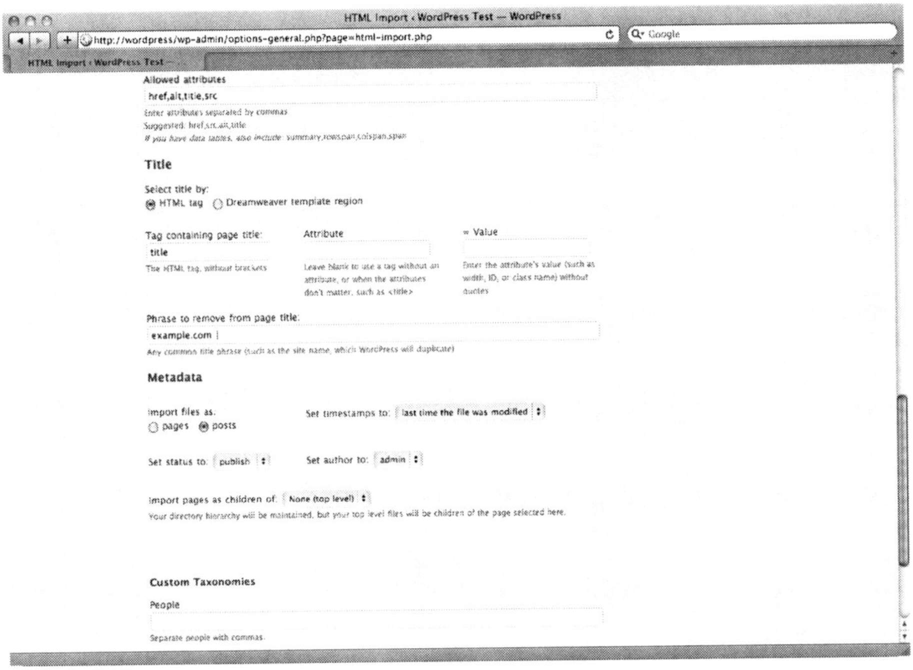

Figure 5-15. HTML Import: choosing the title and metadata

You can select the title tag the same way you chose your content area, as shown in Figure 5-15. You can have the importer remove common words or phrases from your titles. Remember that your site title will be added automatically to your WordPress posts and pages (depending on your theme; see Chapter 7). If it's part of your HTML files' <title> tags, for example, you'll need to remove it now to avoid duplication on your WordPress site.

The metadata section (also shown in Figure 5-15) is where you can specify all the little details: whether you want to import the files as posts or pages, which user should be listed as the author, and what the categories and tags (for posts) or page parent (for pages) should be. You can also choose whether to use the meta description tag's contents as excerpts.

If you have created custom taxonomies for your site (which I'll go over in Chapter 12), you'll see fields for those as well.

Once you've filled in all that information, press the Import button at the bottom of the page and sit back! If you have many files, this might take a minute or two. When the importer has finished, it will display a list of the imported files (Figure 5-16) with any errors noted. It will also give you a set of rewrite rules that, with some slight modifications, you can use in your .htaccess file to redirect visitors from your old files to your new WordPress posts or pages. The original paths won't be exact, especially if you moved the files into a temporary directory while importing them, but you should be able to correct them with a simple search and replace.

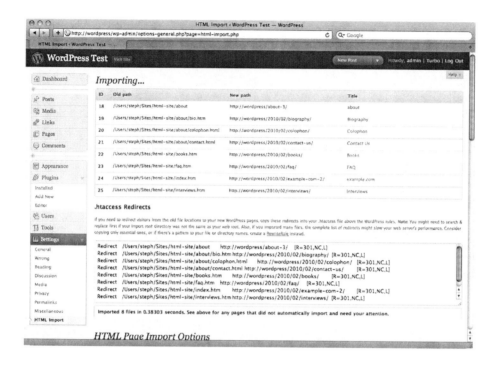

Figure 5-16. The imported files and .htaccess rewrite rules

If the site you're importing has a news section, keep in mind that you could import those files as posts, then remove them from your import directory, and import the rest of the files as pages.

After Importing: Fixing What's Broken

No matter which import tool you used, there's a good chance you'll see some errors in your newly imported content. If you've switched domains, you'll need to change all your internal links and media file paths. There's also a common (and particularly nasty) problem with posts that are garbled or cut off mid-sentence after importing.

Link URLs

If the site you imported lived on another domain, your content is probably full of internal links that contain the old URL. You'll need to search and replace the URL in your old posts and pages. If you've installed the Search & Replace plugin, this will be easy. The plugin's search screen is located at Settings → Search & Replace. Choose the content field, then skip to the bottom of the screen and enter first your old URL, then your new one. See Figure 5-17 for an example.

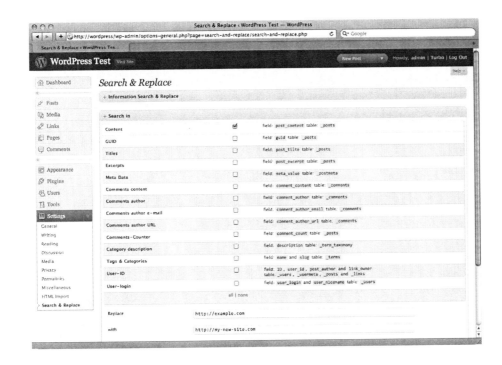

Figure 5-17. Replacing URLs in the content field using the Search & Replace plugin

Paths to Linked Files

Most of the importers will copy the contents of your posts verbatim. That means that if you have any files linked within your old content (images, MP3s, documents), those links won't change. In addition to changing the domain, if necessary, you'll need to update the paths to your files (Figure 5-18).

If all your links were root-relative (/images/photo.jpg), it should be easy to perform a search and replace to accommodate any changes in your directory structure, or you could simply copy your old files to your new site with the directory structure intact. If, however, you had file-relative links (../../images/photo.jpg), you'll have to do a couple of passes to change them all. Do yourself a favor and take this opportunity to make them root-relative!

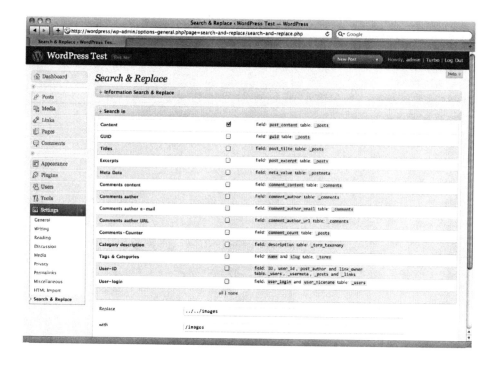

Figure 5-18. Replacing paths in the content field using the Search & Replace plugin

Truncated or Garbled Content

After importing from another site, you might find that some of your posts or pages are filled with garbage characters or inexplicably cut off. What happened?

The key to the problem is this line in your `wp-config.php` file:

```
define('DB_CHARSET', 'utf8');
```

Most likely, your old database used a different character set than your new one. Garbage characters can appear when the import script incorrectly translates the character sets. Your posts might also be truncated at the point where an unrecognized character appeared: a curly quote, an em dash, anything that might have been stored as text and not an encoded HTML equivalent.

There's no easy way to fix this once it's happened. If you don't think the truncation problem is widespread, find one of the truncated articles and take a look at the original version from your old database. Find the character that's causing the problem, and search your old site for it. For all the results you find, just copy the remainder of the article by hand. WordPress does know how to handle special characters, and will encode them correctly once you save your post or page.

If the problem *is* widespread, there's nothing to do but start over. Try to convert the original database's character set to the same one your WordPress database is using. (Make a backup first!) Then run your import again.

Summary

In this chapter you've learned how to import content from WordPress.com, Blogger, Joomla (or Mambo), Drupal and other MySQL-based content management systems, and even static HTML files. I've also shown you how to clean up broken links and truncated content in your imported data.

Now that you have moved all your old content into WordPress, it's time to begin dressing up your new site. In the next chapter, you'll learn how WordPress theme files work and how to create your own custom theme.

CHAPTER 6

■ ■ ■

Creating a Basic Theme

Now that you've configured your site and created some content, it's time to make it look good! First, you'll learn a few ways to change your site's appearance without modifying theme files: using widgets, the menu manager, and uploading custom header and background images. Then you'll create a basic custom theme, starting with a standard HTML file. I'll walk you through the various WordPress template files you can use to make parts of your site look different based on context, and finally I'll show you child themes—a powerful way to customize existing WordPress themes while keeping the original code intact.

Using Widgets

Widgets offer a powerful way to change up your site without touching a line of code. WordPress comes with a baker's dozen of built-in widgets. You can download many more from the plugin repository, and some themes come with their own widgets. Figure 6-1 shows the basic widgets you'll find under Appearance → Widgets.

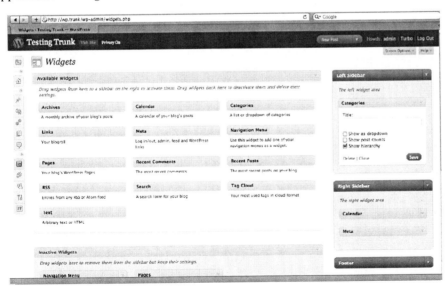

Figure 6-1. The widget management screen

On the main page, you'll see a bank of available widgets. Below the available widgets, there's another bank of inactive widgets. On the right, you'll see a drop zone for each sidebar—that is, each widget area defined in your theme, regardless of whether they actually appear on the sides. The number of sidebars varies; some themes have just one, while others (like Twenty Ten) have five or six. Sidebars can include descriptions to help you keep track of which is which, but the description is optional, as you'll see in Chapter 7, and not all theme or plugin authors will include them.

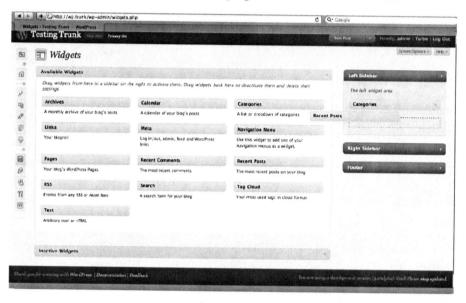

Figure 6-2. Dragging widgets into place

To get started, drag a widget from the available bank into one of the sidebars, as shown in Figure 6-2. Once you've placed the widget in the sidebar, the widget options screen will open. Some widgets don't have any options, and all you can do is close the options screen or remove the widget. (You can also remove widgets from the sidebar by dragging it elsewhere, either back to the available area or into the inactive bank). Other widgets have some options that let you customize their display. For example, the category widget lets you turn the plain linked list into a dropdown, or show the categories in nested lists reflecting the parent/child hierarchy, or include the number of posts assigned to each category. Once you've changed the options, be sure to press the Save button. Otherwise, your changes will be lost when you leave the widget manager screen.

When you drag a widget to the inactive area, it will no longer be displayed in your theme, but all its settings will be preserved. This is useful when you want to temporarily disable a widget or try out an alternative without losing your previous work. When you change your theme, all the active widgets you were using will be moved to the inactive area. All their settings will be saved, so all you have to do is drag them back into the appropriate sidebars in your new theme.

WordPress 2.8 introduced a new way of creating widgets. Any widgets created using the new API, including all the default widgets, can be used as many times as you want. Some older plugins and themes might not use the new multiwidget features, and their widgets can be used only once.

You'll learn how to create your own widgets in Chapter 8.

Using Menus

WordPress 3.0 introduced a new menu feature. If you've downloaded your theme from WordPress Extend (`wordpress.org/extend/themes/`), it might not support the new menus yet, but later in this chapter I'll show you how to modify your theme to enable this feature.

Creating a Menu

To get started with your custom menu, go to Appearance → Menus. Your first menu will be created for you when you load this page.

Use the checkboxes on the right side of the page to add new items to your menu. You can add almost any kind of content as a menu item. By default, the menu management page shows pages, categories, and custom links to URLs you specify. However, in this page's screen options (Figure 6-3), you can turn on the boxes that will let you add posts, tags, custom content types, and custom taxonomies. (You'll learn how to create custom content types and taxonomies in Chapter 12.) You can add multiple items quickly by checking them all at once and pressing the Add to Menu button.

Be sure to press the blue Save Changes button before leaving this screen! Otherwise your menu changes will be lost.

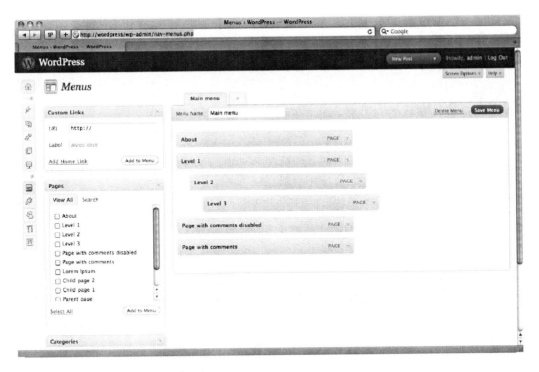

Figure 6-3. Adding a page to a navigation menu

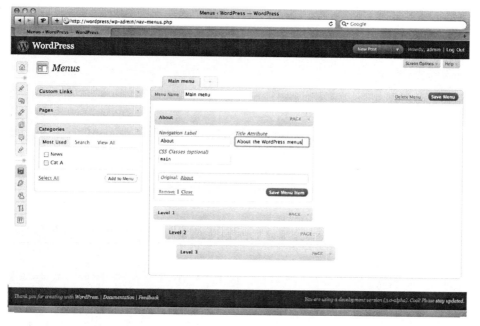

Figure 6-4. Menu item attributes

Editing Menu Items

To edit an item's details or delete it from the menu, use the arrow on the far right side of the item to show the detail editing box (Figure 6-4). By default, the menu item will display the title of the page or the name of the category. However, you can change both the label (the linked text) and the title attribute (the tooltip shown on hover). The original title will always be shown at the bottom of the menu item detail box, so you won't lose track of the item's source.

In the screen options, you can turn on some additional attributes for each menu item: the link target (whether the link opens a new browser window), CSS classes, link relationships (the same sort of XFN data you saw in the link manager in Chapter 4), and a description (which could be displayed below the link if your theme supports it).

You can create multi-level menus, as shown in Figure 6-5. To create a child menu item, simply drag it a little to the right. You'll see its underlying drop zone, drawn in a dashed line, shift over to the right in preset intervals as you move the item.

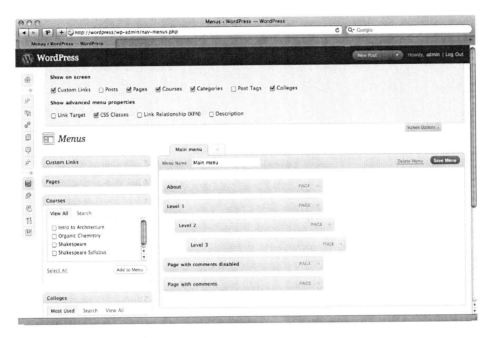

Figure 6-5. Screen options for menus

Creating Multiple Menus

You can create more than one menu. Click the tab containing a plus sign, and you'll see the menu creation screen shown in Figure 6-6. The second menu will become active, and you can begin adding items to it. You can switch back to the first menu using the tab above the drag-and-drop menu item area.

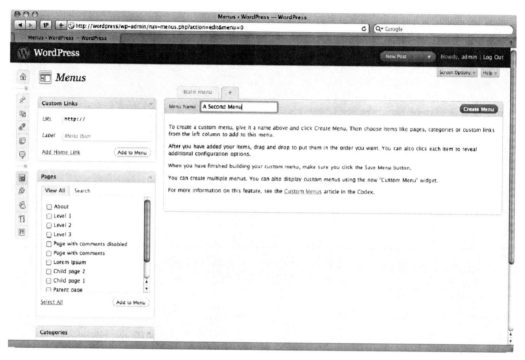

Figure 6-6. Creating a second menu

Using Header and Background Images

If your theme supports custom header and background images, you'll see two additional menu items under Appearance. Let's start with backgrounds. Go to Appearance → Background to get started. Figures 6-7 and 6-8 show the process of uploading a background image and setting the display options.

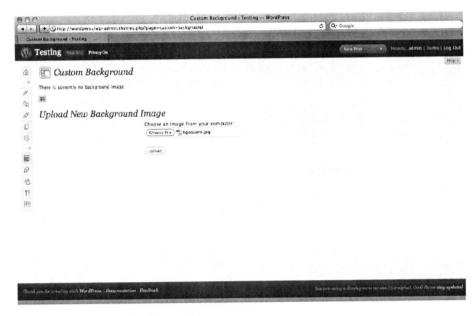

Figure 6-7. Uploading a background image

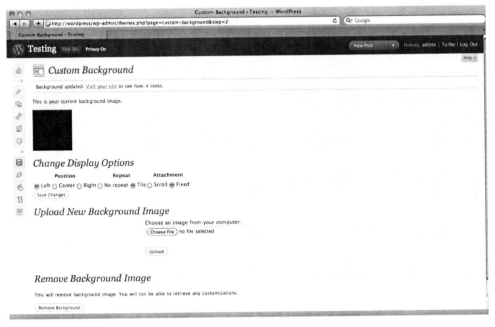

Figure 6-8. Setting the background image display options

The background will be added to your theme using the wp_head() hook. You can specify a background image in your stylesheet, and you'll still be able to replace it using the custom background options. The CSS cascade dictates that styles added directly to a document override those specified in a linked (or imported) stylesheet.

Listing 6-1 shows resulting style block. In this example, you're uploading a file called bgsquare.jpg. This file will be added to the media library, although it is not attached to any particular post.

Listing 6-1. Custom background styles inserted into the theme <head>

```
<meta name="generator" content="WordPress 3.0" />
<style type="text/css">
body {
        background-image:url('http://wordpress/wp-content/uploads/2010/04/bgsquare.jpg');
        background-repeat: repeat;      background-position: top left;  background-attachment:
fixed;}
</style>
</head>
```

Turning HTML into a Theme

WordPress theme files are basically HTML pages with some strategically placed, WordPress-specific PHP functions. While some PHP developers criticize the mingling of languages, preferring a strict separation of logic and layout, the WordPress system is flexible and easy to learn, once you figure out the Loop, which I'll go over in a bit.

A theme is a collection of files in a directory, which will be stored in wp-content/themes in the WordPress directory (unless you have changed this location in wp-config.php). The directory must contain at least two files: style.css, with a header containing some information about the theme, and index.php. There are a number of other optional files that can be used to vary the site's appearance throughout its various sections: archives, pages, search results, and so on.

The best way to demonstrate how a theme file works is to start with a familiar HTML page and show you the tags required to transform it into a WordPress theme file. Listing 6-2 shows the simple XHTML template you'll turn into a theme.

Listing 6-2. A basic XHTML file

```
<!DOCTYPE html PUBLIC "-//W3C//DTD XHTML 1.0 Strict//EN"
        "http://www.w3.org/TR/xhtml1/DTD/xhtml1-strict.dtd">
 <html xmlns="http://www.w3.org/1999/xhtml" xml:lang="en-US">
 <head>
     <title>My Site</title>

     <meta http-equiv="Content-Type" content="application/xhtml+xml;
charset=utf-8" />
     <meta name="description" content="A site about foo." />
     <link rel="stylesheet" href="style.css" type="text/css" />
 </head>
 <body>
 <div id="header">
   <h1>My Site</h1>
 </div> <!-- #header -->
```

```
<div id="main">
   <h2>Foo.</h2>
   <p>Lorem ipsum dolor sit amet, consectetaur adipisicing elit, sed do tempor incididunt ut
labore et dolore magna aliqua. Ut enim ad minim veniam, quis nostrud exercitation ullamco
laboris nisi ut aliquip ex ea consequat.</p>
 </div> <!-- #main -->

 <div id="sidebar">
   <ul>
     <li><a href="#">Page One</a></li>
     <li><a href="#">Page Two</a></li>
     <li><a href="#">Page Three</a></li>
   </ul>
 </div> <!-- #sidebar -->

 <div id="footer">
   <p>&copy; 2010 My Site.</p>
 </div> <!-- #footer -->

 </body>
 </html>
```

The changes are noted in bold in Listing 6-3.

Listing 6-3. The WordPress equivalent

```
<!DOCTYPE html PUBLIC "-//W3C//DTD XHTML 1.0 Strict//EN"
        "http://www.w3.org/TR/xhtml1/DTD/xhtml1-strict.dtd">
<html xmlns="http://www.w3.org/1999/xhtml" <?php language_attributes(); ?>>
<head>
<title><?php bloginfo('name'); ?><?php wp_title(); ?></title>
<meta http-equiv="Content-Type" content="text/html; charset="<?php bloginfo('charset'); ?>" />
<meta name="generator" content="WordPress <?php bloginfo('version'); ?>" />
        <!-- leave this for stats -->
<meta name="description" content="<?php bloginfo('description'); ?>" />
<link rel="stylesheet" href="<?php bloginfo('stylesheet_url'); ?>" type="text/css" />
<link rel="alternate" type="application/rss+xml" title="RSS Feed" href="<?php
bloginfo('rss2_url'); ?>" />
<link rel="alternate" type="application/atom+xml" title="Atom Feed" href="<?php
bloginfo('atom_url'); ?>" />
<link rel="pingback" href="<?php bloginfo('pingback_url'); ?>" />
<?php wp_head(); ?>
</head>
<body <?php body_class(); ?>>
<div id="header">
   <h1><?php bloginfo('name'); ?></h1>
</div> <!-- #header -->
<div id="main">
        <?php if (have_posts()) : while (have_posts()) : the_post(); ?>
        <h2 id="post-<?php the_ID(); ?>" class="<?php post_class(); ?>">
```

```
                <a href="<?php the_permalink() ?>" rel="bookmark" title="Permanent link
to <?php the_title_attribute(); ?>"><?php the_title(); ?></a>
            </h2>
            <?php the_content(); ?>
            <?php wp_link_pages(); ?>
            <div class="commentblock">
                        <?php comments_template(); ?>
            </div><!--commentblock-->
            <?php  endwhile; ?>
        <div class="navigation">
            <div class="alignleft"><?php posts_nav_link(); ?></div>
            <div class="clear"><!-- --></div>
        </div><!-- .navigation -->
            <?php else: ?>
            <h2>Not Found</h2>
            <p>The posts you were looking for could not be found.</p>
            <?php endif; ?>
</div> <!-- #main -->

<div id="sidebar">
<?php if ( !dynamic_sidebar('Sidebar') ) : endif; ?>
</div> <!-- #sidebar -->
<div id="footer">
    <p>&copy; <?php echo date('Y '); bloginfo('name'); ?></p>
</div> <!-- #footer -->
<?php wp_footer(); ?>
</body>
</html>
```

I'll go over each section in turn.

Header

First, rather than specifying a single language, you use the language_attributes function to print the language code corresponding to the setting in your wp-config.php file (US English, unless you changed it).

In the title tag, first you print the title—which could be the title of a post or page, category, or date archive, depending on where this file is used—and then the name of the site. I'll talk more about why I've arranged the title this way in the next chapter.

For the character set, again you use the blog's setting rather than specifying one. Like the language, the character set is specified in the wp-config.php file.

The meta generator tag is somewhat controversial. On the one hand, it provides search engines with an easy means of counting the number of WordPress sites in the world. On the other hand, if you are not conscientious about keeping up with security releases, the generator tag will tell the whole world when you're running outdated, insecure version of the software. Whether or not you include this tag is your choice; it will not affect WordPress's functionality in any way.

The meta description tag is filled in here with the blog description you entered under Settings → General ("Just another WordPress blog," unless you changed it). In the "Search Engine Optimization" section of the next chapter, I'll show you how to generate a unique meta description for every page of your site.

In the next line, `bloginfo('stylesheet_url')` prints the URL of the current theme's stylesheet. As you'll see later, there's a similar bit of code you can use to link to other files in the theme directory.

The next two lines print links to the RSS2 and Atom feeds for the site. There are a number of other feeds you might link here; see Chapter 4 for a complete list.

The pingback URL simply prints a link to your site's XML-RPC file (`http://example.com/xmlrpc.php`), which allows the trackback feature to function.

The `wp_head()` function should appear just before the closing `</head>` tag. It's a hook, which means that it does not print anything directly, but serves as a placeholder function. Developers can add their own code to this hook when they need to insert something—an extra stylesheet or script, for example—to the page header. There are a few built-in functions that hook into `wp-head()`, mostly to call JavaScript files.

Body

The body of your page will generally contain your post or page content, any comments or trackbacks visitors have left, and any sidebars you have defined. I'll go through each of those three areas in turn. First, though, I'll show you the template tags that add styles to your body tag and posts, giving you fine-grained control over the styling of each.

Body and Post Classes

The `body_class()` function prints a series of class names based on the content of the page being viewed. Listings 6-4 through 6-7 show a few examples of the function's output in various contexts.

Listing 6-4. The classes on a single post

```
<body class="single postid-63">
```

This tells you that you're looking at a single post, specifically post ID 63.

Listing 6-5. The classes on a page

```
<body class="page page-id-1952 page-parent page-child parent-pageid-1086 page-template page-template-default logged-in">
```

This tells you that:

- You're looking at a page, specifically page 1952.

- It's a parent of another page.

- It's a child of another page, specifically page 1086.

- It's using a page template, specifically the default template.

- The viewer is logged in.

Listing 6-6. The classes on page 2 of a category archive

```
<body class="archive paged category category-news paged-2 category-paged-2">
```

This tells you that:

- You're looking at an archive page.

- It's a category archive, specifically the news category.

- The archive has more than one page, and you're looking at page 2.

Listing 6-7. Adding classes to the body_class() function

```
<body <?php body_class('main extra-class'); ?>>
// output:
<body class="single postid-63 main extra-class">
```

To add your own classes to the list, provide them as an argument of the body_class() function, as shown in Listing 6-7. They will be appended to the list of automatically generated classes.

The post_class() function, shown attached to the <h2> tag in Listing 6-8, works exactly the same way. It prints attributes about the individual post, including a microformat-specific class (hentry) that lets search engines know that this bit of content on the page is a blog entry. (See microformats.org for more on microformats.)

Listing 6-8 shows the post classes printed for a sticky post with an ID of 188, several tags (tag1, tag2, tag3) and categories (cat-a, cat-b, cat-c, uncategorized, aciform).

Listing 6-8. Sample output of the post_class() function

```
<h2 class="post-188 post type-post hentry category-cat-a category-cat-b category-cat-c
category-uncategorized category-aciform tag-tag1 tag-tag2 tag-tag3">
```

As you can see, these styles offer many opportunities to style posts differently based on their categories, tags, and sticky status. I encourage you to set apart your sticky posts somehow; you could give them a slightly different background color, for example. The rest of the classes are there if you need them.

Content: The Loop

The Loop (Listing 6-9) makes up the main part of a WordPress template. It is essentially a PHP loop wrapped in an if/else statement: if I have posts, then while there are posts, print some information about each one; otherwise print an error message. Figure 6-9 illustrates a typical Loop. What's confusing is that you never see where the posts come from. WordPress performs a database query based on the context—that is, which page you're looking at—and the choices you made in Settings → Reading (regarding the number of posts to display). This query is stored in the $query global variable, and the resulting posts are stored in $posts.

Inside the Loop, the global $post holds the information about each post. All the functions that call a particular piece of information—the_title(), the_content(), and so on—refer to this post, unless otherwise specified (as you'll see in the next chapter). These functions are meant to be used inside the Loop, and generally do not work correctly outside the Loop unless you do a bit of extra work to set up the post data (also in the next chapter).

In most templates, you'll never need to interact directly with $query, $post, or any of the other global variables that define the page; you just need to work with the results. Just as the body classes did, the contents of the Loop will change depending on which page is being viewed. On the home page, either your most recent posts or a single page will be displayed, depending on your choices in the Settings. On a category archive page, the most recent posts in that category appear. Even the search page depends on an invisible database query.

Listing 6-9. The Loop

```
<?php if (have_posts()) : while (have_posts()) : the_post(); ?>
        <h2 id="post-<?php the_ID(); ?>" class="<?php post_class(); ?>">
        <a href="<?php the_permalink() ?>" rel="bookmark" title="Permanent link
to <?php the_title(); ?>"><?php the_title(); ?></a>
        </h2>
        <?php the_content(); ?>
        <?php wp_link_pages(); ?>
        <div class="commentblock">
                <?php comments_template(); ?>
        </div><!--commentblock-->
        <?php endwhile; ?>
    <div class="navigation">
        <div class="alignleft"><?php posts_nav_link(); ?></div>
        <div class="clear"><!-- --></div>
    </div><!-- .navigation -->
 <?php endif; ?>
```

Let's break down the Loop a little.

The first line is a bit complicated; it contains both the conditional (if I have posts) and the beginning of the Loop itself (while I have posts, do something with them). From there to the endwhile() statement, you're inside the Loop, and you can use all the post-specific template tags (or functions). Here you use the_title(), the_content(), wp_link_pages() (which prints page numbers when a post contains multiple pages), and comments_template. This prints a very minimal amount of information about each post. For a complete list of template tags, visit codex.wordpress.org/Template_Tags/.

After the Loop has ended, but before you're completely done with your posts, you need to print some navigation tags. The posts_nav_link() function provides links to older posts (and newer ones if you're viewing an archive page). Note that this tag works only for posts.

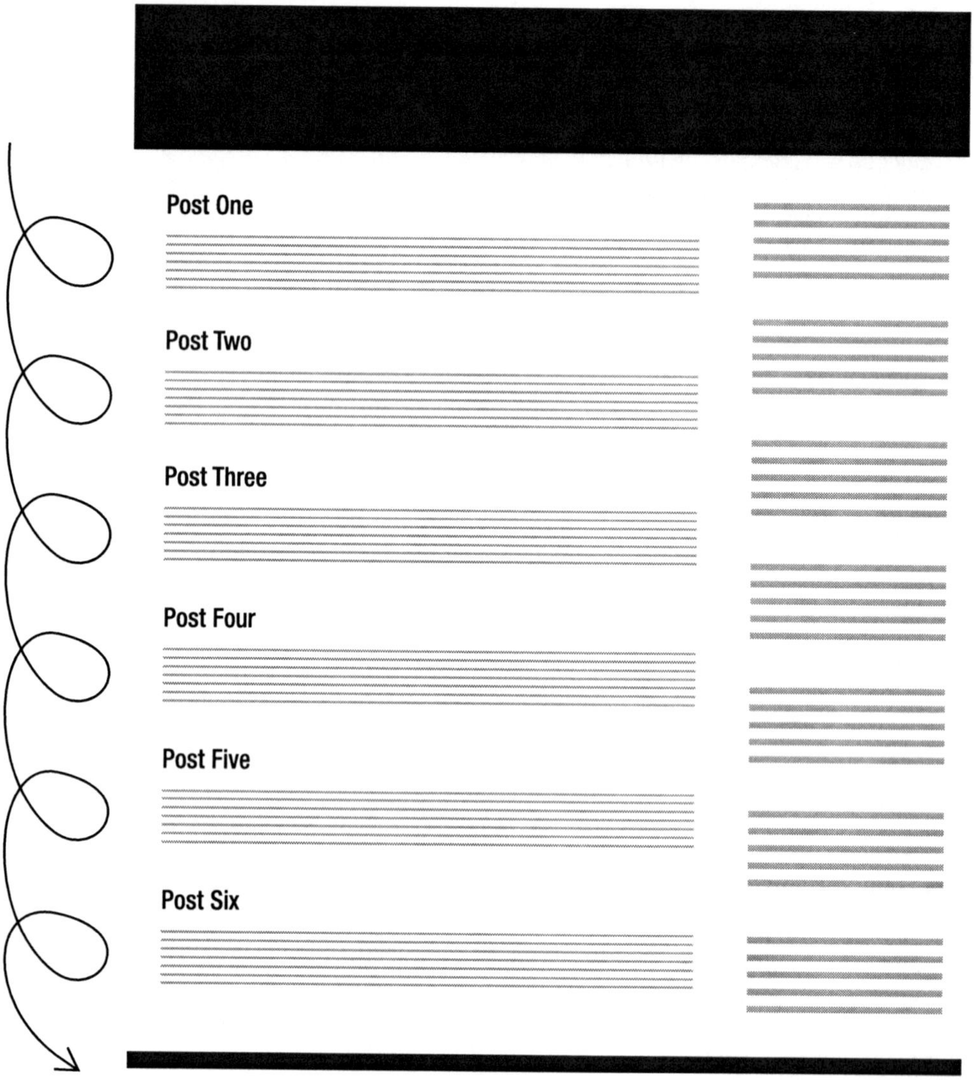

Figure 6-9. The Loop

There are a couple of arguments you can use to modify the way the_content displays your content. The most commonly used is the "more" text string—that is, the text that will be displayed if you have used the <!--more--> tag to break up your post (see Chapter 4). Listing 6-10 shows how to modify the text.

Listing 6-10. Changing the "more" link text

```php
<?php the_content("Continue reading..."); ?>
```

Comments

The `comments_template()` function works like an `include()` statement, but it's specific to one file: `comments.php`. (Some older themes might instead use `comments-popup.php`, which opened comments in a pop-up window.) On the home page or an archive list, it doesn't print anything. On a single post or page, it will display the list of comments and trackbacks (if there are any) and the comment form (if comments are allowed).

Comments can be displayed using the `wp_list_comments()` tag. Listing 6-11 shows a simple list of comments. (This is just a small part of the `comments.php` file.) While this tag offers less fine-grained control over your comment display, it does allow you to take advantage of the options under Settings → Discussion.

Listing 6-11. The comment list

```php
<h3 id="comments"><?php comments_number('No Comments', 'One Comment', '% Comments' );?> to
&#8220;<?php the_title(); ?>&#8221;</h3>

<div class="navigation">
        <div class="alignleft"><?php previous_comments_link() ?></div>
        <div class="alignright"><?php next_comments_link() ?></div>
</div>

<ol class="commentlist">
<?php wp_list_comments(); ?>
</ol>

<div class="navigation">
        <div class="alignleft"><?php previous_comments_link() ?></div>
        <div class="alignright"><?php next_comments_link() ?></div>
</div>
```

Listing 6-12 shows how comments can instead be displayed using a Loop. This is how comments were displayed prior to version 2.7, and some themes still contain this deprecated code. The Loop code offers more control over the individual elements of the comment list, but it also requires more work on your part if you want to modify things. For example, this code displays comments and trackbacks mixed together; if you want to separate them, you have to duplicate the loop and add conditional statements checking the comment type (comment or trackback). You also have to modify this code if you want to enable Gravatars, style the post author's comments differently, or use alternating background colors for every comment. If you use `wp_list_comments()`, all these features are built in, and you just need to style them in your CSS file.

If you display comments using a Loop, you will not be able to take advantage of the settings involving comment threading, paging, or ordering—the last three options under Settings → Discussion.

Listing 6-12. Displaying comments with a loop

```
<h3 id="comments">Comments</h3>
<ol>
<?php foreach ($comments as $comment) : ?>
        <?php $comment->comment_content)) : ?>

                <li id="comment-<?php comment_ID() ?>">
                <div class="comments-body"><?php comment_text() ?></div>
                        <p class="comments-post">Posted by <?php comment_author_link() ?> on
<a href="#comment-<?php comment_ID() ?>" title=""><?php comment_date('F j, Y') ?> at <?php
comment_time() ?></a> <?php edit_comment_link('e','',''); ?></p>
                </li>
        <?php endif; ?>
<?php endforeach; ?>
</ol>
```

The code above constitutes just a small part of the comments.php template. See "Listing Comments" later in this chapter for a complete comments template.

Sidebar

The name of the sidebar must match the name of the widget defined in functions.php. See the "Theme Functions" section of this chapter for more information on setting up widget areas.

The code in Listing 6-13 provides a basic sidebar with one widget area. If you wish, you can check whether any widgets are registered and provide some default sidebar content if they are not. Here, if there are no widgets defined, the viewer will see a search form and a list of archives.

Listing 6-13. The widget area in sidebar.php

```
<div id="sidebar" class="widget-area">
<ul>
<?php if ( !dynamic_sidebar('first-widget-area') ) : // the ID of the sidebar ?>
        <li id="search" class="widget-container widget_search">
                <?php get_search_form(); ?>
        </li>

        <li id="archives" class="widget-container">
                <h3 class="widget-title"><?php _e( 'Archives'); ?></h3>
                <ul>
                        <?php wp_get_archives('type=monthly'); ?>
                </ul>
        </li>

<?php endif; // end primary widget area ?>
</ul>
</div><!-- first .widget-area -->
```

Note that widgets do not have to be placed in a sidebar. While that's their traditional location, widgets can be placed anywhere on the page. The new Twenty Ten default theme has four widget areas in the footer in addition to the two in the sidebar.

You can define multiple sidebar files in your theme by giving them unique names. In addition to sidebar.php, you might have sidebar-page.php and sidebar-author.php. You can call these sidebars in your theme files using the get_sidebar() function, as shown in Listing 6-14. This feature might be most useful when you're customizing the appearance of various archive types, as I'll discuss later in this chapter.

Listing 6-14. Including multiple sidebar files

```php
<?php get_sidebar(); ?>            // sidebar.php
<?php get_sidebar('page'); ?>    // sidebar-page.php
<?php get_sidebar('author'); ?> // sidebar-author.php
```

Footer

In place of a hard-coded copyright year, add the PHP date() function, set to display the current year. It will auto-update on January 1, so you don't have to remember to change it over the holidays. Next to it, use the same bloginfo() function you saw in the header to print the name of the site.

The wp_footer() function is a hook. It might display nothing in a basic installation, but plugins may use it to add code to the theme file. For example, the Google Analytics plugin uses wp_footer() to add the Analytics script to the bottom of the page. Unlike wp_head(), wp_footer() does not (as of this writing) have any built-in functions hooking into it.

Stylesheet

Along with index.php, style.css is one of the two required files in a WordPress theme. You're free to include additional CSS files in your theme, but there must be one with this filename.

Not only is the file required, but it should also begin with a comment block containing the theme's name, URL, description, author name, and version number. Listing 6-15 shows the Twenty Ten theme's header, containing all the relevant information.

Listing 6-15. The theme stylesheet header

```css
/*
Theme Name: Twenty Ten
Theme URI: http://wordpress.org/
Description: The 2010 default theme for WordPress.
Author: the WordPress team
Version: 0.7
Tags: black, blue, white, two-columns, fixed-width, custom-header, theme-options, threaded-
comments, sticky-post, translation-ready, microformats, rtl-language-support
*/
```

This comment block is not absolutely required; your theme will be recognized and listed under Appearance → Themes without it, with the directory name used for the theme name. The tag list is useful only for themes that will be distributed through wordpress.org, where the tags allow users to browse themes by feature or color.

If you're working with a design that wasn't created for WordPress, you need to add a number of styles to your CSS files to account for things that might not have been in the original design, like comments, avatars, and tag and category links for each post. It can be tricky to account for all these elements if your site doesn't yet contain content! The WordPress developers have provided a sample content set for designers. You can download it at codex.wordpress.org/Theme_Development_Checklist#Theme_Unit_Test, import it into a test site, and use it to make sure your theme contains all the styles it needs.

Template Tags

There is a template tag for every piece of information you can enter into a post or page. Figure 6-10 shows the tags that can be used to display the information from the Posts → Edit screen.

Figure 6-10. Template tags for a post

As you'll see throughout this chapter, there is a vast number of template tags you can use to customize your theme. I'll go over most of the essentials, but please visit codex.wordpress.org/Template_Tags/ for a complete list of available tags plus detailed documentation about each one. The conditional tag reference (codex.wordpress.org/Conditional_Tags) is also essential. You'll look at several conditional tags as you dig in to the different theme files that are used to display various kinds of archives.

Date and Time Tags

The date and time tags, the_date() and the_time(), are based on PHP's date() function. If they are called without arguments, they use the date and time formats you chose under Settings → General.

These two tags work exactly the same way, except for one thing: when the_date() appears inside the Loop, it will print the date only once for each set of posts that fall on that date. This behavior makes sense when you're using dates as headers, but it doesn't work so well when you have the date listed alongside the post's other meta data (author, categories, tags, etc.). In the latter case, you need to use the_time() and specify the date format you want. For example, the_time("F j, Y"); will print the month, day, and year in the common American format: May 1, 2010. To use the date format you chose in Settings → General, use the get_option() function as shown in Listing 6-16.

Listing 6-16. the_date and the_time in the Loop

```php
<?php if (have_posts()) : while (have_posts()) : the_post(); ?>
<h3 class="date"><?php the_date(); // prints once per day ?></h3>
        <h2 id="post-<?php the_ID(); ?>" class="<?php post_class(); ?>">
        <a href="<?php the_permalink() ?>" rel="bookmark" title="Permanent link
to <?php the_title(); ?>"><?php the_title(); ?></a>
        </h2>
        <?php the_content(); ?>
        <?php wp_link_pages(); ?>
<p class="postmeta">Posted on
<?php
// these dates and times will print for every post
the_time(get_option("date_format")); // uses date format instead of time
?>
at <?php the_time(); // uses time format by default ?>
</p>
        <div class="commentblock">
                <?php comments_template(); ?>
        </div><!--commentblock-->
        <?php endwhile; ?>
    <div class="navigation">
        <div class="alignleft"><?php posts_nav_link(); ?></div>
        <div class="clear"><!-- --></div>
    </div><!-- .navigation -->
  <?php endif; ?>
```

Theme Files

I've shown you a sample index.php file, but as I mentioned earlier, there are many other theme files you can use to customize various portions of your site. Table 6-1 lists the files.

Table 6-1. Required files and reserved file names.

Required	Optional Includes	Optional Archives and Pages
		404.php
		archive.php
		author.php
		author-*id*.php
		author-*nickname*.php
		category.php
		category-*id*.php
		category-*slug*.php
	comments.php	
	comments-popup.php	
		date.php
	footer.php	
		functions.php
	header.php	
		home.php
index.php		
		links.php

		page.php
		page-*id*.php
		page-*name*.php
		screenshot.png
		search.php
	searchform.php	
	sidebar.php	
	sidebar-*name*.php	
		single.php
		single-*content-type*.php
style.css		
		tag.php
		tag-*slug*.php
		taxonomy.php
		taxonomy-*name*.php
		taxonomy-*name-term*.php

Theme File Hierarchy

In all of the cases below, `index.php` serves as the fallback. If a more specific template is not present, `index.php` will be used. See `codex.wordpress.org/Template_Hierarchy` for more information about the theme file hierarchy.

Sometimes it's hard to tell which file is being used to display a particular page. If you've made changes to a template, but they don't seem to be taking effect, most likely WordPress is not using the template you thought it was. You can use the Show Template plugin to find out. The plugin prints a comment in the footer identifying the theme file that was used to generate the page, as shown in Listing 6-17.

Listing 6-17. The Show Template plugin in action

```
<div id="footer" role="contentinfo">
       <p>
               Testing is proudly powered by
               <a href="http://wordpress.org/">WordPress</a>
               <br /><a href="http://wordpress/feed/">Entries (RSS)</a>
               and <a href="http://wordpress/comments/feed/">Comments (RSS)</a>.
               <!-- 14 queries. 0.169 seconds. -->
       </p>
</div>
</div>

<!-- Active Template: /Users/steph/Sites/wordpress/wp-content/themes/default/single.php -->
</body>
</html>
```

The Home Page

If you have chosen to show your most recent posts on your home page, home.php will be used (if it exists) instead of index.php. It's also possible to use index.php as a unique home page template if your theme contains all the other possible archive templates, so that index.php is never used for any other page display.

If you have chosen a specific page as your site's home page, the appropriate page template will be used instead, even if home.php exists.

Single Posts

For individual post archives, WordPress will use single.php, if it exists. If not, index.php will be used.

Pages

The most specific page template is the one you chose in the Page Template dropdown option on the Edit Page screen. If you haven't chosen a template, WordPress will first look for page-slug.php, where slug is the page's slug. For example, page-about.php would be used for your About page.

If page-slug.php does not exist, WordPress will move on to page-id.php, where id is the ID of the page. For example, if you did not remove the About page that was installed with WordPress, its template would be page-2.php.

Failing all of that, WordPress will use the generic page template, page.php. If that does not exist, index.php will be used instead.

Custom Content Types

If you have any custom content types (see Chapter 12 to learn how to create them), WordPress will look for a file called single-name.php, where name is the slug of the custom type. For example, if you created a post type called Movies with the slug movies, the specific theme file for that type would be (ungrammatically) single-movies.php.

If there is no theme file specific to the content type, `single.php` will be used, with `index.php` as the fallback.

Category Archives

Much like page archives, WordPress will look for first the slug, then the ID, then a generic category template, and finally `archive.php` and `index.php`.

1. `category-slug.php`
2. `category-id.php`
3. `category.php`
4. `archive.php`
5. `index.php`

Tag Archives

Tags work much like categories: slug, then ID, then tag, then `archive.php` and `index.php`.

1. `tag-slug.php`
2. `tag-id.php`
3. `tag.php`
4. `archive.php`
5. `index.php`

Custom Taxonomy Archives

I show you how to create custom taxonomies in Chapter 12. If you'd like a preview, you can download the Taxes plugin (`core.trac.wordpress.org/attachment/ticket/6357/taxes.php`) that creates a "people" taxonomy for tagging your friends and family in your posts and photos.

Once you have created custom taxonomies, you have several options for displaying them. WordPress will first look for a `taxonomy-taxonomy-term.php` file. To use Taxes as an example, the taxonomy is "people" and the slug for Andy's tag might be "andy". WordPress would look for `taxonomy-people-andy.php`. If an archive for Andy doesn't exist, WordPress will look for a generic "people" archive, `taxonomy-people.php`. If that doesn't exist, it will try `taxonomy.php`, then `archive.php`, and finally `index.php`.

Author Archives

It's possible to create a different archive template for every individual author. WordPress will look for author-nickname.php first. If your username is Admin and the nickname is admin, author-admin.php is the most specific theme file for your archives. If that file does not exist, WordPress will then look for author-id.php, making author-1.php the file for your archives.

If neither of those files exists, WordPress will use the generic author template, author.php. Failing that, it will use archive.php, and then index.php as a last resort.

Date-Based Archives

There is just one date-specific archive file, date.php. There are no individual template files for month, year, or day displays. If date.php does not exist, archive.php or index.php will be used.

Search Results

The search.php file will display your search results if it exists. Otherwise, index.php will be used.

Make sure your search.php file contains the posts_nav_link() function. Otherwise, your visitors will have no way to reach any pages of search results other than the first!

Error 404 (File Not Found) Page

There is just one file, 404.php, that could be used to display a "File not found" error message. If this file does not exist, the contents of the else() statement of the other files' Loops will be displayed, as shown in Listing 6-18.

Listing 6-18. Displaying the "not found" error message in theme files other than 404.php

```php
<?php if (have_posts()) : while (have_posts()) : the_post(); ?>
        <h2 id="post-<?php the_ID(); ?>">
        <a href="<?php the_permalink() ?>" rel="bookmark" title="Permanent link
to <?php the_title(); ?>"><?php the_title(); ?></a>
</h2>
        <?php the_content(); ?>
        <?php wp_link_pages(); ?>
        <div class="commentblock">
                <?php comments_template(); ?>
        </div><!--commentblock-->
        <?php  endwhile; ?>
    <div class="navigation">
        <div class="alignleft"><?php posts_nav_link(); ?></div>
        <div class="clear"><!-- --></div>
    </div><!-- .navigation -->
<?php else: ?>
        <h2>Not Found</h2>
        <p>The posts you were looking for could not be found.</p>
<?php endif; ?>
```

Attachment Pages

When you upload media files, you have the option of linking them to a post page rather than the file URL. Attachment pages are shown when files are linked to post pages.

You can create different attachment pages for different media types. The name of the MIME type will be the name of your file; you could have image.php, video.php, audio.php, and application.php as well as a generic attachment.php file.

If no attachment page file exists, single.php will be used, and as a last resort, index.php.

Listing Comments

Listing comments is simple; it takes just one function. The comments template, however, is complicated. That's because it needs to check for a lot of different conditions: whether comments are allowed, whether they've been closed, whether there are any comments, whether the user is logged in, and so forth. Listing 6-19 shows the comments.php file from Simplex Flex, which is almost identical to the comments.php file in Twenty Ten.

Listing 6-19. The Simplex Flex comments.php template

```
<div id="comments">
<?php if ( post_password_required() ) : ?>
<div class="nopassword"><?php _e( 'This post is password protected. Enter the password to view
any comments.', 'simplex-flex' ); ?></div>
</div><!-- .comments -->

<?php
        return;
endif;
?>

<?php // Display the header for the comment section ?>

<?php if ( have_comments() ) : // if there are comments ?>
<h3 id="comments-title"><?php comments_number(
sprintf(__('No Responses to %s', 'simplex-flex'), '<em>' . get_the_title() . '</em>'),
sprintf(__('One Response to %s', 'simplex-flex'), '<em>' . get_the_title() . '</em>'),
sprintf(__('%% Responses to %s', 'simplex-flex'), '<em>' . get_the_title() . '</em>')
); ?> </h3>

<?php // Display navigation for paged comments, at the top of the list ?>

<?php if ( get_comment_pages_count() > 1 ) : // if there is more than one page... ?>
<div class="navigation">
<div class="nav-previous"><?php previous_comments_link( __('&larr; Older Comments', 'simplex-
flex') ); ?></div>
<div class="nav-next"><?php next_comments_link( __('Newer Comments &rarr;', 'simplex-flex') );
?></div>
</div>
<?php endif; ?>
```

```php
<?php // Display the list of comments ?>

<ol class="commentlist">
        <?php wp_list_comments(); ?>
</ol>

<?php // Display navigation for paged comments, at the bottom of the list ?>

<?php if ( get_comment_pages_count() > 1 ) : // if there is more than one page... ?>
<div class="navigation">
<div class="nav-previous"><?php previous_comments_link( __('&larr; Older Comments', 'simplex-
flex') ); ?></div>
<div class="nav-next"><?php next_comments_link( __('Newer Comments &rarr;', 'simplex-flex') );
?></div>
</div>
<?php endif; ?>

<?php else : // else there are no comments yet... ?>

<?php if ( comments_open() ) : // If comments are open, but there are no comments (nothing to
do here) ?>

<?php else : // if comments are closed ?>
<p class="nocomments"><?php _e('Comments are closed.', 'simplex-flex'); ?></p>

<?php endif; ?>
<?php endif; ?>

<?php // Display the comment form ?>

<?php comment_form(); ?>

</div><!-- #comments -->
```

There's a lot going on here, so I'll take it one piece at a time.

First, if the post is password protected and the reader has not already entered the password, you have to prevent them from seeing the comments. This if statement prints an error message to the reader and exits without printing any comments.

Once that's out of the way, you can begin a comment Loop. You do the usual check to see if there are any comments before you print anything, but if there are, you print a header containing the number of comments. This is done with PHP's sprintf() function, which has an odd syntax. You don't need to change this section, so I won't go into detail here, but you can always refer to the documentation at php.net/sprintf if necessary.

The next section checks to see if there's more than one page of comments. This depends entirely on the settings you chose back in Settings → Discussion. If you chose not to split comments into multiple pages, nothing will happen here. If you did, however, this section prints the page navigation. This block of code will be repeated below the comments list as well.

Finally, you display the comments themselves. Here, you see the wp_list_comments() function; however, as you saw earlier in this chapter, you can write your own comments loop if you wish.

Once you print the navigation again, you're done with the if (have_comments()) portion of this Loop, but you're not done yet! You could print something in the event that there are no comments yet, but in this case you've chosen to just leave the comment area blank. However, next you need to print a message if comments have been closed. This is the message your readers will see if you turned off comments on an individual post after allowing them for a while, or if you chose to automatically close comments on older posts.

Once you have taken care of all that, you can print the comment form. The `comment_form()` function prints out a standard form and performs all the necessary checks to see whether comments are open. You could instead use a hand-crafted form, as all themes did prior to version 3.0, but I recommend using the `comment_form()` tag with whatever styles you need to make its appearance match your theme.

Including Additional Files

WordPress 3.0 includes a new include function, `get_template_part()`. This function can take two arguments. Listing 6-20 shows two uses of this function.

Listing 6-20. Using the get_template_part function

```
get_template_part('loop');              // loop.php
get_template_part('loop', 'index');   // loop-index.php
```

With the `get_template_part()` function, you can create your own hierarchy of included files that works just like the sidebars. With one argument, the slug, the function will include a filename matching that slug. If a second argument, the name, is included, WordPress will first look for `slug-name.php`, and if it doesn't exist, it will substitute the more generic `slug.php` file.

Styling Content

Styling your theme is almost entirely up to you, but every theme should include the styles required to make image alignment work as expected. You might recall from Chapter 4 that when you upload an image, you're offered four alignment choices: left, right, centered, or none. When you insert the image into your post or page, WordPress assigns classes to the image based on your selection. Of course, by themselves, those classes don't actually do anything. You'll need to insert the styles in Listing 6-21 (or something similar to them) in your theme's stylesheet.

Listing 6-21. Basic styles necessary to support aligned images and image galleries

```
img.alignright {float:right; margin:0 0 1em 1em}
img.alignleft {float:left; margin:0 1em 1em 0}
img.aligncenter {display: block; margin-left: auto; margin-right: auto}
a img.alignright {float:right; margin:0 0 1em 1em}
a img.alignleft {float:left; margin:0 1em 1em 0}
a img.aligncenter {display: block; margin-left: auto; margin-right: auto}
```

Changing Appearance Based on Context

You've already seen how the body and post class functions can be used to apply different styles based on which content is being viewed. However, sometimes styling isn't enough. There are a number of ways to modify the content itself. You can take advantage of the theme file hierarchy to modify content in different contexts, and within a single file you can use conditional tags.

Conditional Tags

Conditional tags can be used in any template, but they're especially useful in the include files—the header, sidebar, and footer—where using conditional tags let you handle alternatives without creating separate files. Table 6-2 lists the conditional tags and their arguments. In the next few sections, you'll see several ways of using these conditional tags.

There are four classes of conditionals: is*, in*, has*, and *open. Is_sticky() and is_paged() refer to properties of individual posts or pages. All the other is* functions are true if the currently viewed page is of that type. For example, is_single() returns true if it appears in a single post archive template. The is_front_page() function returns true if you're viewing the site's home page, whether you've set the Reading options to display blog posts or a single page, whereas is_home() is true only on the main blog posts page.

The in*, has*, and *open functions refer to properties. For example, comments_open() is true if displayed on the archive page for a post that allows comments. The in_category() function is true only if a post has been assigned directly to the category in question; the function does not check subcategories. (You'll make use of this trait just a few pages from now, when you want to separate subcategory posts in the category archive template.)

Like all WordPress template tags, conditionals are really just functions. Most of these functions can be used inside the Loop or in a specific archive template without arguments. Outside the Loop—that is, in an advanced theme function like you'll see in the next chapter, or in a plugin—you need to provide some identifying information about the post, page, author, tag, category, or taxonomy term you're interested in. Table 6-2 lists the various arguments that each function accepts.

Table 6-2. Arguments accepted by the conditional tags

Conditional	ID	Slug	Title	Array	Other
is_single	X	X	X	X	
is_sticky	X				
is_page	X	X			
is_page_template					Filename
is_category	X	X	X	X	
in_category	X				
is_tag		X	X	X	
has_tag		X	X	X	
is_tax		X	X	X	

is_author	X	Username	Nickname	X	
has_excerpt	X				
The following tags do not accept arguments; they are true if the corresponding archive template is being used to display the current page.					
is_home	is_search	is_day	is_feed	is_404	is_comments_popup
is_front_page	is_time	is_month	is_attachment	is_trackback	is_active_sidebar
is_archive	is_date	is_year	is_singular	is_preview	is_admin
The following tags do not accept arguments. They return information about the currently viewed page.					
comments_open	pings_open	is_paged	in_the_loop		

Posts vs. Pages

Most themes use separate files to display posts and pages rather than using index.php for both. There are simple changes, like removing the category and tag listings from the page display or moving the date tag (or removing it altogether). There are many other changes you could make, though. For example, you could use the conditional tags if_page() and if_single() in your sidebar to display different widget areas for posts and pages. That way, you can display post-related things like archives, categories, and tag clouds only on your post archives and use the page sidebars to list the page's children (if it has any) or media attachments. Listing 6-22 shows a sidebar.php file that includes various sidebars depending on the type of page being viewed.

Listing 6-22. A sidebar.php file that calls other sidebar files conditionally

```
<div id="sidebar">
<?php get_sidebar('nav'); ?>
<?php
if ($post->ID == 2675)
        get_sidebar('book');
if (is_page())
        get_sidebar('pages');
}
?>
</div>
```

Categories

Earlier, you saw how category-specific classes are added to the body tag and the individual post. With category archives, you can customize your category display even further. For example, I often use the_excerpt() on most category archives to provide a quick overview my readers can easily skim.

However, in some situations, like a podcast category, you want the archive to look just like a complete blog home page. In that case, you duplicate category.php and call it category-podcast.php. You then alter category.php to use the_excerpt() while keeping the_content() in the podcast category. You can also use the conditionals again (in_category()) to include podcast-specific information in your sidebar: schedules, donation links, etc.

Category archives have a little quirk: if you're looking at a category that has subcategories, posts from those subcategories will be mixed in with the posts from the parent category. Listing 6-23 shows a category archive template that first lists the child categories, then shows the posts assigned only to the parent category using the in_category() conditional.

Listing 6-23. Listing subcategories and limiting the loop to the parent category

```
<h2 class="pagetitle"><?php single_cat_title(); ?></h2>
<?php
        $catid = get_query_var('cat');
?>
<ul class="subcategories">
        <?php $cats = get_categories('order=desc&title_li=&child_of='.$catid);
                foreach ($cats as $cat) { ?>
                <li>
                    <h4><a href="<?php echo get_category_link( $cat->cat_ID ); ?>" rel="bookmark"
title="<?php echo $cat->cat_name; ?>"><?php echo $cat->cat_name; ?></a></h4>
                </li>
                <?php }
                ?>
</ul>
<?php if (have_posts()) : while (have_posts()) : the_post(); ?>
<?php if (in_category($catid) ) : ?>
        <h2 <?php post_class(); ?>><a href="<?php the_permalink() ?>" rel="bookmark"
title="Permanent Link to <?php the_title_attribute(); ?>"><?php the_title(); ?></a></h2>
        <?php the_content(); ?>
<?php endif; endwhile; ?>
```

Here, you use the get_query_var() function to find out which category you're looking at. You can use this function to retrieve any of the variables that make up the invisible Loop query, but since you know you're working with a category archive, it's the category ID you're interested in.

Once you have the ID, you can use get_categories() to print a list of all the current category's subcategories. Then you can go into your typical Loop, but you've added a conditional tag (which is discussed later in this chapter) to print the title and content only if the post is in the parent category, not any of its subcategories.

Author Archives

Earlier, you saw how to include multiple sidebars using the get_sidebar() function. Listing 6-24 shows how sidebars might be included in an author.php template.

Listing 6-24. Including a sidebar file with author information

```
<?php get_sidebar(); ?>           // sidebar.php
<?php get_sidebar('author'); ?> // sidebar-author.php
```

In an author sidebar, you might use a text widget to provide a short bio of the author in question. You'll see how to access the author profile information directly in Chapter 10.

Search Results

If your search results use the same loop as your home page, your visitors will see the full text of your posts and pages in the list of results. That might be a lot of text! Instead, consider using the_excerpt().

Pages don't have excerpts, so this will require a little setup. Remember that posts and pages share the same database table, which means they really have all the same fields, even if you don't see them in the edit screens. The PJW Page Excerpt plugin adds the excerpt box to the Page → Edit screen. With this in place, you can write brief summaries of your pages for the search results list.

In your search.php file, replace the_content() with the_excerpt(). You should see a much shorter, more user-friendly search results page.

Creating Navigation Menus

Prior to version 3.0, most themes used either page or category lists as menus. Of course, you can still create menus this way, although this method is less flexible than the navigation menu. I'll go through all three of the common methods of creating menus: the new menu tag, page lists, and category lists.

Custom Navigation Tag

By default, the class on the surrounding <div> tag will be "menu", but you can change this in the function parameters. In fact, you can change the <div> tag to something else entirely, as shown in Listing 6-25.

Listing 6-25. Using the wp_nav_menu function

```
<?php wp_nav_menu( 'sort_column=menu_order&format=ul&menu_class=nav' ); ?>
```

Because wp_nav_menu() is a new feature, there are several fallback functions that will be used when the user has not yet created a menu, or when a theme that includes wp_nav_menu() is installed on an older version of WordPress. If wp_nav_menu() is called but there are no menus defined, wp_page_menu() is substituted. If you would prefer another substitute, such as wp_list_categories, you can add the name of your preferred function using the fallback_cb() parameter, as shown in Listing 6-26.

Listing 6-26. Changing the wp_nav_menu fallback function

```
<?php wp_nav_menu( 'sort_column=menu_order&fallback_cb=wp_list_categories' ); ?>
```

Page Lists and Page Menus

The wp_list_pages() function supports several parameters that allow you to change the way pages are listed. By default, all pages will be listed in alphabetical order. Listing 6-27 shows several alternatives. See codex.wordpress.org/Template_Tags/wp_list_pages for the full list of available parameters and their default settings.

Listing 6-27. Using the wp_list_pages function

```
<!-- all pages in alphabetical order -->
<ul> <?php wp_list_pages(); ?> </ul>
<!-- all pages in menu order -->
<ul> <?php wp_list_pages('sort_column=menu_order'); ?> </ul>
<!-- to exclude a single page (in this case, the one with an ID of 12) -->
<ul> <?php wp_list_pages('sort_column=menu_order&exclude=12'); ?> </ul>
```

There's a second function that you can use for a few extra options in your page lists: wp_page_menu(). This is essentially a clone of wp_list_pages() that has just a few extra features. It includes the <ul> tags, so you don't have to specify those separately. It includes a menu_class parameter so you can still style the list using your own class names. This function also adds a "Home" link to the page list, as shown in Listing 6-28.

Listing 6-28. Using the wp_page_menu function

```
<!-- all pages in menu order, then alphabetically by page title -->
<?php wp_page_menu(); ?>
<!-- the above, plus a 'home' link, with a different class on the <ul> -->
<?php wp_page_menu('show_home=true&menu_class=nav'); ?>
```

These parameters give you a great deal of flexibility in creating your navigation menus, but you will quickly discover that WordPress's page management features are a little lacking when it comes to creating the navigation for a complicated site. Changing the page order, choosing which pages are included or excluded, and linking to external sites are all much harder to accomplish with page lists than with the navigation menus.

Changing the Page Order

To rearrange pages, simply change the number in the Order box, as shown in Figure 6-11. It's a little like writing a program in BASIC: if you need to insert a page between the existing ones, you'll have to redo the numbering on the entire sequence.

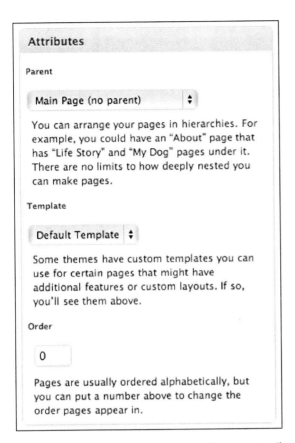

Figure 6-11. The menu order field in the page Attributes box

My Page Order

Choose a page from the drop down to order its subpages or order the pages on this level by dragging and dropping them into the desired order.

Order Subpages

[Parent page ⬍] [Order Subpages]

Order Pages

About
About
Parent page
Lorem Ipsum
Page with comments
Page with comments disabled
Level 1
About

[Click to Order Pages]

Figure 6-12. The My Page Order plugin

The Quick Edit feature makes it a little easier to order several pages at a time, but editing a field for each page is still more tedious than it ought to be. There are a few plugins that make the process much easier.

My Page Order is the simplest way to reorganize your pages in WordPress. It provides a drag-and-drop editing screen (Figure 6-12) for all your top-level pages and a dropdown list of all the pages that have subpages. Choose one of those, and you can rearrange all the pages on that level as well.

PageMash (Figure 6-13) offers a similar drag and drop interface. It expands the first level of subpages and gives you arrows to expand others as needed. You can change not only the order but the depth of each page by dragging it under another page in the list.

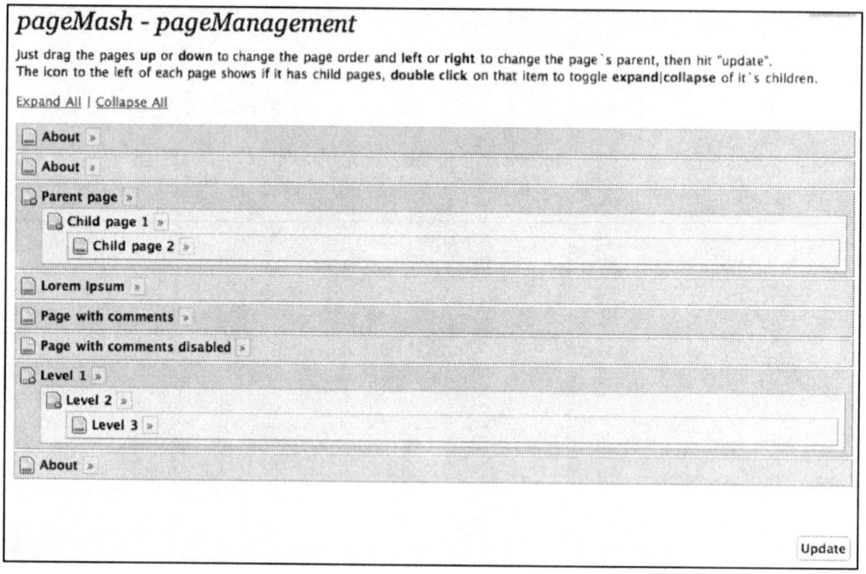

Figure 6-13. The PageMash plugin

Changing Which Pages are Listed

Rather than changing your theme files every time you need to exclude another page from the menu, consider installing a plugin that will allow you to exclude pages from all page list template tags.

Exclude Pages, shown in Figure 6-14, provides a checkbox on the page editing screen that will allow you to decide whether the page should be included in menus.

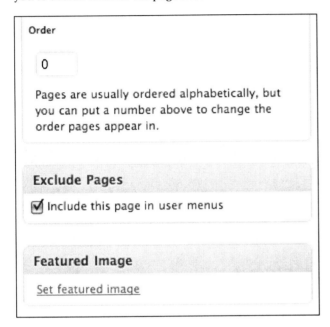

Figure 6-14. The Exclude Pages plugin

Page Lists Plus offers a long list of useful global settings, such as Exclude children of excluded pages. It also allows administrators to specify which options will appear to content authors on individual pages. In addition to choosing whether the page will appear in menus, the author can change the link text, specify custom classes, and even redirect visitors to some other URL.

Including Links to Things Outside WordPress

Sometimes you need to link to something other than a WordPress page in your navigation menu. Perhaps you've built a photo gallery in ZenPhoto. How do you get it into your menu without hand-coding the link every time the menu appears in a theme file?

The Page Lists Plus plugin mentioned above includes just such a feature, but if you want something simpler, try Page Links To (Figure 6-15). Install the plugin, then create a blank post or page with the title of your desired menu item. Scroll down to the Page Links To section of the edit screen and enter the URL of your external page.

Figure 6-15. The Page Links To plugin

The disadvantage of this plugin is that it clutters up your Page → Edit screens with a bunch of placeholder pages.

Category Lists

Much like `wp_list_pages()`, `wp_list_categories()` lets you customize the category list in a number of ways. By default, it lists all your categories in alphabetical order. A few of the function's optional parameters are shown in Listing 6-29.

Unlike pages, categories don't have a menu order. You can add this feature with the My Category Order plugin.

Listing 6-29. Using the wp_list_categories function

```
<!-- all categories in alphabetical order -->
<ul> <?php wp_list_categories(); ?> </ul>
<!-- all categores in menu order: My Category Order plugin required -->
<ul> <?php wp_list_pages('sort_column=menu_order'); ?> </ul>
<!-- show only parent categories -->
<ul> <?php wp_list_categories('depth=1'); ?> </ul>
```

You could combine page and category lists by using a filter. I'll talk more about filters in Chapter 10, but in the meantime, Listing 6-30 shows a quick filter function that could be placed in your `functions.php` file.

Listing 6-30. Appending the category list to your page lists

```
function add_category_list($pagelist) {
        $cats = wp_list_categories('echo=0&title_li=');
        return $pagelist.$cats;
}
add_filter('wp_list_pages', 'add_category_list');
```

Theme Functions

In the last few chapters, you've seen some examples of code that can be placed in a theme's `functions.php` file in order to add or modify WordPress features: changing user contact fields, changing roles, even adding and removing roles. Here, you'll learn more basic uses of the `functions.php` file.

You've probably realized by now that PHP functions can be placed in any theme file. That means you can create functions right in your template; however, if it's something you'll want to reuse in other templates, it's best to put it in the theme functions file or a plugin (which I'll talk about in Chapter 9).

Enabling Widgets

The functions.php file was added to the theme hierarchy in order to support the widget feature in WordPress 1.5. For each widget area you want in your theme, you need to register an array telling WordPress what the area should be called and what code should be displayed before and after the widget block and title.

Let's look at an example. The code in Listing 6-31 defines two widget areas. The results are shown in Figure 6-16.

Listing 6-31. Defining two widget areas

```
function my_widgets_init() {
	register_sidebar( array(
			'name' => 'First Widget Area',
			'id' => 'first-widget-area',
			'description' => __( 'The first widget area'),
			'before_widget' => '<li id="%1$s" class="widget-container %2$s">',
			'after_widget' => "</li>",
			'before_title' => '<h3 class="widget-title">',
			'after_title' => '</h3>',
	) );
	register_sidebar( array(
			'name' => 'Second Widget Area',
			'id' => 'second-widget',
			'description' => __( 'The second widget area'),
			'before_widget' => '<li id="%1$s" class="widget-container %2$s">',
			'after_widget' => "</li>",
			'before_title' => '<h3 class="widget-title">',
			'after_title' => '</h3>',
	) );
}

// Add the widget areas
add_action( 'init', 'my_widgets_init' );
```

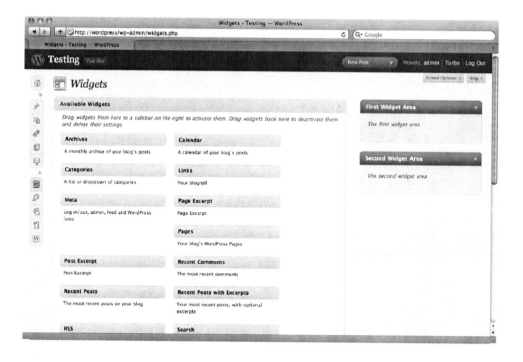

Figure 6-16. *The widgets defined by Listing 6-31*

The classes and IDs in the widget code follow the PHP sprintf() syntax and allow each widget to have a unique ID and a class based on the widget type. For example, a text widget placed third in a widget area, after two other widgets, would open with the list item tag shown in Listing 6-32.

Listing 6-32. *A text widget generated by Listing 6-30*

```
<li id="text-3" class="widget-container widget_text">
        <h3 class="widgettitle">This is a widget</h3>
        <div class="textwidget">
                <p>And this is its text!</p>
        </div>
</li>
```

You can define as many widget areas as you like. Don't forget to make a place for your widgets in your sidebar.php file (or elsewhere in your theme), as described previously in the Sidebar section of this chapter.

Enabling Menus

Navigation menus are a big new feature in version 3.0. If you want to support them in your new theme, or if you're modifying an older theme for 3.0, you'll need to add the code in Listing 6-33 to your theme files.

Listing 6-33. Enabling navigation menus

```
// in functions.php:
add_theme_support('nav-menus');
// wherever your current menu tag is located, replace it with:
<?php wp_nav_menu( 'sort_column=menu_order' ); ?>
```

If you prefer, you can use the new Navigation Menu widget rather than placing the menu tag in your templates.

Enabling Featured Images

If you don't see a Featured Image box on your Edit Posts screen, you can enable one by adding the code in Listing 6-34 to your functions.php file. Featured images were known as post thumbnails prior to version 3.0, and the theme functions still use the old terminology.

Listing 6-34. Enabling featured images

```
add_theme_support( 'post-thumbnails' );
```

Figure 6-17. The featured image meta box in the Post → Edit screen

This will make the box shown in Figure 6-17 appear. It will also enable you to add thumbnails to your post, but the thumbnails won't actually appear on your site until you've edited your other theme files. Find the spot where you'd like the images to appear and add the code in Listing 6-35.

Listing 6-35. *Using the featured image in a template*

```php
<?php the_post_thumbnail( 'thumbnail' ); ?>
```

Enabling Custom Backgrounds and Headers

It's very easy to enable custom backgrounds for your theme. Just add the line in Listing 6-36 to your theme's functions.php file.

Listing 6-36. *Enabling custom backgrounds in functions.php*

```php
add_custom_background();
```

That's all! Once you save this change, you'll see a new menu item under Appearance: Custom Background, and you can go choose your background image. You don't have to add anything to your stylesheet. The styles in Listing 6-1 (at the beginning of this chapter) are automatically added via wp_head().

Adding support for custom headers is a bit more complicated. Because the header is added as an <img> tag and not a background, the changes aren't just styles. You need to define some defaults: an image to be shown if the user hasn't yet chosen one, the image dimensions, and whether the text (site title and description) should be displayed in addition to the image. Listing 6-37 shows everything you need to add to your functions.php file; Listing 6-38 shows the relevant portion of header.php.

Listing 6-37. *Enabling custom headers in functions.php*

```php
define('HEADER_TEXTCOLOR', '');
define('HEADER_IMAGE', '%s/images/header.jpg'); // %s is theme directory uri
define('HEADER_IMAGE_WIDTH', 800 );              // in pixels
define('HEADER_IMAGE_HEIGHT', 200 );
define('NO_HEADER_TEXT', true );

function simplex_header_styles() { ?>
<style type="text/css">
#headimg {
    height: <?php echo HEADER_IMAGE_HEIGHT; ?>px;
    width: <?php echo HEADER_IMAGE_WIDTH; ?>px;
}
<?php if (NO_HEADER_TEXT) { ?>
#header h1, #header #desc {
    text-indent: -99999px;
}
<?php } ?>
</style>
<?php
}
```

```
add_custom_image_header( '', 'simplex_header_styles' );
add_action('wp_head', 'simplex_header_styles');
```

Listing 6-38. Printing the custom header in header.php

```
<div id="header">
<img src="<?php header_image(); ?>" width="<?php echo HEADER_IMAGE_WIDTH; ?>" height="<?php
echo HEADER_IMAGE_HEIGHT; ?>" alt="" id="header-bg" />
<a href="<?php echo get_settings('home'); ?>"><h1><?php bloginfo('name'); ?></h1></a>
<p id="desc"><?php bloginfo('description'); ?></p>
</div>
```

The styles function will include a few CSS rules in the page header. Since they will be inserted at the wp_head() hook, after the theme stylesheet link, they'll override its values.

Enabling Shortcodes in Text Widgets

As you saw in Chapter 4, shortcodes are bracketed placeholders you can use while editing your content that will be replaced with some other, more complicated content (like an embedded video or image gallery) when your post is displayed to visitors. Unfortunately, shortcodes are processed only in post/page content. You can use them in text widgets, however, if you enable theme in the theme functions as shown in Listing 6-39.

Listing 6-39. Enabling shortcode parsing in text widgets

```
add_filter('widget_text', 'shortcode_unautop');
add_filter('widget_text', 'do_shortcode');
```

The first line ensures that a shortcode placed by itself on its own line won't be surrounded by paragraph tags. The second line actually parses the shortcode. Figure 6-18 shows how the shortcode could be used in the widget.

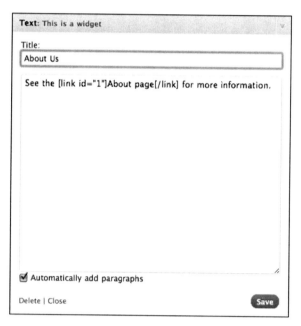

Figure 6-18. A shortcode in a text widget.

Changing Excerpt Length and Ellipsis

Listing 6-40 shows a bit of code from the functions.php file in the new Twenty Ten theme in version 3.0. The first set of functions changes the excerpt length simply by returning the desired number of words as an integer. The second set replaces the default text appended to auto-generated excerpts ('[...]') with a link to the complete post.

Listing 6-40. Changing excerpt length and adding "read more" link

```
// Control excerpt length
function twentyten_new_excerpt_length( $length ) {
        return 40;
}
add_filter( 'excerpt_length', 'twentyten_new_excerpt_length' );

// Make a nice read more link on excerpts
function twentyten_new_excerpt_more($more) {
        return ' &hellip; <a href="'. get_permalink() . '">' .
'Continue reading <span class="meta-nav">&rarr;</span>' . '</a>';
}
add_filter( 'excerpt_more', 'twentyten_new_excerpt_more' );
```

Figure 6-19 shows an excerpt from a theme that does not include the excerpt_length() and excerpt_more() filters. Figure 6-20 shows the same excerpt in the Twenty Ten theme, using the two filters in Listing 6-40.

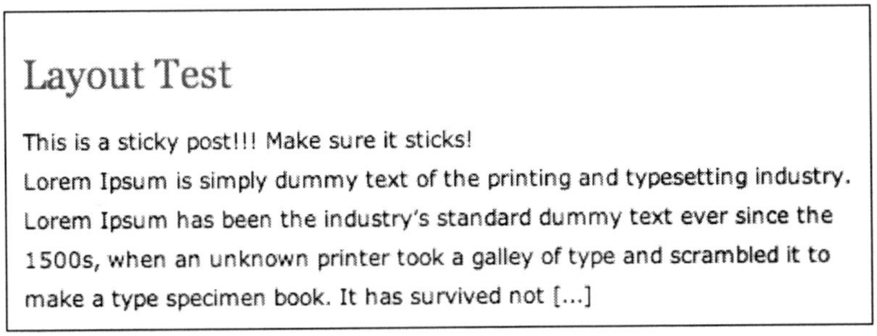

Figure 6-19. *The unfiltered excerpt*

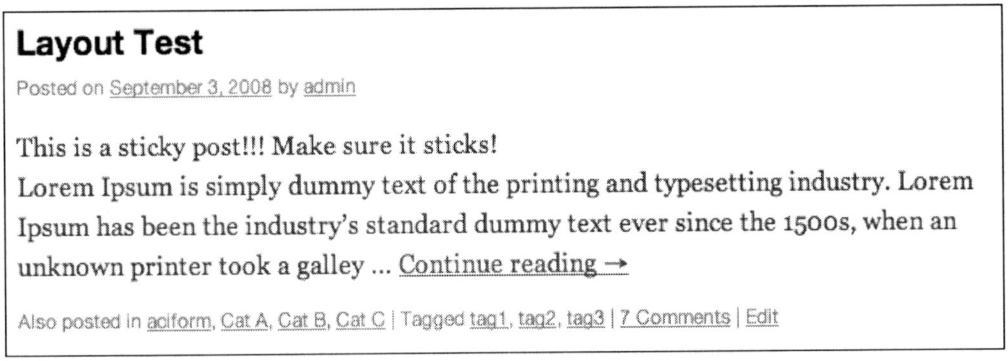

Figure 6-20. *The filtered excerpt*

Other Uses

The theme functions file can be a sandbox for plugin development. You can experiment with advanced functions, like creating shortcodes or taxonomies. You'll see more examples of this in the next few chapters. For more simple theme functions, see Appendix 2.

You need to think strategically about your theme functions. If you were to change themes, would you want to keep any of the functions? If so, consider creating a custom plugin (see Chapter 9) for them instead of keeping them in your theme's functions.php file.

Child Themes

Sometimes it's much easier to modify someone else's theme than it is to create one from scratch. Creating a child theme is a good way to learn the basics of WordPress themes. Child themes are also useful if you've downloaded a theme from the repository and you want to keep up with any updates the author releases, but you need to customize it for your own site.

Child themes are modifications of other themes. They have their own directories and you upload them just like a separate theme, but they depend on their parent themes, and they won't work if the parent is not installed. All your modifications to the original theme will take place in the child theme, so the parent theme remains untouched—and you can update it without wiping out your changes.

Child Theme File Hierarchy

Child themes must include at least a `style.css` file. All other files are optional, even `index.php`. If a required file is not present in the child theme directory, WordPress will look for the file in the parent theme directory. In other words, you need to create files only when you want to override the parent theme's display. To demonstrate how child themes work, I'll go over my own theme, Cub Reporter, a child of the Journalist theme by Lucian E. Marin.

The child theme's comment block requires one additional line: the Template. This should be the name of the directory containing your parent theme, as shown in Listing 6-41.

Listing 6-41. Importing the parent theme styles

```
/*
    Theme Name: Cub Reporter
    Theme URI: http://sillybean.net
    Description: A child theme for Journalist, by <a href="lucianmarin.com">Lucian E.
Marin</a>
    Author: Stephanie Leary
    Author URI: http://sillybean.net
    Template: journalist
    Version: 1.0
    License: GPL
*/
@import url(../journalist/style.css);
```

Child themes' stylesheets take advantage of the cascade feature of CSS. The first line of your child theme, after the required comment block, should import the parent theme's stylesheet. If the parent theme contains multiple stylesheets, you should include them all, unless you plan to replace them with your own.

The beauty of the cascade is that any duplicate style declarations occurring later in the stylesheet will override the original declaration. In a child theme, that means that once you've imported the parent styles, you can modify them easily by duplicating the selectors and replacing the style declarations.

For Cub Reporter, I wanted to change just a few things about Journalist:

- Use the black bubble style for the comment count instead of the site description.
- Add a background image.
- Move the title outside the white area.
- Add unique IDs to the sidebar widgets.
- Add styles for tables and definition lists.
- Change the image caption display.

Figure 6-21 shows the original Journalist theme, and Figure 6-22 shows the Cub Reporter child theme. These changes took just a few lines of CSS.

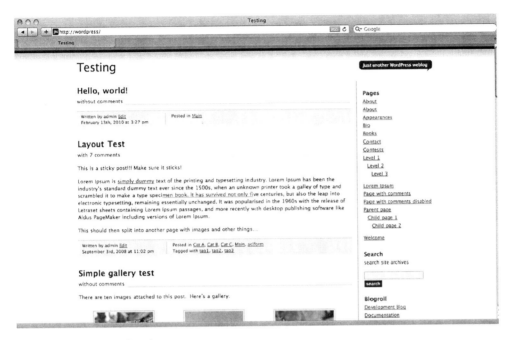

Figure 6-21. The Journalist theme

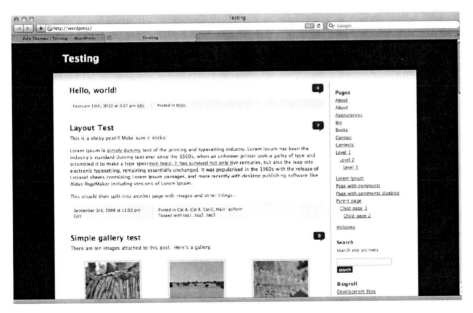

Figure 6-22. The Cub Reporter theme, a child of Journalist

Aside from style.css, which is required, you may replace as many of the parent theme's template files as you like—or none at all, if your changes can be accomplished with CSS alone. Be careful with the theme functions file! If you include one in the child theme, *both* functions.php files will be executed, so be careful not to duplicate any functions from the parent theme, or you'll see fatal errors. If the functions in the parent theme have been wrapped in if (function_exists(…)) statements, you can safely replace them with your own, since your theme functions file will be called first. For example, Twenty Ten's header styles function can be overridden. Listing 6-42 shows the original function and a possible replacement, which uses a more accessible method of hiding the site title and description.

Listing 6-42. Replacing a parent theme's functions

```
// in Twenty Ten's functions.php
if ( ! function_exists( 'twentyten_admin_header_style' ) ) :
function twentyten_admin_header_style() {
?>
<style type="text/css">
#headimg {
        height: <?php echo HEADER_IMAGE_HEIGHT; ?>px;
        width: <?php echo HEADER_IMAGE_WIDTH; ?>px;
}
#headimg h1, #headimg #desc {
        display: none;
}
</style>
<?php
}
endif;

// in your child theme's functions.php
function twentyten_admin_header_style() {
?>
<style type="text/css">
#headimg {
        height: <?php echo HEADER_IMAGE_HEIGHT; ?>px;
        width: <?php echo HEADER_IMAGE_WIDTH; ?>px;
}
#headimg h1, #headimg #desc {
        text-indent: -99999px;
}
</style>
<?php
}
```

A typical child theme might contain three files: style.css, archive.php, and functions.php. The style and functions files from both themes are used. The archive file in the child theme replaces the parent theme's archive file. All the other files not present in the child theme are filled in using the files from the parent theme.

In summary:

- The style.css files in both themes will be used.

- If the child theme contains a functions.php file, both it and the parent theme's functions file will be used.

- For all other templates, if the file exists in the child theme, it will be used. Otherwise, the corresponding file in the parent theme will be used instead.

The bloginfo() function has four possible arguments that will print URLs to the two theme directories. Listing 6-43 shows the four possibilities and their results.

Listing 6-43. Getting URLs for parent and child theme stylesheets and directories

```php
<?php
bloginfo('stylesheet_directory');    // Child theme directory
bloginfo('stylesheet_url');          // Child theme stylesheet
bloginfo('template_directory');      // Parent theme directory
bloginfo('template_url');            // Parent theme stylesheet
?>
```

Child themes are not, as of this writing, accepted into the listing on WordPress Extend. You can download Cub Reporter from my site, sillybean.net/code/themes/.

Troubleshooting Themes

If you accidentally introduce a syntax or fatal error in one of your template files, you'll probably see the dreaded white screen of death when you visit your home page. In some cases, even the admin screens will go blank. The best way to figure out what happened is to turn on debugging (as you saw back in Chapter 2) by adding define('WP_DEBUG', true); to your wp-config.php file. You can also check your PHP error log. Look for the last error shown and try to correct it.

If your theme has gone horribly wrong and you just want to switch back to another one, but you can't access the admin screens to change it, don't panic. Simply delete or rename your active theme's directory. When WordPress can't find it, it will revert to the default theme.

Summary

In this chapter, I've shown you the basic structure of a theme file, the Loop, and all the optional files that can make up a theme. I've gone over basic template tags, conditional tags, and the various tags used to include other files. You've learned how to enable widgets and navigation menus, and you've seen the older methods used to create menus from page and category lists. I've shown you how to create a child theme.

In the next chapter, I'll show you how to dissect and replicate the Loop to create even more complex themes. I'll also show you how to access post data outside the Loop, and I'll show you how to create theme option screens using the theme functions file.

CHAPTER 7

■ ■ ■

Creating an Advanced Theme

In the previous chapter, you learned how to create a theme with one basic Loop in each template file. In this chapter, you'll see how the Loop can be modified to display slightly different information: only one category, or all the categories except one, or even showing pages instead of posts.

To create a more advanced layout, you may need more than one Loop. In this chapter, you'll learn several ways of using multiple Loops. You'll also see how to add extra scripts and stylesheets to your theme and how to create an options form that allows your users to choose different layouts or color schemes from a few predefined choices.

Modifying the Loop

Normally, the Loop generates a list of posts based on the context of the page being viewed (home page, archive, search results) and your Reading settings. To modify what the Loop displays, you need to change the invisible database query that defines your Loop. The `query_posts()` function, when called before your Loop, lets you do just that. This function has a huge set of possible parameters:

- post_type
- post_status
- offset
- showposts [deprecated; use posts_per_page]
- posts_per_page
- paged
- caller_get_posts [excludes stickies if true]
- post_parent
- order

- orderby
- year
- monthnum
- w [week number, 0-53]
- day
- hour
- minute
- second
- post__in [ar
- ray]

- post__not_in [array]
- p [post ID]
- name
- page_id
- pagename
- author
- author_name
- cat
- category_name
- category__in [array]

- category__not_in [array]
- category__and [array]
- tag
- tag__and [array]
- tag__in [array]
- tag_slug__and [array]
- tag_slug__in [array]
- meta_key
- meta_value
- meta_compare [operator]

You can combine most of these arguments to further customize your Loops. I'll demonstrate a handful of the most common Loop modifications. Hopefully, these examples will give you the foundation you need to create your own custom Loops. For more information about query_posts() and all its possible arguments, see codex.wordpress.org/Template_Tags/query_posts.

Excluding a Category from the Home Page

In order to modify the existing Loop rather than creating a new one from scratch, you need to preserve the original query and then add something to it. Listing 7-1 shows how to remove one category (with an ID of 7) from $query_string (the variable that holds the original query) by placing a minus sign before the category ID. Keep in mind that this query string assigns values to variables. It doesn't perform comparisons, so remember not to use the more familiar comparison syntax, such as cat!=7, in a query string.

In this case, you combine query_posts() with the is_home() conditional you saw in the previous chapter to make sure that the posts from category 7 are excluded only on the home page. You wouldn't want to run this on the archive for category 7!

Listing 7-1. Excluding a category from the home page

```php
<?php if ( is_home() ) {
      query_posts( '&cat=-7' );
}
// your usual Loop can go here
?>
```

Showing Only One Category on the Home Page

Perhaps instead of excluding a category, you want to show only one category. That's easy, too, as Listing 7-2 shows.

Listing 7-2. Showing only one category

```php
<?php if ( is_home() ) {
        query_posts( '&cat=7' );
}
// your usual Loop can go here
?>
```

The difference between Listing 1 and Listing 2 is tiny! In the previous example, you used -7 to remove category 7 from the home page. Here, by removing the minus sign, you ensure that *only* category 7 is displayed.

Be careful, and proofread your Loops!

Showing Most Recent Pages Instead of Posts

One of the possible arguments of query_posts() is post_type. You can use this to retrieve pages instead of posts. Listing 7-3 shows a home page template that displays the five most recent pages. The query_posts() line is in bold. Pages are usually sorted alphabetically, so you explicitly set the orderby parameter to date. The default order is descending, and it is not changed here; you could change it to ascending if you wish by adding &order=asc to the query string.

Listing 7-3. Showing the five most recent pages on the home page

```php
<?php
/*
Template Name: Home Page
*/
?>
<?php get_header(); ?>

<div id="main">
<?php query_posts( 'post_type=page&orderby=date&posts_per_page=5' ); ?>

<?php if (have_posts()) : while (have_posts()) : the_post(); ?>
<div class="post" id="<?php echo $post->post_name; ?>">
        <h2><a href="<?php the_permalink(); ?>"
                title="<?php the_title_attribute(); ?>"><?php the_title(); ?></a>
        </h2>
        <?php the_content(); ?>

</div><!-- .post -->
<?php endwhile; ?>
<?php else: ?>
        <p>Sorry, these posts could not be found.</p>
<?php endif; ?>
</div><!-- #main -->
```

```php
<?php get_sidebar(); ?>
<?php get_footer(); ?>
```

As you'll see in Chapter 12, you can use the post_type attribute to list custom post types as well as pages or attachments.

Looping Through All Children of a Page

This query illustrates how to combine several arguments. Here, you want to list pages instead of posts, so use post_type to grab those. You don't want all the pages, just the children of page ID 1364, so use the post_parent attribute. Then you need to sort them by menu_order, an attribute unique to pages, and list them in ascending order, rather than the default descending. Finally, to make sure you get all the children of 1364 without bumping into the per-page limit set in the Reading Settings screen, set posts_per_page to -1. Setting posts_per_page to a negative value removes the per-page limit, thus showing all the posts at once.

Listing 7-4. A home page template file with a Loop showing children of page ID 1364

```php
<?php
/*
Template Name: Home Page
*/
?>
<?php get_header(); ?>

<div id="main">
<?php query_posts(
'post_type=page&orderby=menu_order&order=asc&post_parent=1364&posts_per_page=-1' );
?>

<?php if (have_posts()) : while (have_posts()) : the_post(); ?>
<div class="post" id="<?php echo $post->post_name; ?>">
        <h2><a href="<?php the_permalink(); ?>"
                title="<?php the_title_attribute(); ?>"><?php the_title(); ?></a>
        </h2>
        <?php the_content(); ?>

</div><!-- .post -->
<?php endwhile; ?>
<?php else: ?>
        <p>Sorry, these posts could not be found.</p>
<?php endif; ?>
</div><!-- #main -->

<?php get_sidebar(); ?>
<?php get_footer(); ?>
```

You might find that you need to create an empty parent page as a placeholder in the hierarchy. I often add the extra code in Listing 7-5 to my page template Loops. First, I use get_the_content(), which returns the post content for use in PHP functions rather than echoing it to the screen. If get_the_content() returns nothing, a linked list of its child pages will be shown instead. Here, since I just want to print a linked list rather than a complete Loop, I've used wp_list_pages() instead of query_posts(). I'm also returning the list to a variable, $children, so I can check to see whether the list is empty before printing the surrounding markup.

Listing 7-5. Listing children of the current page if the content is empty

```php
<?php
/*
Template Name: Home Page
*/
?>
<?php get_header(); ?>

<div id="main">
<?php
query_posts(
  'post_type=page&orderby=menu_order&order=asc&post_parent=1364&posts_per_page=-1' );
?>

<?php if (have_posts()) : while (have_posts()) : the_post(); ?>
<div class="post" id="<?php echo $post->post_name; ?>">
        <h2><a href="<?php the_permalink(); ?>"
                title="<?php the_title_attribute(); ?>"><?php the_title(); ?></a>
        </h2>

<?php
$content = get_the_content();
if (empty($content)) {
        $children = wp_list_pages(
          'title_li=&depth=1&child_of='.$post->ID.'&echo=0&sort_column=menu_order' );
        if ($children) { ?>
                <ul id="childpages">
                <?php echo $children; ?>
                </ul>
        <?php }
}
else {
        the_content();
}
?>

</div><!-- .post -->
<?php endwhile; ?>
<?php else: ?>
        <p>Sorry, these posts could not be found.</p>
<?php endif; ?>
</div><!-- #main -->

<?php get_sidebar(); ?>
<?php get_footer(); ?>
```

You could use similar code to list the page's attached media files.

Listing Attached Files

You can display all the attached files of a post without going to the trouble of inserting each one into the post content. The required code looks very much like a second Loop, as shown in Listing 7-6. This could be placed inside the main Loop, perhaps just after the_content().

Listing 7-6. Listing a post's attached files inside the Loop

```php
<?php
    $attachments = get_children(array(
        'post_type' => 'attachment',
        'numberposts' => -1,
        'post_status' => null,
        'post_parent' => $post->ID
        ));
    if ($attachments) { ?>
        <ul class="attachments"> <?php
        foreach ($attachments as $attachment) {
                if (substr($attachment->post_mime_type, 0, 5) != 'image') {
                        $type = str_replace('/', '-', $attachment->post_mime_type);
                        echo "<li class='$type'>";
                        the_attachment_link($attachment->ID, false);
                        echo '</li>';
                }
        }
    ?> </ul>
<?php } ?>
```

The get_children() function can also be used to display child pages, but here you've used the post_type argument to limit the list to attachments. Setting the numberposts argument to -1 ensures that you get all attachments, and the post_parent argument is set to the current post's ID so that you get only those attachments that were uploaded to this particular post.

As you loop through the returned attachment objects, you need to skip over the images, since those will work better with the [gallery] shortcode shown in Chapter 4. (You could use a similar if() statement to exclude any other type of file.) For the rest of the attached files, you need to clean up the MIME type a little bit for use with CSS. You use the attachment's MIME type as the list item class, which allows you to style each link with a file icon background image. In order to get a valid class name, however, you replace the slash in the original MIME type (e.g. application/pdf) with a dash using PHP's str_replace() function.

You separate the_attachment_link() instead of placing it in the echo statement because it echoes by default.

Listing 7-7 provides a few examples of the CSS you might use to style the attachment links, assuming a 16-pixel icon such as FamFamFam's free Mini set (www.famfamfam.com/lab/icons/mini/). The end result is shown in Figure 7-1.

Listing 7-7. CSS for Listing 7-6

```
ul.attachments li {
      list-style: none;
}
ul.attachments li a {
      padding-left: 20px;
      line-height: 18px;
      background-position-top: 0;
      background-position-left: .5em;
      background-repeat: no-repeat;
      background-image: url(img/icons/attachment.gif);  /* default */
}
ul.attachments li.application-pdf a {
      background-image: url(img/icons/pdf.gif);
}
ul.attachments li.application-zip a {
      background-image: url(img/icons/zip.gif);
}
```

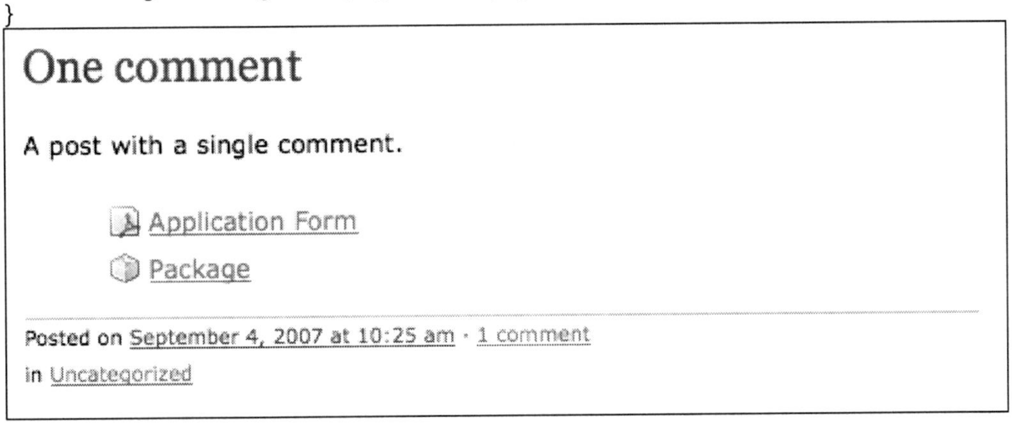

One comment

A post with a single comment.

🗋 Application Form

📦 Package

Posted on September 4, 2007 at 10:25 am · 1 comment

in Uncategorized

Figure 7-1. The styled list of post attachments

Multiple Loops

Now that you know how to create specialized Loops, the next logical step is to display several of these loops on your home page. Showing multiple, modified Loops is the key to "magazine" layouts, like the Magazeen theme shown in Figure 7-2. Most of these layouts treat categories like departments or columns in magazines and newspapers. Each category gets its own section of the page. I'll show you how to do this, but first, let's reset the Loop query.

Figure 7-2. Magazeen, a magazine theme using multiple Loops

Resetting the Query

Once you've modified a Loop query, it stays modified! Therefore, before you start a new Loop, you need to reset the query. Otherwise, your new modifications will operate on the posts already returned by your first query—and that leads to some very unpredictable results. Fortunately, resetting the query takes just one line of code, as shown in Listing 7-8.

Listing 7-8. Resetting the query

```php
<?php wp_reset_query(); ?>
```

That's it! Remember to reset the query in between each of your Loops to avoid strange errors in your advanced layouts.

Earlier, I showed you how to preserve the original query while adding your modifications. If you want to save the original query for use after your new queries, save it to a variable (like $original_query), then reassign it when you're done, as shown in Listing 7-9.

Listing 7-9. Preserving the original query

```php
    <?php
    $original_query = $query_string;
    // query from Listing 7-3
    query_posts( 'post_type=post&orderby=date&posts_per_page=5' );

    if (have_posts()) : while (have_posts()) : the_post(); ?>
        // the contents of your Loop goes here
    <?php endwhile; endif; ?>

<?php

wp_reset_query();

// Another Loop could go here.
// query_posts($original_query);

?>
```

This technique will be important when you try to fetch post information outside the Loop later in this chapter.

A Loop for Each Category

Now that you've reset your query, it's time to create that magazine layout. There are various ways to accomplish this, depending on how you've set up your content. Perhaps you've created a hierarchy of pages, and you want to show those instead. For the moment, however, let's assume that you're using categories to segregate your posts into different departments, since this is the most common scenario. Once you see how this works, you should be able to adapt this code to your needs using some of the other Loop examples in this chapter.

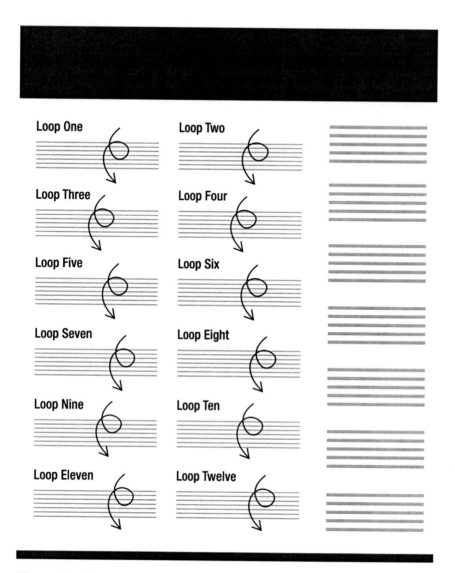

Figure 7-3. A layout with multiple Loops

You could use get_all_category_ids() to fetch an array of IDs, and then loop through each one. However, this is not a very flexible solution. If you have a deep hierarchy of categories, it's unlikely that you actually want to loop through every one of them on your home page. More likely, you really want a box for every top-level category, as illustrated in Figure 7-3.

In order to better control which categories you'll work with, use the get_categories() function instead, as shown in Listing 7-10. This will require a bit more code, since this function returns an array of category objects rather than simple IDs, but that's OK. You can make use of that object data, and if you really need to pass the ID as a parameter to some other function, hey, that's part of the object, too.

Listing 7-10. Creating a Loop for each top-level category

```php
<?php
    $categories = get_categories();

    foreach ($categories as $cat) : ?>
    <div class="category_box">
    <?php
    // get most recent post in cat
    query_posts('posts_per_page=1&cat='.$cat->cat_ID);
    if (have_posts()) : while (have_posts()) : the_post();
     ?>
    <h2><a href="<?php the_permalink(); ?>" title="<?php the_title_attribute(); ?>"><?php
the_title(); ?></a></h2>
        <?php the_content('continue reading...'); ?>
        <?php
            endwhile;
            endif;
            wp_reset_query();
            // get 4 most recent posts in cat offset by 1
            query_posts('posts_per_page=4&offset=1&cat='.$cat->cat_ID);
            if (have_posts()) : ?>
                <ul class="more-stories">
                <?php
                while (have_posts()) : the_post();
                 ?>
                <li><a href="<?php the_permalink(); ?>" title="<?php
the_title_attribute(); ?>"><?php the_title(); ?></a></li>
                <?php
            endwhile; ?>
            </ul> <!-- .more-stories -->
            <?php
            endif;
            wp_reset_query();
            ?>
    </div> <!-- .category_box -->
    <?php endforeach; ?>
```

In this example, you use get_categories() to retrieve a list of all the categories. This function can take a number of arguments to limit the list it returns, but in this case you want the complete list. The function returns the categories as objects, so you use the object notation (object->property) to get the category IDs for the query function.

As you loop through each category, call another Loop with the query set to show only posts in that category. Inside this Loop, print the title and excerpt of the first post only. Then you perform yet another query to get the next four posts, skipping the first. (Note that it might be more efficient to get all five posts in one query and use a true/false flag to determine whether the surrounding markup is a paragraph or a list item, but for now, the multiple query demonstration is more important than efficiency.)

You could, of course, modify the above code to create a Loop for all the children of a certain category, or any other scenario you can think of. See codex.wordpress.org/Function_Reference/ get_categories for all the possible arguments of the get_categories() function.

183

Figure 7-4. *A loop per category*

Showing the Author's Other Recent Posts

In Twenty Ten, there's a footer in `single.php` that displays the author's Gravatar, bio, and a link to all their posts. You can enhance this to show a list of the author's most recent posts using the code shown in Listing 7-11. The results are shown in Figure 7-5.

Listing 7-11. Displaying the post author's five most recent other posts inside the Loop

```php
<?php
$original_query = $query_string;

query_posts( 'post_type=post&orderby=date&posts_per_page=5&exclude'.$post-
>ID.'&author='.$post->post_author );

if (have_posts()) : ?>
<ul class="authorposts">
        <?php while (have_posts()) : the_post(); ?>
        <li><a href="<?php the_permalink() ?>" rel="bookmark" title="'Permanent link to <?php
the_title_attribute(); ?>">
                <?php the_title(); ?></a></li>
                <?php endwhile; ?>
</ul>
<?php endif;

wp_reset_query();
?>
```

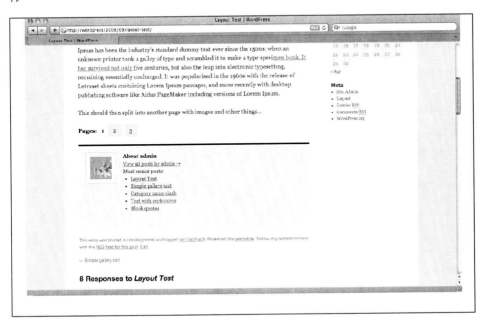

Figure 7-5. Listing the author's most recent posts in Twenty Ten

Accessing Post Information Outside the Loop

Most of the post-related template tags seen in the previous chapter (the_title(), the_content(), and so on) are available only inside the Loop. So what do you do when you need to access information outside the Loop? Use global variables! WordPress has a number of globals that store information about the current state of the application: the current post or page, user, database, and more. All these variables are available to you in your own functions and theme files.

You can access post data using the $post global. Listing 7-12 shows how to display the post's tags in a single post template's sidebar, outside the Loop.

Listing 7-12. Setting up post data to use template tags outside the Loop

```
<div id="sidebar">
<?php
setup_postdata($post);
?>
<h3><a href="<?php the_permalink(); ?>"><?php the_title(); ?></a></h3>
<p class="post-tags"><?php the_tags(); ?></p>
</div>
```

Here, you can see how important it is to make sure that you have properly reset your query after modifying your Loops. If you didn't, the information you collect outside the Loop will refer to the last post returned by your modified Loop query, not the original query! For example, let's say you listed the author's four most recent posts at the bottom of a single post archive and didn't reset the query afterward. In your sidebar (which will come after this query in the code), you then try to display related posts based on the current post's categories and tags. If you didn't reset your query, you'll get the related posts of the author's fifth most recent rather than the one currently displayed by your single archive template.

If you aren't sure whether you're inside the Loop or not, you can use the in_the_loop() conditional tag to check. If you are inside the Loop, this function will return true, as shown in Listing 7-13.

Listing 7-13. Checking whether you're inside the Loop

```
<p>Am I inside the Loop? <?php if (in_the_loop()) echo "yes"; else echo "no"; ?></p>
```

Search Engine Optimization (SEO)

Because the CSS-based theme system encourages standards-based design, and because most themes use proper HTML heading tags for post and page titles, WordPress sites tend to do well in search engine rankings. Of course, there are improvements you can make to your own themes. In this section I'll go over four common concerns: title tags, meta descriptions, meta keywords, and canonical URLs.

Improving the Title Tag

In many WordPress themes, the title tag looks something like Listing 7-14.

Listing 7-14. The usual title tag and its output

```
<title><?php wp_title(); ?><?php bloginfo('name'); ?></title>

<title>example.com &raquo; Howdy, stranger.</title>
```

Good SEO dictates that the more specific information—the post title—should come first, followed by the site name. You can switch the order (and in the process, change the style and position of the separator) using the code in Listing 7-15 instead.

Listing 7-15. The revised title tag and its output

```
<title><?php wp_title('|', true, 'right'); ?><?php bloginfo('name'); ?></title>

<title>Howdy, stranger. | example.com</title>
```

The wp_title() function prints various things depending on the context. For posts and pages, it prints the title. For categories and tags, it prints the name. On the 404 error page, it prints "Page not found."

Titles can be altered using filters—custom functions in plugins or theme functions files. Chapter 9 covers filters and how they work.

Using Categories and Tags as Keywords

If you need to add meta keywords to your single post archive template, you have all the data you need: your categories and tags. All you have to do is get a combined list, separated by commas.

In this example, you first use a conditional tag to make sure this code is used only on single post archives. (Pages don't have categories or tags, and the get_the_tags() and get_the_category() functions won't work correctly on archive pages containing multiple posts.) Then, for each tag and category, you force the name to all lowercase and add it to an array of keywords. As you print the <meta> tag, you remove duplicates from the array with array_unique() and convert the array to a comma-separated string using implode().

Listing 7-16 shows how to build the array of keywords and print it as the content of the <meta> tag.

Listing 7-16. Creating meta keywords tag from post categories and tags in header.php

```php
<?php if (is_single()) {
  foreach((get_the_tags()) as $tag) {
    $keywords[] = strtolower($tag->name);
  }
  foreach((get_the_category()) as $category) {
    $keywords[] = strtolower($category->cat_name);
  }
?>
<meta name="keywords" content="<?php echo implode(", ", array_unique($keywords)); ?>" />
<?php } ?>
```

Using the Excerpt as a Description

Listing 7-17 shows how to use the excerpt as the meta description tag for single posts and pages. Since the_excerpt() prints directly to the screen and can't be passed to other PHP functions, you can't wrap it in the esc_attr() function, as you normally would when using a template tag as an HTML attribute. Instead, you use the_excerpt_rss(). This function formats the excerpt for RSS feeds, but in this case it will work equally well in your description attribute, since excerpts can't contain HTML.

Listing 7-17. Using the_excerpt as a meta description

```php
<?php
if (is_singular()):
global $post;
setup_postdata($post);
?>
<meta name="description" content="<?php the_excerpt_rss(); ?>" />
<?php endif; ?>
```

Short Links and Canonical URLs

Those long URLs containing your post titles are great for improving your search results, but they're awfully long! If you're sharing links on social media networks, e-mailing them, or including them in printed documents, you're probably interested in ways to shorten your links.

The default permalink structure always works, even if you've changed your permalinks to some other structure. Listing 7-18 shows how to include the default permalink in your Loop using the new the_shortcode() tag in 3.0, the results of which are shown in Figure 7-6. If you have installed the WordPress.com Stats plugin, you can take advantage of the wp.me link shortener feature. There are a number of other link shortener plugins you can install if neither of these appeals to you.

Listing 7-18. Displaying the default permalink in a Loop

```php
<?php if (have_posts()) : while (have_posts()) : the_post(); ?>
<h2><a href="<?php the_permalink(); ?>"
        title="<?php the_title_attribute(); ?>"><?php the_title(); ?></a>
</h2>
<?php the_content(); ?>
<p>Sharing this post? <?php the_shortlink(); ?></p>
<?php endif; ?>
```

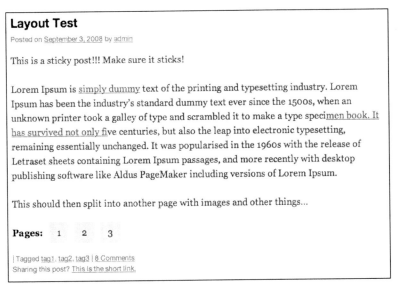

Layout Test

Posted on September 3, 2008 by admin

This is a sticky post!!! Make sure it sticks!

Lorem Ipsum is simply dummy text of the printing and typesetting industry. Lorem Ipsum has been the industry's standard dummy text ever since the 1500s, when an unknown printer took a galley of type and scrambled it to make a type specimen book. It has survived not only five centuries, but also the leap into electronic typesetting, remaining essentially unchanged. It was popularised in the 1960s with the release of Letraset sheets containing Lorem Ipsum passages, and more recently with desktop publishing software like Aldus PageMaker including versions of Lorem Ipsum.

This should then split into another page with images and other things...

Pages: 1 2 3

| Tagged tag1, tag2, tag3 | 8 Comments
Sharing this post? This is the short link.

Figure 7-6. the_shortcode() in the post footer

Google sometimes penalizes sites for duplicating content. However, a single post on your WordPress site might appear on the home page, a date-based archive, a category archive, and the single post archive. It might also have three or four valid URLs if you're using a short link format. To resolve the duplicate content problem, Google recommends that you specify a canonical URL for each post—its home base, where all the archived copies will lead. As of version 2.9, WordPress automatically adds a canonical URL header as part of the wp_head() function. As of 3.0, it also adds the shortlink, as shown in Listing 7-19.

Listing 7-19. Canonical and shortlinks in the <head> section

```
<link rel='canonical' href='http://wordpress/2008/09/layout-test/' />
<link rel='shortlink' href='http://wordpress/?p=188' />
```

Adding Scripts and Stylesheets

WordPress includes several popular JavaScript libraries, including jQuery and Prototype. It's easy to integrate plugins for these libraries, as long as you're careful to avoid conflicts. You also need to use the built-in functions to add scripts and stylesheets to your themes rather than simply hard-coding the <script> and <style> tags in your header file.

Using JavaScript Libraries

WordPress includes a number of JavaScript libraries because it uses those libraries in the administration screens. They're available for you to use in your themes and plugins as well. The libraries include jQuery, Prototype, Scriptaculous, SWFUpload, and Thickbox. See codex.wordpress.org/Function_Reference/wp_enqueue_script for a complete list of the scripts available, along with their handles.

Listing 7-20 shows how to add the built-in jQuery and UI core libraries to your theme.

Listing 7-20. Including jQuery

```php
<?php
function add_jquery() {
        wp_enqueue_script('jquery');
        wp_enqueue_script('jquery-ui-core');
}
add_action('wp_head', 'add_jquery');
?>
```

Using jQuery in WordPress is a bit tricky. Most jQuery scripts rely on a dollar sign function. For example, $("div.main").addClass("wide"); would add the wide class to a div that already had the main class. However, several other libraries, including Prototype, use this same convention. Because WordPress also uses Prototype, the jQuery library is loaded in "no conflict" mode (docs.jquery.com/Using_jQuery_with_Other_Libraries).

You have two options. You can use 'jQuery' in place of the dollar sign function ('$') throughout your script, or you can wrap your script in an extra function. Both methods are shown in Listing 7-21.

Listing 7-21. Using jQuery in WordPress

```javascript
jQuery("div.main").addClass("wide");

jQuery(document).ready(function($) {
    // $() will work inside this function; otherwise use jQuery()
    $("div.main").addClass("wide");
});
```

Adding Your Own Scripts

When you need to add a JavaScript file to your theme, it's tempting to simply paste the <script> tag into header.php, dust off your hands, and move on to your next task. However, this is the wrong way to add scripts to a WordPress theme. You might recall from Chapter 3 that you can specify the location of the wp-content directory. If someone who has moved wp-content() tries to use this theme, the scripts will never load.

Adding the <script> tags via the wp_head() action, as shown in Listing 7-22, is also not a good idea.

Listing 7-22. How not to link scripts

```php
function slider_scripts() { ?>
    <script type="text/javascript" src="<?php bloginfo('url'); ?>/wp-content/themes/test-theme/jquery.js"></script>
    <script type="text/javascript" src="<?php bloginfo('url'); ?>/wp-content/themes/test-theme/jquery-slider.js"></script>
<?php }
add_action('wp_head', 'slider_scripts');
```

This will get the job done, but it's inefficient. You might have a plugin that has already called the jQuery library; now it will be included twice. It's also a bad idea to hard-code the path to the theme directory.

The correct way to add scripts is to use the wp_enqueue_scripts() function. This function adds your script to the header using the wp_head() hook. Listing 7-23 shows how to enqueue a script in the header using a small function and an action hook in functions.php.

Listing 7-23. Enqueueing scripts

```
function add_header_scripts() {
        wp_enqueue_script('header-script', <?php bloginfo('stylesheet_directory');
?>'/js/header-script.js', array('jquery'), '1.0', false);
}
add_action('wp_head', 'add_header_scripts');
```

The wp_enqueue_scripts() function requires several arguments. First, you need to give your script a unique handle, or name. This allows you to refer to it later and ensures that only one script of that name will be included in the page. Next, you need to provide the URL to your script file. Third, if your script relies on any libraries (like jQuery), you need to provide the handles of those dependencies in an array. Fourth, if you need to call a specific version, provide its number. (To use the most recent version, use an empty string for this argument.) Finally, you need to tell WordPress whether the script should be loaded in the footer via wp_footer(). In this case, you want to load the script in the header, so this argument should be false (or blank).

Conditionally Adding Scripts

The wp_enqueue_scripts() function will add your script to every page on your site. What if it's a large script and you want to include it only if a shortcode or some other text is present in the post or page content? One of my favorite theme tricks is to include a script that stripes table rows and turns the table headers into links that trigger a sort function. However, I want to include it only if the post or page content contains a table tag. Listing 7-24 shows how it works.

Listing 7-24. Adding sortable.js if the content contains a table

```
function add_sortable($posts) {
        if (empty($posts)) return $posts;
        $found = false;
        foreach ($posts as $post) {
                if (stripos($post->post_content, '<table') === false) {
                        $found = true;
                        break;
                }
        }
        if ($found) {
                wp_enqueue_script('sortable',
get_bloginfo('stylesheet_directory').'/js/sortable.js');
        }
        return $posts;
}
add_filter('the_posts', 'add_sortable');
```

Here, I've used the filter the_posts(), which lets me pass the array of posts to my function. Then I can loop through the posts, checking to see if the opening table tag is present. If it is, I queue up the table script.

WordPress developer Joost de Valk recently published an updated version of Stuart Langridge's classic table sort script. It turns <th> tags into links. Clicking a heading sorts the table rows, alphabetically or numerically, according to the contents of that column. The updated version of the script also adds alternate row background colors. You can download it at yoast.com/articles/sortable-table/.

Adding Stylesheets

If you need to add stylesheets other than your theme's main style.css file, enqueuing is the proper method for many of the same reasons. The wp_enqueue_style() function is shown in Listing 7-25. Notice that it's very similar to the one you used for scripts.

Listing 7-25. Enqueuing styles

```
function add_header_styles() {
        wp_enqueue_style( 'print-styles',
get_bloginfo('stylesheet_directory').'/css/pring.css', false, false, 'print');
}
add_action('wp_head', 'add_header_styles');
```

The arguments for the function are: a handle for the stylesheet, the file's URL, any dependencies, the version number, and the media type for which this stylesheet should be added. In this case, there are no dependencies or version numbers, so you used false for both arguments.

Outside the Theme Hierarchy: Database Errors and Maintenance Messages

There are also a few files that live outside the theme directory but still affect how your site looks at times. For example, you can create a file called db-error.php in your wp-content directory and use it to style your database connection error message, as shown in Listing 7-26.

Listing 7-26. Basic db-error.php file

```
<html>
<head>
<title>Database Error | MySite.com</title>
</head>
<body>
<h1>Database Error</h1>
<p>The database is not responding, and this site is unavailable. We're sorry! Please try again later.</p>
</body>
</html>
```

You can dress this up to match the rest of your site by copying the contents of your theme's header.php, sidebar.php, and footer.php files into the appropriate locations, but remember to remove any WordPress-specific functions, since they won't work if the database is unavailable. You can also link directly to the stylesheet in your theme directory; just remember to change it if you switch themes.

You can also customize your maintenance mode file, maintenance.php (Listing 7-27). This is also located in your wp-content directory and is shown to your visitors while you're upgrading WordPress core files or plugins. Note that it's a hidden file on UNIX-based operating systems, so you might have trouble seeing it in some applications unless you turn on the option to view hidden files (if there is one).

Listing 7-27. Maintenance mode file

```php
<?php
$protocol = $_SERVER["SERVER_PROTOCOL"];
if ( 'HTTP/1.1' != $protocol && 'HTTP/1.0' != $protocol )
        $protocol = 'HTTP/1.0';
header("$protocol 503 Service Unavailable", true, 503 );
header('Content-Type: text/html; charset=utf-8' );
?>
<html>
<head>
<title>Down for Maintenance | MySite.com</title>
</head>
<body>
<h1>Down for Maintenance</h1>
<p>This site is temporarily unavailable due to scheduled maintenance. Please try again
later.</p>
</body>
</html>
<?php die(); ?>
```

Theme Options

Many themes include options allowing the user to select layouts, color schemes, or other alternatives to the theme's default settings. I'll demonstrate using the Simplex Flex theme I created as a demo for this chapter.

Theme options work just like plugin options, so you'll see many of the same concepts again in Chapter 9. You can also refer to codex.wordpress.org/Settings_API for more details on storing options in the WordPress database.

If you want to add options to your theme, you need to add a page in the Appearance section of the navigation menu and construct the form itself. Unless otherwise noted, all of the following code examples should be placed in the theme's functions.php file.

Adding an Options Page

First, add the options screen to the admin navigation menu, as shown in Listing 7-28.

Listing 7-28. Adding a theme options page to the admin menu

```
function simplex_menu() {
        add_theme_page('Simplex Flex Options', 'Simplex Options', 'edit_theme_options',
__FILE__, 'simplex_options_page');
}
add_action('admin_menu', 'simplex_menu');
```

Actually, that's really all it takes! The `simplex_menu()` function will contain several other things in just a moment, but for now it holds only the `add_theme_page()` function. This function requires several arguments:

- The title of the options page, to be used in the `<title>` tag

- The title of the page as it will appear in the menu

- The capability users should have in order to access this page (see Chapter 10 for more on roles and capabilities); either `edit_themes` or `manage_options` would be a good choice for a theme options page.

- The path to the file containing the options page (in this case, it'll be this file)

- The name of the function containing the options form

Once that's done, you have to add your `simplex_menu()` function to the admin menu. There's an action hook for that, so all you have to do is call `add_action()`.

Note that you haven't created the `simplex_options_page()` function yet. That's OK; the menu option will show up without it, and will take you to a blank page. Before you fill in the form, you need to think about what options your theme will have.

Registering Options

For the purposes of this chapter, Simplex Flex has four options: width (fixed or flexible), columns (two or three, and in which order), whether the site title and description will be shown in addition to the custom header image, and an option to manually enter additional CSS rules.

You'll have to register your option with WordPress or it won't get saved. You should also set some default values. For now, I'll just mention which lines are essential in order to get your options saved and updated correctly in the database.

Listing 7-29 shows the expanded function; it now registers your settings and creates some default values. The changes from the previous listing are in bold. You store all four theme options in a single database field by using an array. This is the best practice for saving theme and plugin options; it's bad form to use a separate database field for each of your options.

Listing 7-29. Registering a setting and saving the default values

```
function simplex_menu() {
        add_theme_page('Simplex Flex Options', 'Simplex Options', 'edit_theme_options',
__FILE__, 'simplex_options_page');
        register_setting('simplex_options', 'simplex_options');
        // set defaults
        $options = array(
                'width' => 'fixed',
                'cols' => '3',
                'sitename' => 'yes',
                'css' => '',
        );
        add_option('simplex_options', $options, '', 'yes');
}
add_action('admin_menu', 'simplex_menu');
```

The register_setting() function shown here has two arguments. First, you have to assign your setting to a group. When you begin building the form, you call each group in turn. In this case, since you have just a few options, you use just one group, with the same name as the option itself. The second argument is the name of the option that will be stored to the database.

Once you registered the setting, you need to save some default values. You create the $options array to hold the four values. Then you can use the add_options() function to store your array. The first argument is, again, the name of the option field in the database. The second argument is the array containing the options to be stored. The third argument should always be empty; it's a deprecated argument that's still present for backward compatibility. The fourth argument, the autoload value, determines whether or not these options will be cached on each page load. This should almost always be "yes."

Creating an Options Form

Now that you have your options in place, you need to build the form that will let users edit them. Figure 7-7 shows the form for Simplex Flex. The code to create this form is shown in Listing 7-30.

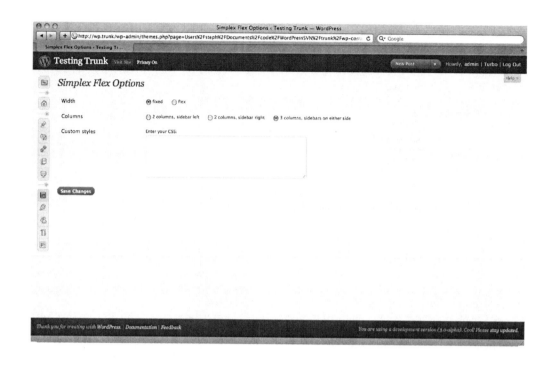

Figure 7-7. *The Simplex Flex options screen*

Listing 7-30. *The theme options form*

```php
function simplex_options_page() { ?>
  <div class="wrap">
  <h2>Simplex Flex Options</h2>
  <form method="post" action="options.php">
        <?php settings_fields('simplex_options'); ?>
        <?php $options = get_option('simplex_options'); ?>
  <table class="form-table">
  <tr valign="top">
  <th scope="row">Width</th>
  <td><label><input type="radio" name="simplex_options[width]" <?php checked('fixed',
$options['width']); ?> value="fixed" /> Fixed</label>
                <label><input type="radio" name="simplex_options[width]" <?php checked('flex',
$options['width']); ?> value="flex" /> Flex</label>
        </td>
  </tr>
<tr valign="top">
  <th scope="row">Columns</th>
  <td><label><input type="radio" name="simplex_options[cols]" <?php checked('left2',
$options['cols']); ?> value="left2" /> 2 columns, sidebar left</label>
```

```
        <label><input type="radio" name="simplex_options[cols]" <?php checked('right2',
$options['cols']); ?> value="right2" /> 2 columns, sidebar right</label>
        <label><input type="radio" name="simplex_options[cols]" <?php checked('col3',
$options['cols']); ?> value="col3" /> 3 columns, sidebars on either side</label>
        </td>
  </tr>
  <tr valign="top">
  <th scope="row">Header text and image</th>
  <td><label><input type="checkbox" name="simplex_options[sitename]" <?php checked('yes',
$options['sitename']); ?> value="yes" />
        Display site name and description superimposed over the header image?</label>
  </td>
  </tr>
        <tr valign="top">
  <th scope="row">Custom styles</th>
  <td><label>Enter your CSS:</label><br />
        <textarea name="simplex_options[css]"><?php echo $options['css']; ?></textarea>
  </td>
  </tr>
  </table>

  <p class="submit">
        <input type="submit" class="button-primary" value="Save Changes" />
  </p>
  </form>
  </div>
<?php }
// the ?> should be at the end of the functions.php file
```

First, you wrap your form in a <div> tag with the wrap class. This is standard for all the options pages in WordPress, and you'll see it again when you create plugin option pages. Next, you open the <form> tag. The ID is optional, but the action must be options.php so your registered settings will be processed and saved to the database.

Inside the form, the first item should be the title of your options page. Then you call the settings_fields() function to make sure your options are handled correctly and to set up the necessary security checks. Also, you need to get the stored options using get_option() so you can populate the fields with any values that have already been saved.

The markup of the form fields is up to you. The table shown here matches the built-in WordPress settings screens. Be sure to follow accessibility practices with your form fields; use labels appropriately.

The checked() and selected() Functions

You'll see the checked() function again in Chapter 9. It can be used to print the appropriate checked attribute for checkboxes and radio buttons. Its first argument is the value you want to match; the second argument is the variable containing your stored option. For dropdown boxes, you could use the similar selected() function.

Listing 7-31 shows one instance of the checked() function used in the Simplex Flex theme options, then shows the longer version of the same code that would be needed if you were to use an if() statement instead.

Listing 7-31. Using checked() vs if

```
<label><input type="radio" name="simplex_options[cols]" <?php checked('left2',
$options['cols']); ?> value="left2" /> 2 columns, sidebar left</label>

<label><input type="radio" name="simplex_options[cols]" <?php if ($options['cols'] == 'left2')
{ ?> value="left2" <?php } ?> /> 2 columns, sidebar left</label>
```

As you can see, the second version is somewhat harder to read.

Saving Form Input into a Single Variable

You could use a separate name for each field, but by using the name of the single registered option and putting the individual field names in brackets, you've taken advantage of a handy PHP shortcut: all those fields will be saved as an array called $simplex_options—exactly the thing you want to store in the database. You don't have to do any processing at all, since the form's handler, options.php, will automatically save those fields to the array and update the database option.

To take advantage of this shortcut, always use a common name for your form fields and put their unique identifiers in brackets, as shown in Listing 7-32.

Listing 7-32. Using common form field names to store values in an array

```
<label><input type="checkbox" name="simplex_options[sitename]" <?php checked('yes',
$options['sitename']); ?> value="yes" />
       Display site name and description superimposed over the header image?</label>

<label>Enter your CSS:</label><br />
       <textarea name="simplex_options[css]"><?php echo $options['css']; ?></textarea>
```

Adding a Stylesheet to the Options Page

Sometimes you need to add styles to your options pages. You could do everything with inline styles, but that's hardly efficient!

Listing 7-33 shows the function that will display the styles in the options page's <head> area. In this case, you have very little to add, so you won't go to the trouble of creating a separate stylesheet for Simplex Flex. However, it would be easy to do so; just include a link to a separate stylesheet, admin-styles.css, which would be located in the simplex-flex theme directory.

Listing 7-33. Styles for the options page

```
function simplex_flex_admin_css() { ?>
       <style type="text/css">
              textarea { width: 32em; height: 8em; }
       </style>
       <link rel="stylesheet" type="text/css" src="<?php bloginfo('stylesheet_directory');
?>/admin-styles.css">
<?php
}
```

Now you have to add this function to the admin pages somehow. You could use the admin_head() hook, but that puts the styles on every page. It would be much better to add it only to the theme options page.

In addition to admin_head(), there's another hook that's specific to each page, admin_head-filename. The filename should include the extension. For example, if you wanted to add a stylesheet to the Dashboard, the hook would be called admin_head-index.php.

Now you just need the name of the current theme options page, without the preceding path that you'd get with the __FILE__ constant. As it turns out, that's easy. The add_theme_page() function returns the file name of the theme page that gets added. In Listing 7-29, you didn't need the returned value, but now you can make use of it.

Listing 7-34 shows the necessary changes to the simplex_menu() function.

Listing 7-34. Adding a stylesheet to the options page

```
function simplex_menu() {
        $file = add_theme_page('Simplex Flex Options', 'Simplex Options',
'edit_theme_options', __FILE__, 'simplex_options_page');
        add_action("admin_head-$file", 'simplex_flex_admin_css');
        register_setting('simplex_options', 'simplex_options');
        // set defaults
        $options = array(
                'width' => 'flex',
                'cols' => '3',
                'sitename' => 'yes',
                'css' => ''
        );
        add_option('simplex_options', $options, '', 'yes');
}
add_action('admin_menu', 'simplex_menu');
```

Putting it All Together

Listing 7-35 shows the complete theme options code, which results in the screen in Figure 7-7. In Simplex Flex, this code appears in functions.php, along with the widget definitions, header and background image support, and other theme functions.

Listing 7-35. A complete theme options page

```
<?php
function simplex_menu() {
        $css = add_theme_page('Simplex Flex Options', 'Simplex Options', 'edit_theme_options',
__FILE__, 'simplex_options_page');
        add_action("admin_head-$css", 'simplex_flex_admin_css');
        register_setting('simplex_options', 'simplex_options');
        // set defaults
        $options = array(
                'width' => 'flex',
                'cols' => '3',
```

```php
                        'sitename' => 'yes',
                        'css' => ''
                );
                add_option('simplex_options', $options, '', 'yes');
        }
add_action('admin_menu', 'simplex_menu');

function simplex_options_page() { ?>
    <div class="wrap">
    <h2>Simplex Flex Options</h2>
    <form method="post" action="options.php">
            <?php settings_fields('simplex_options'); ?>
            <?php $options = get_option('simplex_options'); ?>
    <table class="form-table">
    <tr valign="top">
    <th scope="row">Width</th>
    <td><label><input type="radio" name="simplex_options[width]" <?php checked('fixed',
$options['width']); ?> value="fixed" /> Fixed</label>
                    <label><input type="radio" name="simplex_options[width]" <?php checked('flex',
$options['width']); ?> value="flex" /> Flex</label>
            </td>
    </tr>
<tr valign="top">
    <th scope="row">Columns</th>
    <td><label><input type="radio" name="simplex_options[cols]" <?php checked('left2',
$options['cols']); ?> value="left2" /> 2 columns, sidebar left</label>
            <label><input type="radio" name="simplex_options[cols]" <?php checked('right2',
$options['cols']); ?> value="right2" /> 2 columns, sidebar right</label>
            <label><input type="radio" name="simplex_options[cols]" <?php checked('col3',
$options['cols']); ?> value="col3" /> 3 columns, sidebars on either side</label>
            </td>
    </tr>
    <tr valign="top">
    <th scope="row">Header text and image</th>
    <td><label><input type="checkbox" name="simplex_options[sitename]" <?php checked('yes',
$options['sitename']); ?> value="yes" />
            Display site name and description superimposed over the header image?</label>
    </td>
    </tr>
            <tr valign="top">
    <th scope="row">Custom styles</th>
    <td><label>Enter your CSS:</label><br />
            <textarea name="simplex_options[css]"><?php echo $options['css']; ?></textarea>
    </td>
    </tr>
    </table>

    <p class="submit">
            <input type="submit" class="button-primary" value="<?php _e('Save Changes') ?>" />
    </p>
    </form>
```

```
    </div>
<?php }
?>
```
Be sure your theme works correctly with the default options! Many users will activate the theme and go on their merry way without ever looking at the options screen.

Theme Frameworks

There are a number of advanced WordPress themes that allow users to build very customized layouts by choosing options rather than writing code. They also provide a solid framework for developers to build complex sites. These theme frameworks are all different, but they have a few things in common. They use theme options pages to make choices simpler for users. They take advantage of the template file hierarchy, which you learned about in the previous chapter, to create rich context in archives. They include their own widgets or even full plugins using the theme functions file. They use child themes to let site owners customize the themes while maintaining the originals separately, allowing the developers to offer upgrades without destroying those modifications.

A framework could provide a good basis for your project, or you might just look into their inner workings for inspiration. Some of these frameworks are not free, and not all of them comply with the WordPress GPL license. Paid ("premium") themes are marked with the $ symbol. Other frameworks might be free to download, but require payment for support.

Carrington: carringtontheme.com/

Genesis ($): www.studiopress.com/themes/genesis/

Hybrid: themehybrid.com/themes/hybrid/

Sandbox: www.plaintxt.org/themes/sandbox/

Thematic: wordpress.org/extend/themes/thematic/

Thesis ($): diythemes.com/thesis/

Whiteboard: plainbeta.com/2008/05/20/whiteboard-a-free-wordpress-theme-framework/

Distributing Themes

If you want to publish your theme on the official theme repository at WordPress Extend, you need to make sure your theme meets a long list of requirements (see the checklist below). You also need to localize your theme so it can be translated. I'll talk about localization and internationalization in Chapter 9 in the context of plugins. The process of localizing themes is very similar, so I won't repeat it here. Also in Chapter 9, I'll explain how to use Subversion to maintain different versions of your theme.

Theme Checklist

The theme developer center at wordpress.org includes an extensive checklist (codex.wordpress.org/Theme_Development_Checklist). If you prefer, there's an interactive checklist at www.wplover.com/lab/theme-development-checklist where you can check off each item as you go and keep track of your progress, as shown in Figure 7-8. If you don't plan to distribute your theme to the public, don't sweat over each and every one of the 146 items on the checklist! Just glance at it to make sure you haven't overlooked anything essential.

As of this writing, neither checklist has been updated to include the new features in version 3.0. You should check to see whether your theme includes:

- `wp_nav_menu()` in the theme templates and `add_theme_support('nav-menus')` in `functions.php`. (See `codex.wordpress.org/Function_Reference/wp_nav_menu`)

- `add_custom_background()` in `functions.php` if you want to allow the user to upload her own background image. (See `codex.wordpress.org/Function_Reference/add_custom_background`)

- `the_shortlink()` somewhere inside the Loop if you want to publicize it. (See `codex.wordpress.org/Template_Tags/the_shortlink`)

- `comment_form()` instead of the `<form>` tag and its contents in `comments.php`. (See `codex.wordpress.org/Template_Tags/comment_form`)

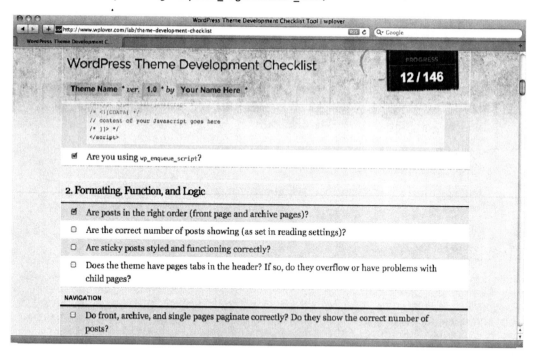

Figure 7-8. The theme checklist

Summary

In this chapter, you've learned all the essential steps to creating a complex theme. I've shown you how to modify the Loop and run multiple Loops per page—the key to complicated "magazine" layouts such as Mimbo and Magazeen. I've shown you how to access post information outside the Loop, which is especially useful in your sidebars (and widgets, in the next chapter). I've also gone over some changes you can make to your theme's header file to improve search engine optimization. I've discussed the proper way to include scripts and extra stylesheets in your themes, including how to use the built-in jQuery library. I've also shown you how to create options pages for advanced themes.

In the next chapter, you'll learn how to create custom widgets that could be included with your theme.

CHAPTER 8

■ ■ ■

Creating Widgets

Widgets are the building blocks of WordPress sidebars. They can be created in a theme's functions file or in a plugin.

In this chapter, I'll show you how I created two of my plugins, Recent Posts From Category and Dashboard Notepad. You'll see how to create these widgets as part of a theme's functions file, and in the next chapter I'll show you how to transform them into plugins.

While these two plugins create widgets, note that plugins can do any number of other things. Widgets are limited to displaying a bit of content inside the widget areas you defined in your theme's functions.php file back in chapter 6.

Basic Widgets

WordPress widgets are classes, which makes them easy to duplicate, even if you've never worked with object-oriented programming before. A class provides a blueprint for objects that will be reused in various ways. Creating a new widget is a matter of copying the basic widget class, then adjusting the enclosed functions to output the content you have in mind. The widget class contains four functions: one that registers the widget, one that prints the widget output, one that updates the widget options, and one that displays the options form.

Examining the Calendar Widget

Before I go into the details of custom widgets, let's take a look at the code for one of the simplest built-in widgets, the calendar (Figure 8-1). The code (from wp-includes/default-widgets.php) is given in Listing 8-1. Things you would change in your own widget are in bold.

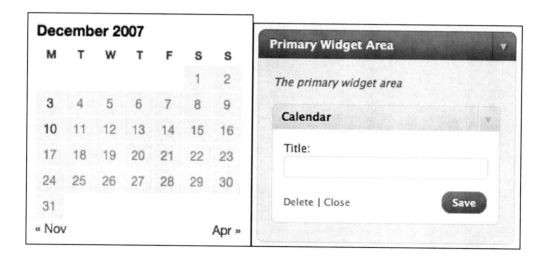

Figure 8-1. The calendar widget in the widget manager area and the Twenty Ten theme

Listing 8-1. The built-in calendar widget

```
class WP_Widget_Calendar extends WP_Widget {

        function WP_Widget_Calendar() {
                // define widget title and description
                $widget_ops = array('classname' => 'widget_calendar',
                        'description' => __( 'A calendar of your blog&#8217;s posts') );
                // register the widget
                $this->WP_Widget('calendar', __('Calendar'), $widget_ops);
        }

        // display the widget in the theme
        function widget( $args, $instance ) {
                extract($args);
                // apply filters to the given title, or print non-breaking space if empty
                $title = apply_filters('widget_title', empty($instance['title']) ?
                        ' ' : $instance['title'], $instance, $this->id_base);
                // before/after code for widget and title were defined in functions.php
                echo $before_widget;
                if ( $title )
                        echo $before_title . $title . $after_title;
                // print the inner widget, the part that makes this widget unique
                echo '<div id="calendar_wrap">';
                get_calendar();
                echo '</div>';
                echo $after_widget;
        }
```

```
        // update the widget when new options have been entered
        function update( $new_instance, $old_instance ) {
                $instance = $old_instance;
                // replace old with new
                $instance['title'] = strip_tags($new_instance['title']);

                return $instance;
        }

        // print the widget option form on the widget management screen
        function form( $instance ) {
                // combine provided fields with defaults
                $instance = wp_parse_args( (array) $instance, array( 'title' => '' ) );
                $title = strip_tags($instance['title']);
                // print the form fields
?>
                <p><label for="<?php echo $this->get_field_id('title'); ?>">
                        <?php _e('Title:'); ?></label>
                        <input class="widefat" id="<?php echo $this->get_field_id('title'); ?>"
name="<?php echo $this->get_field_name('title'); ?>" type="text" value="<?php echo
esc_attr($title); ?>" /></p>
<?php
        }
}
```

Look how little you have to change! Now, I did say that this is one of the simplest widgets. Your widgets might have more options, and therefore a longer form and more fields to update. Still, this is going to be pretty easy, right?

I'll go through each piece of this widget, starting with the form and working backwards.

The Options Form

The form function defines what will appear in the widget manager under Appearance → Widgets. In the case of the calendar widget, there are no options other than the title, so the form shown in Listing 8-1 was unchanged. In your own widgets, you'll probably have an option or two, and you'll need to create a few more form fields. Let's review the form function by itself (Listing 8-2).

Listing 8-2. The form function

```
        // print the widget option form on the widget management screen
        function form( $instance ) {
                // combine provided fields with defaults
                $instance = wp_parse_args( (array) $instance, array( 'title' => '' ) );
                $title = strip_tags($instance['title']);
                // print the form fields
?>
                <p><label for="<?php echo $this->get_field_id('title'); ?>">
<?php _e('Title:'); ?></label>
                        <input class="widefat" id="<?php echo $this->get_field_id('title'); ?>"
name="<?php echo $this->get_field_name('title'); ?>" type="text" value="<?php echo
esc_attr($title); ?>" /></p>
```

```php
<?php
    }
```

First, let's think about what this widget will display in the theme. The get_calendar() tag is pretty simple. It takes just one possible argument, the format of the days' names in the table heading. You don't need the argument here; the tag respects the time and date settings you chose in your General Settings screen. The tag, and thus the widget, simply prints a calendar, as shown in Figure 8-1. Therefore, you don't need any widget options other than the title of the widget itself. Were you generating a more complicated bit of code, you would need more options, as you'll see in the Random Posts from Category widget later in this chapter (Listing 8-7), and you would add those form fields here in the form function.

In the first line of the form function, you parse the arguments passed in the $instance variable and merge it with a second array containing the default values for your options. Then, before you display the title on the widget manager screen, you need to strip HTML tags. Widget titles are strictly defined; you saw this back in Chapter 7 when you defined the widget areas in functions.php. You need to keep stray HTML tags from interfering with the widget output, not to mention widget manager itself.

Now it's time to display the form fields. There's no need for a <form> tag; that will be taken care of for you. You just need to wrap the title in a <label> tag and provide an input field for each option—in this case, just the title itself.

To convert the stored value of a widget option into attribute-friendly strings, pass the name of the option to the get_field_id() and get_field_name() functions. For the value itself, use the $title variable again, this time passed through the esc_attr function.

And you're done with the form! The submit button will be added automatically.

The Update Function

The first thing to do in any widget update function is to save the old values, in case any of them didn't change. Then, go through each of the fields from your form, do any required processing on them, and save them to the new form instance.

In this case, the only thing you need to do with your widget title is, once again, strip any HTML tags. Listing 8-3 shows the isolated update function.

Listing 8-3. The update function

```php
// update the widget when new options have been entered
function update( $new_instance, $old_instance ) {
        $instance = $old_instance;
        // replace old with new
        $instance['title'] = strip_tags($new_instance['title']);

        return $instance;
}
```

The Widget Output

Listing 8-4 shows the isolated widget output function.

Listing 8-4. The widget function

```
        // display the widget in the theme
        function widget( $args, $instance ) {
                extract($args);
                // apply filters to the given title, or print non-breaking space if empty
                $title = apply_filters('widget_title', empty($instance['title']) ?
' ' : $instance['title'], $instance, $this->id_base);
                // before/after code for widget and title were defined in functions.php
                echo $before_widget;
                if ( $title )
                        echo $before_title . $title . $after_title;
                // print the inner widget, the part that makes this widget unique
                echo '<div id="calendar_wrap">';
                get_calendar();
                echo '</div>';
                echo $after_widget;
        }
```

The $args variable passed to the widget function is an array of all the fields in the form. To make them easier to work with, the first line extracts them into separate variables.

The next line is a bit complicated. It's an if/else statement using the ternary operator syntax. If you're not familiar with the ternary operator, it can be confusing to read. Unpacked, this line would look more like Listing 8-5.

Listing 8-5. *A less compact way of processing the widget title*

```
// First, you'll provide a non-breaking space if the title field was left empty.
if (empty($instance['title']))
        $title = ' ';
else
        $title = $instance['title'];
// Then, you need to apply filters, in case another plugin needs to alter widget titles
$title = apply_filters('widget_title', $title, $instance, $this->id_base);
```

First, you provide a non-breaking space if the title field was left empty. Then, by calling apply_filters(), you allow plugins to modify the widget titles.

Once you have the title, you need to kick off the widget with $before_widget. Then you print the title using $before_title and $after_title. Recall that you defined all the before and after options back in Chapter 7 when you set up the widget areas in functions.php.

Now it's time to print the heart of the widget. In this case, you use just one template tag, get_calendar(), surrounded by a <div> tag (which might be useful for styling the widget). As you'll see later in this chapter, you could do something much more complicated here.

Once you're finished with the widget output, you print $after_widget, and you're done.

Setting up the Widget

Finally, the setup function is shown by itself in Listing 8-6.

Listing 8-6. The setup function

```
function WP_Widget_Calendar() {
        // define widget title and description
        $widget_ops = array('classname' => 'widget_calendar',
'description' => __( 'A calendar of your blog&#8217;s posts') );
        // register the widget
        $this->WP_Widget('calendar', __('Calendar'), $widget_ops);
    }
```

The name of the first function in the class should match your widget name. This function provides the information about the widget WordPress needs to display on the widget manager screen.

You could accomplish all this in one line, but for readability, you'll create an array of the widget's properties (class name and description). Then you just need to initalize the widget with an internal name (calendar), a label (Calendar), and the array of properties.

■ **Note:** the description and label are shown wrapped in the __() function (that's two underscores and nothing else). As you will see in the next chapter, this function is used to translate the given strings into the user's chosen language.

Creating Your Own Widget

To create your own widget, you need to duplicate the widget class and add your own logic and form fields. Then you just need a few extra lines to register your widget and make it available on the widget manager screen. Listing 8-7 shows a simplified version of my Random Posts from Category plugin (Figure 8-2). For simplicity's sake, I've removed the extra code required for internationalizing the strings and supporting the the_excerpt Reloaded plugin as well as the built-in the_excerpt() function. Other than that, this really is the whole plugin. If you want, you can flip ahead to the next chapter and see how to set up the comment block necessary to use this as a plugin. Otherwise, paste this into your theme's functions.php file, and you'll see a new widget available under Appearance → Widgets.

The things that are unique to this widget are shown in bold.

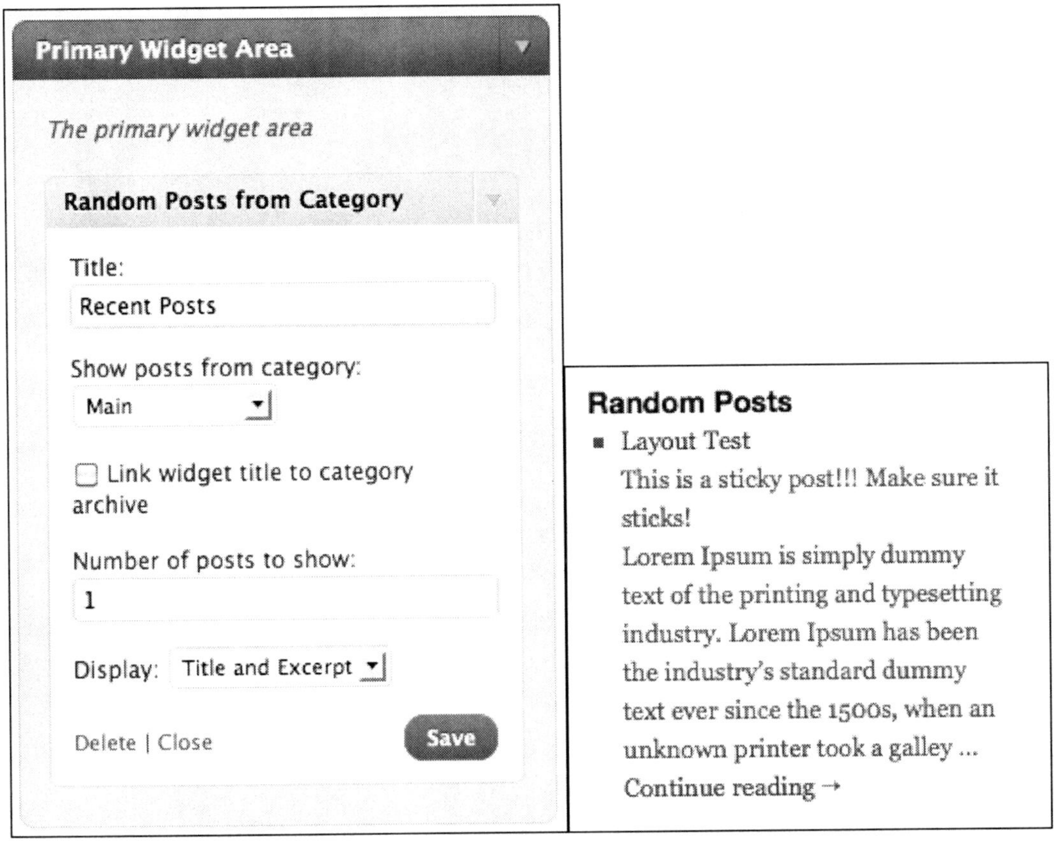

Figure 8-2. The Random Posts from Category widget manager and output in the Twenty Ten theme

Listing 8-7. The Random Posts from Category widget

```
class RandomPostsFromCategory extends WP_Widget {

function RandomPostsFromCategory() {
        $widget_ops = array('classname' => 'random_from_cat', 'description' => 'random posts
from a chosen category');
        $this->WP_Widget('RandomPostsFromCategory', 'Random Posts from Category',
$widget_ops);
}


function widget( $args, $instance ) {
        extract( $args );
```

```php
        $title = apply_filters('widget_title', empty( $instance['title'] ) ) ? 'Random Posts' :
$instance['title']);

        echo $before_widget;
        if ( $title) {
                if ($instance['postlink'] == 1)  {
                        $before_title .= '<a
href="'.get_category_link($instance['cat']).'">';
                        $after_title = '</a>'.$after_title;
                }
                echo $before_title.$title.$after_title;
        }
        ?>
        <ul>
        <?php
        query_posts("cat=".$instance['cat']."&showposts=".$instance['showposts']."&orderby=r
and");
        // the Loop
        if (have_posts()) : while (have_posts()) : the_post(); ?>
                <li><a href="<?php the_permalink(); ?>" title="<?php the_title_attribute();
?>"><?php the_title(); ?></a>
                <?php
                  if ($instance['content'] == 'excerpt')
                        the_excerpt();
                  elseif ($instance['content'] == 'content')
                        the_content();
        endwhile; endif;
        ?>
        </ul>
        <?php
        echo $after_widget;
        wp_reset_query();
}


function update( $new_instance, $old_instance ) {
        $instance = $old_instance;
        $instance['title'] = strip_tags($new_instance['title']);
        $instance['cat'] = $new_instance['cat'];
        $instance['showposts'] = $new_instance['showposts'];
        $instance['content'] = $new_instance['content'];
        $instance['postlink'] = $new_instance['postlink'];
        return $instance;
}

function form( $instance ) {
        //Defaults
                $instance = wp_parse_args( (array) $instance, array(
                        'title' => 'Random Posts',
                        'cat' => 1,
                        'showposts' => 1,
```

```php
                                'content' => 'title',
                                'postlink' => 0));
?>

<p>
<label for="<?php echo $this->get_field_id('title'); ?>">Title:</label>
<input class="widefat" id="<?php echo $this->get_field_id('title'); ?>"
        name="<?php echo $this->get_field_name('title'); ?>" type="text" value="<?php echo
$instance['title']; ?>" />
</p>

<p><label for="<?php echo $this->get_field_id('cat'); ?>">Show posts from category:</label>
<?php wp_dropdown_categories(array('name' => $this->get_field_name('cat'), 'hide_empty'=>0,
'hierarchical'=>1, 'selected'=>$instance['cat'])); ?></label>
</p>

<p>
<input id="<?php echo $this->get_field_id('postlink'); ?>" name="<?php echo $this-
>get_field_name('postlink'); ?>"
        type="checkbox" <?php checked($instance['postlink'], 1); ?> value="1" />
<label for="<?php echo $this->get_field_id('postlink'); ?>">Link widget title to category
archive</label>
</p>

<p><label for="<?php echo $this->get_field_id('showposts'); ?>">Number of posts to
show:</label>
<input class="widefat" id="<?php echo $this->get_field_id('showposts'); ?>" name="<?php echo
$this->get_field_name('showposts'); ?>"
        type="text" value="<?php echo $instance['showposts']; ?>" />
</p>

<p>
<label for="<?php echo $this->get_field_id('content'); ?>">Display:</label>
<select id="<?php echo $this->get_field_id('content'); ?>" name="<?php echo $this-
>get_field_name('content'); ?>" class="postform">
        <option value="title"<?php selected( $instance['content'], 'title' ); ?>>Title
Only</option>
        <option value="excerpt"<?php selected( $instance['content'], 'excerpt' ); ?>>Title
and Excerpt</option>
        <option value="content"<?php selected( $instance['content'], 'content' ); ?>>Title
and Content</option>
</select>
</p>

<?php
        } // function form
} // widget class
```

This time, I'll go through the functions in order, beginning with the setup function alone in Listing 8-8.

Listing 8-8. The widget setup function

```
function RandomPostsFromCategory() {
        $widget_ops = array('classname' => 'random_from_cat', 'description' => 'random posts
from a chosen category');
        $this->WP_Widget('RandomPostsFromCategory', 'Random Posts from Category',
$widget_ops);
}
```

In the first function, the names have changed. The classname and description are up to you; just make sure the classname is a valid name for a class in CSS (see www.w3.org/TR/CSS21/syndata.html#characters for details). When you call $this->WP_Widget, you need to pass it three arguments: the name of this widget (which should match this function's name), its title (for the widget manager screen), and the array of options you created in the previous line.

In the widget function (Listing 8-9), you first check to see if the option to make the title a link has been checked. If it has, you need to add the link markup to the $before_title and $after_title variables. Then you move on to the heart of the widget output, which is in this case a Loop. Just as you did in the previous chapters on themes, you'll use query_posts() to get the posts from the selected category and show the chosen number of posts. In this query, rather than getting the most recent posts, you're ordering them at random. And of course, once you're finished with the widget output, you need to reset the query.

Listing 8-9. The widget function

```
function widget( $args, $instance ) {
        extract( $args );

        $title = apply_filters('widget_title', empty( $instance['title'] ) ? 'Random Posts' :
$instance['title']);

        echo $before_widget;
        if ( $title) {
                if ($instance['postlink'] == 1)  {
                        $before_title .= '<a href="'.get_category_link($instance['cat']).'">';
                        $after_title = '</a>'.$after_title;
                }
                echo $before_title.$title.$after_title;
        }
        ?>
        <ul>
        <?php
        query_posts("cat=".$instance['cat']."&showposts=".$instance['showposts']."&orderby=ran
d");
        // the Loop
        if (have_posts()) : while (have_posts()) : the_post(); ?>
                <li><a href="<?php the_permalink(); ?>" title="<?php the_title_attribute();
?>"><?php the_title(); ?></a>
                <?php
                        if ($instance['content'] == 'excerpt')
                                the_excerpt();
```

```
                elseif ($instance['content'] == 'content')
                        the_content();
        endwhile; endif;
        ?>
        </ul>
        <?php
        echo $after_widget;
        wp_reset_query();
}
```

The update function (Listing 8-10) changes very little, except that you've added the new options to the array.

Listing 8-10. The update function

```
function update( $new_instance, $old_instance ) {
        $instance = $old_instance;
        $instance['title'] = strip_tags($new_instance['title']);
        $instance['cat'] = $new_instance['cat'];
        $instance['showposts'] = $new_instance['showposts'];
        $instance['content'] = $new_instance['content'];
        $instance['postlink'] = $new_instance['postlink'];
        return $instance;
}
```

In the form function (Listing 8-11), you need to add the new options' default values to this array as well. Then it's just a matter of adding form inputs for each of the additional options. For the category, you can make use of WordPress's wp_dropdown_categories() function. In the checkbox and select fields, you might have noticed two interesting functions: checked() and selected(). These allow you to compress the code required to see whether or not the relevant option has already been selected or not. The checkbox code, for example, is much simpler than the alternative, shown in Listing 8-12.

Listing 8-11. The form function

```
function form( $instance ) {
        //Defaults
                $instance = wp_parse_args( (array) $instance, array(
                        'title' => 'Random Posts',
                        'cat' => 1,
                        'showposts' => 1,
                        'content' => 'title',
                        'postlink' => 0));
?>

<p>
<label for="<?php echo $this->get_field_id('title'); ?>">Title:</label>
<input class="widefat" id="<?php echo $this->get_field_id('title'); ?>"
```

```
            name="<?php echo $this->get_field_name('title'); ?>" type="text" value="<?php echo
$instance['title']; ?>" />
</p>

<p><label for="<?php echo $this->get_field_id('cat'); ?>">Show posts from category:</label>
<?php wp_dropdown_categories(array('name' => $this->get_field_name('cat'), 'hide_empty'=>0,
'hierarchical'=>1, 'selected'=>$instance['cat'])); ?></label>
</p>

<p>
<input id="<?php echo $this->get_field_id('postlink'); ?>" name="<?php echo $this-
>get_field_name('postlink'); ?>"
        type="checkbox" <?php checked($instance['postlink'], 1); ?> value="1" />
<label for="<?php echo $this->get_field_id('postlink'); ?>">Link widget title to category
archive</label>
</p>

<p><label for="<?php echo $this->get_field_id('showposts'); ?>">Number of posts to
show:</label>
<input class="widefat" id="<?php echo $this->get_field_id('showposts'); ?>" name="<?php echo
$this->get_field_name('showposts'); ?>"
        type="text" value="<?php echo $instance['showposts']; ?>" />
</p>

<p>
<label for="<?php echo $this->get_field_id('content'); ?>">Display:</label>
<select id="<?php echo $this->get_field_id('content'); ?>" name="<?php echo $this-
>get_field_name('content'); ?>" class="postform">
        <option value="title"<?php selected( $instance['content'], 'title' ); ?>>Title
Only</option>
        <option value="excerpt"<?php selected( $instance['content'], 'excerpt' ); ?>>Title and
Excerpt</option>
        <option value="content"<?php selected( $instance['content'], 'content' ); ?>>Title and
Content</option>
</select>
</p>

<?php
        } // function form
```

Listing 8-12. The alternative to checked(); not recommended

```
<?php if ($instance['postlink']) { ?> checked="checked" <?php } ?>
```

That's about all there is to widgets! The widget function could contain almost anything. Just keep in mind that widgets are (usually) outside the Loop, so you'll need to access post data accordingly or create your own Loop (as shown in Listing 8-9).

More Widget Examples

Widgets are one of the most popular plugin categories on wordpress.org. Of the many great offerings, there are two that really show the breadth and depth of what a widget can do. The Section widget (Figure 8-3) allows you to display a bit of HTML on selected pages or category archives. It makes use of all the conditional tags I've talked about in the last few chapters, but it lets you create context-aware content without coding. The Query Posts widget (Figure 8-4) allows you to display a list of posts or pages using all the options available in the query_posts() function—again, without coding.

Figure 8-3. The Section widget

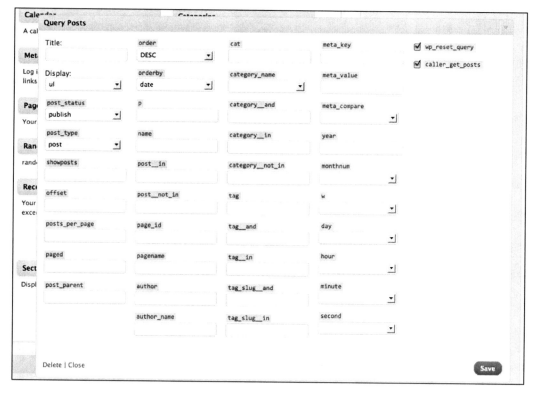

Figure 8-4. The Query Posts widget

Dashboard Widgets

Creating new Dashboard widgets is not quite as elegant as creating sidebar widgets. For a very basic Dashboard widget, you'll have two essential functions, the widget itself (dashboard_notepad_widget()) and the setup function (dashboard_notepad_widget_setup()). Here, since the code for setting option defaults is used in both those functions, it has been pulled out into its own function, dashboard_notepad_widget_options(). Finally, you use the add_action() function to add your new widget to the Dashboard setup process using the wp_dashboard_setup() hook.

My Dashboard Notepad plugin creates an extremely simple Dashboard widget. Anything you enter into the form is saved there until you clear it out. It's great for jotting down ideas for future posts or sharing reminders with other site administrators. In this simplified version, it really has just one option: the note text.

The Dashboard Notepad widget is shown in Figure 8-5, and the source code is given in Listing 8-13. Take a look at the code, and then I'll walk through each piece.

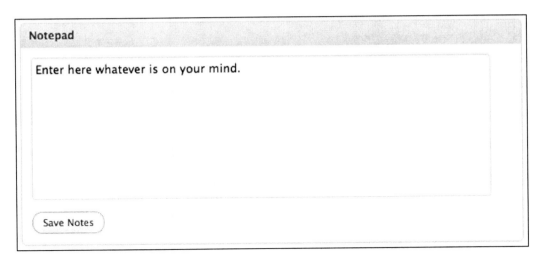

Figure 8-5. The Dashboard Notepad widget

Listing 8-13. The Dashboard Notepad widget source code

```
function dashboard_notepad_widget() {
        $options = dashboard_notepad_widget_options();
        if (!empty($_POST['dashboard_notepad_submit']) ) {
                $options['notes'] = stripslashes($_POST['dashboard_notepad']);

                update_option('dashboard_notepad', $options);
        } else
                $dashboard_notepad = htmlspecialchars($options['notes'], ENT_QUOTES);
        $form = '<form method="post" action="'.$_SERVER['PHP_SELF'].'">';
        $form .= '<textarea id="dashboard_notepad" name="dashboard_notepad" style="width: 95%;
height: 12em; background: #fcfcfc;"';
        $form .= '>'. $options['notes'].'</textarea>';
        $form .= '<p><input type="submit" value="Save Notes" class="button widget-control-
save"></p>';
        <input type="hidden" name="dashboard_notepad_submit" value="true" />';
        $form .= '</form>';
        echo $form;
}

function dashboard_notepad_widget_setup() {
        $options = dashboard_notepad_widget_options();
        if (!is_array($options)) $options = array('notepad_title' => 'Notepad');
        wp_add_dashboard_widget( 'dashboard_notepad_widget_id', $options['notepad_title'],
'dashboard_notepad_widget');
}

function dashboard_notepad_widget_options() {
        $defaults = array( 'notes' => 'Enter here whatever is on your mind.',
                'notepad_title' => 'Notepad');
```

219

```
                $options = get_option('dashboard_notepad');
                if (!is_array($options)) $options = array();
                return array_merge( $defaults, $options );
        }

add_action('wp_dashboard_setup', 'dashboard_notepad_widget_setup');
```

■ **Caution:** The example in Listing 8-13 has been vastly simplified for the purposes of demonstration. The full plugin version includes a number of additional checks on users' permissions, such as whether they're allowed to post unfiltered HTML. **Do not use the simplified code on a live site; download the plugin instead.**

Configuration Screens

As you saw in Chapter 2, some widgets have options. If yours does, you'll need to create a configuration screen.

Listing 8-14 is an expanded version of the Dashboard Notepad widget, this time with several options. You'll let the administrator change the widget title. You'll also put some role checking in place so that the administrator can decide who gets to edit the notes. The changes from Listing 8-13 are in bold. Figure 8-6 shows the resulting configuration screen.

Listing 8-14. Dashboard Notepad widget with options configuration screen

```
function dashboard_notepad_widget() {
        $options = dashboard_notepad_widget_options();
        if (!empty($_POST['dashboard_notepad_submit']) ) {
                $options['notes'] = stripslashes($_POST['dashboard_notepad']);
                update_option('dashboard_notepad', $options);
        } else
                $dashboard_notepad = htmlspecialchars($options['notes'], ENT_QUOTES);
        if (current_user_can($options['can_edit'])) $admin = TRUE;
        else $admin = FALSE;
        $form = '<form method="post" action="'.$_SERVER['PHP_SELF'].'">';
        $form .= '<textarea id="dashboard_notepad" name="dashboard_notepad" style="width: 95%;
height: 12em; background: #fcfcfc;"';
        if (!$admin) $form.= ' readonly="readonly"';
        $form .= '>'. $options['notes'].'</textarea>';
        if ($admin) $form .= '<p><input type="submit" value="Save Notes" class="button widget-
control-save"></p>
                <input type="hidden" name="dashboard_notepad_submit" value="true" />';
        $form .= '</form>';
        echo $form;
}

function dashboard_notepad_widget_setup() {
        $options = dashboard_notepad_widget_options();
```

```php
        if (!is_array($options)) $options = array('notepad_title' => 'Notepad');
        if (current_user_can($options['can_read'])) {
                wp_add_dashboard_widget( 'dashboard_notepad_widget_id',
$options['notepad_title'], 'dashboard_notepad_widget', 'dashboard_notepad_widget_control' );
        }
}

add_action('wp_dashboard_setup', 'dashboard_notepad_widget_setup');

function dashboard_notepad_widget_options() {
        $defaults = array( 'notes' => 'Enter here whatever is on your mind.', 'can_edit' =>
'edit_dashboard', 'can_read' => 'read', 'notepad_title' => 'Notepad');
        $options = get_option('dashboard_notepad');
        if (!is_array($options)) $options = array();
        return array_merge( $defaults, $options );
}

function dashboard_notepad_widget_control() {
        $options = dashboard_notepad_widget_options();
        if ( 'post' == strtolower($_SERVER['REQUEST_METHOD']) && isset( $_POST['widget_id']
) && 'dashboard_notepad_widget_id' == $_POST['widget_id'] ) {
                if ( isset($_POST['can_edit']) )
                        $options['can_edit'] = $_POST['can_edit'];
                if ( isset($_POST['can_read']) )
                        $options['can_read'] = $_POST['can_read'];
                if ( isset($_POST['notepad_title']) )
                        $options['notepad_title'] = $_POST['notepad_title'];
                update_option( 'dashboard_notepad', $options );
        }
?>
        <p><label for="notepad_title">Widget title:</label>
                <input type="text" id="notepad_title" name="notepad_title" value="<?php echo
$options['notepad_title']; ?>" /></p>
        <p>
        <select id="can_edit" name="can_edit">
                <option value="edit_dashboard" <?php selected('edit_dashboard',
$options['can_edit']); ?>>Admins</option>
                <option value="edit_pages" <?php selected('edit_pages',
$options['can_edit']); ?>>Editors</option>
                <option value="publish_posts" <?php selected('publish_posts',
$options['can_edit']); ?>>Authors</option>
                <option value="edit_posts" <?php selected('edit_posts',
$options['can_edit']); ?>>Contributors</option>
                <option value="read" <?php selected('read', $options['can_edit']);
?>>Subscribers</option>
        </select>
        <label for="can_edit">and above can <strong>edit</strong> the notes.</label>
        </p>
    <p>
        <select id="can_read" name="can_read">
```

```
                <option value="edit_dashboard" <?php selected('edit_dashboard',
$options['can_read']); ?>>Admins</option>
                <option value="edit_pages" <?php selected('edit_pages',
$options['can_read']); ?>>Editors</option>
                <option value="publish_posts" <?php selected('publish_posts',
$options['can_read']); ?>>Authors</option>
                <option value="edit_posts" <?php selected('edit_posts',
$options['can_read']); ?>>Contributors</option>
                <option value="read" <?php selected('read', $options['can_read']);
?>>Subscribers</option>
        </select>
        <label for="can_read">and above can <strong>read</strong> the notes.</label>
        </p>
<?php
}
```

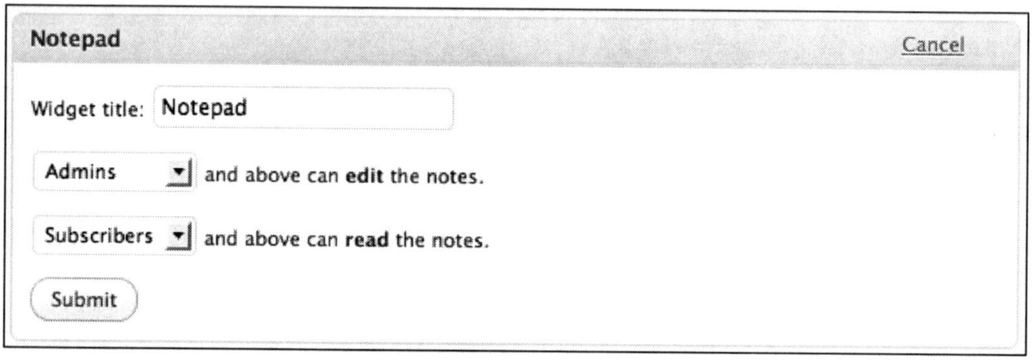

Figure 8-6. Dashboard Notepad configuration screen

The biggest change is, of course, the `dashboard_notepad_widget_control()` function. The first thing you need to do in this function is get the existing options from the database, then run through the data posted from the form and update any options if necessary using the `update_options` function. (This function is more often used for theme and plugin options, and you'll see it again in the next chapter.) Once that's done, just print form fields for each option, with the stored options shown as the field defaults. As with the sidebar widgets, you don't have to include the form tag or the submit button; those are taken care of automatically.

The control function has to be added to the widget setup function. The name of the control function is the last argument passed to `wp_add_dashboard_widget()`. As you saw in Listing 8-13, if this argument is not present, the widget will not have a configuration screen.

Most of the other changes to the functions simply involve adding checks for your new options. There is one unusual thing about the revised `dashboard_notepad_widget_setup()` function. Since you're now checking to see whether the user can read the notes, the entire `wp_add_dashboard_widget()` function is now wrapped in an `if()` statement. You could have put this in the `dashboard_notepad_widget()` function, checking only whether the user gets to see the textarea containing the notes. However, in that case, users who don't have permission to read the notes would have a useless widget cluttering up their Dashboards. By placing this check in the setup function instead, you hide the widget altogether if the user can't see its contents.

Summary

In this chapter you've learned how to create widgets for both themes and the Dashboard. Along the way, you've seen some functions you'll look at more closely in the next chapter: actions, setting and retrieving options, and checking user capabilities.

CHAPTER 9

■ ■ ■

Creating Plugins

While theme functions are quite powerful, they aren't very portable. If you ever wanted to switch themes, you would have to copy all your essential functions from one theme to another. There's another option: many of the theme functions you've seen throughout this book could become plugins. Plugins offer much better control over functions, since you can activate and deactivate them as needed. The plugin manager also provides some safeguards, since plugins containing errors will fail to activate, whereas errors in a theme functions file will affect your site immediately. You can do any number of things with plugins: modify or replace existing functions (filters), add your functions in predetermined locations (actions), create new template tags and shortcodes, and more.

Throughout this chapter, I'll show you examples from two of my plugins, Next Page and Dashboard Notepad. You saw Dashboard Notepad in the previous chapter; it's the plugin that adds a textarea for taking notes on the Dashboard screen. Next Page fills in a gap in the WordPress template tags: the previous and next post navigation tags work only for posts, not for pages. Next Page provides template tags and shortcodes for page navigation that work just like the post navigation. You can find the most current versions of these plugins at WordPress Extend. I'll begin by showing you simplified versions of the various functions, and I'll gradually add complexity as we go through the chapter.

Getting started

Let's assume that you've decided what your plugin should do. Perhaps you have a bit of existing PHP code that you'd like to integrate into WordPress, or maybe you've been playing around with a new function as part of a theme file and you'd like to make it more portable. In any case, you have something in mind for the core of your plugin. Now you need to know how to package it as a plugin, create some options, and perhaps even submit it to the official plugin repository.

The first step is to create your plugin files. While you can create a plugin that's just one file—like the Hello, Dolly plugin included in the WordPress download package—most plugins contain multiple files (even if it's just one PHP file and a readme.txt), so it's a good idea to start by creating a directory for your plugin. It should go inside your /wp-content/plugins directory.

To begin the Next Page plugin, I created a directory and file. The file is saved as /wp-content/plugins/next-page/next-page.php. The first thing that goes into this file is the header comment block, as shown in Listing 9-1. The title and description will appear in your list of plugins. If you provide a URL in addition to your name as the author, your name will be linked to that URL. You may also provide a URL for the plugin, if it has its own page on your website. You should also include a license, either as a single line (as shown) or as a separate comment block (if, for example, you are including the standard GNU Public License header).

Listing 9-1. The Next Page plugin header comment block

```
<?php
/*
Plugin Name: Next Page
Plugin URI: http://sillybean.net/code/wordpress/next-page/
Description: Provides shortcodes and template tags for next/previous navigation in pages.
Version: 1.0
License: GPLv2
Author: Stephanie Leary
Author URI: http://sillybean.net/
*/
?>
```

There are a few additional requirements for plugins distributed through the official repository. If you intend to submit your plugin, you'll need to include a readme.txt file, some screenshots (optional), and a few extra functions that will allow your plugin to be translated into other languages (also optional, but preferred). These steps are detailed at the end of this chapter.

Once you've created your files, you need to plan your approach to the code itself. You should identify the things that users might want to change and plan to turn those things into options. Then you'll need to create the option page containing the form where users can save their options to the database. You can then go through the parts of your code you identified as potential options and replace them with the variable containing your stored options. To demonstrate, I'll show you the Next Page plugin without its options, then add the options page, and replace the appropriate variables. First, however, I'll show you how to create a very basic template tag.

Creating a Template Tag

By now, you've probably realized that template tags in WordPress are just plain old PHP functions. Some take arguments, some don't. Some echo their results by default; others return the results for use in other functions. Creating a new template tag for your plugin is as simple as deciding what sort of function you need to write and whether it should return a value or echo it to the screen. Listing 9-2 shows a very simple example, and Figure 9-1 shows the results.

Listing 9-2. A simple template tag

```
function today() {
        $format = get_option('date_format');
        echo date($format);
}
```

*Figure 9-1. **The results of the today() tag when placed above the Loop***

Creating Template Tags with Arguments

Your template tags can accept arguments in strings or arrays just like WP template tags do. The wp_parse_args() function is the key to WordPress's argument magic. This function takes in your arguments and converts them to an array if they aren't already. If you want, it can also merge your arguments with an array of default values. Then it passes the cleaned-up, merged array back to you for use in your template tag function.

You can use wp_parse_args() to provide a more flexible template tag that can override the settings you chose on the plugin options page. For example, let's extend the simple today() template tag. Perhaps you'd like to let the user specify a date format in the template tag, but use the stored option if no format is provided. You could also add an option to print some text before the date. Listing 9-3 shows the revised template tag function.

Listing 9-3. A today() template tag with arguments

```
function today($args = '') {
        $defaults = array('format' => get_option('date_format'), 'before' => '');
        $args = wp_parse_args($args, $defaults);
        echo $args['before'] .' '. date($args['format']);
}
```

Now you can use the today() tag in either of the ways shown in Listing 9-4, and you'll get the date preceded by "Today is: ". If you don't provide any arguments, it will print the date without a prefix, using the formatting option chosen in Settings → General, just as it did before.

Listing 9-4. Using the new today() template tag

```
<h3>
<?php
// arguments as a string
today('format=l, M j, Y&before=Today is:');

// array would work too
// today(array('format' => 'l, M j, Y', 'before' => 'Today is:'));
?>
</h3>
```

Making Room for Options

For a more complex example, let's look at the Next Page plugin, which provides three template tags. They print links to the previous, next, and parent pages of the currently viewed page. The corresponding functions are very similar to one another, but I'll show you all three so you can see the minor differences. There's a fourth function as well, a utility that's called by the previous_link() and next_link() functions. It gets a list of all pages, minus those explicitly excluded, and returns them in a flat array.

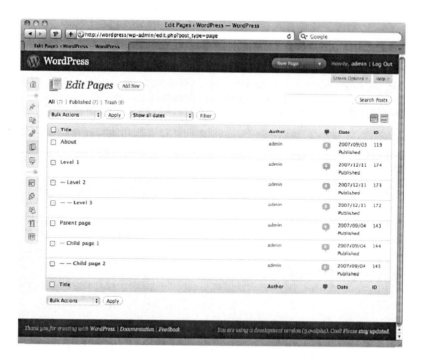

Figure 9-2. Page IDs

To illustrate, Figure 9-2 shows a set of pages and their IDs (using the Simply Show IDs plugin). The flattened array would be (119,174,173,172,143,144,145), and the next/previous tags would display the pages in that order.

Listing 9-5 shows the Next Page template tag functions.

Listing 9-5. The three Next Page template tag functions

```
// next_link tag

function next_link() {
        global $post;
// exclude page IDs 1, 2, and 3
        $exclude = array(1,2,3);
        $pagelist = next_page_flatten_page_list($exclude);
        $current = array_search($post->ID, $pagelist);
        $nextID = $pagelist[$current+1];

        $linkurl = get_permalink($nextID);
        $title = get_the_title($nextID);
        $after_link = '&rarr;';

        $link = '<a href="' . $linkurl . '">' . $title . '</a>' . $after_link;
        echo $link;
}

// previous_link tag

function previous_link() {
        global $post;
// exclude page IDs 1, 2, and 3
        $exclude = array(1,2,3);
        $pagelist = next_page_flatten_page_list($exclude);
        $current = array_search($post->ID, $pagelist);
        $prevID = $pagelist[$current-1];

        $before_link = '&larr;';
        $linkurl = get_permalink($prevID);
        $title = get_the_title($prevID);

        $link = $before_link . '<a href="' . $linkurl . '">' . $title . '</a>';
        echo $link;
}

// parent_link tag

function parent_link() {
        global $post;
        $parentID = $post->post_parent;

// exclude page IDs 1, 2, and 3
        $exclude = array(1,2,3);
        if (in_array($parentID, $exclude)) return false;
```

```
        else {
                $linkurl = get_permalink($parentID);
                $title = get_the_title($parentID);

                $link = '<a href="' . $linkurl . '">' . $title . '</a>';
                echo $link;
        }
}

// utility function

function next_page_flatten_page_list($exclude = '') {
        $args = 'sort_column=menu_order&sort_order=asc';
        if (!empty($exclude)) $args .= '&exclude='.$exclude;
        $pagelist = get_pages($args);
        $mypages = array();
        foreach ($pagelist as $thispage) {
            $mypages[] = $thispage->ID;
        }
        return $mypages;
}
```

Once you have the flattened array, it's easy to find the pages adjacent to the current one: you just increase or decrease the array key by one, grab the value, and use that page ID to build a permalink.

You could insert Listing 9-5 into your plugin file (next-page/next-page.php), activate it, and use next_link() and previous_link() in your templates. However, what if you wanted to use a character other than an arrow as part of the link text? What if you want to use "Next" and "Previous" in place of the page titles? You'd have to edit the plugin.

To allow users to change the linked text as well as the characters shown before or after the page titles, you need to add some options. Listing 9-6 shows the revised plugin code, using a single $options array in place of the hard-coded values used in Listing 9-5.

Listing 9-6. Using option variables

```
// next_link tag

function next_link() {
        global $post;
        $options = get_option('next_page');
        $exclude = $options['exclude'];
        $pagelist = next_page_flatten_page_list($exclude);
        $current = array_search($post->ID, $pagelist);
        $nextID = $pagelist[$current+1];

        $before_link = stripslashes($options['before_next_link']);
        $linkurl = get_permalink($nextID);
        $title = get_the_title($nextID);
        $linktext = $options['next_link_text'];
        if (strpos($linktext, '%title%') !== false)
                $linktext = str_replace('%title%', $title, $linktext);
        $after_link = stripslashes($options['after_next_link']);
```

```
        $link = $before_link . '<a href="' . $linkurl . '" title="' . $title . '">' .
$linktext . '</a>' . $after_link;
        echo $link;
}

// previous_link tag

function previous_link() {
        global $post;
        $options = get_option('next_page');
        $exclude = $options['exclude'];
        $pagelist = next_page_flatten_page_list($exclude);
        $current = array_search($post->ID, $pagelist);
        $prevID = $pagelist[$current-1];

        $before_link = stripslashes($options['before_prev_link']);
        $linkurl = get_permalink($prevID);
        $title = get_the_title($prevID);
        $linktext = $options['prev_link_text'];
        if (strpos($linktext, '%title%') !== false)
                $linktext = str_replace('%title%', $title, $linktext);
        $after_link = stripslashes($options['after_prev_link']);

        $link = $before_link . '<a href="' . $linkurl . '" title="' . $title . '">' .
$linktext . '</a>' . $after_link;
        echo $link;
}

// parent_link tag

function parent_link() {
        global $post;
        $options = get_option('next_page');
        $parentID = $post->post_parent;

        $exclude = array($options['exclude']);
        if (in_array($parentID, $exclude)) return false;
        else {
                $before_link = stripslashes($options['before_parent_link']);
                $linkurl = get_permalink($parentID);
                $title = get_the_title($parentID);
                $linktext = $options['parent_link_text'];
                if (strpos($linktext, '%title%') !== false)
                        $linktext = str_replace('%title%', $title, $linktext);
                $after_link = stripslashes($options['after_parent_link']);

                $link = $before_link . '<a href="' . $linkurl . '" title="' . $title . '">'
. $linktext . '</a>' . $after_link;
                echo $link;
        }
```

```
    }

// utility function

function next_page_flatten_page_list($exclude = '') {
        $args = 'sort_column=menu_order&sort_order=asc';
        if (!empty($exclude)) $args .= '&exclude='.$exclude;
        $pagelist = get_pages($args);
        $mypages = array();
        foreach ($pagelist as $thispage) {
            $mypages[] = $thispage->ID;
        }
        return $mypages;
}
```

Now that you know how the user will be able to modify the template tags' output using options, you need to build the form that will let them save those options to the database.

Adding an Options Page

Almost every WordPress plugin involves some sort of option, and that means you'll need to create the form that lets users manage those options. If you went through the process of creating theme functions back in Chapter 7, the process for plugins will look very much the same.

To add an options page to the main navigation menu, you need two functions. One will display the content of the options page, and the other is a container for the add_options_page() function. Finally, you'll need to add your container function to the admin_menu() hook using add_action().

Listing 9-7 is taken from my Next Page plugin. I'll use this plugin as an example for the next several sections of this chapter, as it illustrates options pages, shortcodes, and template tags. Here, I've shown the bare minimum that's required to add an options page. In the next section, I'll show you how to fill in the form fields and process the input data into WordPress options.

Listing 9-7. An empty options page

```
// Add a new submenu under Options:
add_action('admin_menu', 'next_page_add_pages');

function next_page_add_pages() {
        add_options_page('Next Page', 'Next Page', 'manage_options', 'next-page',
'next_page_options');
}

// displays the options page content
function next_page_options() { ?>
<div class="wrap">
<form method="post" id="next_page_form" action="options.php">
    <h2>Next Page Options</h2>

        <p> the form fields will go here </p>

        <p class="submit">
```

```
            <input type="submit" name="submit" class="button-primary" value="Update Options" />
            </p>
</form>
</div>
<?php
} // end function next_page_options()
```

Unlike the widgets you created in the previous chapter, on the plugin options pages, you do have to define the form and its submit button. The form should always be posted to `options.php`. This file processes all the WordPress options. Once you have registered your plugin's options (which I'll show you in the next section), you can use just two lines to your form to process them.

The wrapper element (`<div class="wrap">`) is essential to the layout of all WordPress admin pages, so you must include it in your options forms. The form tags should go inside the wrapper. The id attribute is optional, but your form method should be `post` and the action should always be `options.php` (the file that processes all WordPress options).

The results of Listing 9-7 are shown in Figure 9-3.

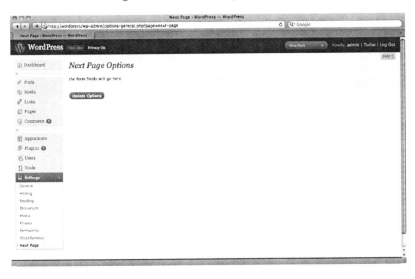

Figure 9-3. The skeleton options page

Your form button styles should conform to WordPress standards. You should have one primary button (the one that saves the options, publishes the post, etc.) and it should be styled with the `button-primary` class. All other buttons should use the `secondary` class. These styles are consistent throughout the WordPress administration screens. The QuickPress Dashboard widget, shown in Figure 9-4, illustrates the contrast between the two button styles.

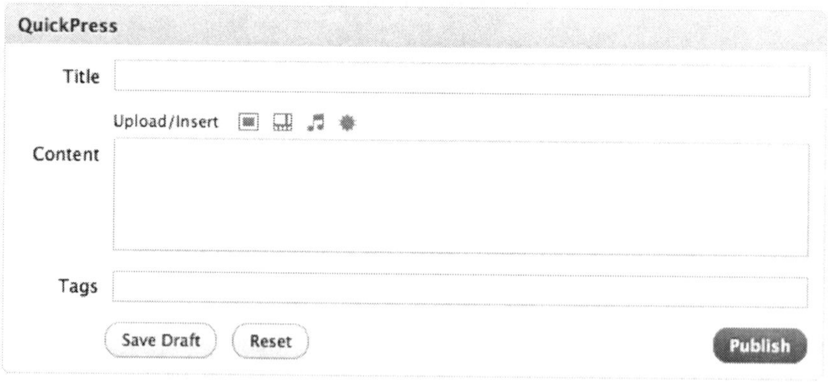

Figure 9-4. *The secondary (Save Draft, Reset) and primary (Publish) button styles*

Now that you have an options page in place, it's time to add some fields to the form.

The Settings API

WordPress provides a complete framework for setting, updating, and deleting plugin and theme options in the database. The settings API handles a lot of security issues for you (although there are still things for you to check). It also handles most of the work of saving options to the database. All you have to do is register the settings you plan to use, so WordPress knows which ones it should handle. For more information on the Settings API, visit the Codex page at codex.wordpress.org/Settings_API.

Registering Settings and Creating Defaults

Prior to version 2.7, you could create options without registering them with WordPress, but then you had to do a lot of manual security checks and updates. With the new settings API, all of that is much easier, but you *must* register your settings in order for them to work.

You may register a separate setting for each variable you need to store, but it's impolite to take up lots of database rows with your plugin's options. Instead, group your variables into arrays, each of which can be stored in a single database row. Listing 9-8 shows the code required to register a single setting. The first argument is the setting's name; the second is the name of the group in which it appears. In this case, you'll have just one group, so the names are the same.

Listing 9-8. Registering a setting

```
function register_next_page_options() {
        register_setting( 'next_page', 'next_page' );
}
add_action('admin_init', 'register_next_page_options' );
```

Registering the setting lets WordPress know that you plan to use it, but it doesn't do anything about setting default values. You'll have to do that yourself. You can use the activation hook to make sure your options are set as soon as the plugin is activated. Listing 9-9 shows a function that sets default option values, stored in a single array, when the plugin is activated.

Listing 9-9. Setting default options on activation

```
function next_page_activation() {
        // set defaults
        $options = array();
        $options['before_prev_link'] = '<div class="alignleft">';
        $options['prev_link_text'] = __('Previous:', 'next-page').' %title%';
        $options['after_prev_link'] = '</div>';

        $options['before_parent_link'] = '<div class="aligncenter">';
        $options['parent_link_text'] = __('Up one level:', 'next-page').' %title%';
        $options['after_parent_link'] = '</div>';

        $options['before_next_link'] = '<div class="alignright">';
        $options['next_link_text'] = __('Next:', 'next-page').' %title%';
        $options['after_next_link'] = '</div>';

        $options['exclude'] = '';

        // set new option
        add_option('next_page', $options, '', 'yes');
}
register_activation_hook(__FILE__, 'next_page_activation');
```

The code here is fairly simple; it's just an array in which each element contains the default values for one of the options. Note the use of the add_option() function to save the options array to the database. The add_option() function requires four arguments:

- The name of the option to be saved

- Its value

- An empty string (a deprecated argument kept for backward compatibility)

- The $autoload variable (This last argument determines whether your options should be loaded into WordPress' object cache on each page load. You'll be using these options in template files, so this value should be 'yes'.)

That's it! You've set the default values, and now it's time to build the form that will let you change those values.

Creating the Options Form

In Listing 9-7, you saw the basic outline of the options page. Now you need to create the individual form fields that will allow users to change the plugin settings.

First, you need to tell WordPress that this form will be using the option you registered earlier. You'll also go ahead and load the stored options into a variable so you can use them throughout the form. Listing 9-10 shows these changes to the basic form.

Listing 9-10. Setting up options for use in the form

```
// displays the options page content
function next_page_options() { ?>
<div class="wrap">
<form method="post" id="next_page_form" action="options.php">
<?php
    settings_fields('next_page');
    $options = get_option('next_page');
?>
    <h2>Next Page Options</h2>

        <-- the form fields will go here -->

        <p class="submit">
        <input type="submit" name="submit" class="button-primary" value="Update Options" />
        </p>
</form>
</div>
<?php
} // end function next_page_options()
```

Now that you have your options, you can use them to print the default values for each form field. Listing 9-11 shows the form fields for the Next Page options. This should look fairly similar to the theme options form you saw in Chapter 7, except this time I've created my own form layout instead of using the standard WordPress tables. You may lay out your plugin options pages however you wish. The table method is required only if you are adding options to an existing page. Otherwise, you're free to create the layout that best serves your form, as shown in Listing 9-11.

Listing 9-11. Adding the options fields

```
// displays the options page content
function next_page_options() { ?>
<div class="wrap">
<form method="post" id="next_page_form" action="options.php">
<?php
settings_fields('next_page');
$options = get_option('next_page');
?>
    <h2>Next Page Options</h2>

<-- the form fields go here -->

        <p><label>Exclude pages:<br />
        <input type="text" name="next_page[exclude]" id="exclude"
                value="<?php echo $options['exclude']; ?>" /><br />
        <small>Enter page IDs separated by commas.</small></label></p>
```

```
<div id="previous-page">
    <h3>Previous Page Display:</h3>
    <p><label>Before previous page link: "<br />
    <input type="text" name="next_page[before_prev_link]" id="before_prev_link"
            value="<?php echo stripslashes(htmlentities($options['before_prev_link']));
?>" /> </label></p>

    <p><label>Previous page link text: <small>Use %title% for the page title</small><br />
    <input type="text" name="next_page[prev_link_text]" id="prev_link_text"
            value="<?php echo stripslashes(htmlentities($options['prev_link_text'])); ?>"
/> </label></p>

    <p><label>After previous page link:<br />
    <input type="text" name="next_page[after_prev_link]" id="after_prev_link"
        value="<?php echo stripslashes(htmlentities($options['after_prev_link'])); ?>" />
</label></p>
    <p>Shortcode: <strong>[previous]</strong><br />
    Template tag: <strong>&lt;?php previous_link(); ?&gt;</strong></p>
</div>

<div id="parent-page">
    <h3>Parent Page Display:</h3>
    <p><label>Before parent page link:<br />
    <input type="text" name="next_page[before_parent_link]" id="before_parent_link"
            value="<?php echo stripslashes(htmlentities($options['before_parent_link']));
?>" /> </label></p>

    <p><label>Parent page link text: <small>Use %title% for the page title</small><br />
    <input type="text" name="next_page[parent_link_text]" id="parent_link_text"
            value="<?php echo stripslashes(htmlentities($options['parent_link_text']));
?>" /> </label></p>

    <p><label>After parent page link:<br />
    <input type="text" name="next_page[after_parent_link]" id="after_parent_link"
            value="<?php echo stripslashes(htmlentities($options['after_parent_link']));
?>" /> </label></p>
    <p>Shortcode: <strong>[parent]</strong><br />
    Template tag: <strong>&lt;?php parent_link(); ?&gt;</strong></p>
</div>

<div id="next-page">
    <h3>Next Page Display:</h3>
    <p><label>Before next page link:<br />
    <input type="text" name="next_page[before_next_link]" id="before_next_link"
            value="<?php echo stripslashes(htmlentities($options['before_next_link']));
?>" /> </label></p>

    <p><label>Next page link text: <small>Use %title% for the page title</small><br />
    <input type="text" name="next_page[next_link_text]" id="next_link_text"
            value="<?php echo stripslashes(htmlentities($options['next_link_text'])); ?>"
/> </label></p>
```

```
    <p><label>After next page link:<br />
    <input type="text" name="next_page[after_next_link]" id="after_next_link"
            value="<?php echo stripslashes(htmlentities($options['after_next_link'])); ?>"
/> </label></p>
    <p>Shortcode: <strong>[next]</strong><br />
    Template tag: <strong>&lt;?php next_link(); ?&gt;</strong></p>
</div>

<!-- end form fields -->

        <p class="submit">
        <input type="submit" name="submit" class="button-primary" value="Update Options" />
        </p>
</form>
</div> <!-- .wrap -->
<?php
} // end function next_page_options()
```

For each of the fields, you can use the get_option() function to retrieve the stored value. However, you have to run that value through some clean-up functions before you can display it as an attribute of an HTML tag, so here you've wrapped each one in the htmlentities() and stripslashes() PHP functions.

You can add a stylesheet to the options page, just as you did with the theme options in Chapter 7. Once again, you'll piggyback onto the function you used to add the options page to the menu, and grab the resulting filename to pass to the plugin-specific admin_head() hook, as shown in Listing 9-12. The changes to the next_page_add_pages() function are in bold, and the next_page_css() function is new.

Listing 9-12. Adding a stylesheet to this options page, not all the admin screens

```
function next_page_add_pages() {
    // Add a new submenu under Options:
        $file = add_options_page('Next Page', 'Next Page', 'manage_options', 'next-page',
'next_page_options');
        add_action("admin_head-$file", 'next_page_css');
}

function next_page_css() { ?>
<style type="text/css">
#next-page, #parent-page, #previous-page { float: left; width: 30%; margin-right: 5%; }
#next-page { margin-right: 0; }
</style>
<?php
}
```

All of this results in the options form shown in Figure 9-5.

Figure 9-5. The Next Page plugin options form

Updating Options

If you've registered your options and called settings_fields() in your form, WordPress updates the options for you. Sometimes, though, you need to make additional changes. You can update the options manually as shown in Listing 9-13.

Listing 9-13. Updating an option manually

```
function change_options() {
        $options = get_option('my_option');
        // do something with $options here
        update_option('my_option', $options);
}
```

You might recall the Dashboard Notepad widget control function from Chapter 8. Since widget forms don't automatically process options like plugin pages do, in that function you had to update the widget's options using the $_POST form input, as shown in Listing 9-14. First, you grabbed the existing option values. Then you checked to make sure the posted information came from the Dashboard Notepad form and not some other widget's form. If that was the case, then for each form field, you assigned the posted value to the corresponding item in the options array. Finally, you called update_option() with the updated array.

Listing 9-14. Processing options in Dashboard Notepad (partial)

```
function dashboard_notepad_widget_control() {
        $options = dashboard_notepad_widget_options();
```

```
        if ( 'post' == strtolower($_SERVER['REQUEST_METHOD']) && isset( $_POST['widget_id'] )
    && 'dashboard_notepad_widget_id' == $_POST['widget_id'] ) {
            if ( isset($_POST['can_edit']) )
                    $options['can_edit'] = $_POST['can_edit'];
            if ( isset($_POST['can_read']) )
                    $options['can_read'] = $_POST['can_read'];
            if ( isset($_POST['notepad_title']) )
                    $options['notepad_title'] = $_POST['notepad_title'];
            $options['autop'] = $_POST['autop'];
            update_option( 'dashboard_notepad', $options );
        }
// <form> ... </form> goes here
}
```

Deleting Options

It's a good practice to remove your plugin's options from the database when the user uninstalls it. You do this by deleting it from the Plugins screen, and it's very easy to do, as you can see in Listing 9-15.

Listing 9-15. Removing the Next Page plugin options on deactivation

```
// when uninstalled, remove option
register_uninstall_hook( __FILE__, 'next_page_delete_options' );

function next_page_delete_options() {
        delete_option('next_page');
}
```

No, really, that's all there is to it! Be a good citizen and add uninstall functions like this to your WordPress plugins. Your users will thank you for not cluttering up their database options tables with unneeded rows.

Wrapping Up

Once you've completed all your functions, activate your plugin and try it out! Make sure there is no extra white space after your closing ?> tag, or WordPress will give an error on activation.

Listing 9-16 shows the completed Next Page plugin and Figure 9-6 is a screenshot of the plugin.

Listing 9-16. The complete Next Page plugin

```
<?php
/*
Plugin Name: Next Page
Plugin URI: http://sillybean.net/code/wordpress/next-page/
Description: Provides shortcodes and template tags for next/previous navigation in pages.
Version: 1.4
License: GPLv2
Author: Stephanie Leary
Author URI: http://sillybean.net/
```

```
*/

add_action('admin_menu', 'next_page_add_pages');

register_activation_hook(__FILE__, 'next_page_activation');
function next_page_activation() {
        // set defaults
        $options = array();
        $options['before_prev_link'] = '<div class="alignleft">';
        $options['prev_link_text'] = __('Previous:', 'next-page').' %title%';
        $options['after_prev_link'] = '</div>';

        $options['before_parent_link'] = '<div class="aligncenter">';
        $options['parent_link_text'] = __('Up one level:', 'next-page').' %title%';
        $options['after_parent_link'] = '</div>';

        $options['before_next_link'] = '<div class="alignright">';
        $options['next_link_text'] = __('Next:', 'next-page').' %title%';
        $options['after_next_link'] = '</div>';

        $options['exclude'] = '';

        // set new option
        add_option('next_page', array_merge($oldoptions, $options), '', 'yes');
}

// when uninstalled, remove option
register_uninstall_hook( __FILE__, 'next_page_delete_options' );

function next_page_delete_options() {
        delete_option('next_page');
}

// i18n
if (!defined('WP_PLUGIN_DIR'))
        define('WP_PLUGIN_DIR', dirname(dirname(__FILE__)));
$lang_dir = basename(dirname(__FILE__)). '/languages';
load_plugin_textdomain( 'next_page', 'WP_PLUGIN_DIR'.$lang_dir, $lang_dir );


add_action('admin_init', 'register_next_page_options' );
function register_next_page_options(){
        register_setting( 'next_page', 'next_page' );
}

function next_page_add_pages() {
    // Add a new submenu under Options:
        $css = add_options_page('Next Page', 'Next Page', 'manage_options', 'next-page',
'next_page_options');
        add_action("admin_head-$css", 'next_page_css');
}
```

```php
function next_page_css() { ?>
<style type="text/css">
#next-page, #parent-page, #previous-page { float: left; width: 30%; margin-right: 5%; }
#next-page { margin-right: 0; }
</style>
<?php
}

// displays the options page content
function next_page_options() { ?>
    <div class="wrap">
        <form method="post" id="next_page_form" action="options.php">
                <?php settings_fields('next_page');
                $options = get_option('next_page'); ?>

    <h2><?php _e( 'Next Page Options', 'next-page'); ?></h2>

    <p><label><?php _e("Exclude pages: ", 'next-page'); ?><br />
    <input type="text" name="next_page[exclude]" id="exclude"
            value="<?php echo $options['exclude']; ?>" /><br />
        <small><?php _e("Enter page IDs separated by commas.", 'next-page');
?></small></label></p>

    <div id="previous-page">
    <h3><?php _e("Previous Page Display:", 'next-page'); ?></h3>
    <p><label><?php _e("Before previous page link: ", 'next-page'); ?><br />
    <input type="text" name="next_page[before_prev_link]" id="before_prev_link"
            value="<?php echo stripslashes(htmlentities($options['before_prev_link']));
?>" /> </label></p>

    <p><label><?php _e("Previous page link text: <small>Use %title% for the page
title</small>", 'next-page'); ?><br />
    <input type="text" name="next_page[prev_link_text]" id="prev_link_text"
            value="<?php echo stripslashes(htmlentities($options['prev_link_text'])); ?>"
/> </label></p>

    <p><label><?php _e("After previous page link: ", 'next-page'); ?><br />
    <input type="text" name="next_page[after_prev_link]" id="after_prev_link"
        value="<?php echo stripslashes(htmlentities($options['after_prev_link'])); ?>" />
</label></p>
    <p><?php _e('Shortcode:'); ?> <strong>[previous]</strong><br />
    <?php _e('Template tag:'); ?> <strong>&lt;?php previous_link(); ?&gt;</strong></p>
    </div>

    <div id="parent-page">
    <h3><?php _e("Parent Page Display:", 'next-page'); ?></h3>
    <p><label><?php _e("Before parent page link: ", 'next-page'); ?><br />
    <input type="text" name="next_page[before_parent_link]" id="before_parent_link"
            value="<?php echo stripslashes(htmlentities($options['before_parent_link']));
?>" /> </label></p>
```

```php
    <p><label><?php _e("Parent page link text: <small>Use %title% for the page title</small>",
'next-page'); ?><br />
    <input type="text" name="next_page[parent_link_text]" id="parent_link_text"
            value="<?php echo stripslashes(htmlentities($options['parent_link_text']));
?>" /> </label></p>

    <p><label><?php _e("After parent page link: ", 'next-page'); ?><br />
    <input type="text" name="next_page[after_parent_link]" id="after_parent_link"
            value="<?php echo stripslashes(htmlentities($options['after_parent_link']));
?>" /> </label></p>
    <p><?php _e('Shortcode:'); ?> <strong>[parent]</strong><br />
    <?php _e('Template tag:'); ?> <strong>&lt;?php parent_link(); ?&gt;</strong></p>
    </div>

    <div id="next-page">
    <h3><?php _e("Next Page Display:", 'next-page'); ?></h3>
    <p><label><?php _e("Before next page link: ", 'next-page'); ?><br />
    <input type="text" name="next_page[before_next_link]" id="before_next_link"
            value="<?php echo stripslashes(htmlentities($options['before_next_link']));
?>" /> </label></p>

    <p><label><?php _e("Next page link text: <small>Use %title% for the page title</small>",
'next-page'); ?><br />
    <input type="text" name="next_page[next_link_text]" id="next_link_text"
            value="<?php echo stripslashes(htmlentities($options['next_link_text'])); ?>"
/> </label></p>

    <p><label><?php _e("After next page link: ", 'next-page'); ?><br />
    <input type="text" name="next_page[after_next_link]" id="after_next_link"
            value="<?php echo stripslashes(htmlentities($options['after_next_link'])); ?>"
/> </label></p>
    <p><?php _e('Shortcode:'); ?> <strong>[next]</strong><br />
    <?php _e('Template tag:'); ?> <strong>&lt;?php next_link(); ?&gt;</strong></p>
    </div>

        <p class="submit">
        <input type="submit" name="submit" class="button-primary" value="<?php _e('Update
Options', 'next-page'); ?>" />
        </p>
        </form>
        </div>
<?php
} // end function next_page_options()

// make the magic happen
function next_page_flatten_page_list($exclude = '') {
        $args = 'sort_column=menu_order&sort_order=asc';
        if (!empty($exclude)) $args .= '&exclude='.$exclude;
        $pagelist = get_pages($args);
        $mypages = array();
        foreach ($pagelist as $thispage) {
            $mypages[] = $thispage->ID;
```

```
            }
            return $mypages;
    }

    function next_link() {
            global $post;
            $options = get_option('next_page');
            $exclude = $options['exclude'];
            $pagelist = next_page_flatten_page_list($exclude);
            $current = array_search($post->ID, $pagelist);
            $nextID = $pagelist[$current+1];

            $before_link = stripslashes($options['before_next_link']);
            $linkurl = get_permalink($nextID);
            $title = get_the_title($nextID);
            $linktext = $options['next_link_text'];
            if (strpos($linktext, '%title%') !== false)
                    $linktext = str_replace('%title%', $title, $linktext);
            $after_link = stripslashes($options['after_next_link']);

            $link = $before_link . '<a href="' . $linkurl . '" title="' . $title . '">' .
$linktext . '</a>' . $after_link;
            echo $link;
    }

    function previous_link() {
            global $post;
            $options = get_option('next_page');
            $exclude = $options['exclude'];
            $pagelist = next_page_flatten_page_list($exclude);
            $current = array_search($post->ID, $pagelist);
            $prevID = $pagelist[$current-1];

            $before_link = stripslashes($options['before_prev_link']);
            $linkurl = get_permalink($prevID);
            $title = get_the_title($prevID);
            $linktext = $options['prev_link_text'];
            if (strpos($linktext, '%title%') !== false)
                    $linktext = str_replace('%title%', $title, $linktext);
            $after_link = stripslashes($options['after_prev_link']);

            $link = $before_link . '<a href="' . $linkurl . '" title="' . $title . '">' .
$linktext . '</a>' . $after_link;
            echo $link;
    }

    function parent_link() {
            global $post;
            $options = get_option('next_page');
            $parentID = $post->post_parent;

            $exclude = array($options['exclude']);
```

```
        if (in_array($parentID, $exclude)) return false;
        else {
                $before_link = stripslashes($options['before_parent_link']);
                $linkurl = get_permalink($parentID);
                $title = get_the_title($parentID);
                $linktext = $options['parent_link_text'];
                if (strpos($linktext, '%title%') !== false)
                        $linktext = str_replace('%title%', $title, $linktext);
                $after_link = stripslashes($options['after_parent_link']);

                $link = $before_link . '<a href="' . $linkurl . '" title="' . $title . '">' .
$linktext . '</a>' . $after_link;
                echo $link;
        }
}
?>
```

Figure 9-6. The previous and next page links

Plugin Possibilities

Creating template tags is just one of the things you can do in a plugin. The possibilities are quite literally endless! If you need inspiration, take a look at the WordPress Ideas forum at wordpress.org/extend/ideas/ for features WordPress users have requested.

Now that you've seen the basic framework of a plugin, I'll demonstrate a few more things you can do with plugins: shortcodes and role-dependent content.

The Shortcode API

Creating shortcodes in WordPress is a matter of creating the function that prints out what you want, and then defining it as a shortcode. In the case of Next Page, the shortcodes are just alternatives to the template tags—they do the same thing. Since that's the case, and there are no arguments to be dealt with, creating the shortcodes takes all of three lines, as shown in Listing 9-17.

Listing 9-17. Creating the three Next Page shortcodes

```
add_shortcode('previous', 'previous_link');
add_shortcode('next', 'next_link');
add_shortcode('parent', 'parent_link');
```

That's it! Add these lines to the end of the Next Page plugin file, and you can now use [previous] in the post or page content as an alternative to using previous_link() in a theme file.

Of course, shortcodes can be more complicated. They can accept arguments, and you can have opening and closing shortcodes that surround a bit of text. Since Next Page doesn't demonstrate all that, I'll show you the shortcode processing function from another plugin of mine, Simple Internal Links, which lets you easily link to content within your WordPress site. This plugin provides the shortcodes shown in Listing 9-18. The corresponding plugin function is shown in Listing 9-19.

Listing 9-18. The Simple Internal Links shortcodes

```
/*
// creates a link to post/page ID 6180 and uses its title as the linked text
[link id="6180"]

// uses the given text instead of the post/page title
[link id="6180"]link text[/link]

// links to post/page using the slug instead of the ID
[link name="post-slug"]
[link name="post-slug"]link text[/link]

// links to post/page using the title
[link title="About Us"]
[link title="About Us"]link text[/link]

// links to a category by slug
[link cat="cat-slug"]
[link cat="cat-slug"]link text[/link]

// links to a tag by slug
[link tag="tag-slug"]
[link tag="tag-slug"]link text[/link]
/**/
```

Listing 9-19. Simple Internal Links shortcodes

```
function create_anylink($atts, $content = null) {
        //extract page id from the shortcode attributes
```

```
        extract(shortcode_atts(array( 'id' => 0, 'name' => null, 'cat' => null, 'tag' => null
), $atts));
        $link = '';

        // do categories first
        if (!empty($cat)) {
                $catobj = get_category_by_slug($cat);
                $link = get_category_link($catobj->term_id);
                if (empty($content)) $content = get_cat_name($catobj->term_id);
        }
        // then tags
        elseif (!empty($tag)) {
                $tagobj = get_term_by( 'slug', $tag, 'post_tag' );
                $link = get_tag_link($tagobj->term_id);
                if (empty($content)) $content = $tagobj->name;
        }
        elseif (!empty($title)) {
                $thepost = get_page_by_title($title);
                if (!$thepost) {   // there is no get_post_by_title, so we'll sanitize and try
it as a slug
                        global $wpdb;
                        $id = $id = $wpdb->get_var( $wpdb->prepare(
                                    "SELECT ID FROM $wpdb->posts WHERE post_name = %s AND
(post_type = 'post' OR post_type = 'page') ", sanitize_title($title) ));
                        $thepost = get_post($id);
                }
                if (empty($content)) {
                        $thepost = get_post( $id ); // will get all post types
                        $content = $thepost->post_title;
                }
                $link = get_permalink($id);
        }
        else {
                // if no ID, get post/page by name or title
                if (empty($id)) {
                   global $wpdb;
                   $id = $wpdb->get_var( $wpdb->prepare(
                                "SELECT ID FROM $wpdb->posts WHERE post_name = %s AND
(post_type = 'post' OR post_type = 'page') ", $name ));
                }

                // use $content for the title if it exists; otherwise fetch page/post title
                if (empty($content)) {
                        $thepost = get_post( $id ); // will get all post types
                        $content = $thepost->post_title;
                }
                $link = get_permalink($id);
        }

        if (!empty($link))
                return '<a href="'.$link.'">'.$content.'</a>';
        else
```

```
                    return $content; // no cat, ID, or name provided; ignore this shortcode
}
add_shortcode('link', 'create_anylink');
```

The `create_anylink()` function takes two arguments: the attributes of the shortcode and the content enclosed by the shortcode. Since some shortcodes, like [gallery], stand alone, you can assume that `$content` is empty. The extract function merges the array of default values and the array that was passed and extracts them into named variables. Then you see which argument you got. For each possible argument, you see whether a title was provided, and if not, you fill in the link text with the post/page/category/tag title.

The method of finding the permalink varies depending on which arguments were used. Most notably, there is no `get_post_by_title()` function. Instead, I've sanitized the given title using the same function that creates automatic permalink slugs on the Edit screens. Unless the user has changed the post slug manually, this should give you a slug that you can use to find the post ID.

For more information on shortcodes, see the Codex page at `codex.wordpress.org/Shortcode_API`.

Checking for Capabilities

In WordPress, each user is assigned to a role. Each role has a list of capabilities that users may perform. The roles and capabilities are covered in depth in Chapter 10. For now, here's a quick overview:

Administrators can do anything in the WordPress administration area: write, edit, and delete posts, pages, links, and comments; upload media files of any type; import content; manage the Dashboard; create, edit, and delete other users; enable and configure plugins and themes; change the site's theme; and manage all the available options.

Editors can publish, edit, and delete posts and pages written by any user. They can upload some kinds of files, and they can write HTML without restrictions. They can manage links and categories, and they can moderate comments. Editors and administrators are also the only users allowed to read private posts and pages.

Authors can publish, edit, and delete their own posts. They cannot write pages. They can upload some kinds of media files, and they are allowed to use only a limited set of HTML tags.

Contributors can write their own posts, but may not publish or delete them. Their HTML will be limited to a few HTML tags (see Listing 10-1), and they cannot upload media files.

Subscribers can manage their own profiles, but can do virtually nothing else in the administration area.

Visit `codex.wordpress.org/Roles_and_Capabilities` for a detailed list of all the capabilities assigned to each role.

The function that you'll use to check for your user's capabilities is `if_user_can()`. This function takes one argument: the capability you want to check.

You generally don't need to do this on option pages. WordPress automatically checks for the capability you specified as the minimum when you added the options page. However, there are lots of other places where it would be a good idea to check capabilities before you allow the user to do something.

Creating an Editorial Comment Shortcode

You can use the `if_user_can()` function to create a shortcode for notes that only editors and administrators can see, as shown in Listing 9-20.

Listing 9-20. An editorial comment shortcode

```
// Usage: [ed]this is a note only editors can read.[/ed]

function editorial_note($content = null) {
    if (current_user_can('edit_pages') && is_single())
        return '<span class="private">'.$content.'</span>';
    else return '';
}
add_shortcode( 'ed', 'editorial_note' );
```

In this case, there are no attributes to worry about. The only argument for your shortcode function is the enclosed content, which you'll assume is empty by default. In addition to checking for the appropriate capability ('edit_pages', in this case), you've decided that these notes should appear only on single pages and post archives, so you've added a check for the is_singular() conditional. If the user has the right capability and you're on the right kind of page, you'll wrap the enclosed content in a span (so you can style it later, if you want to) and return it.

See the Dashboard Notepad widget in Chapter 8 for more examples with if_user_can().

Listing Private Pages

One odd little quirk of WordPress is that private pages aren't included in the page lists and navigation menus, even if the user is logged in and has permission to read them. The filter function in Listing 9-21 adds the private pages only if the user has the appropriate capability. This is not a perfect function by any means. It adds the private pages in a flat list, ignoring the parent/child hierarchy. However, the code necessary to create a true hierarchical private page menu is well beyond the scope of this book.

Listing 9-21. Adding private pages to the page lists and nav menus

```
function private_suite_add_menu($pagelist) {
        if (current_user_can('read_private_pages')) {
                global $wpdb;
                $list = '';
                $pageresults = $wpdb->get_results(wpdb_prepare("SELECT id, post_title,
post_parent FROM $wpdb->posts WHERE post_status=%s AND post_type=%s" ,'private','page'));

                foreach ($pageresults as $privatepage) {
                        $list .= '<li class="page_item private"><a
href="'.get_permalink($privatepage->id).'" title="'.esc_attr($privatepage->post_title).'">'
                                .$privatepage->post_title.'</a></li>';
                }
                return $pagelist.$list;
        }
        else return $pagelist;
}
add_filter('wp_list_pages', 'private_suite_add_menu');
add_filter('nav_menu', 'private_suite_add_menu');
```

As you can see, if the user doesn't have permission to read private pages, the rest of the function is bypassed entirely and the filter returns the unchanged list of pages.

Hooks: Filters and Actions

You've seen several add_filter() and add_action() functions by now. These two functions allow you to take advantage of the hooks scattered throughout WordPress. For a complete list of available actions and filters, visit codex.wordpress.org/Plugin_API/Action_Reference and codex.wordpress.org/Plugin_API/Filter_Reference.

Filters allow you to modify or replace the output existing functions. For example, you could append ads or a copyright notice to content in feeds, or search and replace a word or phrase in your post/page content.

Actions allow you to add your own functions in predetermined locations. For example, you can add a lightbox effect to your photo galleries by adding the appropriate JavaScript file to your theme's <head> tag, or you could send an e-mail notification to all users when a new post is published.

Actions

You've seen a number of add_action() functions called when adding things to wp_head() or admin_head() in themes and plugins. Each add_action() function required two arguments: the name of the action hook and the name of your custom function.

Action hooks are like empty paper cups in the giant Rube Goldberg machine that is WordPress. Imagine a gumball being dropped into the top of your page. This is your page request, and it's going to pass through a number of gizmos before it reaches the bottom. Some of those gizmos include paper cups that will tip over when the gumball falls into them. Adding your own functions to action hooks is like dropping pennies into those paper cups before you let the gumball go. Not only will the gumball fall out and continue on its path when the cup tips over, but your pennies will, too.

Notable actions include:

- Init: one of the first things done on every page, both front end and administration

- admin_init: the first thing done on every administration page

- wp_head: the last thing done in the theme <head> section

- admin_head: the last thing done in the administration page's <head> section

- admin_head-$filename: the same, but for a specific administration page

- admin_menu: constructing the navigation menu in the administration pages

- template_redirect: occurs just before the theme template file is chosen, allowing you to override that choice

- wp_enqueue_scripts: printing the list of scripts in the theme header

- `wp_print_styles`: printing the list of stylesheets in the theme header

- `widgets_init`: constructing the list of active widgets

- `loop_start` and `loop_end`: surrounding the Loop

- `wp_footer`: the last thing done before the theme's closing `</body>` tag

Creating Private Categories

Since you've already seen so many examples of actions, I'll show you just one more. The function in Listing 9-22 creates private categories using the save_post() action, which occurs on the Edit → Post page after the new or updated post has been saved to the database.

Listing 9-22. Creating private categories

```
function set_private_categories($postid) {
        if ($parent_id = wp_is_post_revision($postid))
                $postid = $parent_id;
        $privatecats = get_option('private_categories'); // array of category IDs
        if (!is_array($privatecats))
                $privatecats = array($privatecats);
        foreach ($privatecats as $cat) {
                if (in_category($cat, $postid)) {
                        $updated = array();
                        $updated['ID'] = $postid;
                        $updated['post_status'] = 'private';
                        wp_update_post($updated);
                }
        }
}
add_action('save_post', 'set_private_categories');
```

In this function, you'll assume that there's an option stored somewhere containing the IDs of the categories that should be private. (This function is part of my Private Suite plugin, and there, the private categories are part of the plugin's options array.)

The very first thing to do is see if you're saving a revision—that is, if this is happening during an autosave. If so, you really want the ID of the revision's parent—the current revision—rather than the revision ID.

Next, you'll get the array of category IDs. If it isn't an array for some reason, you'll make it one.

Then, for each private category in the array, you'll check to see if this post has been assigned to that category. If it has, you need to change the post status. The wp_update_post() function requires an array containing the post's ID and any fields that need to be updated, so your array has just two elements.

To use this code example on your site, you might want to combine it with the examples in Chapter 10 on choosing which roles may read private posts. Otherwise, just like your editorial comment shortcode, the content in these categories will be limited to editors and administrators.

Filters

Filters are actions that are performed on strings or other variables. The big difference in your function is that you'll have an argument; the filter function will pass you some piece of content to work with. You can filter many of WordPress's built-in strings: author names, links, post titles and content, category names, and so on; and you can filter things like arrays of pages and categories. Your filter function will take the original variable as its argument, and it will return the altered variable. You could append something, prepend something, or perform a search and replace on a string.

Some of the filters you'll see often include:

- wp_title: allows the <title> tag to be altered or replaced

- the_title: allows the title of the post or page to be altered or replaced

- the_content: alters the content of the post or page

- wp_autop: automatically turns line breaks into paragraph tags

- do_shortcodes: processes shortcodes

- the_excerpt_length: determines the length (in characters) of the_excerpt()

- the_excerpt_more: determines what's shown at the end of the_excerpt()

- wp_list_pages: allows the list of pages to be modified

Listing 9-23 shows a simple filter that appends a post author's name to the content of the post, effectively adding a signature of sorts.

Listing 9-23. Appending an author name to the post content using a filter

```
function post_signature($content) {
        global $post;
        $author_id = $post->post_author;
        $author = get_userdata($author_id);
        $name = '<p>'.$author->display_name.'</p>';
        return $content.name;
}
add_filter('the_content','post_signature');
```

The code here is pretty simple. Since this function takes place outside the Loop but doesn't include all of the post information in the arguments, you need to declare the global $post object so you can find the author. The author's ID will be stored in $post, so you'll grab that and pass it to the get_userdata() function. That returns yet another object, this one containing all of the author's information. You'll pull out the display name, wrap it in a paragraph tag, and append it to the content. Then you'll return the altered content back to the Loop, where it will be printed after going through any other the_content() filters.

Appending a List of Child Pages

Back in Chapter 8, I showed you how to include a list of child pages in a page template. You could do so using a filter, so you could maintain the code in functions.php rather than individual template files.

Listing 9-24 shows how to create the child pages filter. In this case, you'll assume that the filter should operate only on single page archives; if the page content is shown as part of a Loop, you probably don't want to clutter the Loop display with a bunch of page lists.

Listing 9-24. Appending child pages using a filter

```
function append_child_pages($content) {
        if (is_page()) {
                global $post;
                $children = '<ul>'.wp_list_pages('title_li=&child_of'=$post->ID).'</ul>';
        }
        return $content.$children;
}
add_filter('the_content','append_child_pages');
```

This is even simpler than the previous example. Again, you need the global $post object. Since wp_list_pages() prints list items without the surrounding list tags, you have to add those manually. Then you pass the content and the page list back to the Loop as one big string.

You could easily alter this function to print the child pages only if the parent page's content is empty, as shown in Listing 9-25. The changes from the previous example are in bold.

Listing 9-25. Appending child pages only if the parent page is empty

```
function append_child_pages($content) {
        if (is_page() && (empty($content))) {
                global $post;
                $children = '<ul>'.wp_list_pages('title_li=&child_of'=$post->ID).'</ul>';
        }
        return $content.$children;
}
add_filter('the_content','append_child_pages');
```

Changing the "Private" and "Password Protected" labels

If you've used the private or password-protected status for posts or pages, you've probably noticed that WordPress adds labels to the titles, and there is no setting allowing you to change it. In Listing 9-26, you'll do a search and replace on the private page's title to replace the default "Private: " label with your own "Members Only" label.

Listing 9-26. Removing the "Private" prefix from private pages

```
function custom_private_title($title) {
        return str_replace(__("Private: "), 'Members Only: ', $title);
}
add_filter('private_title_format', 'custom_private_title');
```

In this case, I've left in the internationalization function (the two underscores) which I'll explain in more detail later in this chapter. When you're filtering built-in WordPress strings like this, it's important to use translatable strings. In this case, you're searching for the word Private followed by a colon, but if this were a plugin that you intended to distribute on WordPress Extend, you'd quickly find that your replacement wouldn't appear to users who've set up WordPress in another language.

Other Filters

Strings aren't the only things you can filter. One of the more interesting filters introduced in version 2.9 is user_contactmethods(). This filter lets you work with the array of contact fields listed in the user profile page. In Chapter 10, I show you how to use this filter to remove the default instant messenger fields and add a Twitter account and a phone number.

Prioritizing and Troubleshooting Actions and Filters

Both actions and filters can take an optional third argument: the priority. If left out, this argument will default to 10, and your hooked functions will occur after all the built-in ones have completed. However, you can set the priority to any number at all. Set it to a lower number if you need your function to operate before the built-in actions and filters.

If you have installed plugins that use filters, or you've written your own filter, it can be hard to tell where the original content ends and the filtered addition begins. Sometimes it's also not clear when certain actions take place. The Hooks & Filters Flow plugin (planetozh.com/blog/my-projects/wordpress-hooks-filter-flow/) is a great way to list all the actions and filters that are operating on your content. Unlike most plugins, this one must be placed in your WordPress root directory or wp-admin. You have to enter its URL into your browser, because there is no link to it from your admin menu.

Figure 9-7 shows the plugin's report on my test installation, which has a few plugins installed. You'll see several functions belonging to my HTML Import and Dashboard Notepad plugins mixed in with default WordPress functions. Hooks & Filters Flow is a great way to see if your plugin is interfering with another filter, or if you need to adjust its priority.

Figure 9-7. The Hooks & Filters Flow plugin

Variations on Option Pages

I've demonstrated how to add your option page to the Settings menu, which is the conventional location for plugin options. You have several other choices available, though. You can add your page in another section of the navigation menu (Tools, for example). You can create a top-level menu for your plugin, which is especially useful if your plugin requires more than one option page. You can even add your options to one of the existing pages rather than creating a whole new one.

Adding Other Submenus

Most plugins' option pages are placed in the Settings portion of the menu. However, if you feel that another section would be more appropriate for your plugin's page, you can simply change the add_options_page() function to one of the others shown in Listing 9-27.

Listing 9-27. Submenu functions

```
//Settings
add_options_page (page_title, menu_title, capability, handle);
// Tools
add_management_page (page_title, menu_title, capability, handle);
// Appearance
add_theme_page (page_title, menu_title, capability, handle);
// Posts
add_posts_page (page_title, menu_title, capability, handle);
// Pages
add_pages_page (page_title, menu_title, capability, handle);
// Users
add_user_page (page_title, menu_title, capability, handle);
```

All the functions require the same arguments you saw in Listing 9-7; the only difference is the location of the resulting option page.

Adding a Top-level Menu Item

Unless your plugin requires several options pages, it's best to add your options page under the Settings menu as shown in Listing 9-7. However, if you do have a number of separate pages, you can create a top-level menu item for your plugin as shown in Listing 9-28. This code would replace the first few lines of Listing 9-7.

Listing 9-28. Adding a top-level menu item

```
add_action('admin_menu', 'next_page_add_pages');

function next_page_add_pages() {
    add_menu_page('Next Page Options', 'Next Page', 'manage_options', __FILE__,
'next_page_options');
}
```

This add_menu_page() function looks quite a bit like the add_options_page() function in Listing 9-7. The arguments for both functions are:

- Page title: the <title> of your options page

- Heading: the heading shown above your options form

- Capability: the minimum user capability required to access the page (usually manage_options)

- File handle: an identifier for your plugin file (in this case, the file name)

- Options form function: the name of the function that displays the options <form>

- Menu icon (optional in add_menu_page()): you can specify the file location of an icon for your menu item

The results of Listing 9-28 are shown in Figure 9-8.

Figure 9-8. *The top-level menu item*

Adding a Section to an Existing Options Page

If you have just a few settings to work with and it would make sense to include them on an existing page rather than creating a whole new one, you can do so. For example, if you had an option related to privacy, you could use the code in Listing 9-29 to add your option to that page.

*Listing 9-29. **Adding an option to the Privacy page***

```
function add_extra_privacy_options() {
    add_settings_field('extra_privacy', 'Extra Privacy Option', 'extra_privacy_options',
'privacy', $section = 'default', $args = array());
    register_setting('privacy','extra_privacy');
}

add_action('admin_init', 'add_extra_privacy_options');

// displays the options page content
function extra_privacy_options() { ?>
        <p> the form fields will go here </p>
<?php
}
```

Keep in mind that the standard WordPress options pages are laid out using tables. The contents of your display function will appear inside a table cell.

The results of Listing 9-29 are shown in Figure 9-9.

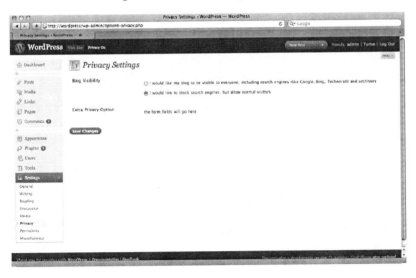

Figure 9-9. An extra option on the Privacy page

See codex.wordpress.org/Adding_Administration_Menus for more examples of adding options pages to various parts of the admin menu.

Publishing a Plugin

If you've been using the examples in this book to develop your own theme or plugin, you probably have a bunch of files stashed in a directory somewhere. You could just zip them up and dump them onto your web server, but that's not an ideal solution. Will you maintain copies of the older versions as you develop new ones? How will you alert users when updates are available? What happens to your code if you decide to stop developing for WordPress?

The repository at WordPress Extend takes care of all those problems for you. In order to use it, you're going to have to get familiar with source control using Subversion. First, however, you need to create your readme file.

Readme Files and Screenshots

Along with the PHP file(s) containing your plugin's code, you are required to include a readme.txt file in plugins uploaded to WordPress Extend. Readme files use the Markdown syntax. Each main heading is surrounded by two equal signs ('==') and will become a linked tab on the plugin page. Subheadings use fewer equal signs. Listing 9-30 shows an empty readme file with all the possible headings. If you prefer filling in form fields to dealing with Markdown, you can use the online readme file generator at sudarmuthu.com/wordpress/wp-readme.

On the Contributors line, list your username on wordpress.org along with the usernames of any collaborators you have. If you have a page on your own site for your plugin, give the URI in the Plugin URI line; otherwise you can omit the line or use the address of the plugin's Extend page. If you accept donations, use the Donate link line to provide the URI of the page where users can send you donations.

The Version line refers to the version of the plugin accompanying this copy of the readme file. You could upload an alpha version for testers, in which case the Version would be something like 1.1-alpha while the Stable tag remains 1.0. This way, your alpha version would be available under "Other versions" but end users would not be prompted to upgrade from the Plugins screen.

"Requires at least" and "Tested up to" refer to the versions of WordPress on which this plugin is known to work.

Listing 9-30. A sample readme.txt file

```
=== My Plugin ===

Plugin Name: My Plugin
Contributors: sillybean
Plugin URI: http://example.com
Author URI: http://example.com
Donate link: http://example.com
Requires at least: 2.8
Tested up to: 3.0
Stable tag: 1.0
Version: 1.0
Tags: posts, pages

== Description ==

Describe your plugin here.
```

```
[wpvideo fft9IGgw]

== Installation ==

1. Upload the plugin directory to `/wp-content/plugins/`
1. Activate the plugin through the 'Plugins' menu in WordPress
1. Go to Settings &rarr; My Plugin to set the options

== Upgrade Notice ==

You should upgrade to 1.0 immediately because there was a serious bug in 0.9.

== Screenshots ==

1. The caption for screenshot-1.png
1. The caption for screenshot-2.png

== Changelog ==

= 1.0 =
* New feature X
= 0.9 =
* Beta release for testers

== Frequently Asked Questions ==

= Question? =

Answer.

= Question 2? =

Answer 2.
```

Note that numbered lists can use "1" for each list item. Markdown will correct the numbering so you don't have to renumber your entire list if you add a step in the middle. If you prefer, you can number your lists the usual way. You may also use HTML (including entities like →) if you wish.

See wordpress.org/extend/plugins/about/readme.txt for a readme.txt file filled with dummy text. It has a number of Markdown syntax examples. See daringfireball.net/projects/markdown/ for a complete guide to Markdown.

You may embed video files in your readme. If you have published a screencast to YouTube or Vimeo video, simply enter the video's URL. If your video is hosted on wordpress.tv, enter the video's ID, as shown in the Description section above.

When you're finished with your readme file, you should run it through the validator (wordpress.org/extend/plugins/about/validator/) to avoid unexpected formatting problems on your Extend page.

If your plugin includes an option page or generates some kind of output (a template tag, a JavaScript effect, etc.), you should take a screenshot or two and include them in your plugin directory. They should be named screenshot-1.png, screenshot-2.png, and so on. The dimensions are up to you.

Subversion (SVN)

If you've never used Subversion before, getting your plugin listed at WordPress Extend can be a little daunting. I'll go over the process for all the major operating systems.

First, go to the Plugin Development Center (wordpress.org/extend/plugins/about/) and sign up to have your plugin added. You'll have to give it a name, a description, and a URL. The name will be shortened to a slug for your plugin's address on Extend; otherwise, all these things can be changed later. You can take this step even if you haven't figured out Subversion yet, because it might take a while to get the plugin approved—anywhere from a few hours to a week, because a real person has to look at your submission and determine that you are not a spammer. Eventually, you'll receive an e-mail containing your repository URL. In the meantime, keep reading. I'll explain the basic concepts of Subversion and walk you through the whole process of submitting your plugin.

Basic Concepts

Subversion is a form of source control. Like CVS and Git, Subversion lets you keep track of all the changes you've made to your code. A Subversion repository is a web-accessible archive of those changes. Ever wished you could undo several days' worth of work and roll back to an earlier iteration? If you've kept your local copy in sync with your repository, you can. Furthermore, you can make all those versions—the current release as well as the whole history of the project—available to the public, as shown in Figure 9-10. WordPress plugins and themes are distributed using a Subversion repository, as is the core WordPress software.

Figure 9-10. A plugin page with the stable version and links to other versions

Working with a repository breaks down into three common steps: checking out, updating, and committing. If you're new to Subversion, this will make more sense in the context of an established project, like WordPress itself, rather than the new one you're submitting. Let's say that you wanted to check out a nightly version of WordPress to use as the basis for your development. You'd go to wordpress.org/download/svn/ and locate the address of WordPress's trunk:

core.svn.wordpress.org/trunk/. You'd enter this into your client (covered in more detail later) and check out an initial copy. Then, let's say a week or so later, you realize that there have probably been some updates since you checked out your copy, and you'd like to stay in sync. You'd tell your client to update your copy, and it would download all the files that had changed since your initial checkout. If you had changed any of those files in your local copy, your client would alert you to the conflict and ask you what to do. Now, if you're reading this, I'm guessing that you are probably not a WordPress core developer. If you were, though, you'd be able to upload your changes to the repository, making them available to everyone, by committing your altered files.

That's how Subversion works for an existing project. When you first submit your plugin to Extend, you'll receive the address of your repository, and you'll check out an initial copy. This seems nonsensical, because you haven't submitted anything yet, so what is there to check out?

Branches, Tags, and Trunk

WordPress Extend conforms to the Subversion convention of splitting software projects (like plugins or themes) into three major subdirectories: branches, tags, and trunk. When you check out a copy of the code from the repository, these are the three directories you'll download. For a new project, like your plugin or theme, all the directories will be empty—just a framework to help you organize your files. To help illustrate, Figure 9-11 shows the tag and trunk directories for my Next Page plugin.

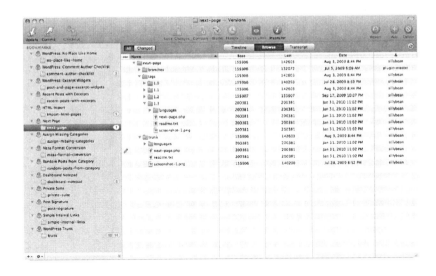

Figure 9-11. Tag and trunk files for the Next Page plugin

The trunk directory is your working copy. On a public repository, like the one for WordPress itself, the nightly builds are snapshots of the trunk. This is the copy of the code that's in active development, so it's generally not considered stable, and it's not recommended for public use. It is useful for alpha and beta testers.

Branches are for major releases. For WordPress, these are the versions that get jazz nicknames and press releases: 2.8, 2.9, 3.0. When you're ready to release a major version, create a new subdirectory under branches using the version number as the directory name. Copy the files from trunk into the branch directory and commit your changes.

The tags are the individual, minor version releases of your plugin or theme. For WordPress itself, these are the point releases containing bug fixes and security updates: 2.9.1, 2.9.2. For each minor version of your theme or plugin, you'll create a corresponding tag directory. When your trunk reaches a stable point, you'll copy the files into a new tag directory, update the readme file, and commit your changes. After that, leave the directory alone! You should maintain each release as an archival copy, not to be altered. If you want to release more changes, create a new tag.

If you're constantly improving your plugins and themes, the difference between branches and tags might be academic. If you wish, you can ignore the branches directory and keep all your releases in tags. As long as you tag the release numbers correctly in your readme files, the repository will be able to keep everything straight.

Client Software

While you're waiting to hear back about your plugin submission, you need to install a Subversion client.

Macs: If you use a Mac running OS 10.5 or higher, the command line interface for Subversion is already installed, and you can use it via the Terminal. If you prefer a graphic interface, Versions by Sofa Software is an excellent client. You can also use Subversion through several code editors and IDEs. Textmate is one of the most popular.

Windows and Linux: You can download Subversion from subversion.apache.org. If you're on Windows and you prefer a graphic interface, try TortoiseSVN (tortoisesvn.tigris.org), which integrates with Windows Explorer. This is by far the most popular choice among Windows users.

From this point on, things look very different depending on which client you're using. I'll demonstrate using Versions and Tortoise. If you prefer the command line, visit markjaquith.wordpress.com/2005/11/02/my-wordpress-toolbox/ for a quick overview of the most common Subversion commands.

Mac: Versions

When you open Versions, you'll be presented with two big choices. You need to create a new repository bookmark. You'll be asked to fill in the address of the repository (Figure 9-12). This should be the URL you received in your e-mail. You should also enter your wordpress.org username and password. You can connect anonymously, but you won't be able to upload any changes.

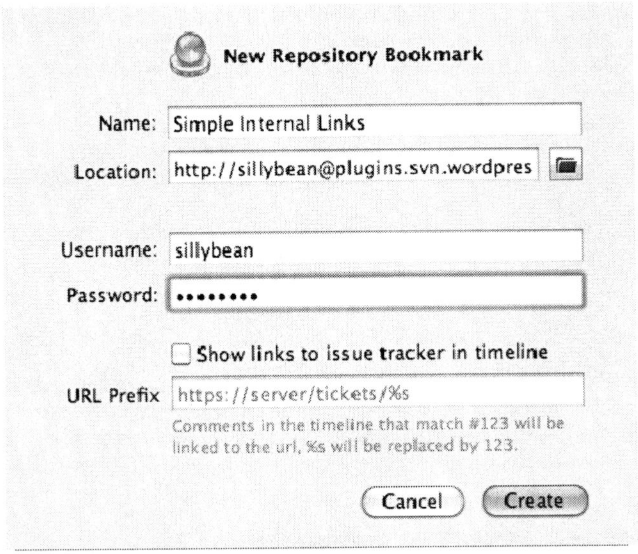

New Repository Bookmark

Name: Simple Internal Links

Location: http://sillybean@plugins.svn.wordpres

Username: sillybean

Password: ••••••••

☐ Show links to issue tracker in timeline

URL Prefix: https://server/tickets/%s

Comments in the timeline that match #123 will be
linked to the url, %s will be replaced by 123.

Cancel   Create

Figure 9-12. Creating a repository bookmark in Versions

When you press Create, the bookmark will appear in a list on the left side of the Versions window. Highlight it and press Checkout in the upper left corner. Since this is the first checkout, you'll be asked to choose a folder on your computer where the local copies of the files will be stored. Do so, and you'll have three new, empty subdirectories: branches, tags, and trunk, as shown in Figure 9-13.

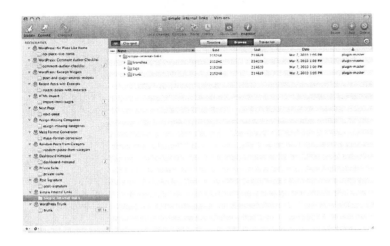

Figure 9-13. The files from the initial checkout

From this interface, you can open up the files in your editor of choice and make whatever changes you need. When you're finished making changes in trunk, you can highlight the files and press the Commit button in the upper left corner. Versions will upload the files to the repository, and within fifteen minutes or so, they'll be available to the world.

When you add a new file to a source-controlled directory (like a new branch or tag), you'll have to explicitly add it to the repository. Highlight the new file or directory and press the green Add button in the upper right corner. Likewise, when you need to remove a file, you'll have to highlight it and press the red Delete button.

If you've made a lot of changes throughout your project, just highlight the top-level directory and hit Commit. Versions will go through the subdirectories recursively and find all the changed files.

Windows: TortoiseSVN

TortoiseSVN is unusual in that it doesn't open in its own application window. Instead, it provides a set of contextual menu items in Windows Explorer. To perform your initial checkout, create the local folder where you'd like to store your plugin versions. Right-click this folder and choose SVN Checkout. A window will pop up where you'll be asked for the repository URL. Enter the one you received by e-mail, as shown in Figure 9-14.

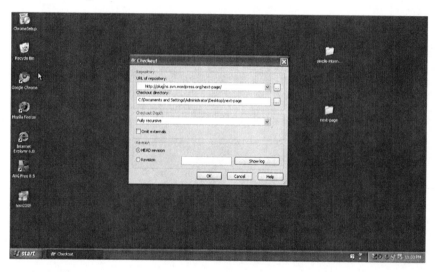

Figure 9-14. The initial checkout with Tortoise

If you have your plugin files ready, create a new folder under Tags and give it a number—let's say it's 1.0. Copy your files into the 1.0 folder. Make sure the version number in the plugin header and the readme file match this number. Then right-click the 1.0 folder and choose Add from the TortoiseSVN submenu. Once the plus icon appears on your folder, right-click it again and choose SVN Commit from the contextual menu, as shown in Figure 9-15.

Figure 9-15. Committing a tagged folder with Tortoise

You'll get a warning message about using tags instead of branches or trunk. Click OK. Next, you'll be prompted for your username and password. Enter your credentials for wordpress.org. The next prompt asks you for a commit message. This can be whatever you want for the initial checkin; for later updates, it's a good idea to summarize what changed since the previous version.

Enter your commit message and press OK. You'll see filenames scroll past you as the files are uploaded, and when it's done, the plus sign on your folder will change to a big green check, and you'll see the success message shown in Figure 9-16.

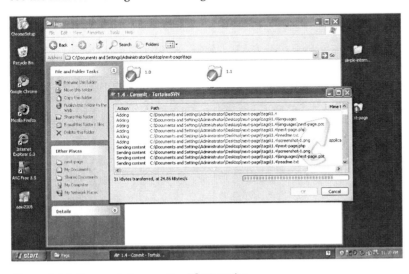

Figure 9-16. Successful commit with Tortoise

Localization and Internationalization

WordPress uses standard PHP gettext functions to allow string translations. To make your plugin available for translation, you have to localize all your strings.

The process of localizing strings is simple, but tedious. Each string must be wrapped in one of two functions. Echoed strings should be wrapped with _e(), while strings passed as arguments to other functions should be wrapped in __(). Additionally, each wrapper function must have a second argument, the text domain of your plugin. Most plugin authors use the directory name as the text domain. Finally, you need to generate a separate file containing all those wrapped strings, which translators will use as a template.

There are tools on WordPress Extend to help you with most of this. You'll still have to wrap the strings in the appropriate functions, but once that's done, you can automate the processes for the text domain and the language files.

■ **Note:** Because "internationalization" is a twenty-letter word that takes a while to type, it's often abbreviated as "i18n," with the middle 18 letters omitted. Similar abbreviations include localization (l10n) and accessibility (a11y).

Wrapping Strings in Gettext Calls

Listing 9-31 shows the Next Page options form you created in Listing 9-11, but this time, all the strings have been wrapped in the appropriate translation functions. This is the file you'll need to upload to the tools on WordPress Extend.

*Listing 9-31. **Next Page options with translation wrappers***

```
function next_page_options() { ?>
    <div class="wrap">
        <form method="post" id="next_page_form" action="options.php">
                <?php settings_fields('next_page');
                $options = get_option('next_page'); ?>

    <h2><?php _e( 'Next Page Options'); ?></h2>

    <p><label><?php _e("Exclude pages: "); ?><br />
    <input type="text" name="next_page[exclude]" id="exclude"
                value="<?php echo $options['exclude']; ?>" /><br />
        <small><?php _e("Enter page IDs separated by commas."); ?></small></label></p>

    <div id="previous-page">
    <h3><?php _e("Previous Page Display:"); ?></h3>
    <p><label><?php _e("Before previous page link: "); ?><br />
    <input type="text" name="next_page[before_prev_link]" id="before_prev_link"
                value="<?php echo stripslashes(htmlentities($options['before_prev_link']));
?>" />  </label></p>
```

```php
    <p><label><?php _e("Previous page link text: <small>Use %title% for the page
title</small>"); ?><br />
    <input type="text" name="next_page[prev_link_text]" id="prev_link_text"
            value="<?php echo stripslashes(htmlentities($options['prev_link_text'])); ?>"
/>  </label></p>

    <p><label><?php _e("After previous page link: "); ?><br />
    <input type="text" name="next_page[after_prev_link]" id="after_prev_link"
        value="<?php echo stripslashes(htmlentities($options['after_prev_link'])); ?>" />
</label></p>
    <p><?php _e('Shortcode:'); ?> <strong>[previous]</strong><br />
    <?php _e('Template tag:'); ?> <strong>&lt;?php previous_link(); ?&gt;</strong></p>
    </div>

    <div id="parent-page">
    <h3><?php _e("Parent Page Display:"); ?></h3>
    <p><label><?php _e("Before parent page link: "); ?><br />
    <input type="text" name="next_page[before_parent_link]" id="before_parent_link"
            value="<?php echo stripslashes(htmlentities($options['before_parent_link']));
?>" />  </label></p>

    <p><label><?php _e("Parent page link text: <small>Use %title% for the page
title</small>"); ?><br />
    <input type="text" name="next_page[parent_link_text]" id="parent_link_text"
            value="<?php echo stripslashes(htmlentities($options['parent_link_text']));
?>" />  </label></p>

    <p><label><?php _e("After parent page link: "); ?><br />
    <input type="text" name="next_page[after_parent_link]" id="after_parent_link"
            value="<?php echo stripslashes(htmlentities($options['after_parent_link']));
?>" />  </label></p>
    <p><?php _e('Shortcode:'); ?> <strong>[parent]</strong><br />
    <?php _e('Template tag:'); ?> <strong>&lt;?php parent_link(); ?&gt;</strong></p>
    </div>

    <div id="next-page">
    <h3><?php _e("Next Page Display:"); ?></h3>
    <p><label><?php _e("Before next page link: "); ?><br />
    <input type="text" name="next_page[before_next_link]" id="before_next_link"
            value="<?php echo stripslashes(htmlentities($options['before_next_link']));
?>" />  </label></p>

    <p><label><?php _e("Next page link text: <small>Use %title% for the page title</small>");
?><br />
    <input type="text" name="next_page[next_link_text]" id="next_link_text"
            value="<?php echo stripslashes(htmlentities($options['next_link_text'])); ?>"
/>  </label></p>

    <p><label><?php _e("After next page link: "); ?><br />
    <input type="text" name="next_page[after_next_link]" id="after_next_link"
            value="<?php echo stripslashes(htmlentities($options['after_next_link'])); ?>"
/>  </label></p>
```

```
<p><?php _e('Shortcode:'); ?> <strong>[next]</strong><br />
<?php _e('Template tag:'); ?> <strong>&lt;?php next_link(); ?&gt;</strong></p>
</div>

        <p class="submit">
        <input type="submit" name="submit" class="button-primary" value="<?php _e('Update
Options'); ?>" />
        </p>
        </form>
        </div>
<?php
} // end function next_page_options()
```

Adding the Gettext Domain

At this point, if you haven't already signed up for your Subversion repository, go ahead and do so. You won't have access to the automated tools until you've checked in the first copy of your plugin. If you don't want the plugin to be available to the public until the translation features are done, give the plugin file header a lower version number than the stable version listed in the readme file.

Once you've checked in the first copy of your plugin, log in to Extend and visit your plugin's page. Under the Admin tab, you'll see a list of handy links and two translation sections: Generate POT File and Add Domain to Gettext Calls. Figure 9-17 shows the Admin screen for Next Page.

Figure 9-17. The Next Page Admin screen on Extend

First, you'll add the domain to the gettext calls. If the domain shown is not the one you want to use, replace it in the text field. Then, choose your plugin file from your computer and press Get domainified file. The modified file will be downloaded back to your computer automatically. Save it over the original, and check it in to Subversion. You can leave it in the trunk for now rather than creating a new tag. Each gettext call should now have the domain added as a second argument, as shown in Listing 9-32.

Listing 9-32. A gettext call with the text domain

```php
<?php _e("Exclude pages: ", 'next-page'); ?>
```

Creating the .POT File

You might have to wait a few minutes for your domainified file to appear in the Subversion repository. (You can use the link to the Trac browser at the top of the Admin page to check the file's modification time.) Once it's there, you can use it to create the POT (Portable Object Template) file. This is the file that will contain all the translatable strings for your future translators to work with.

Choose the trunk or the appropriate tag from the dropdown menu and press Get POT. The POT file will be downloaded to your computer. Place it somewhere in your plugin directory. I like to create a languages subdirectory to hold the POT file and any translations, but this is entirely up to you.

Adding the i18n Function Block

The very last thing you need to do is to load the plugin's text domain. This is the function that makes the translation go; it passes all your gettext-wrapped strings through the language file (if it exists) matching the user's language as set in his or her configuration. The necessary code is shown in Listing 9-33.

Listing 9-33. The i18n functions

```php
if (!defined('WP_PLUGIN_DIR'))
        define('WP_PLUGIN_DIR', dirname(dirname(__FILE__)));
$lang_dir = basename(dirname(__FILE__)). '/languages';
load_plugin_textdomain( 'next_page', 'WP_PLUGIN_DIR'.$lang_dir, $lang_dir );
```

First, you've defined the WP_PLUGIN_DIR constant, in case it doesn't exist, for backward compatibility. Next, you need to tell WordPress which directory your language files will be stored in. Finally, you've called the load_plugin_textdomain() function, which requires three arguments: the domain (as chosen when you added the gettext calls), the full path to the language directory, and path to the language directory relative to the plugin directory. The last two arguments are redundant, and again are present for backward compatibility. If you don't need your plugin to be compatible with pre-2.6 versions of WordPress, you may leave the second argument blank.

Once you've made all your localization changes, increment your plugin's version number and commit the updates. Your plugin is now ready for translators!

There is not yet an automated process by which translators can submit their work to you for inclusion in the plugin. Be sure to provide an e-mail address in the plugin's readme file so translators can send you their files. For each language, they will generate a PO (Portable Object) and MO (Machine Object) file. The .po file is human-readable; the .mo file is a compressed binary for faster loading. When you receive them, add them to the same directory where you stored your .POT file. You can then update your plugin version with the new translations.

Summary

In this chapter, I've shown you all the basics of WordPress plugin development: adding options forms, creating template tags and shortcodes, checking user capabilities, filtering content, and adding your own functions to action hooks. I've also gone over the process of publishing a plugin on WordPress Extend, including how to create a `readme.txt` file, localize your plugin, and upload it using Subversion.

While I have by no means shown you everything you will ever need to know about writing plugins for WordPress, I hope I have given you a solid foundation for further research. As always, the Codex should be your first stop when you need to find a function or look up an action hook. If the relevant Codex is incomplete—and I'm sorry to say the end-user documentation is far more complete than that for developers—try searching the forums, Google, the PHPdocs, and the Xref documentation.

In this chapter, I've shown you very briefly how to check for users' capabilities in your plugins. In the next chapter, you'll learn all about the built-in roles and capabilities in WordPress. You'll also learn how to change them to suit your needs.

CHAPTER 10

■■■

Users and Roles

WordPress has five built-in user roles with escalating permissions. The basic role and notification systems work well for many blogs, but they're too limited for more complex content management. Fortunately, the developers have indicated that the roles will be overhauled in an upcoming version (perhaps 3.1). In the meantime, they can be modified if you're willing to dig into some PHP or install a couple of plugins: you can change the fields in the basic user profile, modify roles, and create whole new roles. I'll look at all the code (or plugin settings) required to make these changes.

Users

If you changed your password just after you installed WordPress, you've already seen the user profile page (Figure 10-1). You can reach it by going to Users → Your Profile in the navigation menu. You might not have noticed, but you were assigned the administrator role.

Figure 10-1. A user profile

In the personal options section, you can determine how the WordPress administration screens will work for you. You can disable the visual (rich text) editor on the content editing screens and you can switch the color scheme to blue. See codex.wordpress.org/Keyboard_Shortcuts for the full list of comment moderation shortcuts you'll have if you enable keyboard shortcuts for comment moderation.

Note that the username you chose when you installed WordPress cannot be changed unless you edit the database field directly (with PHPMyAdmin, for example). You could also create another user, give it the administrator role, and log in with that account instead.

The first and last name fields should be self-explanatory. The nickname field works much like a post's slug. It's used in the URL to your author archive page (which we talked about in Chapter 6) and can be used in some functions that retrieve user profile data.

The display name setting determines how your name will appear on your site: in your post/page bylines, on your author archive pages, and in your comments (f you're logged in when you leave a comment).

Your e-mail address will be used for all the notifications you, personally, will receive from WordPress. While the e-mail you specified in Settings → General will be used for system notifications, you'll be notified at the address you provide here about every comment on posts you've written, if you've checked the appropriate setting in Settings → Discussion. If you forget your password, you'll be able to reset it by having a new one sent to this address. Note that users can't have duplicate e-mail addresses; if you need to create additional accounts for yourself as you test various features, you'll have to use a different address for each one.

The URL you enter here will be used if your theme supports author links in bylines. Your name will also be linked to this URL if you are logged in when commenting.

The biography field is not often used in themes, but some display it as a post footer in a multi-author blog or in the sidebar of the author archive template. This field accepts a limited set of HTML tags—the same ones allowed in comments, in fact. All other tags will be removed. The allowed tags (and attributes) in all filtered HTML fields are shown in Listing 10-1.

Listing 10-1. HTML tags and attributes allowed in filtered HTML fields

```
<a href="" title="">
<abbr title="">
<acronym title="">
<b>
<blockquote cite="">
<cite>
<code>
<del datetime="">
<em>
<i>
<q cite="">
<strike>
<strong>
```

WordPress uses Gravatars (gravatar.com) for its user avatars. If a user has a Gravatar associated with his or her e-mail address, it will be shown in the administration screens and in any theme that supports avatars.

As an administrator, you can edit other users' profiles as well as your own. No other role has this capability.

Displaying a User's Information

To display a user's information inside the Loop, you don't need to find their user ID; all the user functions will assume that you're talking about the current post author and fill in the ID automatically.

You can use the the_author_meta() function to display user information. There's also get_the_author_meta(), which returns information for use in PHP rather than displaying it to the screen. Listing 10-2 shows how to create a footer for posts in a multi-author blog that displays the author's avatar, display name, and bio. This code should be placed in a theme's single.php file somewhere after the post content. Figure 10-2 shows how the resulting author information block appears in the Twenty Ten theme.

Listing 10-2. Displaying user information in a post footer

```
<div id="entry-author-info">
        <div id="author-avatar">
                <?php echo get_avatar(get_the_author_meta('user_email')); ?>
        </div>
        <div id="author-description">
                <h2>About <?php the_author(); ?></h2>
                <?php the_author_meta('description'); ?>
                <div id="author-link">
                        <a href="<?php echo get_author_posts_url( $authordata->ID ); ?>"
title="View all posts by <?php get_the_author(); ?>">
                        View all posts by <?php the_author(); ?> &rarr;</a>
                </div>
        </div>
</div>
```

Figure 10-2. The user information as displayed in the Twenty Ten theme

273

Extending User Profiles

WordPress user profiles include several contact fields: an e-mail address, a URL, and three instant messenger accounts: AIM, Yahoo, and Google Talk (or Jabber). You can change these fields with just a few lines of code in a theme functions file or a plugin. You can also change the fields outside the Contact Info group, although it takes a bit more work.

Changing Contact Fields

The built-in contact fields are not always terribly useful. Business users need to add job titles, some social networks value Twitter usernames over instant messenger accounts, and so on.

WordPress has a filter function that allows you to change the fields that appear in the Contact Info section. The code is fairly simple, as shown in Listing 10-3. Place it in your theme's functions.php file or in a new plugin (as you saw in in Chapter 9).

Listing 10-3. Changing user profile contact fields

```
// change user contact fields
function change_contactmethod( $contactmethods ) {
  // Add some fields
  $contactmethods['twitter'] = 'Twitter Name (no @)';
  $contactmethods['phone'] = 'Phone Number';
  $contactmethods['title'] = 'Title';
  // Remove AIM, Yahoo IM, Google Talk/Jabber
  unset($contactmethods['aim']);
  unset($contactmethods['yim']);
  unset($contactmethods['jabber']);
  // make it go!
  return $contactmethods;
}
add_filter('user_contactmethods','change_contactmethod',10,1);
```

This function accepts an associative array of contact fields. You've added three new fields, where the array key is a short name for the field and the value is the label that will appear in the form. Then you've removed the array items containing the fields you no longer want—all three instant messenger accounts, in this case. Of the default contact fields, these are the only three you can remove; the e-mail and URL fields must remain.

Finally, you need to call the filter. The add_filter() function takes four arguments: the name of the built-in filter ('user_contactmethods'), the name of the custom function ('change_contactmethod'), a priority (10, in this case, means the filter has a low priority and will be called after most other filters), and finally the number of arguments the custom function requires (in this case, just one).

Once you place the above code into your functions.php file, you'll see the new contact fields displayed when you view a user's profile, as shown in Figure 10-3.

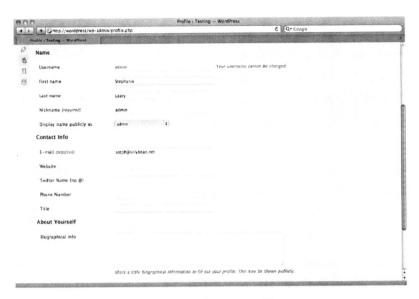

Figure 10-3. The new contact fields in the user profile

Creating More Profile Fields

Because the code above works only on contact fields, you'll need to work a little harder to add fields elsewhere in the profile. In Listing 10-4, I've created a profile field for the user's birth year. You'll need to edit the code to reflect the field(s) you want to use. You can see the results in Figure 10-4.

Listing 10-4. Adding user profile fields

```php
<?php
/*
Plugin Name: Stephanie's Extra User Profile Fields
Plugin URI: http://sillybean.net/
Description: Adds an extra field (the birth year) to the user profile. Loosely based on PJW
User Meta by Peter Westwood.
Author: Stephanie Leary
Version: 1.0
Author URI: http://sillybean.net/
*/
// Usage: the_author_meta('birth_year'); will display the birth year in templates

// Show new fields in the form
add_action( 'show_user_profile', 'show_more_profile_fields' );
add_action( 'edit_user_profile', 'show_more_profile_fields' );

// Save the new fields when the profile is edited
add_action( 'personal_options_update', 'save_more_profile_fields' );
add_action( 'edit_user_profile_update', 'save_more_profile_fields' );
```

```
function show_more_profile_fields( $user ) { ?>

        <h3>Other information</h3>
        <table class="form-table">
                <tr>
                        <th><label for="birth_year"><?php _e('Birth Year'); ?></label></th>
                        <td><input type="text" name="birth_year" id="birth_year" value="<?php
echo esc_attr(get_user_meta($user->ID, 'birth_year', true) ); ?>" /></td>
                </tr>
        </table>

<?php }
function save_more_profile_fields( $user_id ) {
        update_user_meta( $user_id, 'birth_year', $_POST['birth_year'], get_user_meta($user-
>ID, 'birth_year', true));
}
?>
```

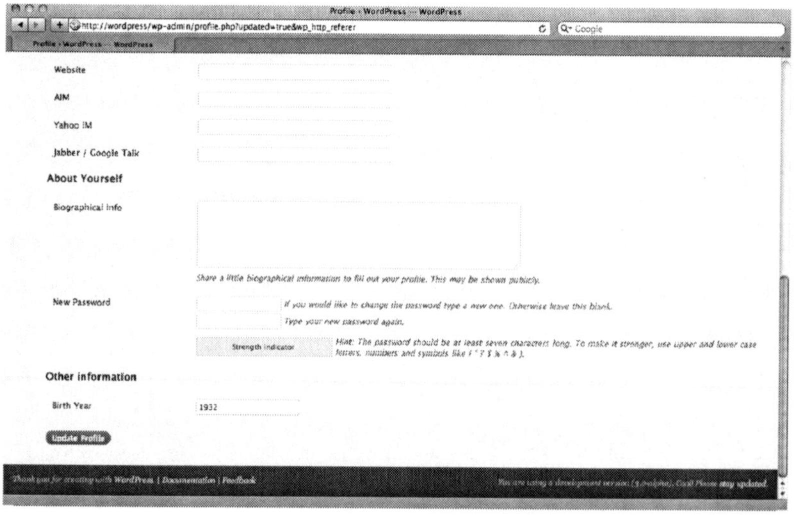

Figure 10-4. The added profile field

Displaying All Users' Information

WordPress provides an archive template that displays all posts, but there is no template that displays a list of all users. Let's say that you are building a business site, and you want to take advantage of the new contact fields you defined above to display a user directory that will automatically reflect any changes your users make to their contact information. To do so, create a new page template containing the code shown in Listing 10-5. This code should be placed more or less where the_content() would usually go; you'll need to add the surrounding markup to match your site's theme.

In this example, you get all user IDs of your blog with the get_users_of_blog() function. Then, to make it easier to loop through them, you go through all the user objects returned by that function and create a simple array. Finally, you loop through the array and display each field in a table cell.

Notice that the object field names for the new contact fields match the short names you used when you created them.

Figure 10-5 shows the resulting directory page.

Listing 10-5. Building a user directory

```php
<?php
/*
Template Name: Staff Directory
*/
    //get all registered users
    $blogusers = get_users_of_blog();
    foreach ($blogusers as $bloguser) {
        //get data about each user as an object
        $user = get_userdata($bloguser->user_id);
        // create a flat array with only the fields we need
        $allusers[$user->ID] = array(
                'name' => $user->display_name,
                'title' => $user->title,
                'phone' => $user->phone,
                'twitter' => $user->twitter
        );
}
?>
<table id="staff-directory" class="sortable">
<thead>
        <tr>
          <th>Name</th>
          <th>Title</th>
          <th>Phone</th>
          <th>Twitter</th>
        </tr>
</thead>
<tbody>
<?php
foreach ($allusers as $auser) {   ?>
        <tr>
          <td><?php echo $auser['name']; ?></td>
          <td><?php echo $auser['title']; ?></td>
          <td><?php echo $auser['phone']; ?></td>
          <td><a href="http://twitter.com/<?php echo $auser['twitter']; ?>">
              @<?php echo $auser['twitter']; ?></a></td>
        </tr>
<?php } ?>
</tbody>
</table>
```

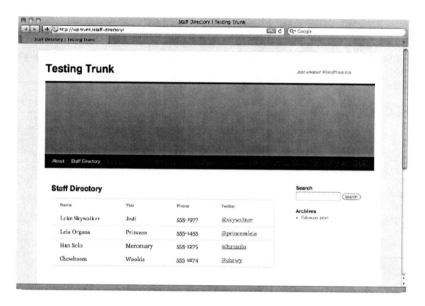

Figure 10-5. The resulting Staff Directory

See `sillybean.net/?p=2715` for a more complex version of this user directory, including a method of creating downloadable vCard address book files for each user using microformats.

Roles

WordPress has five built-in user roles. Each has a set of capabilities (or permissions). They are:

Administrators can do anything in the WordPress administration area: write, edit, and delete posts, pages, links, and comments; upload media files of any type; import content; manage the Dashboard; create, edit, and delete other users; enable and configure plugins and themes; change the site's theme; and manage all the available options.

Editors can publish, edit, and delete posts and pages written by any user. They can upload some kinds of files, and they can write HTML without restrictions. They can manage links and categories, and they can moderate comments. Editors and administrators are also the only users allowed to read private posts and pages.

Authors can publish, edit, and delete their own posts. They cannot write pages. They can upload some kinds of media files, and they are allowed to use only the limited set of HTML tags shown in Listing 10-1.

Contributors can write their own posts but may not publish or delete them. Their HTML is limited to the set of allowed tags and they cannot upload media files.

Subscribers can manage their own profiles, but can do virtually nothing else in the administration area.

Visit `codex.wordpress.org/Roles_and_Capabilities` for a detailed list of all the capabilities assigned to each role.

Features that are not available to users will not appear in their administration screens. See Figure 10-6, where the navigation menu is fully expanded to show the options available to authors.

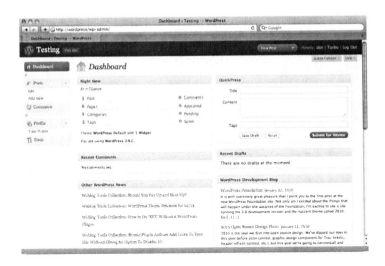

Figure 10-6. *The Dashboard as it appears to an author*

Roles in Action: Notifications, Moderation, and Workflow

For administrators and editors, publishing posts and pages is simple: write the content, press Publish. For authors, it's a little more complicated. Since they are not allowed to publish their own posts, they must submit them for review, as shown in Figure 10-7. Editors and administrators will then see the pending posts on the Posts → Edit screen, as shown in Figure 10-8. They will not get an e-mail notification unless you add a plugin, as you'll see in the next section.

Figure 10-7. *Writing a post as an author*

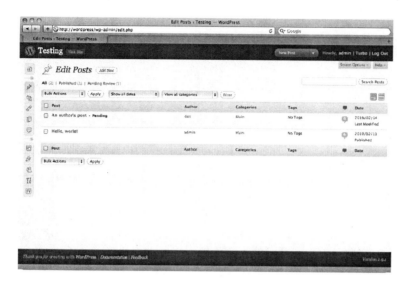

Figure 10-8. Pending posts from the administrator's view

Any comments on the post will trigger e-mail notifications, depending on the choices made under Settings → Discussion. Notifications will be sent to the post author as well as the administrator e-mail account specified under Settings → General. If you have activated the Akismet plugin, some comments may be held for moderation, as shown in Figure 10-9.

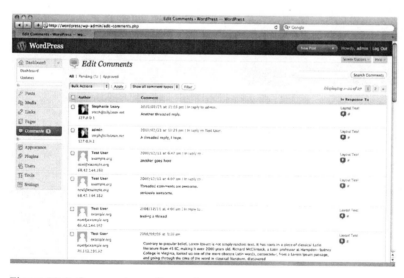

Figure 10-9. Comments pending review

■ **Note:** E-mail notifications rely on the server's mail settings. PHP uses sendmail on most UNIX-based operating systems. If you're on Windows, or sendmail doesn't work, install a plugin to send mail via SMTP instead. See Appendix 1 for a list of possible plugins.

Improving Workflow with Plugins

For very busy sites with many authors and editors, the built-in notifications and post scheduling features often prove inadequate. There are several plugins you can install to provide your users with a more robust workflow.

Notification of Posts Pending Review

WordPress does not send e-mail notifications to editors and administrators when a post is pending review; the pending posts simply wait under Posts → Edit until a reviewer logs in. If you do want e-mails of pending posts, install the Peter's Collaboration E-mails plugin. It allows you to add administrators to the general notification list, and it provides options to set up notifications for categories or groups of users, as shown in Figure 10-10.

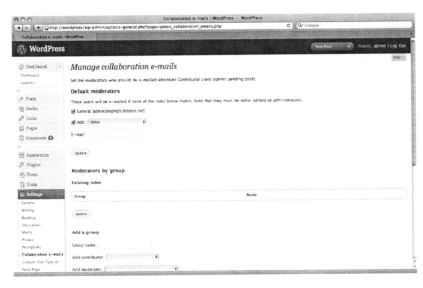

Figure 10-10. Peter's Collaboration E-mails options

Notifying All Administrators

If you are sharing administration duties with a partner, you might become frustrated with the fact that comment notifications are sent only to the address saved in Settings → General. If you want all administrators to get an e-mail, add the Notifications to All Administrators plugin. It has no options; just install it and wait for the notification e-mails to arrive.

Viewing Scheduled Posts

Normally, posts scheduled for future publication are displayed in the same list as your other posts, under Posts → Edit. When you have many future posts, this listing becomes unwieldy. The Editorial Calendar plugin allows you to visualize your scheduled posts. It places a new screen under the Posts menu (Figure 10-11) where you'll see a few weeks' worth of posts at a time. (You can configure the number in the Screen Options tab.) Move your cursor near the top or bottom of the calendar to scroll through additional dates.

You can add a post by clicking a day's header, and if you hover over the posts on the calendar, you'll see a row of links allowing you to edit, delete, or view the post. To reschedule a post, click and drag its title to another day.

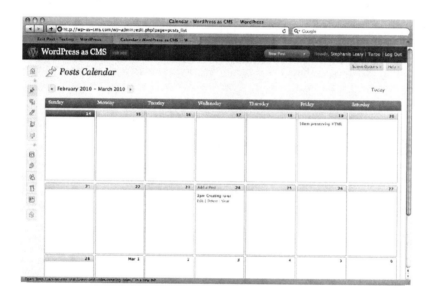

Figure 10-11. Scheduled posts on the editorial calendar

Complete Workflow

Even with Peter's Collaboration E-mails, the notification features are just not what they should be. For example, when an editor approves a post for publication, the author isn't notified! The creators of the Edit Flow plugin aim to collect all of the missing role and notification features into a single plugin. Designed for newsrooms, Edit Flow includes custom post statuses (Figure 10-12), including Assigned, Pitch, and Waiting for Feedback; editorial comments on the post editing screen; and e-mail notification any time a post's status changes. The plugin allows you to create groups of users (Figure 10-13) that can subscribe to updates on a post and configure recipients for all the notifications (Figure 10-14).

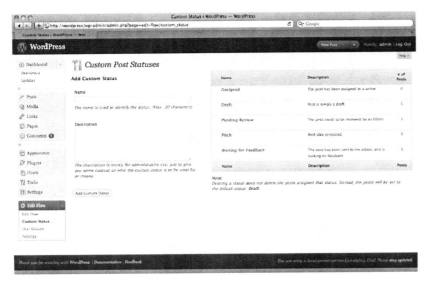

Figure 10-12. Custom post statuses in Edit Flow

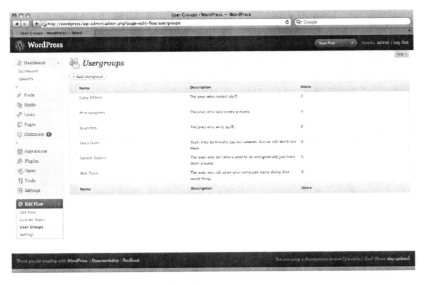

Figure 10-13. User groups in Edit Flow

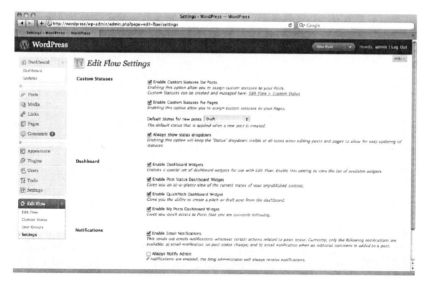

Figure 10-14. *Edit Flow settings*

Changing, Creating, and Removing Roles

Assuming the built-in user roles haven't been altered by a plugin, the higher roles contain all the capabilities of the lower roles. In other words, an author can do everything a contributor can do, plus a few other things. This means that if you want to modify roles, you don't have to change a capability for every possible role. Change the lowest role, and the others will inherit the new capabilities. However, it's possible to create new roles that are not cumulative, as you'll see later in this section.

Modifying Roles

If you need to change one or two capabilities, it's relatively easy to do so with a few lines of code in a plugin (see Chapter 9) or your theme functions (see Chapter 7). For example, if you want to allow any logged-in user to view your private posts and pages, you need to grant them two additional capabilities, as shown in Listing 10-6. This bit of code should go in your theme functions file or in a new plugin.

Listing 10-6. Modifying an existing role

```php
<?php
// allow subscribers to view private posts and pages
$PrivateRole = get_role('subscriber');
$PrivateRole -> add_cap('read_private_pages');
$PrivateRole -> add_cap('read_private_posts');
?>
```

The first line fetches the existing subscriber role (as an object) and assigns to it a variable. In the next two lines, you add the capabilities to read private posts and pages to our variable. That's it! Any subscribers can now read your private content—and so can authors and contributors, whose roles include all the capabilities of subscribers. (Remember that editors and administrators already had these particular capabilities.)

Creating Roles

Sometimes, rather than adding capabilities to an existing role, you need to create a whole new role. The code to do so is relatively easy. Again, place the lines in Listing 10-7 in your theme's functions.php file.

Listing 10-7. Creating a new role

```php
<?php
add_role('privatereader', 'Private Reader', array(
        'read' => 1,
        'level_0' => 1,
        'read_private_pages' => 1,
        'read_private_posts' => 1,
    ));
?>
```

The add_role() function requires three arguments: the role's name (for internal use), the display name, and an array of the role's capabilities. (See codex.wordpress.org/Roles_and_Capabilities for a complete list of the capabilities in WordPress.) Here, you've given the role the same two capabilities a subscriber starts out with, 'read' and 'level_0.' (The *level_n* capabilities exist for backward compatibility; very early versions of WordPress used a 1-10 scale instead of named roles.) Then, you've added the two roles relating to private content.

The functions that check for the presence of a capability in the role array will test for Boolean values. You could use true or false, but most WordPress developers prefer to use 1 or 0.

That's all it takes! Now, if you add a new user or edit an existing one, your role dropdown should include the Private Reader option, as shown in Figure 10-15.

Figure 10-15. Adding a user with the custom role

If you want to modify your new role, use the same code as before, but change the get_role() function's argument to your role's internal name, as shown in Listing 10-8.

Listing 10-8. Modifying the new role

```php
<?php
// remove ability to read private pages
$PrivateRole = get_role('privatereader');
$PrivateRole -> remove_cap('read_private_pages');
?>
```

In this example, it makes sense to create a new role only if you want to keep the subscriber role as-is; otherwise; it's simpler to just modify the subscriber role.

When *would* it make sense to create a new role?

Creating a Role for Designers

Let's imagine a new scenario. You're building a large site, and you, the programmer, are sharing responsibilities with a graphic designer. You want to give your designer complete control over the content and theme design, but you don't want him editing other users, adding plugins, or importing content from other sites.

You could create a whole new role and enumerate every capability you want the designer to have, as you did above for the private reader, but this role will be similar to the administrator's, and that's a lot of capabilities! Instead, duplicate the admin role and remove the eight or nine capabilities you don't want the designer to have, as shown in Listing 10-9.

Listing 10-9. Creating a designer role

```php
<?php
$admin = get_role('administrator');

// get_role returns an object.
// We want the capabilities piece, which is an array.
$caps = $admin->capabilities;

// Remove the stuff we don't want in the new role.
unset($caps['activate_plugins']);
unset($caps['edit_plugins']);
unset($caps['update_plugins']);
unset($caps['delete_plugins']);
unset($caps['install_plugins']);
unset($caps['edit_users']);
unset($caps['delete_users']);
unset($caps['create_users']);
unset($caps['import']);

// Add the new role.
add_role('designer', 'Designer', $caps);
?>
```

Note that WordPress's admin menus and screens don't always behave exactly as you'd expect. In this case, even though you've removed all capabilities involving plugins, the designer will still be able to access the Plugins → Add New screen, search for plugins, and install them — but s/he won't be able to activate the new plugin or see the list of installed plugins. These menu problems are currently under discussion in the WordPress bug database and will be addressed when the user/role system is rewritten.

Removing Roles

It takes just one line of code, Listing 10-10, to remove a role.

Listing 10-10. Removing a role

```php
<?php
remove_role('designer');
?>
```

If the deleted role has any users assigned to it, their role will be set to "None" until you assign them another one. You can use the Bulk Edit feature to reassign many users at once.

■ **Caution:** I do not recommend removing any of the five built-in roles, even if you don't plan to use them. Each of the administration screens (and the menu items leading to them) appears only if you have the capability to see it. If you remove the built-in roles, you'll need to make certain you have created other roles with those capabilities, or you'll find yourself locked out of your site.

Managing Roles with Plugins

As you can see, changing a lot of capabilities for various roles would involve a cumbersome amount of code. And writing the code by hand means you can't easily delegate the task to other adminstrators, unless they're as proficient with PHP as you are. Fortunately, there are several plugins that make role management a much easier task by providing a complete user interface. Members is the most complete and up to date.

Members Plugin

Justin Tadlock's plugin aims to replace the venerable Role Manager plugin. Role Manager was for a long time the best choice for managing roles and capabilities, but it has not been updated since WordPress 2.6 was released, and some of its features no longer work. The Members plugin is a wonderful replacement. In addition to managing roles, it adds other features, such as private content control. Figure 10-16 shows the Members screen allowing you to edit the administrator role.

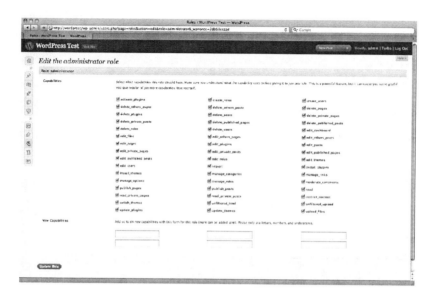

Figure 10-16. Editing the administrator role with the Members plugin

Summary

In this chapter, I've looked at the built-in user profiles. I've shown you a few ways to change and extend the profiles, and how to display user information in themes. I've also covered the built-in roles, how roles define the editorial workflow, and how to change that workflow with plugins. Finally, you learned how to modify, create, and remove roles.

In the next chapter, I'll go over some of the common performance and security issues you'll find in a typical WordPress installation, and I'll show you some plugins and configuration settings that can speed up and secure your site.

CHAPTER 11

■ ■ ■

Performance and Security

WordPress is database-driven, so it's not quite as fast at serving up individual pages as a CMS that writes static files to the server, like Movable Type. However, there are a number of things you can do to improve its performance, starting with caching dynamic output to static pages. I'll explain how caching works and show you how to set it up. I'll also look at some ways to identify performance problems in your installation.

The down side of being the most popular CMS in the world is that WordPress attracts a lot of attention from would-be hackers. The development team does a great job of responding to newly discovered vulnerabilities quickly, so staying up to date with the latest release is the most important thing you can do to protect yourself from attacks. However, there are a number of other little things you can do, and I'll walk you through them in the second half of this chapter.

Caching

If you've ever seen a Slashdotted, Dugg, or Fireballed site suddenly fail to respond, you've witnessed the consequences of insufficient caching. A dynamic site has to query the database several times to assemble each page a visitor requests. Queries for a typical WordPress page include the `bloginfo()` options (site title, description, language, theme stylesheet URL), the post or page title and contents, the comments, and the sidebar widgets. If you're using multiple Loops, you're using even more queries. Servers can generally handle all those MySQL queries and PHP page-building functions for sites with low traffic, but when your site gets its fifteen minutes of fame—or gets hit with a denial of service attack—your server will probably buckle under the sudden demand.

The solution is to cache the assembled pages—that is, to store copies as static files in a hidden directory and to redirect incoming visitors to those copies rather than allow them to continually hammer your dynamic site. Not only does this speed things up for your visitors, but if you're on a shared hosting server, it will prevent you from exceeding your allotted CPU usage. Some hosts are nice about helping you keep the site up and running when that happens; others will just shut down your site to protect the other users on the server.

WordPress does not come with built-in caching. (This is perhaps the biggest criticism leveled at the WordPress project by users of other open-source content management systems.) It *does* come with support for a number of different caching options, and it's up to you to decide which plugin best suits your needs and your hosting environment. Cache plugins available at WordPress Extend include:

- WP Super Cache

- W3 Total Cache

- Batcache

- Hyper Cache

- WP Widget Cache

I'll walk through Super Cache, which is by far the most popular. First, though, take a look at your permalink settings. You *must* use a permalink structure other than the default in order for the caching plugins to work. Super Cache warns you if your permalink structure won't work, as shown in Figure 11-1. All of the cache plugins operate by using rewrite rules in your `.htaccess` file to redirect requests from your dynamic WordPress pages to static files saved in a hidden directory in your installation. If you aren't using permalinks, WordPress hasn't written any rewrite rules to `.htaccess`. If the rewrites never take place, your dynamic pages will be served up to your visitors even though you have installed and activated a caching plugin.

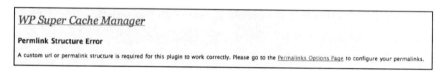

Figure 11-1. WP Super Cache warning message on permalink structures

Setting up Super Cache

Unlike most plugins, Super Cache doesn't start working as soon as you activate it. You have to configure it first. You'll see a red-outlined warning message on your plugin list until you set up caching or deactivate the plugin, as shown in Figure 11-2.

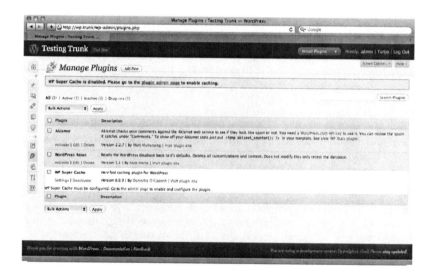

Figure 11-2. WP Super Cache activation

Basic Settings

Go to Settings → Super Cache to configure the plugin (Figure 11-3). The first thing you have to decide is whether to run the plugin in Half On or full On mode. In Half On mode, Super Cache emulates an older plugin, WP-Cache, which stores the cached files as PHP. Your server won't have to process any MySQL queries, but it still has to generate those PHP pages. In On mode, Super Cache saves those files as HTML instead, so there's no PHP processing required to serve them up to your visitors. If you're serving thousands of pages per minute, that small difference goes a long way.

For most sites, Half On mode will be fine for daily use. You can always toggle the status later if you need to.

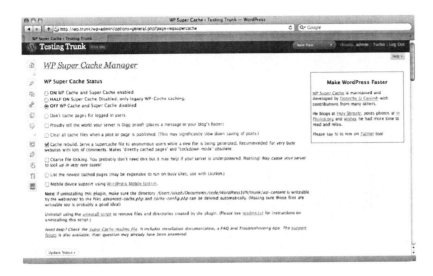

Figure 11-3. Main Super Cache settings

Next, you should probably turn on the option labeled Don't cache pages for logged in users. This will ensure that as you're making changes to the site, you can view them immediately without waiting for the cache to refresh.

The next option will rebuild the cache when you add a post or page. This will ensure that your visitors will see the new content immediately, but it will also slow things down for you and your other users. Every time you publish something, the entire cache will have to be regenerated, and that can take a significant amount of processing power if you have a large site. My recommendation is to try writing a few posts with this option on and see how it goes. If your site becomes unusably slow, turn it off! Your visitors will just have to wait for the old cached pages to expire (within the time limit you'll set in just a moment) before they see your new posts.

Normally, a post's cached page will be rebuilt every time someone adds a comment. However, if you get so many comments that this would be counterproductive, you can turn on the cache rebuild option. New files will still be generated, but if a new comment comes in while the page is being generated, the viewer will see the older copy.

Coarse file locking is no longer recommended but is still available for backward compatibility. This option locks cache files while they are being rebuilt, but Super Cache now uses temporary files during the rebuild process, and coarse file locking is obsolete.

I do not recommend listing the most recently cached pages unless your site traffic is nominal and you're curious as to how the plugin is operating.

I'll talk about the mobile support option in the next section. For now, choose among the options I've gone over and press Update status.

When the page refreshes, you should see a section listing the contents of the cache (Figure 11-4).

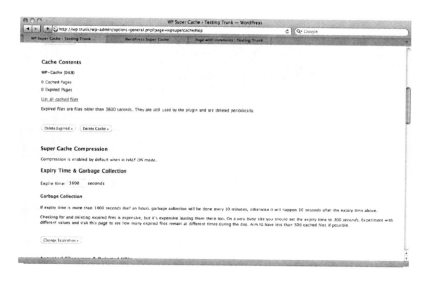

Figure 11-4. Super Cache contents

In this section, you can manually delete the cache. This is helpful when you've changed some of the settings in the first section and you'd like the changes to take effect before the cached pages expire.

Compression

The compression settings determine whether your cached files are stored in compressed (gzipped) format. Modern browsers are capable of unzipping pages after downloading them, so your server can send smaller files. Compression is optional in On mode, but is on by default in Half On mode. If you're running in On mode, you can enable compression. You'll then be shown a list of the rewrite rules that should be added to .htaccess, and if your .htaccess file is writeable, you can press a button to make the changes. Otherwise, you'll need to copy them by hand.

Super Cache compression can cause problems if your server is already compressing output using mod_deflate (on Apache) or PHP compression (zlib). In this case, the doubly-compressed files might appear as garbage characters to some users. You can turn off compression in Super Cache or adjust your server's settings. The plugin FAQ contains information on how to do this; if those instructions don't work, ask your hosting provider about your server's compression settings.

Other Settings

Under Expiry Time & Garbage Collection, you can choose how long your cached pages will last before they should be rebuilt. The default setting is 3600 seconds (one hour). You can lower this, but keep in mind that garbage collection requires server resources, just as rebuilding pages does. You should experiment with different settings to strike a balance between these two processes that doesn't overly tax your server.

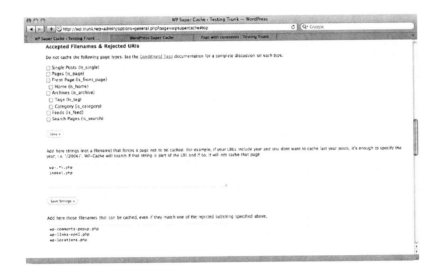

Figure 11-5. Accepted filenames and rejected URIs in WP Super Cache

In the Accepted Filenames and Rejected URIs section of the Super Cache settings (Figure 11-5), you can specify certain pages that should not be cached. The page type options should look familiar; they're identical to the conditional tags you saw in Chapter 7. Of these, I would recommend checking Feeds. You can leave the rest of these settings on their default values in most cases. You'll change them when you enable mobile support in the next section.

At the bottom of the Super Cache settings screen, you'll have the option to directly cache a single file (Figure 11-6). If you write a post or a page that you know will bring in untold numbers of readers, you can head off the impending performance crisis by caching the page not in the usual hidden cache location, but right in your blog directory. How does this work? The WordPress rewrite rules—all of them, including Super Cache's—are set up to rewrite URLs only if the requested file or directory does not exist on the server. Therefore, if you create a cached page in the location that matches the permalink, the cached file will trump all rewrite rules. Since the server doesn't have to look through all those rewrites, it will be a little faster at serving up that particular file. And when you're looking at thousands of requests coming in, "a little faster" multiplies quickly into some significant performance.

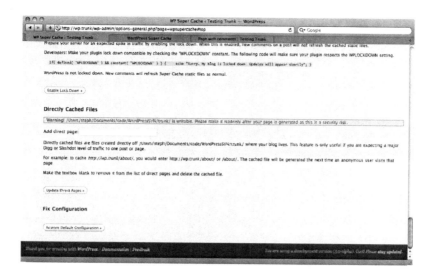

Figure 11-6. Directly caching a popular file in WP Super Cache

Caching and Mobile Stylesheets

The final checkbox in the main set of Super Cache options turns on mobile support. This doesn't mean much unless you're also running a second plugin that provides a mobile version of your site. To demonstrate how this works, I'll walk you through setting up Super Cache to work with WPTouch, the plugin that provides mobile versions of all sites on wordpress.com.

The WPTouch settings screen has a multitude of options. I won't discuss them all here; the ones I'm interested in showing you are in the Advanced Options box. Highlight the user agent strings as shown in Figure 11-7, copy them, and then head back over to the Super Cache settings.

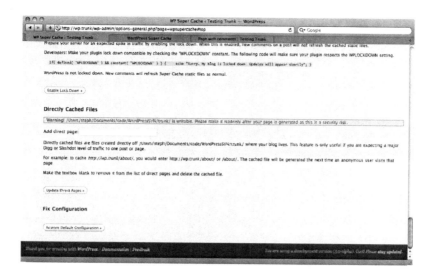

Figure 11-7. User agent strings in the WPTouch Advanced Options

First, in order to support WPTouch, you'll have to select Half On mode. Full On mode circumvents the user agent checking that allows mobile version plugins to work, so you'll have to use Half On mode if you want to use Super Cache alongside a mobile plugin. That's OK; for most sites, Half On is sufficient. Next, check off mobile device support and press Update Status.

Now that mobile device support is on, you need to prevent Super Cache from displaying the cached pages to mobile user agents. Scroll down and find the Rejected User Agents box, as shown in Figure 11-8. Paste the user agent strings you copied from the WPTouch settings screen and remove the commas, placing each user agent on its own line. Press Save UA Strings, and you've enabled mobile support.

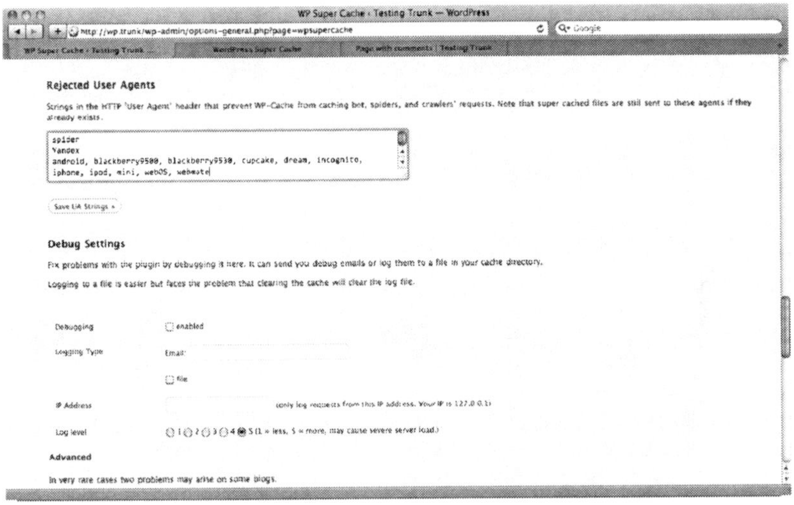

Figure 11-8. Pasting the mobile user agents into the Super Cache list of rejected user agents

However, there's one more step you need to take: deleting the existing cache. Any time you change the Super Cache settings, you need to delete the cache so the cached pages will be rebuilt according to your new settings. Once you've saved the UA strings, scroll back up to the Cache Contents section and press Delete Cache.

WPTouch is not the only mobile version plugin by any means, but mobile support in Super Cache works essentially the same way with all the other plugins.

Permalinks and Performance

When you chose your permalink structure back in Chapter 3, you had a lot of tags you could choose from. However, a few of those tags can cause performance problems on large sites with hundreds of pages. Specifically, permalink structures that begin with the four string-based tags, %category%, %tag%, %postname%, and %author%, are significantly slower than those beginning with numeric tags. The reason is that WordPress has to store rewrite rules in a field in the options table for these less efficient structures. So, instead of using /%category%/%postname%/, you might use /%year%/%category%/%postname%/ instead.

Note that using the No Category Base plugin, as discussed in Chapter 3, only exacerbates this problem.

For a more complete discussion of the permalink performance problem, visit `dougal.gunters.org/blog/2009/02/04/efficient-wordpress-permalinks`.

Tracking Down Performance Problems

If your site is slow, but it's not because of an inefficient permalink structure, tracking down the cause can be bewildering. What are some things that would cause performance problems? Plugins that write a lot of records to the database, like Audit Trail, or anything that *says* it will slow things down, like the Super Cache option to clear the cache every time a post or page is saved. There are several tools you can use to identify the problem.

First, you should make sure it's not just a temporary network or server problem. If your web host has a page or RSS feed where you can check your server's status, take a look at it and see if anything unusual is going on.

Next, see if the slowdown is due to the way your theme is constructed or the way files are being served. The YSlow extension for Firefox can help you figure out whether you just have too many images, whether HTTP compression is working on your server, or whether you have a lot of JavaScript files gumming up the works. (YSlow is, in fact, a plugin of a plugin; first you need to install the Firebug extension, and then add YSlow to it. Both tools are invaluable.)

If it's not the network, and it's not your theme, and it's not your permalinks, it's time to take a look at the database queries that run every time a page is generated on your site. If you're using a caching plugin, either turn it off or make sure that it shows uncached pages to admin users. Then install the WP Tuner plugin and view your home page. Scroll all the way to the bottom, and you'll see a huge information panel telling you everything that's going on with your database.

Look for queries highlighted in yellow. Those are the ones causing problems. Now, if it's the Start marker, as in Figure 11-9, your problem is most likely not with WordPress itself, but with your server. MySQL might not be optimized correctly, or the server hardware itself might not be up to snuff. Either way, talk to your hosting provider about the problem. In this case, all the markers showed fairly long load times. This server was very old and underpowered for the sites it was hosting. Once this site was moved to a more powerful server, all the markers' times decreased dramatically. Solving the Start problem took care of admin_notices as well.

If it's not Start, take a look at where it's coming from. Is it a plugin? Deactivate the plugin and see if your problems go away. Is it a theme? Switch to the default theme and see if the site runs faster. Is it one of the standard hooks (init, admin_head)? Use the Hooks & Filters Flow plugin (planetozh.com/blog/my-projects/wordpress-hooks-filter-flow/), which you saw in Chapter 9, to see what functions are hooked in that spot.

Sometimes, an unresponsive site doesn't mean you've done anything wrong. You could be experiencing a denial of service attack. To stop that, you'll need to work on securing your WordPress site.

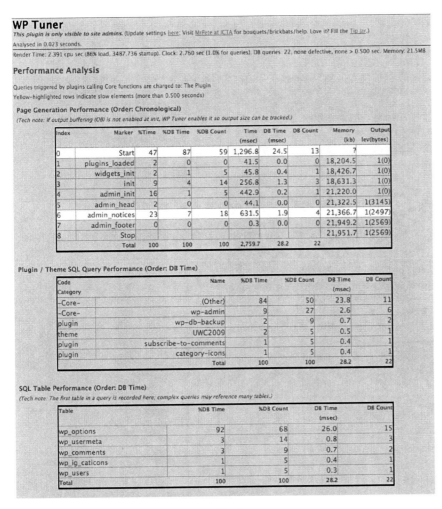

Figure 11-9. WP-Tuner output on an old, slow server

Securing Logins

In older versions of WordPress, the first user account was always named admin. This made it relatively easy for hackers to try to crack the password on the account. As of version 3.0, you can choose your username during the installation process. This cuts down on the scale of the problem, but it doesn't mitigate it entirely. You might still want to lock down your login screens. For even more security, you could force the login process to take place over SSL, thus encrypting your password transmissions. You could even conduct all your administrative tasks over SSL.

Login Lockdown

The Login Lockdown plugin helps protect you from brute force password attacks by disabling the login function for a range of IP addresses after several failed attempts in a short period of time, as shown in Figure 11-10. (Using the default settings, it will lock you out for an hour after you've failed to enter the right password three times in five minutes.) If you're the sort of person who continually forgets your password, this might not be the plugin for you! However, since guessing at administrative passwords is a common method of breaking into WordPress sites, I recommend that you pick a password you can remember and install this plugin.

Figure 11-10. An account locked out by the Login Lockdown plugin

SSL

You have a few options when it comes to SSL. You can force WordPress to use SSL for logins only, or you can use SSL for all administration sessions.

With the SSL login option, your username and password will be handled in a secure transaction. All your other traffic, including the authorization cookies you receive from WordPress, will be sent in the clear.

With SSL-only admin sessions, your username, password, and all your authorization cookies will be encrypted. While this is obviously somewhat more secure, it is slower. For most situations, SSL logins should be sufficient. The login option allows users to choose whether or not to use SSL for the entire admin session or just the login.

Listing 11-1 shows the two lines you may add to `wp-config.php` to enable SSL support. Choose just one of these!

Listing 11-1. SSL settings in wp-config.php

```
// https for all admin sessions:
define('FORCE_SSL_ADMIN', true);

//https required for login; optional for the rest of the admin session:
define('FORCE_SSL_LOGIN', true);
```

The Admin SSL plugin has always been a popular choice for managing SSL options, but as of this writing it has not been updated to work with version 2.9.

Removing The Meta Generator Tag

One of the things `wp_head()` adds to a WordPress theme's header template is a meta generator tag showing which version of WordPress you're using. It helps the WordPress developers know how many WordPress sites there are in the world. However, it's also an advertisement to would-be hackers that your site runs on WordPress—especially if you haven't updated to the latest release. Now, you should always upgrade to the newest release as soon as possible, but of course there will be times when you just can't upgrade immediately. If that's the case, you wouldn't want to advertise to the world that you're running an older, potentially insecure version of WordPress.

You can remove the meta tag altogether using the function shown in Listing 11-2, placed in your theme's `functions.php` file.

Listing 11-2. Removing the meta generator

```
remove_action('wp_head', 'wp_generator');
```

File Permissions

All the files in your WordPress installation should list you as the owner. The files that WordPress needs to write to (`.htaccess`, `wp-content`) should belong to a group that contains the web server user. For example, on a UNIX-based server running Apache, you would need to find out which user owns Apache's processes (usually it's www). On IIS, you need to know which user IIS runs as (SYSTEM). Then make sure that there's a group containing both you and the web server user. That's the group your `wp-`

content and .htaccess files should belong to. On most servers, that's done for you. However, in order to better secure your WordPress site, I recommend that you allow only wp-content to be group writable, and make sure you're the only user who can write to .htaccess.

Securing .htaccess and wp-config.php

There are a number of ways hackers could use your .htaccess file maliciously. They could use rewrite rules to redirect your visitors to a site other than yours, but that's the sort of thing you'd notice immediately, and it doesn't happen very often. A subtle attack is more likely. One particularly nasty hack involves writing a file full of spam links to a writeable subdirectory deep in the WordPress package, then using PHP's auto_prepend_file or auto_append_file directives to include that file in your theme's index.php file. At first, it looks like someone has mauled your theme, but in fact the theme files haven't changed at all. This is the sort of attack that can leave you chasing your tail for hours, unless you realize that .htaccess is a big point of vulnerability in your installation.

WordPress needs write access to your .htaccess file only to make changes to your permalink structure. If you are using WP Super Cache, the plugin also requires write access to add the cache rewrite rules to the file. However, in both cases, if WordPress cannot write to the file, it will print the necessary rules on the screen and ask you to update the file manually. Therefore, I recommend that you adjust permissions on .htaccess so that your user account is the only one allowed to write to it. On UNIX-based operating systems, you can use the chmod 744 command to make sure you can write to it while everyone else can read only.

You can also modify the .htaccess file itself to secure your wp-config.php file. Normally, any visitor requesting your configuration file will just see a blank page, since the file doesn't echo anything to the screen. However, this addition to .htaccess prevents unwanted users from viewing your config file at all.

While .htaccess is not generally accessible through a browser, either, you can apply the same technique to give it a little extra protection, as shown in Listing 11-3. It looks a little recursive, but it works!

Listing 11-3. Securing wp-config.php and .htaccess using .htaccess

```
<Files wp-config.php>
order allow,deny
deny from all
</Files>

<Files .htaccess>
order allow,deny
deny from all
</Files>
```

For more security-related modifications to .htaccess, visit www.josiahcole.com/2007/07/11/almost-perfect-htaccess-file-for-wordpress-blogs/.

Changing File Locations

It's possible to move wp-config.php and the wp-content folder. You can even put the WordPress files other than index.php in a separate subdirectory. All of these things will help minimize attacks that exploit writeable directories in predictable locations.

Moving wp-config.php

Your configuration file contains your database username and password, so it's important to keep this file secure. If you are installing WordPress in your web root directory (such as public_html), you can move your wp-config.php file to the parent directory—one that isn't readable from a browser—without changing any settings, as shown in Figure 11-11. WordPress will automatically recognize the file's new location.

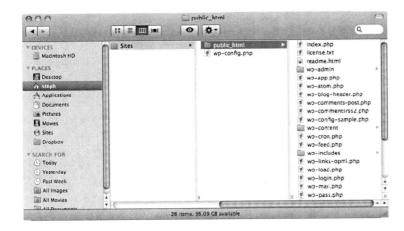

Figure 11-11. Placing wp-config.php outside the public web directory

Giving WordPress Its Own Subdirectory

If you would prefer not to have WordPress's files cluttering up your site's root directory, or you would prefer a nonstandard location for your admin files as a security precaution, you can install WordPress in a subdirectory while keeping your site visible at the original location. For example, you can install WordPress at mydomain.com/blog but have the site appear at mydomain.com.

First, install WordPress *in the subdirectory* as you normally would. Then move the main index.php file and your .htaccess file from that subdirectory into the parent directory. In your example, you would install WordPress in the blog directory, then move index.php and .htaccess into the web root directory.

Open index.php in a text editor and edit the path to wp-blog-header.php. Add your subdirectory to the file path. In this example, you're installing WordPress in the blog subdirectory, so your line would read require('./blog/wp-blog-header.php'); Of course, you can replace 'blog' with anything you wish.

Now log in to the site at its new address: mydomain.com/blog/wp-admin. Go to Settings General and change your WordPress address to the new one: mydomain.com/blog. Leave the Blog address alone, and save your changes. See Figure 11-12 for an example.

WordPress address (URL)	http://wordpress/blog
Blog address (URL)	http://wordpress

Figure 11-12. Changing the WordPress address without changing the blog address

301

Once you've saved these options, you'll be logged out. You'll have to log back in at the new location (`http://example.com/blog/wp-admin/`).

Moving wp-content

You can move your `wp-content` folder elsewhere if you like or rename it to something else. However, there are a number of constants related to the `wp-content` and `plugins` directories. To make sure your plugins continue working correctly, you should define all of these constants in your `wp-config.php` file. Add the constant definitions anywhere in the configuration file, as shown in Listing 11-4.

Listing 11-4. Renaming /wp-content to /files

```
define('WP_CONTENT_DIR', $_SERVER['DOCUMENT_ROOT'] . '/files');
define('WP_CONTENT_URL', 'http://example.com/files');
define('WP_PLUGIN_DIR', $_SERVER['DOCUMENT_ROOT'] . '/files/plugins');
define('WP_PLUGIN_URL', 'http://example.com/files/plugins');
define('PLUGINDIR', $_SERVER['DOCUMENT_ROOT'] . '/files/plugins');
```

Once you've made these changes, you also need to change the location of your uploads directory. You might recall seeing this setting in Chapter 3. Go to Settings Media and change the paths as shown in Figure 11-13.

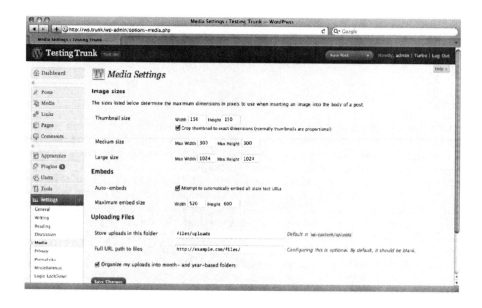

Figure 11-13. Changing the upload paths in Settings Media

Database Security

For the most part, you have to rely on your host to keep your database secure. Of course, you need to protect your database username and password (and choose a good password). There are at least two additional things you can do to help protect your database: change the table prefix and back up the database regularly.

Changing the Table Prefix

Since the default table prefix is well known, changing it is also a good step toward protecting your site from basic SQL injection attacks. If you installed WordPress with your host's one-click installer (like Fantastico), you might not have had a choice about the prefix; otherwise, the prefix is an option you chose when you filled in your database username and password (Figure 2-5).

Changing it after the fact requires you to modify the MySQL tables directly. How to accomplish this depends on what sort of database access your host allows you. I'll demonstrate using PHPMyAdmin, the most popular interface. If you don't have easy access to your database, you can try changing the prefix with the WP Security Scan plugin.

For each table in the database, click either the Browse or Structure icon, then choose Operations from the row of tabs across the top of the screen. You'll see a screen like Figure 11-14. In the Table Options group, you'll see a field where you can rename the table. Replace 'wp' with your new prefix and press the Go button.

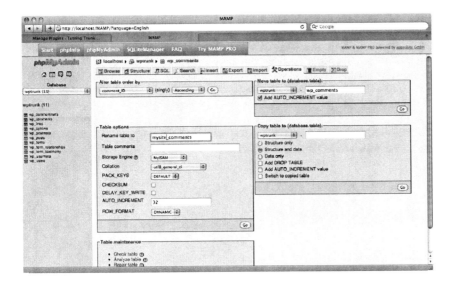

Figure 11-14. Renaming a database table

Once you've changed the tables, you'll need to update `wp-config.php` to reflect the change. The relevant portion of the configuration file is shown in Listing 11-5.

Listing 11-5. The database prefix option in wp-config.php

```
/**
 * WordPress Database Table prefix.
 *
 * You can have multiple installations in one database if you give each a unique
 * prefix. Only numbers, letters, and underscores please!
 */
$table_prefix = 'mysite_';
```

Changing the table prefix will not protect you from a determined hacker; it's basically security through obscurity. It will stop some SQL injection scripts that rely on the ubiquity of standard WordPress installations. Making yours just a little bit different from everyone else's helps. However, you should be prepared to restore your database from a clean backup if something does go wrong.

Backing Up the Database and Files

Keeping regular backups of your database is essential if you want to be able to restore your site after something has gone wrong. Your hosting provider might do this for you, but it's still a good idea to keep your own copies in case something catastrophic happens.

There are several plugins you can use to back up your database right from the WordPress administration screens. My favorite is WP-DB-Backup. Once you've installed it, you'll find a new Backup item under the Tools menu. On the plugin's screen, you'll see checkboxes for each of the tables in your WordPress database. A standard installation will look like Figure 11-15. If your plugins have added tables of their own, those will be shown in the column on the right, and you can choose which ones you want to include in the backup. If you have several installations of WordPress sharing a single database with different table prefixes, the tables with the other prefixes will also appear on the right.

To make a backup, simply check the tables you want to include, decide whether to include spam comments and post revisions, and choose your destination. If you save the backup to the server, a gzipped SQL file will be saved to the directory shown (a subdirectory of `wp-content`).

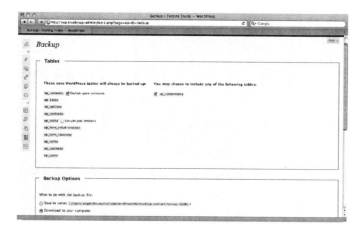

Figure 11-15. Backing up the database with the WP-DB-Backup plugin

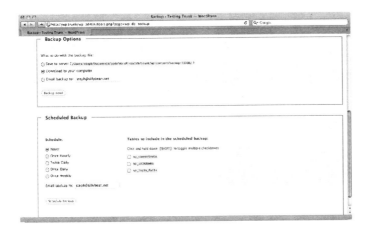

Figure 11-16. Scheduling options with WP-DB-Backup plugin

The lower half of the plugin's option screen (Figure 11-16) lets you schedule regular backups. However, these backups must be emailed to you. Make sure the email account you enter here can handle a lot of attachments (unless you're diligent about deleting old copies when the new one comes in.) The compressed file is not all that large, but over time the size will add up.

■ **Note:** As of this writing, WP-DB-Backup hasn't been updated for WordPress 2.9, so it doesn't automatically back up the new *_commentmeta table. Be sure to check off that table when you make your backups.

To restore from one of these backups, you'll need some sort of interface to your MySQL database other than WordPress itself. If your host offers PHPMyAdmin, for example, you could go to the Import tab and upload your backup file. Check your host's documentation to see how you can import SQL files into your database.

Don't forget to back up your files, too. Your uploaded media files probably wouldn't be very easy to replace, and if you've made any changes to your theme, you'll need copies of those, too. In general, it's a good idea to keep backups of your entire wp-content directory. You can automate this process with a tool like rsync (samba.anu.edu.au/rsync/) if you're feeling geeky, but I just use my FTP client's synchronize feature to download an updated copy every time I log in to make a change.

Monitoring Security Problems

There are several plugins that will help you maintain a secure installation:

WP Security Scan checks your file permissions (Figure 11-17), passwords, database security, and more. It provides tools to fix most of the problems it identifies.

WordPress Firewall monitors HTTP requests for blacklisted phrases and can email you when it finds something suspicious.

Exploit Scanner (Figure 11-18) searches your files and database for any suspicious entries, like files full of spam links.

Audit Trail (Figure 11-19) is also useful for letting you know who's been attempting to log in and what they changed.

See Appendix 1 for more security-related plugins.

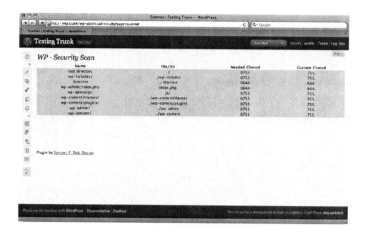

Figure 11-17. Checking file and directory permissions with WP Security Scan

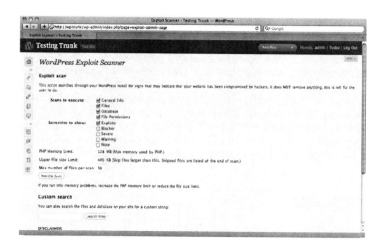

Figure 11-18. Configuring the Exploit Scanner plugin

Figure 11-19. The Audit Trail

Summary

In this chapter, I've shown you how to speed up your WordPress site and how to lock it down. I've covered caching with WP Super Cache, choosing efficient permalink structures, and identifying performance bottlenecks with WP Tuner and YSlow. To secure your site, I've talked about barring users from multiple login attempts, using SSL for logins and/or full admin sessions, and securing both your files and your database. Finally, I've shown you a handful of plugins that help you keep an eye on your installation. Now that you know what to look for, these tools should help you maintain a fast, healthy WordPress site.

Now that you've seen everything involved in managing a standard WordPress site, I'll show you how to customize your content. In the next chapter, you'll learn how to create custom fields to store extra information in each of your articles. You'll also learn how to create custom taxonomies—new sets of tags and categories you can use to organize your content. You'll even create whole new content types.

■ ■ ■

CHAPTER 12

Custom Content Types, Taxonomies, and Fields

In the preceding chapters, I've shown you how to bend posts, pages, categories, and tags to your needs. However, these types of content aren't always sufficient, and sometimes it's just not feasible to have several kinds of content jumbled together under Posts.

In this chapter, I'll show you how to use custom taxonomies to create separate groups of categories and tags for your existing content. Then I'll show you how to create whole new content types. Finally, I'll show you how to extend content types (including posts and pages) with custom fields for even more flexibility.

If you want to get custom post types and/or taxonomies up and running quickly on your site, try the Custom Post Types UI plugin. It provides a simple user interface for managing both content types and taxonomies. If, however, you're creating content types and taxonomies as part of a plugin for a more portable solution, read on!

Custom Taxonomies

First, some terminology. A *taxonomy* is a group of terms. *Terms* are individual choices. For example, Post Tags is a taxonomy, and each tag is a term within that taxonomy. Likewise, Post Categories is a taxonomy, and each category is a term. Each taxonomy has a label, a slug, and a description. Individual terms also have labels, slugs, and descriptions. You've seen this before when creating a new category.

Custom taxonomies were introduced in version 2.3, but there was no built-in user interface for them until version 2.8, and very few developers used them. In 2.8, UI support for non-hierarchical taxonomies was added. In 3.0, hierarchical taxonomies are now supported as well, which means you don't have to do the work of creating meta boxes and saving taxonomy terms to the database; WordPress does all that for you. All you have to do is register your new taxonomy and define its labels.

Creating a new taxonomy requires just one function: `register_taxonomy()`. However, the arguments can get a little complicated, and there's a bit more work you have to do to make permalinks work. Listing 12-1 shows all the possible arguments for a new taxonomy.

Listing 12-1. Registering a new taxonomy

```
register_taxonomy(
        'people', //Taxonomy name
        array('attachment:image', 'attachment:video', 'attachment:audio', 'post', 'page'),
//Content object type
        array(
                'labels' => array(
```

```
                         'name' => __( 'People' ),
                         'singular_name' => __( 'Person' ),
                         ),
              'helps' => __('Separate names with commas.'),
              'rewrite' => array('slug' => 'person'),
              'query_var' => true,
              'show_ui' => true,
              'show_tagcloud' => true,
              'hierarchical' => false,
         )
    );
```

Let's break down these arguments:

- Taxonomy name: an internal name for the new taxonomy.

- Content object type: the types of content that can use this taxonomy. This argument can be a string containing a single content type or it can be an array of several content types, as shown in Listing 12-1.

- Other arguments: an array containing:

  - labels: an array containing the name (plural) and the singular name. These provide the text for the administration screens' navigation menu item (beneath Categories and Post Tags) leading to the management page for this taxonomy; and the title for the taxonomy's meta box on the Post → Edit screen. (See Figure 12-1.) The singular name ensures that the management page for your taxonomy is grammatically correct. ("Add a new genre" instead of "Add a new genres;" see Figure 12-2.)

  - helps: the instructive text that appears below the entry field on the Post → Edit screen. Applies only to non-hierarchical taxonomies.

  - rewrite: possible values are:

    - False: no permalink rules will be created for this taxonomy.

    - True: the permalink structure will be /?taxonomy=term in the default structure or /taxonomy/term using any other permalink structure.

    - Array containing a slug: the slug will be used in place of the taxonomy name. (See Listing 12-2 for examples of each rewrite method.)

  - query_var: possible values are:

    - False: this taxonomy will not be available in custom queries

- True: you can use the taxonomy name in queries. In this case, query_posts('genre=fantasy'); would return any books tagged with "fantasy" as the genre, as shown in Figure 12-6.

- String: the given string will be the query variable rather than the taxonomy name. (See the Authors taxonomy in Listing 12-2 for the proper syntax.)

- show_ui: whether or not the management screens and meta boxes should be shown for this taxonomy. Defaults to true. You could set this to false if you were creating a hidden taxonomy that would be used in your plugin code, but never by users.

- show_tagcloud: whether this taxonomy should be an option in the tag cloud widget. (See Figure 12-3.) Defaults to the value of show_ui. Applies only to non-hierarchical taxonomies.

- hierarchical: whether this taxonomy should be hierarchical (category-like) or non-hierarchical (tag-like). Defaults to false (tag-like).

The resulting People taxonomy meta box is shown in Figure 12-1.

Figure 12-1. The People taxonomy

You can register as many new taxonomies as you need. Let's start with some tag-like, non-hierarchical ones.

Non-hierarchical Taxonomies

Non-hierarchical taxonomies are just like tags. They don't have parent/child relationships. The meta box added to the Post → Edit screen looks like the tag entry field: a single text input box with an autocomplete feature.

To illustrate, let's create the taxonomies for a hypothetical site listing books that are part of a series. For this project, you want separate taxonomies for the genre, the series status, and the author(s) of the books (as opposed to the post author). Keep the regular post tag field—use it for general keywords associated with the books.

Listing 12-2 shows the new taxonomies you'll use to create the series books site. Since there are three of them, wrap them into a single function, which is called using the `init()` action hook. (This is exactly how the built-in taxonomies are created.)

In addition to creating the taxonomies themselves, you must flush the rewrite rules (which are cached) in order for the new rewrite rules to take effect. Since this needs to be done just once, wrap it up in a plugin activation function. This function calls `create_book_series_tax()` once to get all the new rewrite rules into place, then flushes the rewrite rules. This forces the list of rewrite rules to be rebuilt, and the new ones will be included.

Listing 12-2. Creating the series book taxonomies

```php
<?php
/*
Plugin Name: Series Book Taxonomies
*/

add_action('init', 'create_book_series_tax');
register_activation_hook( __FILE__, 'activate_book_series_tax' );

function activate_book_series_tax() {
        create_book_series_tax();
        $GLOBALS['wp_rewrite']->flush_rules();
}

function create_book_series_tax() {
        register_taxonomy(
                'genre',
                'post',
                array(
                        'labels' => array(
                                'name' => __( 'Genres' ),
                                'singular_name' => __( 'Genre' ),
                        ),
                        'helps' => __('Separate genres with commas.'),
                )
        );
        register_taxonomy(
                'author',
                array('attachment:image', 'attachment:video', 'attachment:audio', 'post',
'page'),
                array(
                        'labels' => array(
```

```
                        'name' => __( 'Authors' ),
                        'singular_name' => __( 'Author' ),
                    ),
                    'helps' => __('Separate authors with commas.'),
                    'rewrite' => array('slug' => 'author'),
                    'query_var' => 'author',
            )
        );
        register_taxonomy(
                'status',
                'post',
                array(
                    'labels' => array(
                            'name' => __( 'Completion Status' ),
                            'singular_name' => __( 'Status' ),
                    ),
                    'helps' => __('Enter the series status (completed, ongoing, etc.).'),
            )
        );
}

?>
```

Here, you omit all the arguments that would be set to their default values (`rewrite`, `query_var`, `show_ui`, `show_tagcloud`, and `hierarchical`) except on the Authors taxonomy, where I've demonstrated how you would change the rewrite and query slugs if you wanted to. I also used the Authors taxonomy to show how you could add a taxonomy to more than one type of content. In this case, it's possible that your site will include photos of an author, or even a video or sound file. You've added all the possible content types. (Custom taxonomies don't work for links.)

Figure 12-2 shows the resulting meta boxes on the Post → Edit screen. Figure 12-3 shows the management page for the status taxonomy, and Figure 12-4 shows the tag cloud widget options once all three taxonomies have been added.

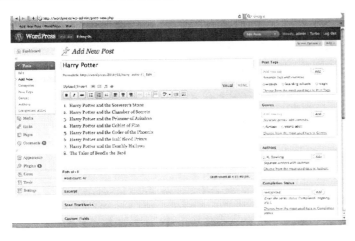

Figure 12-2. The resulting taxonomy boxes, on the right

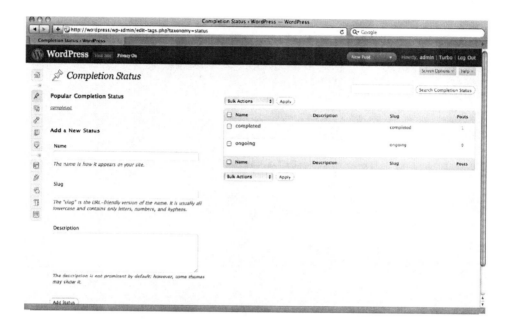

Figure 12-3. The management page for the Completion Status taxonomy

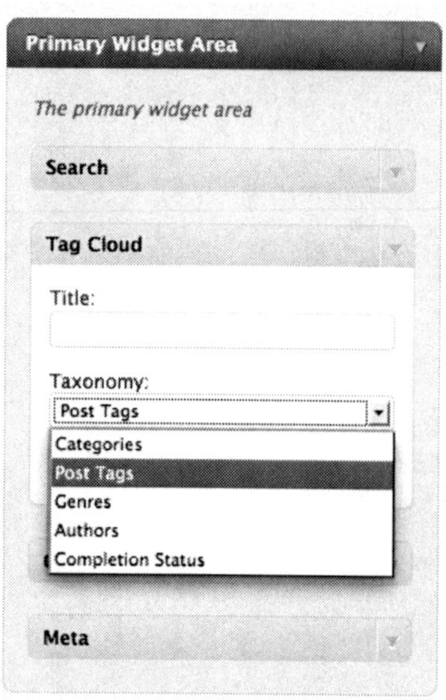

Figure 12-4. The tag cloud widget with the new taxonomy options

Hierarchical Taxonomies

Hierarchical taxonomies are like categories. They can have parents and children, and the meta box on the Post → Edit screen looks just like the category box.

For the book series site, you might want your users to classify things in fine-grained subgenres, not just the major categories one would find in a bookstore. To do this, just add one line of the `register_taxonomy()` arguments, as shown in Listing 12-3. Since helps ("Separate genres with commas") are not shown for hierarchical taxonomies, remove that argument.

Listing 12-3. Changing Genres to a hierarchical taxonomy

```
register_taxonomy(
        'genre',
        'post',
        array(
                'labels' => array(
                        'name' => __( 'Genres' ),
                        'singular_name' => __( 'Genre' ),
                ),
                'hierarchical' => true,
        )
);
```

Figure 12-5 shows a post with the altered Genres taxonomy meta box. You've added a few more genres, too. The Categories meta box is still present; here, it's just out of view, near the bottom of the screen. Figure 12-6 shows the management screen for the Genres taxonomy, which now looks just like the category management screen.

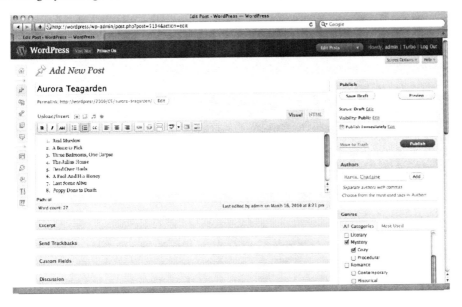

Figure 12-5. A hierarchical taxonomy in Post → Edit

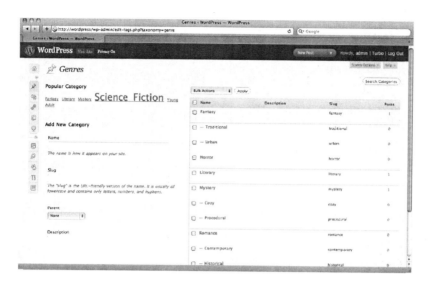

Figure 12-6. The management screen for the Genres taxonomy

Using Custom Taxonomies

If you publish the Harry Potter post shown in Figure 12-2, you can then browse to your archive page using the permalink structure you created and one of the terms you assigned. In this case, /genre/fantasy results in the archive page shown in Figure 12-7.

Figure 12-7. The fantasy genre archive page

As you can see, this archive page is a little generic. The Twenty Ten theme does not include a taxonomy archive template, so the title of the page is simply "Blog Archives." In order to fix it up, you can either add a conditional statement checking `is_tax()` to your generic `archive.php` template, or you can create a `taxonomy.php` template. Let's use the latter option. Listing 12-4 shows a basic taxonomy template for Twenty Ten.

Listing 12-4. A new taxonomy.php file for the Twenty Ten theme

```php
<?php get_header(); ?>

                <div id="container">
                        <div id="content">

<?php the_post(); ?>
                <h1 class="page-title">
                <?php
                        $term = get_term_by( 'slug', get_query_var( 'term' ), get_query_var(
'taxonomy' ) );

                        echo ucwords($term->taxonomy) . ': ' . $term->name;
                ?></h1>

<?php rewind_posts(); ?>

<?php get_generic_template( 'loop', 'archive' ); ?>

                        </div><!-- #content -->
                </div><!-- #container -->

<?php get_sidebar(); ?>
<?php get_footer(); ?>
```

All that's changed from `archive.php` is that you've removed the date-based conditionals and replaced the standard title with a bit of code that fetches the current taxonomy and term. Here, you've added PHP's `ucwords()` function to make sure the taxonomy name is uppercase, no matter how the user entered it. This changes the archive title in Figure 12-6 to "Genre: Fantasy." That's still rather lackluster; you can do better.

Listing 12-5 shows a revised heading tag. You can put this in a `taxonomy-genre.php` file, where you know your grammar will be correct for any of the genre terms.

Listing 12-5. The <h1> heading in taxonomy-genre.php

```php
<h1 class="page-title">
        <?php
        $term = get_term_by( 'slug', get_query_var( 'term' ), get_query_var( 'taxonomy' ) );
        echo 'Posts in the '.$term->name.' '.$term->taxonomy;
?></h1>
```

This gives provides the "Posts in the Fantasy genre" which is much better.

It would also be nice to include the taxonomies in the post's meta data alongside the categories and post tags. You could use `the_taxonomies()`, but this function is indiscriminate and prints *all* the taxonomies, including the built-in ones. There's no way to limit it to a particular taxonomy. Its output for the Harry Potter post is shown in Listing 12-6.

Listing 12-6. Result of the_taxonomies()

```
Categories: Main. Post Tags: boarding schools, magic, and wizards. Genres: Fantasy and Young
Adult. Authors: J. K. Rowling. Completion Status: completed.
```

To list just one taxonomy at a time with better control over the output, add them to the template individually, using `get_the_term_list()` as shown in Listing 12-7. This function won't print anything if there are no terms associated with the post, so you don't need to check first to see if it's empty.

Listing 12-7. Listing the terms of a particular taxonomy alongside categories and tags

```php
<p>Posted in <?php the_category(',') ?>
<?php echo get_the_term_list( $post->ID, 'series', 'in the series ', ', ', '' ); ?></p>
<?php if ( the_tags('<p>Tagged with ', ', ', '</p>') ) ?>
```

WordPress doesn't provide an archive page for a taxonomy as a whole. That is, there's no page automatically built that will list all the terms used in a particular taxonomy; you have to build one yourself. Listing 12-8 shows how to create a linked list of all the terms in a particular taxonomy.

Listing 12-8. Listing taxonomy terms

```php
<ul id="authors">
    <?php
        $authors = get_terms('authors');
        foreach ($authors as $author) { ?>
            <li><a href="<?php echo get_term_link( $author, 'authors') ?>"><?php echo
$author->name; ?></a> <span class="comments"><?php echo $author->description; ?></span>  </li>
    <?php } ?>
</ul>
```

You could turn that into a widget or just put it into a sidebar. For the purpose of demonstration, however, let's add a page template containing this code in place of the content. The result is shown in Figure 12-8.

Figure 12-8. The author term list

There's also no built-in way to display all the taxonomies. The get_taxonomies() function will display them, but it includes all the registered taxonomies, including the defaults, as shown in Listing 12-9.

Listing 12-9. Listing all registered taxonomies

```
<ul id="taxonomies">
<?php
        $taxes = get_taxonomies();
        foreach ($taxes as $tax) echo '<li>'.$tax.'</li>';
?>
</ul>
```

If you're using the series books taxonomies, the list will be:

- category

- post_tag

- nav_menu

- link_category

- genre

- author

- status

To remove the built-in taxonomies from the list and show only the custom taxonomies you've created, use the taxonomies' _builtin argument. It's a private argument intended for WordPress's internal use, but since you're not abusing it to create your own "built-in" taxonomy, you can use it to filter your taxonomy list, as shown in Listing 12-10.

Listing 12-10. Listing only custom taxonomies

```
<ul id="taxonomies">
<?php
        $taxes = get_taxonomies(array('_builtin' => false));
        foreach ($taxes as $tax) echo '<li>'.$tax.'</li>';
?>
</ul>
```

Now the result is more useful:

- genre

- author

- status

319

Other Taxonomy Examples

The Taxes plugin (`core.trac.wordpress.org/attachment/ticket/6357/taxes.php`) was written a few years ago to demonstrate the then-new taxonomy features. It provides a way to tag all your content—posts, pages, and media uploads—with people's names, much like the tagging features on Flickr and Facebook. Figure 12-9 shows what the media uploader looks like with the People taxonomy included.

Figure 12-9. People tagging in the media uploader

The Series plugin is another great example. It's used to organize posts that are part of an ongoing series, as shown in Figure 12-10.

Figure 12-10. A list of posts in the Series plugin

Here you can see why you might want to create taxonomy-specific archive templates. Your site might not be as mixed up as the demo, but here's the genre tag cloud appearing on the tutorial series archive page. If you don't really need to create a whole new template file, you might use conditional tags to include different sidebars for each.

Custom Content Types

While custom taxonomies provide a powerful way to organize posts, sometimes that organization just isn't enough. For a blogger, using posts for movie and book reviews as well as slice-of-life vignettes might suffice, but posts and pages can be too limiting a framework for more complex sites.

WordPress 3.0 provides methods of creating whole new content types. New types can be hierarchical, like pages, or non-hierarchical, like posts. As you create the new types, you can choose which attributes (revisions, thumbnails, etc.) they support. And, of course, you can assign taxonomies to your custom types.

■ **Note:** Custom content types are also referred to as custom *post* types throughout the WordPress documentation, since posts are the underlying basis for all other content types.

Let's consider a real-world scenario: a university department site containing information about specific courses as well as news updates (the blog) and informational pages (hours and location, a staff directory, etc.). Without custom content types, the choice lies between posts and pages. Since the office would like to publish a feed of all the honors courses available (and individual feeds for each college), they have elected to use posts to store the course information. Figure 12-11 shows a typical course post.

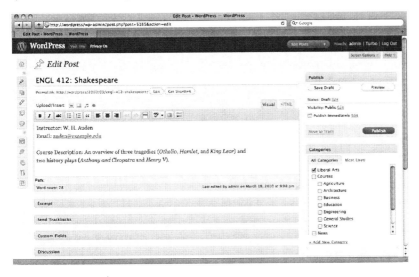

Figure 12-11. The original course post

You can make this office's workflow a lot better using a custom content type for the courses. In WordPress 3.0, creating new content types is as easy as creating new taxonomies. The `register_post_type()` function looks an awful lot like `register_taxonomy()`, and many of its attributes work the same way. Listing 12-11 shows a sample content type with all the possible arguments.

Listing 12-11. Creating a new content type

```
register_post_type(
        'mytype',
        array(
                'labels' => array(
                        'name' => __( 'My Types' ),
                        'singular_name' => __( 'My Type' ),
                ),
                'public' => true,
                'supports' => array(
                        'title',
                        'editor',
                        'author',
                        'excerpts',
                        'custom-fields',
                        'revisions',
                        'thumbnail')
                )
        );
register_taxonomy_for_object_type('category', 'mytype');
register_taxonomy_for_object_type('post-tag', 'mytype');
?>
```

As with taxonomies, the post types are created with a handle and an array of attributes. Here are all of the possible attributes:

- labels: an array containing the names of the content type in their plural ('name') and singular ('singular_name') forms.

- description: a short description of the content type. Empty by default.

- public: whether this content type should be shown in the admin screens. False (hidden) by default.

- exclude_from_search: whether content of this post type should be excluded from search results. By default, inherits the value of public.

- publicly_queryable: whether queries can be performed using the post_type argument. By default, inherits the value of public.

- show_ui: whether Edit and Add New screens should be added for this post type. By default, inherits the value of public.

- inherit_type: if you would like the new type to use the capabilities of an existing type, use this argument to set it.

- capability_type: content type for read_, edit_, and delete_ capabilities. Post is the default type used if no other is specified. You can use this argument to create a whole new set of capabilities specific to the new content type (e.g. 'course').

- capabilities: an array of capabilities ('edit_post,' 'delete_post,' 'publish_posts'). If you created a new capability_type, these values will default to the standard post capabilities with the name of your content type substituted for 'post' (e.g. 'edit_course,' 'delete_course,' 'publish_courses').

- hierarchical: whether the post type is hierarchical (page-like). False (post-like) by default.

- Supports: as a substitute for calling the `add_post_type_support()` function, list supported features here. Defaults to none. The possible features are:

    o   author: the user writing the custom entry

    o   title: whether this content type includes a title

    o   editor: whether the visual/HTML content textarea and media uploader should be used

    o   excerpts: whether the excerpts field should be used

    o   thumbnail: whether this content type should include image thumbnails

    o   comments: whether comments will be accepted for this content type

    o   trackbacks: whether trackbacks will be accepted for this content type

    o   custom-fields: whether the Custom Fields box will be shown and custom fields automatically saved.

    o   revisions: whether revisions will be stored and displayed.

    o   page-attributes: the Page Attributes box, containing the parent, template, and menu order options.

- register_meta_box_cb: the name of a callback function that will set up any custom meta boxes for the edit screens. This function should contain any `remove_meta_box()` and `add_meta_box()` calls.

- Taxonomies: an array of taxonomy names that will be used by the content type. Default is none. You can register taxonomies later with `register_taxonomy()` or `register_taxonomy_for_object_type()`.

Note that `public` is true by default for taxonomies but is false by default for post types. The `query_vars`, `rewrite`, and `show_ui` attributes all inherit from `public`, so be sure to set `public` to true (or turn on each of those items individually).

Non-hierarchical (Post-like) Content Types

Let's start transforming the courses by creating a new content type for a university. Listing 12-12 shows a simple plugin that creates a new nonhierarchical content type—something very similar to posts. As with `register_taxonomy()`, you don't have to include arguments if you plan to use the default values.

Listing 12-12. Creating a non-hierarchical content type for courses

```
function post_type_courses() {
      register_post_type(
            'course',
            array(
                  'labels' => array(
                        'name' => __( 'Courses' ),
                        'singular_name' => __( 'Course' ),
                  ),
                  'public' => true,
                  'supports' => array(
                        'title',
                        'editor',
                        'author',
                        'excerpt',
                        'custom-fields',
                        'revisions',)
                  )
            );
      register_taxonomy_for_object_type('category', 'course');
}
```

In this case, you've decided that the course type should not support comments or trackbacks and will use categories but not tags.

If you activate this little plugin, your navigation menu will immediately gain a new section just below Comments: Courses, with options to edit, add a new course, or manage course categories (Figure 12-12). Tags aren't shown because you didn't add `post_tag` to the list of fields this content type supports. Also, note that "Series" appears under Posts, but not Courses. (The Series plugin was still activated from another project, and the plugin's taxonomy is assigned only to posts.)

Figure 12-12. Activating the course plugin; new Courses menu section now available

Now you need to change your old course posts to the new course content type. All content types are stored in the `wp_posts` table, and the only difference at the database level is the `post_type` field. If you don't want to copy and paste all your old posts into the new content type, you could just edit the database records directly (Figure 12-13) or write a SQL query to do this for all the posts you need to convert.

Figure 12-13. Changing the content type in the wp_posts table

Now, go to Courses → Edit and see all the posts you converted to courses (in this case, just one, as shown in Figure 12-14). If you publish this course, you can see it at its new permalink (Figure 12-15). Note that permalinks for custom content types are not editable; they follow the rewrite rules specified in the `register_post_type()` arguments.

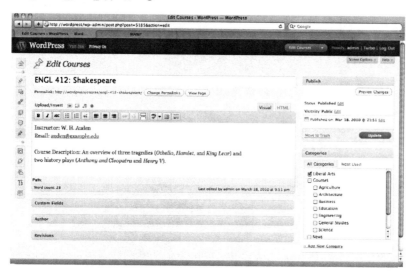

Figure 12-14. Editing the new course

Figure 12-15. The new course as it appears on the site

Now you have a post-like content type for your courses. However, the office might need to create several related entries for each course: a general overview, a syllabus, and a reading list. In that case, it would make more sense to create the courses as hierarchical content types, like pages.

Hierarchical (Page-like) Content Types

A hierarchical content type can have children, just as pages do. Listing 12-13 shows how to revise the plugin created in Listing 12-12 to make courses hierarchical.

Listing 12-13. Creating a non-hierarchical content type for courses

```php
<?php
/*
Plugin Name: Course Post Types
*/

/* Content Types */

add_action('init', 'post_type_courses');

function post_type_courses() {
        register_post_type(
                'course',
                array(
                        'labels' => array(
                                'name' => __( 'Courses' ),
                                'singular_name' => __( 'Course' ),
                        ),
                        'public' => true,
                        'show_ui' => true,
                                'rewrite' => true,
                                'query_var' => true,
                                'hierarchical' => true,
                                'supports' => array(
                                        'title',
                                        'editor',
                                        'author',
                                        'excerpt',
                                        'custom-fields',
                                        'revisions',
                                        'page-attributes',)
                        )
                );
        register_taxonomy_for_object_type('category', 'course');
}
?>
```

Now your editing screen will look more like a page, as shown in Figure 12-16. And, since you now have the Attributes meta box, you can choose parents.

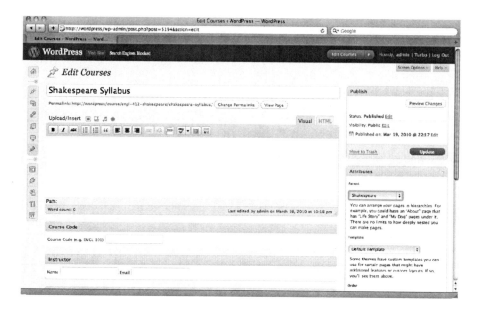

Figure 12-16. Editing the hierarchical content type with attributes meta box

Custom Taxonomies for Custom Content Types

Let's say the department in question is the Honors office. This office tracks the Honors courses offered in each college. Before custom content types came along, they would use categories for each college, but those categories were mixed in with the general blog categories (news, scholarships) and the office's podcast.

You can instead use a custom taxonomy for your colleges. Once you've created the taxonomies, you have to register them for the course content type. Listing 12-14 shows the complete revised plugin. You've removed the standard category taxonomy and replaced it with a new one, colleges, which is defined below.

The resulting changes to the Courses → Edit screen are shown in Figure 12-17. For the rest of this chapter, let's stick with a non-hierarchical content type.

Listing 12-14. Adding custom taxonomies to the course content type

```php
<?php
/*
Plugin Name: Course Post Types
*/

/* Content Types */

add_action('init', 'post_type_courses');

function post_type_courses() {
```

```php
        register_post_type(
                'course',
                array(
                        'labels' => array(
                                'name' => __( 'Courses' ),
                                'singular_name' => __( 'Course' ),
                        ),
                        'public' => true,
                        'supports' => array(
                                'title',
                                'editor',
                                'author',
                                'excerpt',
                                'custom-fields',
                                'revisions',)
                        )
                );
        register_taxonomy_for_object_type('college', 'course');
}

/* Taxonomies */

add_action('init', 'create_course_series_tax');
register_activation_hook( __FILE__, 'activate_course_series_tax' );

function activate_course_series_tax() {
        create_course_series_tax();
        $GLOBALS['wp_rewrite']->flush_rules();
}

function create_course_series_tax() {
                register_taxonomy(
                'college',
                'course',
                array(
                        'labels' => array(
                                'name' => __( 'Colleges' ),
                                'singular_name' => __( 'College' ),
                        ),
                        'hierarchical' => true,
                )
        );
}
?>
```

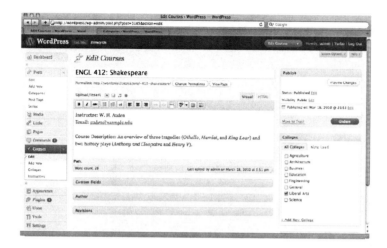

Figure 12-17. Editing a course with the new taxonomy

Changing Edit Screen Columns

Since you've added the college taxonomy to the course content type, it would be great if you could see the colleges on the Edit Courses screen. Adding columns to the edit screen is a two-step process: first, define the column headers, and second, define the contents of the new column.

Changing Column Headers

The code to add a new column is fairly simple. Listing 12-15 shows how to add a column for the college taxonomy to the Edit Courses screen.

Listing 12-15. Changing column headers for the course content type

```
/* Custom Edit Columns */
add_filter("manage_edit-course_columns", "course_taxonomy_columns");

// rearrange the columns on the Edit screens
function course_taxonomy_columns($defaults) {
        // insert college taxonomy column
        $defaults['colleges'] = __('Colleges');
        return $defaults;
}
```

First, you call the appropriate filter, in this case `manage_edit-course_columns()`. (Replace 'course' with the name of your content type.) You're filtering an array containing the names of the column headings. To add a column, all you have to do is add an item to the array. However, that would place this column at the far right side of the table, after the comment and date columns. To make this page look more like the Edit Posts screen, you need to rearrange the columns, as shown in Listing 12-16.

Listing 12-16. Rearranging column headers

```
add_filter("manage_edit-course_columns", "course_taxonomy_columns");

// rearrange the columns on the Edit screens
function course_taxonomy_columns($defaults) {
        // preserve the default date and comment columns
        $comments = $defaults['comments'];
        $date = $defaults['date'];

        // remove default date and comments
        unset($defaults['comments']);
        unset($defaults['date']);

        // insert college taxonomy column
        $defaults['colleges'] = __('Colleges');

        // restore default date and comments
        $defaults['comments'] = $comments;
        $defaults['date'] = $date;

        return $defaults;
}
```

In this example, the first thing you need to do is preserve the contents of the comment and date columns, so you don't have to recreate them from scratch later. (The comment column contains an image rather than just text.) Next, remove these two columns from the array. Then, add your custom column, colleges. Finally, add back the original columns in the order in which you want them to appear.

The resulting column arrangement is shown in Figure 12-18.

Figure 12-18. The new Edit screen column

Displaying Column Contents

Now that your new column is in place, you need to fill it with some information—in this case, the list of colleges chosen for each course. Listing 12-17 shows the necessary filter.

Listing 12-17. Displaying the college taxonomy terms in the new Edit screen column

```
add_action("manage_pages_custom_column", "course_taxonomy_custom_column");
// for non-hierarchical content types, use the following instead:
// add_action("manage_posts_custom_column", "course_taxonomy_custom_column");

// print the college taxonomy terms, linked to filter the posts to this taxonomy term only
function course_taxonomy_custom_column($column) {
        global $post;
        if ($column == 'colleges') {
                $colleges = get_the_terms($post->ID, 'college');
                if (!empty($colleges)) {
                        $thecolleges = array();
                        foreach ($colleges as $college) {
                                $thecolleges[] = '<a
href="edit.php?post_type=course&college='.$college->slug.'>' .
esc_html(sanitize_term_field('name', $college->name, $college->term_id, 'college', 'display'))
. "</a>";
                        }
                        echo implode(', ', $thecolleges);
                }
        }
}
```

Here, you use a couple of if() statements to make sure that you're working with the proper column and that the course is assigned to at least one college. Then, you build an array of links based on the URLs on the Edit screens for other content types. These links would filter the list of courses to the chosen college, just as you'd expect. Finally, once the foreach() loop has finished, you use implode() to print the list of links separated by commas.

Figure 12-19 shows the completed Edit Courses screen.

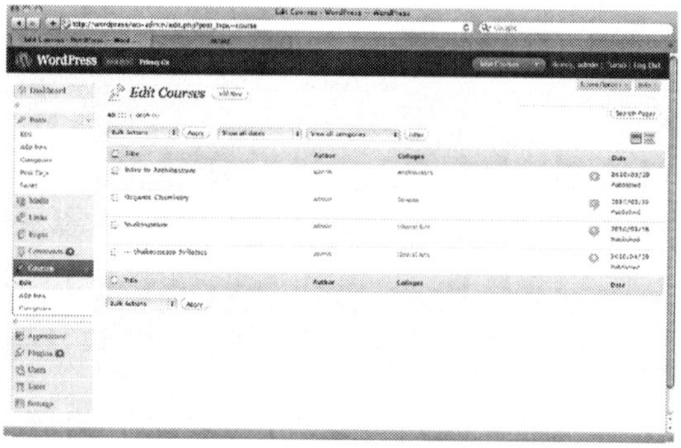

Figure 12-19. The Edit Courses screen with the completed college taxonomy column

Including Custom Content Types in Your Theme

To create a single archive page for a custom content type, all you have to do is create another file in your theme directory, single-*type*.php. However, there is no built-in way to create a dedicated archive for a custom content type. To work around this, you must use a page template. Listing 12-18 shows an example archive template for Twenty Ten. Save this to your theme directory, then create a new page called Course Archives and choose this file as its page template (Figure 12-20).

Listing 12-18. A content archive page template for courses

```php
<?php
/*
Template Name: Custom Content Archive
*/

$wp_query = null;
$wp_query = new WP_Query();
$wp_query->query('post_type=course');
$posts = null;
$posts = $wp_query->posts;
?>

<?php get_header(); ?>


<div id="container">
        <div id="content">

<?php if ($wp_query->have_posts() ) : while ($wp_query->have_posts() ) : $wp_query-
>the_post(); ?>
        <div id="post-<?php the_ID(); ?>" <?php post_class(); ?>>
                <h1 class="entry-title"><?php the_title(); ?></h1>
                <div class="entry-content">
                        <?php the_content(); ?>
                </div><!-- .entry-content -->
        </div><!-- #post-<?php the_ID(); ?> -->
<?php endwhile; endif; ?>

        </div><!-- #content -->
</div><!-- #container -->

<?php get_sidebar(); ?>
<?php get_footer(); ?>
```

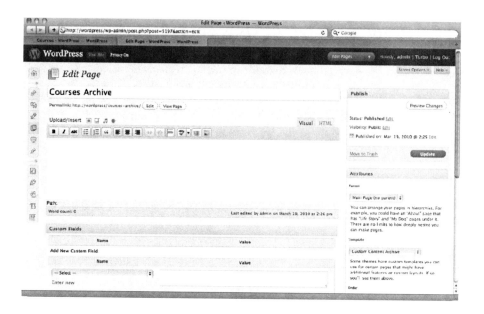

Figure 12-20. Creating the custom content archive page

This template includes an alternative method of creating custom Loops that you haven't seen before. In this case, since you don't want to just modify the standard query—that would get posts as well as courses—you need to create a whole new query object, then call the have_posts() and the_post() functions as methods of this new object. (In fact, those functions always were methods of the $wp_query object, but like most things about the Loop, that part was invisible to you as long as you were working with the standard query.) Once you've set up the_post(), you can use all the usual content-related template tags.

The resulting archive page is shown in Figure 12-21.

Justin Tadlock has demonstrated how to add custom content types to a home page and main feed (justintadlock.com/archives/2010/02/02/showing-custom-post-types-on-your-home-blog-page). You can adapt his code, as shown in Listing 12-19, to show courses in the home page. This function and filter can go in the custom content plugin you created in Listing 12-12 or your theme's functions.php file.

Listing 12-19. Showing the course content type alongside posts on the home page

```
add_filter( 'pre_get_posts', 'my_get_posts' );

function my_get_posts( $query ) {
        if ( is_home() )
                $query->set( 'post_type', array( 'post', 'course' ) );
        return $query;
}
```

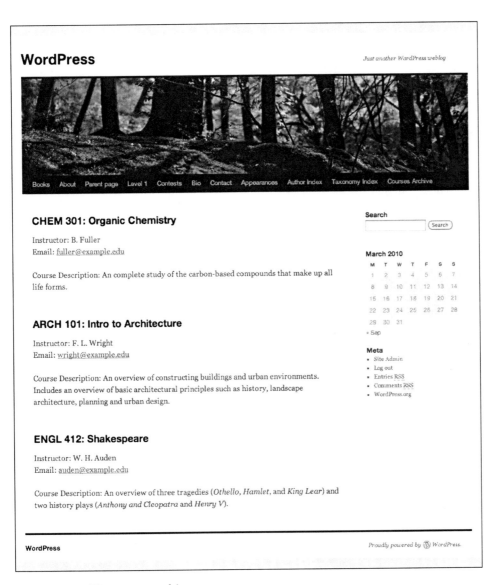

Figure 12-21. The courses archive page

Feeds for Custom Content Types

You can use the `pre_get_posts()` filter to include custom content types in feeds as well as the home page. The required change is shown in Listing 12-20.

Listing 12-20. Showing the course content type alongside posts in the site feed

```
add_filter( 'pre_get_posts', 'my_get_posts' );

function my_get_posts( $query ) {
        if ( is_home() || is_feed() )
                $query->set( 'post_type', array( 'post', 'course' ) );
        return $query;
}
```

However, for the Honors office, it would make more sense to separate the courses from the posts feed, which is used for office news.

As you saw in Chapter 4, there are many feeds that aren't publicized in WordPress. You can use a query string format similar to the one you used for searches to get feeds of your custom content types. The `post_type` parameter given should match the name of your custom content type. You can even combine content types using the parameters instead of filters. Table 12-1 lists some of the possible feed URLs for custom content types.

Table 12-1. Course content type feeds in WordPress

Feed Type	Default URL	Clean URL
RSS 2.0 (default)	/?feed=rss2&post_type=course	/feed/?post_type=course /feed/rss2/?post_type=course
Atom 1.0	/?feed=atom&post_type=course	/feed/atom/?post_type=course
RSS 0.92	/?feed=rss&post_type=course	/feed/rss/?post_type=course
RDF	/?feed=rdf&post_type=course	/feed/rdf/?post_type=course
Combining content types	/?feed=rss2&post_type=course,post,page	/feed/?post_type=course,post,page

Custom Fields in Custom Content Types

Let's take a closer look at the content of the course in Figure 12-17. There are really three distinct pieces of information lumped into that textarea: the instructor's name, his e-mail address, and a brief description of the course. Furthermore, the title field contains the university's internal code (ENGL 412) as well as the actual course title. What if the office asks you to create a table of honors courses with the code and the title in separate, sortable columns? There's no good way to separate that data with the standard WordPress fields.

The course description can stay in the content field, but the course code, instructor name, and e-mail address would all be better off in separate custom fields. However, the standard custom field interface is not very friendly, and the office's administrative assistant is not going to find it intuitive. You ought to provide a better interface for adding this information.

Creating the Custom Fields

First, you have to modify your post type function to add a callback. This is the name of the function that will add (and/or remove) custom meta boxes from the Edit screen. Listing 12-21 shows the change.

Listing 12-21. Updating the post_type_courses() function to include callback argument

```
function post_type_courses() {
        register_post_type(
                'course',
                array(
                        'labels' => array(
                                'name' => __( 'Courses' ),
                                'singular_name' => __( 'Course' ),
                        ),
                        'description' => __('Individual course data'),
                        'public' => true,
                        'show_ui' => true,
                        'register_meta_box_cb' => 'course_meta_boxes',
                        'supports' => array(
                                'title',
                                'editor',
                                'author',
                                'excerpt',
                                'custom-fields',
                                'revisions',)
                        )
                );
        register_taxonomy_for_object_type('college', 'course');
}
```

Then you need to add the course_meta_boxes() function, as shown in Listing 12-22. You'll add a whole new section to the Course Post Types plugin to handle the custom meta boxes, and this will be the first part of that section.

Listing 12-22. The callback function that adds meta boxes

```
/* Custom Fields */

function course_meta_boxes() {
        add_meta_box( 'course_code_meta', __('Course Code'), 'course_code_meta_box', 'course',
'normal', 'high' );
        add_meta_box( 'instructor_meta', __('Instructor'), 'instructor_meta_box', 'course',
'normal', 'high' );
}
```

This function adds two meta boxes, one for the course code and one for the instructor information. The course code box will contain one text field for the code. The instructor box will contain two fields, the name and the e-mail. The arguments of add_meta_box() are:

- Handle: a unique name for this meta box, for your internal use

- Title: the title of the box

- Callback: the name of the function that will print the contents of the box

- Post type: the names of all the post types that will use this box. To have the box appear on a page as well as a course, you would have used `array('course','page')` here.

- Section: which part of the Edit screen this box will appear in by default (normal, advanced, or side)

- Priority: how high the box should appear within its section (high, normal, or low)

Next, create the callback functions that print each meta box, as shown in Listing 12-23.

Listing 12-23. Printing the meta boxes

```
function course_code_meta_box() {
        global $post;
        $code = get_post_meta($post->ID, '_course_code', true);
        if ( function_exists('wp_nonce_field') ) wp_nonce_field('course_code_nonce',
'_course_code_nonce');
?>
        <label for="_course_code">Course Code (e.g. ENGL 101)</label>
        <input type="text" name="_course_code"
                value="<?php echo wp_specialchars(stripslashes($code), 1); ?>" />
<?php
}

function instructor_meta_box() {
        global $post;
        $name = get_post_meta($post->ID, '_instructor_name', true);
        $email = get_post_meta($post->ID, '_instructor_email', true);
        if ( function_exists('wp_nonce_field') ) wp_nonce_field('instructor_nonce',
'_instructor_nonce');
?>
        <label for="_instructor_name">Name</label>
        <input type="text" name="_instructor_name"
                value="<?php echo wp_specialchars(stripslashes($name), 1); ?>" />
        <label for="_instructor_email">Email</label>
        <input type="text" name="_instructor_email"
                value="<?php echo wp_specialchars(stripslashes($email), 1); ?>" />
<?php
}
```

Each function simply prints the form fields within the meta box. To make sure the field values are populated with any previously saved data, call get_post_meta(), which requires three arguments: the post ID, the meta key, and a true/false value determining whether the function should return a single value or all values stored with that key for the post.

The resulting Edit Course screen is shown in Figure 12-22.

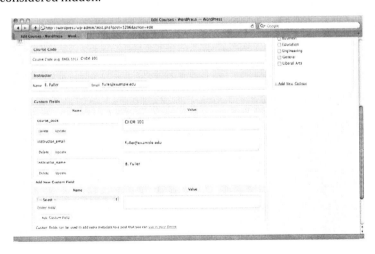

Figure 12-22. *The Edit Course screen with the new custom fields*

In this case, you use meta key names that begin with underscores. If you hadn't, you would see each of these three custom fields in the Custom Fields meta box in addition to your new meta boxes, as shown in Figure 12-23. WordPress will not print meta fields whose keys begin with underscores; they are considered hidden.

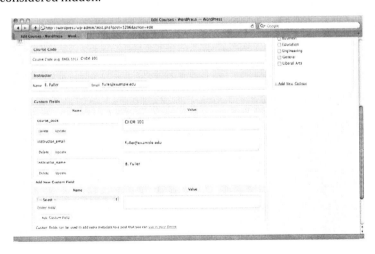

Figure 12-23. *Duplicated custom fields when keys do not begin with underscores*

Verifying and Saving User Input

You might have noticed that these form fields contain nonces
(codex.wordpress.org/Wordpress_Nonce_Implementation). A nonce is a number used once, and it's a
security precaution you didn't have to take when you created plugins because you were using the
settings API, which handled all that for you. Here, you aren't registering any settings. Instead, you are
saving user input directly to the database, and you need to verify that the data in $_POST came from a
valid source. In order to do that, you create a nonce for each box. The wp_nonce_field() function creates
a hidden form field. It can take just one argument, a key you use to check the value later
('course_code_nonce'). If you were using just one nonce, you could leave it at that, and the field's name
would be _wp_nonce by default. However, in this form you have two nonces, and you need to give each
one a unique name, so you use a second argument to do so.

Finally, you have to write a function to save your custom field data when the post is saved. Anything
in the standard meta box would be handled automatically, but custom meta box fields must be updated
manually, as shown in Listing 12-24. You need to make sure this function runs every time a post is
saved, so use the save_post() action hook.

Listing 12-24. Saving the meta box fields

```
add_action( 'save_post', 'save_course_meta_data' );

function save_course_meta_data( $post_id ) {
        global $post;

        // ignore autosaves
        if (defined('DOING_AUTOSAVE') && DOING_AUTOSAVE) return $post_id;

        // check nonces
        check_admin_referer('course_code_nonce', '_course_code_nonce');
        check_admin_referer('instructor_nonce', '_instructor_nonce');

        // check capabilites
        if ( 'course' == $_POST['post_type'] && !current_user_can( 'edit_post', $post_id ) )
                return $post_id;

        // save the custom fields, one by one

        // course code field
        // if the field is empty...
        if (empty($_POST['_course_code'])) {
                // see what the original value was
                $storedcode = get_post_meta( $post_id, '_course_code', true );
                // remove it from the database
                delete_post_meta($post_id, '_course_code', $storedcode);
        }
        // if the field isn't empty, we need to save it
        else
                update_post_meta($post_id, '_course_code', $_POST['_course_code']);

        // instructor name field
        if (empty($_POST['_instructor_name'])) {
```

```
                $storedname = get_post_meta( $post_id, '_instructor_name', true );
                delete_post_meta($post_id, '_instructor_name', $storedname);
        }
        else
                update_post_meta($post_id, '_instructor_name', $_POST['_instructor_name']);

        // instructor email field
        if (empty($_POST['_instructor_email'])) {
                $storedemail = get_post_meta( $post_id, '_instructor_email', true );
                delete_post_meta($post_id, '_instructor_email', $storedemail);
        }
        else
                update_post_meta($post_id, '_instructor_email', $_POST['_instructor_email']);
}
```

First, you need to check whether this save_post action is being called as a result of an autosave. If it is, you don't need to process the custom fields yet, so you return the post ID and exit the function.

Next, you need to check the nonces you created in the form field functions. The check_admin_referer() function would usually take just one argument, the key you provided when you created the nonce. However, since you're using two, you need to use the second argument (the unique identifier). If either nonce fails verification, you again exit the function without saving the fields.

There's one last thing you need to check before you can save the fields: the user's capabilities. Back when you created the course content type, you had the option of specifying an edit capability other than edit_post. Since you didn't, that's the capability you need to check here.

Once you know that you're allowed to save the data, you need to check whether there's anything in each field. If there isn't, you call delete_post_meta() to remove its row from the wp_postmeta table. This function requires three arguments: the post ID, the meta key, and the previously stored value. You can again use get_post_meta() to fetch the stored value so you can pass it to delete_post_meta().

If the fields aren't empty, you need to update them. The update_post_meta() function requires the ID, the meta key, and the new value.

That's it! You can now edit and save the custom fields in their own meta boxes instead of the main Custom Fields box.

All Together

The complete Course Post Types plugin is shown in Listing 12-25. It registers the course post type, adds the college taxonomy, displays the college taxonomy on the Edit Courses screen, and adds the course code, instructor name, and instructor e-mail meta boxes to the Courses → Edit screen.

Listing 12-25. The complete Course Post Types plugin

```php
<?php
/*
Plugin Name: Course Post Types
*/

/* Content Types */

add_action('init', 'post_type_courses');
```

```php
function post_type_courses() {
    register_post_type(
        'course',
        array(
            'labels' => array(
                'name' => __( 'Courses' ),
                'singular_name' => __( 'Course' ),
            ),
            'description' => __('Individual course data'),
            'public' => true,
            'show_ui' => true,
            'register_meta_box_cb' => 'course_meta_boxes',
            'supports' => array(
                'title',
                'editor',
                'author',
                'excerpt',
                'custom-fields',
                'revisions',)
            )
    );
    register_taxonomy_for_object_type('college', 'course');
}

/* Taxonomies */

add_action('init', 'create_course_series_tax');
register_activation_hook( __FILE__, 'activate_course_series_tax' );

function activate_course_series_tax() {
    create_course_series_tax();
    $GLOBALS['wp_rewrite']->flush_rules();
}

function create_course_series_tax() {
    register_taxonomy(
        'college',
        'course',
        array(
            'labels' => array(
                'name' => __( 'Colleges' ),
                'singular_name' => __( 'College' ),
            ),
            'hierarchical' => true,
        )
    );
}

/* Custom Fields */

add_action( 'save_post', 'save_course_meta_data' );
```

```php
function course_meta_boxes() {
        add_meta_box( 'course_code_meta', __('Course Code'), 'course_code_meta_box', 'course',
'normal', 'high' );
        add_meta_box( 'instructor_meta', __('Instructor'), 'instructor_meta_box', 'course',
'normal', 'high' );
}

function course_code_meta_box() {
        global $post;
        if ( function_exists('wp_nonce_field') ) wp_nonce_field('course_code_nonce',
'_course_code_nonce');
?>
        <label for="_course_code">Course Code (e.g. ENGL 101)</label>
        <input type="text" name="_course_code"
                value="<?php echo wp_specialchars(stripslashes(get_post_meta($post->ID,
'_course_code', true)), 1); ?>" />
<?php
}

function instructor_meta_box() {
        global $post;
        if ( function_exists('wp_nonce_field') ) wp_nonce_field('instructor_nonce',
'_instructor_nonce');
?>
        <label for="_instructor_name">Name</label>
        <input type="text" name="_instructor_name"
                value="<?php echo wp_specialchars(stripslashes(get_post_meta($post->ID,
'_instructor_name', true)), 1); ?>" />
        <label for="_instructor_email">Email</label>
        <input type="text" name="_instructor_email"
                value="<?php echo wp_specialchars(stripslashes(get_post_meta($post->ID,
'_instructor_email', true)), 1); ?>" />
<?php
}

function save_course_meta_data( $post_id ) {
        global $post;

        // ignore autosaves
        if (defined('DOING_AUTOSAVE') && DOING_AUTOSAVE) return $post_id;

        // check nonces
        check_admin_referer('course_code_nonce', '_course_code_nonce');
        check_admin_referer('instructor_nonce', '_instructor_nonce');

        // check capabilites
        if ( 'course' == $_POST['post_type'] && !current_user_can( 'edit_post', $post_id ) )
                return $post_id;

        // save fields
        if (empty($_POST['_course_code'])) {
                $storedcode = get_post_meta( $post_id, '_course_code', true );
```

```
                delete_post_meta($post_id, '_course_code', $storedcode);
        }
        else
                update_post_meta($post_id, '_course_code', $_POST['_course_code']);

        if (empty($_POST['_instructor_name'])) {
                $storedname = get_post_meta( $post_id, '_instructor_name', true );
                delete_post_meta($post_id, '_instructor_name', $storedname);
        }
        else
                update_post_meta($post_id, '_instructor_name', $_POST['_instructor_name']);

        if (empty($_POST['_instructor_email'])) {
                $storedemail = get_post_meta( $post_id, '_instructor_email', true );
                delete_post_meta($post_id, '_instructor_email', $storedemail);
        }
        else
                update_post_meta($post_id, '_instructor_email', $_POST['_instructor_email']);
}

/* Custom Edit Columns */

add_filter("manage_edit-course_columns", "course_taxonomy_columns");

// rearrange the columns on the Edit screens
function course_taxonomy_columns($defaults) {
        // preserve the default date and comment columns
        $comments = $defaults['comments'];
        $date = $defaults['date'];

        // remove default date and comments
        unset($defaults['comments']);
        unset($defaults['date']);

        // insert college taxonomy column
        $defaults['colleges'] = __('Colleges');

        // restore default date and comments
        $defaults['comments'] = $comments;
        $defaults['date'] = $date;

        return $defaults;
}

add_action("manage_pages_custom_column", "course_taxonomy_custom_column");
// for non-hierarchical content types, use the following instead:
// add_action("manage_posts_custom_column", "course_taxonomy_custom_column");

// print the college taxonomy terms, linked to filter the posts to this taxonomy term only
function course_taxonomy_custom_column($column) {
        global $post;
        if ($column == 'colleges') {
```

```php
                    $colleges = get_the_terms($post->ID, 'college');
                    if (!empty($colleges)) {
                            $thecolleges = array();
                            foreach ($colleges as $college) {
                                    $thecolleges[] = '<a
href="edit.php?post_type=course&college='.$college->slug.'>' .
esc_html(sanitize_term_field('name', $college->name, $college->term_id, 'college', 'display'))
. "</a>";
                            }
                            echo implode(', ', $thecolleges);
                    }
            }
}

?>
```

Once you've revised the courses to take advantage of the new fields, you also need to modify the single-course.php template. Listing 12-26 shows a revised template that displays the courses in a table, and Figure 12-24 shows the result.

Listing 12-26. The new course archive template using custom fields

```php
<?php get_header(); ?>

<div id="container">
        <div id="content">

<?php if ($wp_query->have_posts() ) : ?>
        <table>
                <thead>
                        <th>Code</th>
                        <th>Title</th>
                        <th>Instructor</th>
                <thead>
                <tbody>
<?php
        while (have_posts() ) : the_post(); ?>
        <tr id="post-<?php the_ID(); ?>" <?php post_class(); ?>>
                <td><?php echo get_post_meta($post->ID, '_course_code', true); ?></td>
                <td><a href="<?php the_permalink(); ?>" title="<?php the_title_attribute();
?>"><?php the_title(); ?></a></td>
                <td><a href="mailto:<?php echo get_post_meta($post->ID, '_instructor_email',
true); ?>"><?php echo get_post_meta($post->ID, '_instructor_name', true); ?></a></td>
        </tr>
<?php endwhile; ?>
                </tbody>
        </table>
<?php endif; ?>

        </div><!-- #content -->
</div><!-- #container -->
```

```php
<?php get_sidebar(); ?>
<?php get_footer(); ?>
```

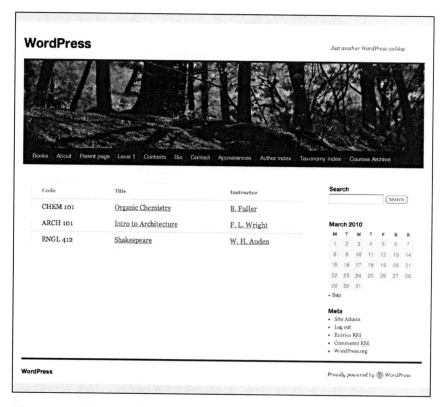

Figure 12-24. The completed course table

Summary

In this chapter, I've shown you how to move beyond the built-in content types in WordPress—way beyond! You can add small custom fields to posts and pages or create entirely new content types of your own, and you can categorize and tag them with many sets of taxonomy terms. You now have all the tools you need to create a completely customized database of content, all with the same user-friendly editing interfaces WordPress is famous for.

Up to this point, you've talked about setting up a single WordPress site. In the next chapter, you'll learn how to create a whole network of WordPress sites from one installation.

CHAPTER 13

■ ■ ■

Setting up the Network

Until version 3.0, there was WordPress, and then there was WordPress MU. WordPress itself could create only one site, while the MU (multi-user) fork could be used to create a network of related sites similar to wordpress.com or edublogs.com. With version 3.0, the two projects have merged once again. When you downloaded WordPress, you gained all the features that used to be specific to MU; they're just hidden until you turn them on.

Even if you don't need to create a whole network of user sites, you could use the network features to manage multiple sites rather than installing WordPress separately for each one. This would be especially useful if your group of sites shares the same pool of users, since they would each have one account instead of several.

While the network-enabled WordPress (known as multi-site mode) looks mostly the same, there are some differences in the requirements, the user management, and plugin and theme activation.

Network Requirements

In general, WordPress's multi-site mode has the same requirements as WordPress itself. However, you'll need to decide how you want your network site's addresses to work. You can choose subdomains (http://subsite.example.com) or subfolders (http://example.com/subsite/), and each requires something a little different.

Subdomains

If you are planning to allow users to sign up for their own sites on your network, you need to set up wildcard DNS, and you must be able to create wildcard aliases.

In most cases, setting up wildcard DNS is something your hosting provider must handle for you. The general idea is that, in addition to accepting requests for example.com and www.example.com, your domain must be able to accept requests for all other subdomains -- *.example.com -- without your having to add each one individually to the DNS record.

Similarly, your server must be set up to direct traffic for all unspecified virtual hosts to your WordPress site. In Apache's configuration, you would add ServerAlias *.example.com to your WordPress site's virtual host definition. Again, this is generally something your hosting provider can help you with.

If you are not planning to allow users to create new sites on their own, you do not need to set up wildcard DNS or aliases. For example, if you are managing a network of university departments, you would not necessarily want any authorized users to be able to create new sites without your approval. In that case, you would want to create the new subdomains one at a time.

Subfolders

We've talked about .htaccess files quite a bit throughout this book, so you probably have one set up. However, if you've gotten away without one until now, you'll need it in order to use the subfolder option on your network. WordPress won't create any new physical subfolders for your new sites; they'll all be virtual folders created using rewrite rules, with all incoming requests routed through WordPress.

Activating the Network

For existing MU sites, you can just upgrade. For single-site installations, you have to add a constant to the wp-config.php file: define('WP_ALLOW_MULTISITE', true); Save the file, and when you log back in to the Dashboard, you'll see that there is now a Network menu under Tools. Go to it, and you'll see the initial page of the network setup process, as shown in Figure 13-1.

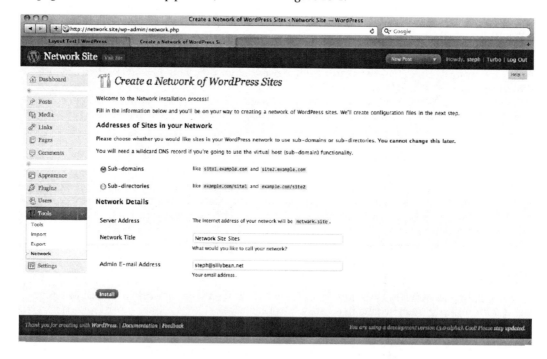

Figure 13-1. *The network setup screen*

First, choose subdomains or subdirectories for your setup, keeping in mind the requirements we've discussed. Then, enter a title for your network. (The one WordPress suggests might not make sense, as shown in Figure 13-1.) You'll be asked to enter an administrator email address again; this one will be used for notifications related to new sites, and it does not have to be the same as the address you chose for your initial WordPress installation (which will be used for comment notifications and so on related to that site only).

Press Install!

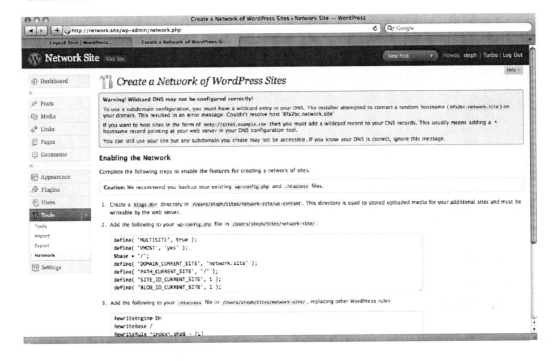

Figure 13-2. The second step of the network setup

On this second screen (Figure 13-2), you'll be given a set of constants to copy into your wp-config.php file. This is not the entire file, so don't overwrite the whole thing! Just add these few constants. I recommend creating a network section.

You'll also be given a new set of rewrite rules for your .htaccess file. Paste these in; they can replace the WordPress section that's already there.

If you get a warning as shown in Figure 13-2, your wildcard DNS setup is not working. If you plan to add each subdomain by hand, as I do on this test installation, you can ignore this warning. Otherwise, contact your server administrator or hosting provider to resolve the problem.

You also need to create a directory called blogs.dir in your wp-content directory. Since your network sites won't have their own uploads directory, blogs.dir is where their uploaded media will be stored. This directory needs to be writeable by the server, just as your uploads directory is.

Once you've saved both files and created blogs.dir, return to the Dashboard. You'll see some new things there, as shown in Figure 13-3.

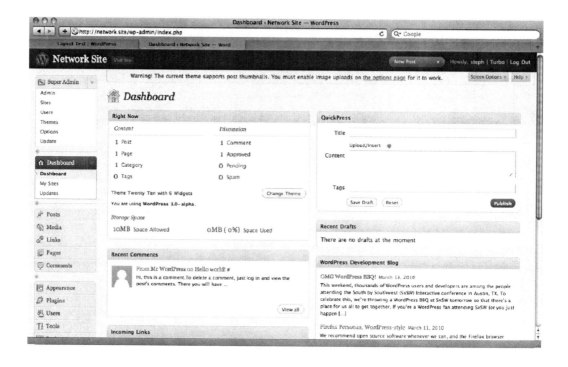

Figure 13-3. *The network-activated Dashboard*

The warning you'll probably see at the top of the screen appears because once you've activated the network, you have to explicitly allow file uploads. If you're using a theme that supports post thumbnails (like Twenty Ten), you'll be warned that file uploads are not yet enabled.

Other than the warning, there are several new items here. On the left, you'll see that there's a whole new section of the navigation menu, Super Admin. The options pages under this section of the menu will allow you to configure your network, and I'll walk you through each of them in a moment.

Under the Dashboard section of the menu, you'll see a new My Sites option. This leads to a page where you'll see all the sites on which you are a user. Of course, you are the Super Administrator for all the other sites, even if they are not listed here.

In the Right Now box, you'll see new statistics related to storage space. Each site, including this main one, is limited to a certain amount of storage space. You'll be able to change this under Super Admin → Options. If you allow network users to upload files, you'll need to set these limits to something your server can handle.

For now, everything else on the Dashboard is just the same as it was before you enabled the Network, so let's start configuring.

Configuring the Network

Go to Super Admin → Options to begin configuring your network. This is a long screen with a lot of options. Figure 13-4 shows the first few sections. We'll go through each section one by one.

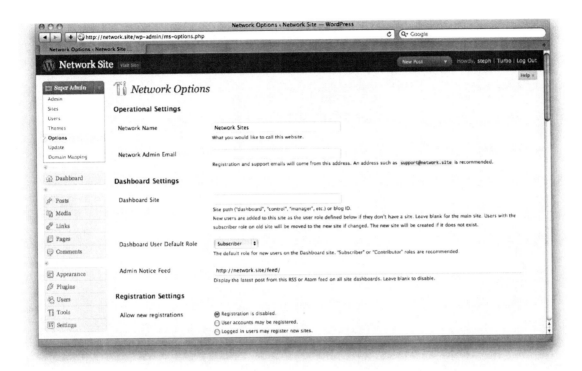

Figure 13-4. Network options

Operational Settings

The network name shown here should be the same as the network title you chose during the network setup. You can change it here.

The network admin email address will be used as the sender for all the registration and support notifications sent to your network users.

Dashboard Settings

When you add new users to the network without specifying a site for them, they will be added to the site you name here. This does not have to be your main site; you can create another one to use as the holding area for new users if you prefer.

New users may be added with any role, but the one you specify here will be the default choice.

You may also specify an RSS feed to be displayed on all the network sites' Dashboards. If you plan to use your initial WordPress site as the news blog for the network, provide its feed URL here. The notice is very prominent, as shown in Figure 13-5, so use this option wisely. Keep in mind that it doesn't have to be your site's main feed; you could dedicate a single category or tag to network announcements.

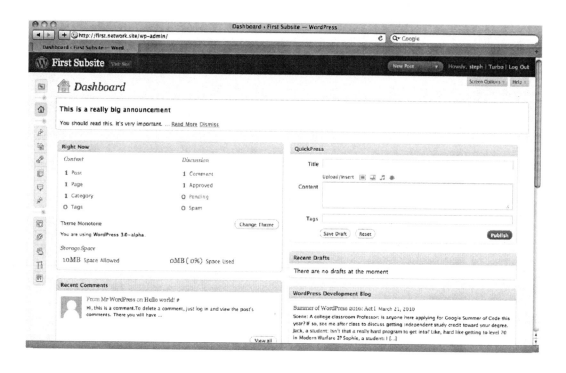

Figure 13-5. An admin notice in a network site's Dashboard

Registration Settings

The registration settings (Figure 13-6) deal with the way users will be added to your network. If registration is disabled, no one can sign up for an account, and you will have to add site administrators manually. To allow people to sign up for accounts but not new sites, choose the second option. (This doesn't necessarily mean everyone in the world can register, as we'll see in a moment.) The third option allows the users you have added manually to create their own sites. The fourth option is the one to use if you want to create a blog network: allow users to register and create sites for themselves.

The next pair of radio buttons determines whether an email notification will be sent to newly registered users. In a later section of this screen, you'll be able to customize the emails.

If you would then like the administrators to be able to add users to their network sites, you can choose 'yes' in the next pair of options.

The list of banned usernames exists to protect you from users who might launch phishing attempts from your site, especially if you have allowed administrators to invite users.

The next option, Limited Email Registrations, allows you to restrict user registration to specified domains. If you are building a site for users in a business or school, this options is the ideal way to limit your user pool.

On the flip side of that, there might be domains of users you don't want registering for your network, and you can specify those in the Banned Email Domains field.

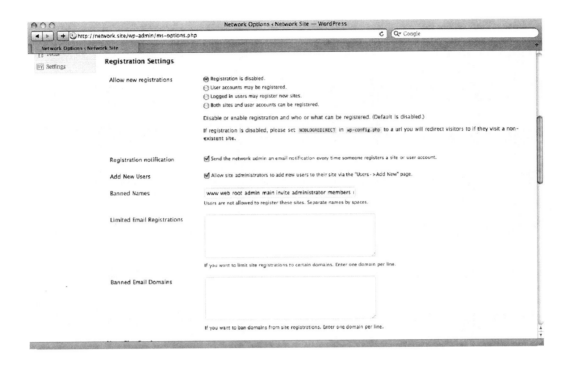

Figure 13-6. Network options (cont.)

New Site Settings

In this section (Figure 13-7), you can rewrite the welcome email, which is sent when a user registers a new site, and the welcome user email, which is sent when a new user is added without creating a site.

You can also alter the first post, first page, first comment, first comment author, and first comment URL. Anything specified here will replace the "Hello, world!" post that appears when a new site is created.

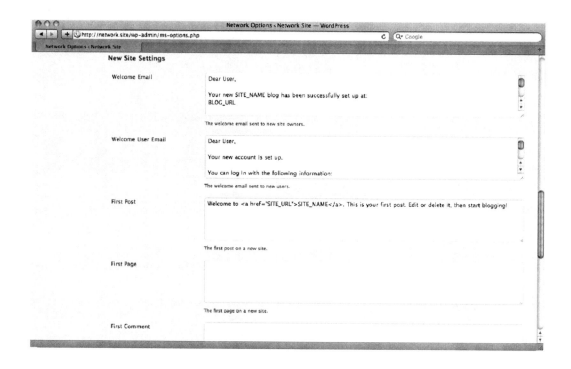

Figure 13-7. Network options (cont.)

Upload Settings

The upload settings determine whether your users are allowed to upload images, video, and music. Note that this affects your main blog as well! If you tried to edit a post and noticed that your media upload icons were gone (Figure 13-8), you need to check these options to get them back. If these options are off, users will still be able to use the general media upload icon to add files, but only of the file types you specify in the Upload File Types field below.

The Site Upload Space option allows you to limit the size of each network site. You will have to determine how much space your hosting account allows you and how that should be divided among your network sites. The Max Upload File Size field allows you to limit the size of individual files added via the media uploader.

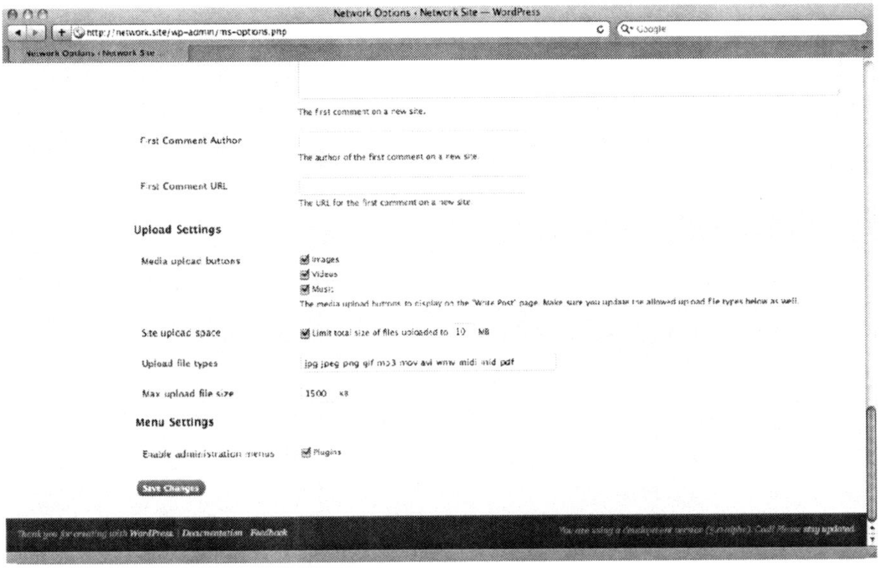

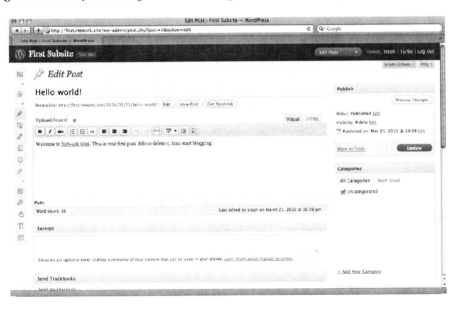

Figure 13-8. *The post editing screen with image, video, and music uploads disabled*

Figure 13-9. *Network options (cont.)*

Menu Settings

In this section, you may choose whether individual site administrators can access the plugin pages. If you do not check this box, they will not be able to activate, deactivate, or install plugins for their network sites.

Creating Additional Network Sites

To create your first new network site, go to Super Admin → Sites. On this screen (Figure 13-10), you'll be able to add, edit, deactivate, or archive an entire network site. In the fields below the list of sites, enter the subdomain, the name of the new site, and the email address of its administrator – for now, yours.

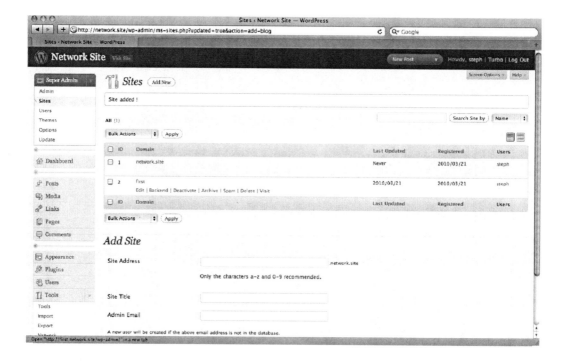

Figure 13-10. *Adding a network site*

Click the "Backend" link below the site's subdomain in the list to visit its Dashboard. You should see a Dashboard that looks exactly like a new WordPress installation (Figure 13-10), except the Super Admin menu will still be visible on the left (because you're still logged in as a superadministrator), and the lastest post from the admin notice feed (if you specified one) will be displayed.

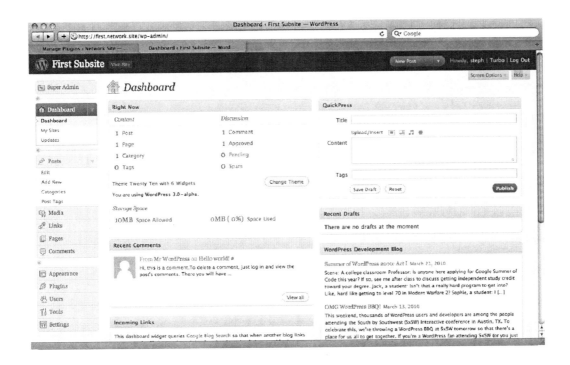

Figure 13-11. The first network site's Dashboard

Network Users

Under Super Admin → Users, you may add more users to your network. They will be added to the site you selected in the Dashboard Settings section of your network options. Individual site administrators can then invite those users to become users of the subsite as well. They can also invite new users by creating a username and sending an email invitation.

To add a user to a subsite, to to Dashboard → My Sites and visit the subsite's Dashboard using the Backend link. Then to go Users → Add New, where you'll see the form shown in Figure 13-12. Enter the user's username, if it exists, or create one for them if they are not already registered. Enter their email address and choose their role.

To invite the user, leave the checkbox blank and press "Add User." They'll receive a confirmation link allowing them to complete the registration process and fill in their account profile.

If you are logged in as a super administrator, you can skip the confirmation email. As soon as you press "Add User," the user will be registered. They will not receive a password, so you'll need to edit their account and create a password, or tell them to use the "forgot password" link on the login page to generate a new one.

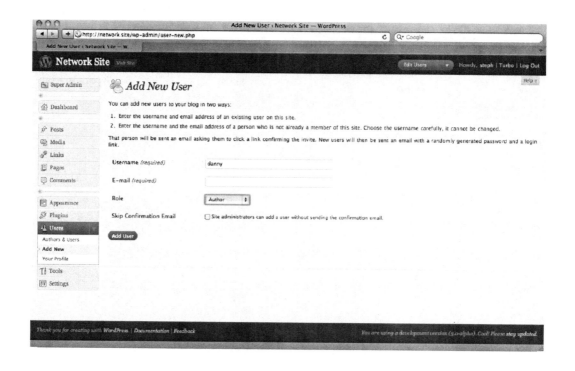

Figure 13-12. *Adding a user to a network site*

Splogs

If you have chosen to allow people to sign up for sites on your network, you are about to discover a whole new kind of spam: splogs. Just as spammers will leave comments on random blogs and sign up for accounts on forums, they will sign up for blogs on your network and fill them with junk.

In the list of sites under Super Admin → Sites, you can mark sites as spam. However, keeping up with splogs could soon consume more of your time than you're willing to spend. There are a number of plugins that help prevent spam user registrations. WP Hashcash is one good choice. Its options are shown in Figure 13-13.

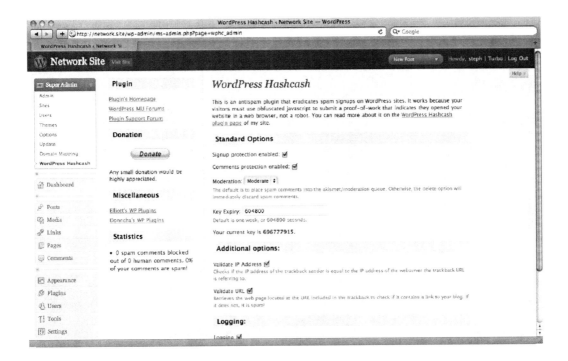

Figure 13-13. WP Hashcash options

Hashcash works by adding JavaScript to your login and comment forms (according to the options you choose). If the script runs, you know the user visited your site in a real browser and was therefore not a spam robot. If the script fails, the user will not be able to sign up.

Since this plugin does rely on JavaScript, it will block anyone who has disabled JavaScript in his or her browser. Consider your audience carefully and decide whether this trade-off is acceptable.

Network Plugins and Themes

Themes installed in your main site will not be available to the network sites until you activate them under Super Admin → Themes, as shown in Figure 13-14. Individual sites' administrators may install themes, but those themes will be available only within that site.

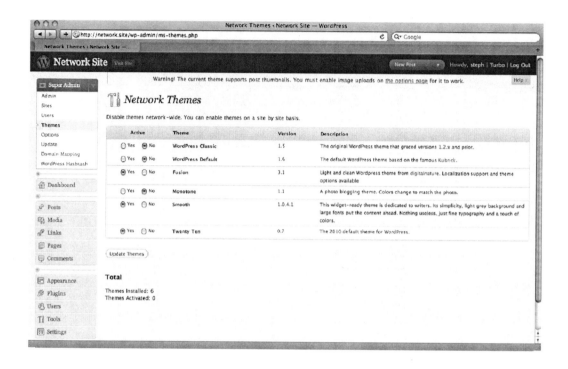

Figure 13-14. *Activating themes for the network*

When you install new plugins in Plugins → Add New, keep in mind that the "activate" link shown will activate for the current site only. To activate it for the whole network, go back to the plugin list without activating and choose "Network Activate" from the plugin list.

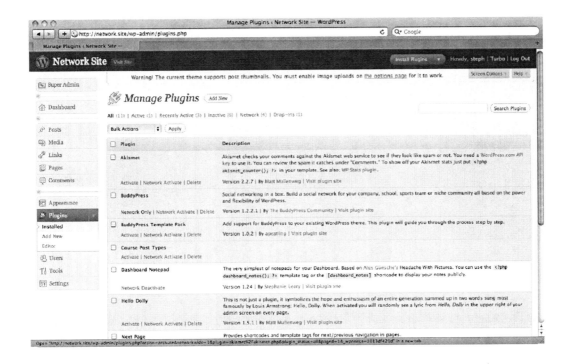

Figure 13-15. Activating a plugin for the network

Plugin and Theme Options

Plugins and themes that use the settings API should work correctly in network sites. Older plugins that handle the options without the help of the settings API might not work.

Plugins and themes that are enabled for all the network sites will be installed on those sites with their default options. There is currently no way to deploy themes or plugins with a set of options you have chosen, unless you set up a single site as a template and use the Blog Templates plugin to create the other network sites, as described in the next section.

Upgrading the Network

To upgrade the sites on your network, first you must upgrade the main site. You can do this as you usually would, by going to Dashboard → Update.

Once the main site has been upgraded, go to Super Admin → Update. Press the button there to upgrade all the network sites in turn, as shown in Figure 13-16.

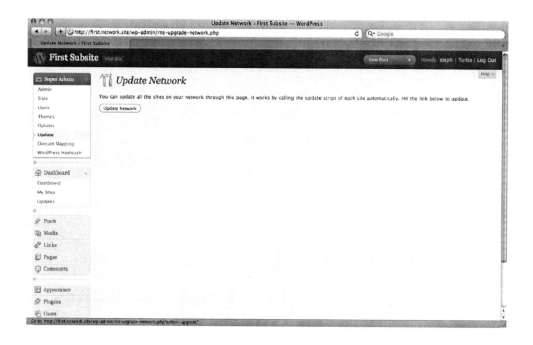

Figure 13-16. *Upgrading the network*

To upgrade network themes and plugins, simply update them as usual from the main network site (Dashboard → Update). No further action is necessary.

Mapping Domains

You can let your users map their own domains to their network sites using the Domain Mapping plugin (`wordpress.org/extend/plugins/wordpress-mu-domain-mapping/`). This creates an options page under Tools → Domain Mapping where users can enter the domain(s) they want to use. This feature might eventually be incorporated into WordPress itself, but was not included in 3.0.

Once you have installed the plugin and enabled it for the network, go to Tools → Domain Mapping. You'll be asked to copy a file, sunrise.php, from the plugin's folder to wp-content. You'll also be asked to uncomment the `SUNRISE` definition from `wp-config.php`. If you created your network from a new WordPress 3.0 installation and were not previously using WordPress MU, your config file won't have a `SUNRISE` definition. Just add the line `define( 'SUNRISE', 'on' );` somewhere in your group of network settings.

Next, you'll be asked to set the IP address or CNAME of your server in the site admin page. Go to Super Admin → Domain Mapping and enter one of the two requested items, as shown in Figure 13-17.

Now you can go back to Tools → Domain Mapping, and you'll be able to enter a domain for your network site, as shown in Figure 13-18. Of course, you need to register this domain before it will work!

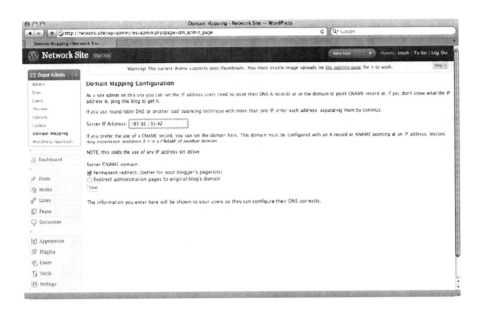

Figure 13-17. Setting the server's IP address

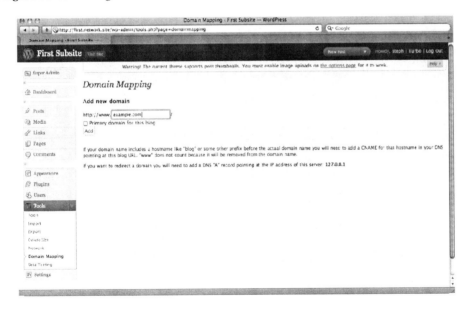

Figure 13-18. Mapping a domain

BuddyPress

BuddyPress is a plugin with some associated themes that, when activated, turns your WordPress installation into a social network. Users can sign up, create profiles, and participate in discussions without ever entering the administration screens. BuddyPress is now available for single-site WordPress installations as well as networks, and includes all the same features except separate blogs for individual users. I'll demonstrate using the network installation.

While BuddyPress can be installed and configured like a simple plugin, it has its own ecosystem of plugins, themes, and hooks. It even has its own Codex, located at http://codex.buddypress.org.

Features

The main BuddyPress features are the activity stream (also known as the wire), groups, forums, friends, and private messages.

Activity Stream

The activity stream, shown in Figure 13-19, is the first page users see when they log in to a BuddyPress network. The stream shows members' profile updates, blog posts and comments, forum posts, new friendship connections, and new site members.

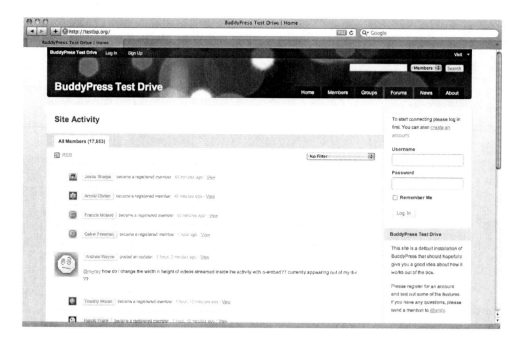

Figure 13-19. The activity stream

Groups

Groups (Figure 13-20) are an incredibly powerful feature for organizations. While the administrator can create starter groups, the real beauty of the feature is that members can create their own groups, effectively organizing themselves into grassroots taxonomies based on their own interests or needs. Each group has its own wire, forum, and member directory, allowing the members to direct the course of the group's conversations.

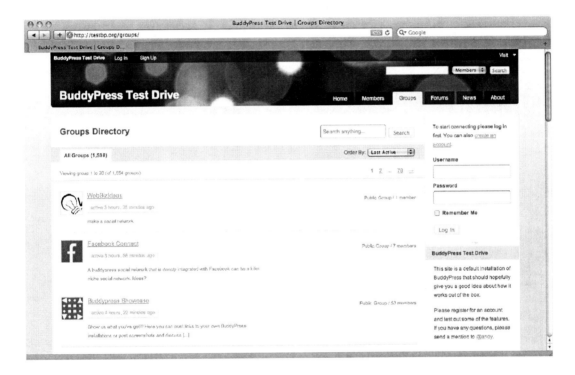

Figure 13-20. The groups listing

Forum

The forum in BuddyPress is based on bbPress, and provides the basic features you'd expect to find in any forum software. The list of all forum topics is shown under the Forum tab (Figure 13-21), but users can navigate through the groups to find group-specific forum topics.

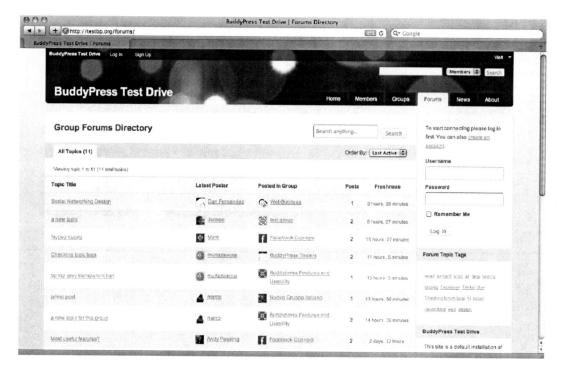

Figure 13-21. The forum

Friends and Private Messages

The friends feature allows you to connect with other network users. Once you have created friendships with other users, you can filter features like the activity stream to show only friends' updates. The friendship connections also enable another important feature: private messages. If you have been confirmed as another user's friend, you may send messages directly to that user rather than posting something publicly on the wire or the forum.

Installation

Unlike most plugins, BuddyPress doesn't have an option to activate it for the main site only; you must activate it for the entire network.

You can install BuddyPress using the normal plugin installer. Once the plugin is activated for the network, you'll also need to activate the default BuddyPress theme (included) or find a child theme at buddypress.org/extend/themes.

General

Once you have installed BuddyPress, you'll find a new set of options under BuddyPress in your navigation menu. I'll go through each screen.

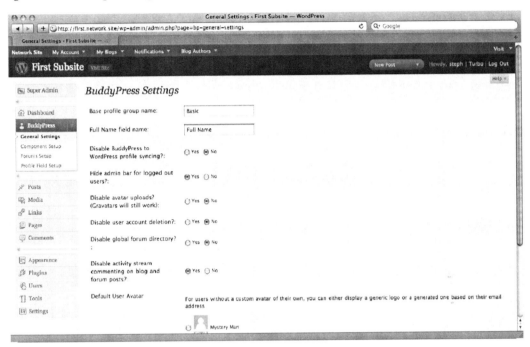

Figure 13-22. General BuddyPress options

On the general settings screen, shown in Figure 13-22, you can change the built-in profile fields and a few user-related settings.

The Base profile group name refers to the group containing the single built-in profile field (the user's name) and any fields you add to that group in the profile settings screen. Here you can also change the title of the name field. I'll talk more about profile fields in the section on the profile settings screen.

By default, BuddyPress syncs basic user profiles to WordPress user profiles. If you would prefer to keep them separate, choose "yes" here to disable the synchronization function.

BuddyPress includes its own avatar feature. If you would prefer to use Gravatars, you can choose "yes" to disable the feature that allows users to upload new avatars specific to their BuddyPress profiles.

Users are generally allowed to delete their own BuddyPress accounts. If you would prefer that they not delete their own accounts, choose "yes" to disable the deletion feature.

Each BuddyPress group will have its own forum topics. By default, users who click the "Forum" tab will first see a listing of all the forum topics. If you would prefer they see only their own groups, you can disable the global directory by choosing "yes."

The next option allows you to choose whether the activity stream includes blog comments and forum posts. If you disable these items, the activity stream will show only blog posts, profile updates, friendship status updates, and posts to the wire.

While BuddyPress allows users to upload their own avatars to their profiles, it uses Gravatars unless they are replaced with other images. The last setting on the general page allows you to choose the avatar that is shown if the user has no Gravatar and has not uploaded another avatar. This setting looks just like the default avatar option in WordPress under Settings → Discussion.

Components

In this screen, you can turn off any portions of BuddyPress you don't intend to use, as shown in Figure 13-23. By default, all components are enabled.

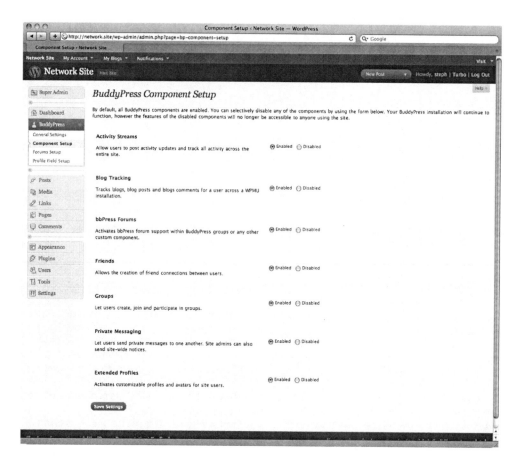

Figure 13-23. BuddyPress component settings

Forums

BuddyPress includes bbPress, the forum part of the WordPress family. You can install bbPress in one click from the BuddyPress Forums option screen, as shown in Figure 13-24.

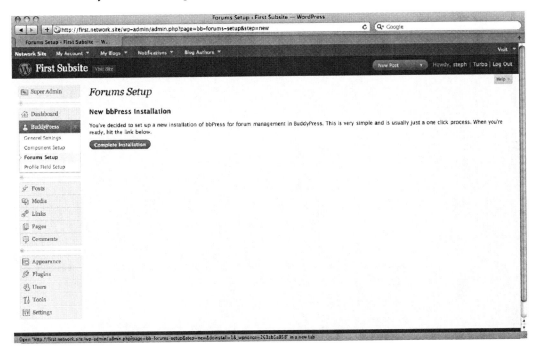

Figure 13-24. Installing bbPress

Profile

You might recall from Chapter 6 that we had to use a little bit of code to extend the basic WordPress user profile. In BuddyPress, extended profiles are built right in, and all you have to do is specify the details of each field as shown in Figure 13-25: the title, the description, whether the field should be required, and what sort of form field it should display. You can rearrange the fields by dragging them around on the Profile options screen.

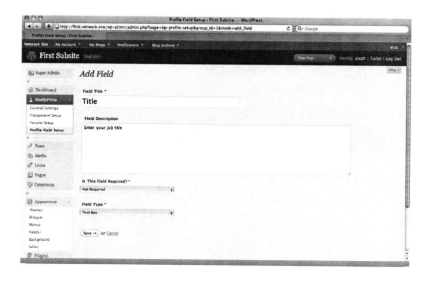

Figure 13-25. Adding a profile field

You can also create whole new groups of profile fields. These will be displayed to the user as tabs or buttons, depending on your theme, as shown in Figure 13-26.

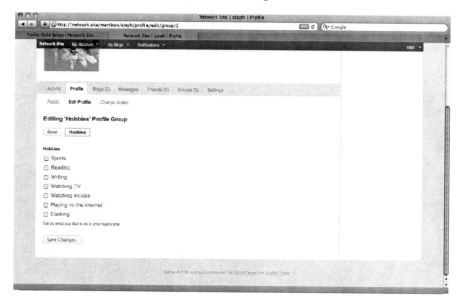

Figure 13-26. Profile field groups as they appear to the user

Note that any fields you added to your main WordPress installation using the contact method filters will not appear in your BuddyPress profiles; the two methods of creating new fields are (at least for now) incompatible.

Using BuddyPress

I've covered just the most basic information on setting up BuddyPress networks. You've probably thought of a few different uses for the software by now. Of course, the most common BuddyPress sites are niche social networks. However, you could also use BuddyPress to create a business intranet, with groups for each department, or a site for a professional organization, with groups for each special interest. If you work for a school, you could use BuddyPress to network students, perhaps creating groups for each club or activity. Churches could use BuddyPress to keep track of members and create group discussions for committees.

Visit buddypress.org/extend/plugins/ to find plugins to extend your BuddyPress site, and buddypress.org/extend/themes/ for additional BuddyPress themes. The possibilities are endless. Create something new!

Summary

In this chapter, you've learned how to apply your knowledge of WordPress to create an entire network of WordPress-based sites. You've learned how to set up the network features, how to install and enable plugins and themes for the network, and how to manage network sites and users. You've seen how to set up domain mapping for your network users and how to block spambots from signing up for accounts.

You've also learned the basics of BuddyPress, and you now know how to create your own WordPress-based social network.

■ ■ ■

Plugin Index

There are thousands of plugins and themes you can use to extend WordPress. You'll find most of them in the official plugin repository at `wordpress.org/extend/`. I've provided URLs only for those plugins that can't be found easily by searching Extend for their names. See Chapter 3 for information on installing and configuring plugins.

Editing: Inline, Rich Text, Reusable Content, and Attachments

Front End Editor and **Inline Editor** allow posts and pages to be edited without having to enter the dashboard.

TinyMCE Advanced allows you to add a number of buttons to the rich text editor, including a complete set of table buttons.

TinyMCE Excerpt provides the rich text editor for the excerpt field. It does not have a visual/HTML switch and will not include any changes to the visual editor made by other plugins.

Post Snippets and **Reusables** allow you to define bits of reusable content that can be included in a post via shortcode and/or rich text editor buttons.

List Child Attachments (code.google.com/p/list-child-attachments/) provides a template tag and shortcode that lists all the files attached to a post or page.

Excerpts

Advanced Excerpt modifies the_excerpt tag. It allows you to preserve HTML in excerpts, define the excerpt length, and change the ellipsis character.

the_excerpt Reloaded (robsnotebook.com/the-excerpt-reloaded/) provides a new template tag for excerpts. You can preserve specified HTML tags in excerpts, define the excerpt length, and choose what 'more…' text to display.

PJW Page Excerpt provides the excerpt box on page write/edit screens and allows you to use the_excerpt for pages.

Custom Post Types, Taxonomies, and Fields

Custom Post Type UI provides an options page that allows you to create and manage both custom post types and custom taxonomies. Post Type Switcher allows you to convert your old posts and pages to new content types.

Taxes (core.trac.wordpress.org/attachment/ticket/6357/taxes.php) demonstrates custom taxonomies by adding a tag field for "people" to posts, pages, and media attachments. It works, but it's out of date; see the Custom Content Types and Taxonomies chapter for an updated version.

PODS (pods.uproot.us) provides a framework for creating and using custom content types.

Custom Field Template, Magic Fields, and **Flutter** all add boxes to edit screens and allow you to define custom post types.

Page Order

My Page Order provides a simple drag-and-drop interface for rearranging the order of pages on any single level of the page hierarchy. A dropdown menu allows you to choose pages that have children and rearrange the pages on that level.

pageMash provides a complex drag-and-drop interface for rearranging the order and hierarchy of pages.

Page Lists & Navigation

Exclude Pages provides a checkbox on the edit page screen that allows you to explicitly include or exclude pages from WP's page list functions.

Page Lists Plus modifies wp_list_pages. You may exclude pages, add a Home link, add rel or nofollow attributes, or redirect pages to another URL.

NAVT allows you to create and arrange menus through a complex drag-and-drop interface. Pages, users, categories, and user-defined options are all available for inclusion.

Page Links To and **Redirection** redirect posts or pages to another URL.

Yoast Breadcrumbs provides a template tag for breadcrumb navigation on both posts and pages. Pages display the page parents; posts display the category hierarchy.

Folding Pages Widget (http://navyroad.com/2007/09/04/folding-pages-widget/) provides parent/child/sibling page navigation.

Alphabetical Sorting

AZ Index creates alphabetical listings of posts by any field: title, category, author, excerpt, tag, etc. Posts may be sorted within the list by some other field, up to three levels deep.

WP-SNAP provides alphabetical listings of posts by title within a category.

Permalinks & Short URLs

No Category Base removes the category base from your permalink format. Note that this plugin can slow performance, since WordPress will have to check for matching category and page titles.

Pretty Link turns your WordPress site into a URL shortening service of your own and can track visitors to the short links.

Short URL provides a shorter URL for every post.

wp.me is WordPress' own URL shortening service, available as part of the WordPress.com Stats plugin.

Feeds

Feedsmith redirects WordPress' built-in feeds to your Feedburner URL.

E-mail Notifications

Subscribe to Comments allows visitors to receive e-mail notifications of follow-up comments on individual posts.

Subscribe2 allows registered users to receive e-mail notifications of new posts.

Clean Notifications reformats e-mail notifications in HTML, removing extraneous information and providing useful links.

Notifications to All Administrators sends all the common notifications to all users with the administrator role, not just the one whose e-mail address is shown under Settings → General.

Peter's Collaboration E-mails sends a message when an author submits a post for review, and when a pending post is approved, scheduled, or changed back to a draft.

Forms

Contact Form 7 allows you to create e-mail contact forms with Akismet spam protection.

MM Forms is a fork of Contact Form 7 that can store form responses in the database as well as e-mailing them.

CForms II can store form responses in the database, upload files, create multi-page forms, limit submissions by date or number, and more.

Gravity Forms (www.gravityforms.com) offers a great user interface, file uploads, e-mail autoresponders, and confirmation pages with data passed from the form input. It allows user-submitted posts (with images, categories, etc.). *Commercial; $39-199.*

Users, Permissions, and Login Screens

Members provides on/off toggles for all capabilities in WP and allows you to define new roles. It also adds several features relating to private content.

Sidebar Login provides a login form widget.

Login Redirect allows you to reroute users (by username or by role) to a specified URL on login.

Members Only requires users to log in before viewing your site.

Private Suite allows you to change the prefixes on private and password-protected post/page titles, set which roles can read private content, and create private categories.

Visitor Statistics

Google Analyticator includes the Google Analytics code in your footer and provides checkboxes for advanced Analytics options, such as AdSense integration, tracking file downloads, outbound links, and admin visitors. It also adds a graph and some information about your most requested pages to your Dashboard.

Wordpress.com Stats provides a graph of visitors and search queries as a dashboard widget.

Podcasts

Podcasting and PowerPress add a file upload box to the post write/edit screen, provide extra fields for iTunes data, and create a new feed that includes the iTunes data.

Podcast Channels allows you to create separate podcasts for individual categories.

Social Media

Wickett Twitter Widget provides a widget that will display your tweets.

Twitter Tools provides a widget that will display your tweets as well as a number of advanced options such as autotweeting when you post to your blog, shortening URLs via bit.ly or other services, and adding a hashtag in tweets.

Sociable adds a configurable row of buttons below your post that will allow users to quickly share your post with specified social networking services.

Social Networks

BuddyPress turns your WordPress site into a complete social network.

Events and Calendars

The Events Calendar allows you to create events (and optionally make a post for each) and display them as a small sidebar calendar, a large calendar in a post, or a sidebar list of upcoming events.

GigPress (gigpress.com) is designed for listing tour performances, but might work for general events. It includes microformats, RSS and iCal feeds, and CSV export.

WP-Calendar (bustatheme.com/wordpress/wp-calendar/) displays a gorgeous large-format calendar with entry titles shown on the days they were posted.

Caching

WP Cache creates cached HTML files of your site and displays them using .htaccess rewrite rules.

WP Super Cache includes WP Cache and adds a number of other features: file locking, GZIP compression, cache rebuild options, and more.

W3 Total Cache uses APC or memcached to cache database queries rather than files.

Performance, Maintenance, and Diagnostics

Maintenance Mode displays a simple maintenance message to everyone except administrators.

WP-DB-Backup provides a button to quickly back up specified database tables and can be scheduled to back up to a specified directory.

Optimize DB performs MySQL's automatic optimization routines on your database from the admin area.

WP Tuner helps you identify performance problems. It appends an information panel to every page, viewable only to administrators, that analyzes queries and database response time.

Search & Replace allows you to replace text in chosen database fields.

SQL Monitor appends an analysis of SQL queries to any screen being viewed by an administrator.

PHP Speedy (http://aciddrop.com/php-speedy/) compresses, combines, and sets expire headers for JavaScript and CSS files.

Broken Link Checker runs a background process that periodically checks your site for broken links.

Changelogger displays a plugin's readme.txt changelog section (if available) on the plugin management screen for all versions between the one you have installed and the current version in the plugin repository.

Show Template lets you know which theme file is being used to generate a particular page.

Hooks & Filters Flow (planetozh.com/blog/my-projects/wordpress-hooks-filter-flow/) lets you see which filters are being applied (and in what order) to various pieces of content in a WordPress template.

Health Check (westi.wordpress.com/2009/12/26/giving-your-wordpress-a-check-up/) is still in development as of this writing. It checks your installation for server configuration errors and suggests improvements.

WP Security Scan monitors file permissions, database security, and user passwords to help mitigate security vulnerabilities.

WordPress Firewall examines incoming requests and rejects those that match well-known attack vectors.

Mobile

WPtouch provides an iPhone app-style theme to mobile users.

Widgets

Query Posts lets you select posts to display in the sidebar with all the power of the `query_posts()` function (and none of the coding).

Section Widgets allows you to display the widget's contents selectively based on the page context.

Random Posts from Category is a widget that allows you to display posts from a selected category in your sidebar.

Dashboard Notepad creates a Dashboard widget where you can store and share notes.

Search Engine Optimization

Google XML Sitemaps generates XML sitemaps (plain and/or gzipped) according to the `sitemaps.org` specification.

All in One SEO Pack reverses the order of the page/post and site names in titles, sets canonical URLs, generates metatags, and more.

Importing Content

Import HTML Pages imports HTML files as posts or pages.

Drupal Import installs an old WP version, imports, then upgrades via PHP or SQL scripts, not plugins. There are three versions:

- 6.x to WP 2.7x: http://tinyurl.com/dru6wp2

- 5.x to WP 2.3x: http://tinyurl.com/dru5wp2

- CCK fields to Pods: http://tinyurl.com/cck2pods

Mambo/Joomla Import (tinyurl.com/joom2wp) is not a plugin, but does provide a web interface. It has been tested with M/J 1.0-1.5x and WP 2.7x.

CSV Importer imports posts from a comma-separated values file and can be used to import content from Excel.

Network Sites

Domain Mapping allows users to map their own domains to their network subdomains.

Multi-Site allows you to create multiple networks from one WordPress installation. Each new network can have its own site administrator and subsites.

■ ■ ■

Theme Functions

This sample theme functions file includes many of the tricks shown throughout this book. Save it as functions.php in your theme directory, or copy the features you need into your existing theme functions file.

```php
<?php
/*
Theme Functions
*/

// Removing the meta generator tag
// (Chapter 11, Performance and Security)
remove_action('wp_head', 'wp_generator');

// Changing excerpt length
// (Chapter 6, Basic Themes)
function change_excerpt_length($length) {
        return 100;
}
add_filter('excerpt_length', 'change_excerpt_length');

// Changing excerpt more
// (Chapter 6, Basic Themes)
function change_excerpt_more($more) {
        return '...';
}
add_filter('excerpt_more', 'change_excerpt_more');

// Add excerpts to pages
// (Chapter 12, Custom Content Types, Taxonomies, and Fields)
function add_page_excerpt_meta_box() {
        add_meta_box( 'postexcerpt', __('Excerpt'), 'post_excerpt_meta_box', 'page', 'normal',
'core' );
}
add_action( 'admin_menu', 'add_page_excerpt_meta_box' );

// Add support for menus
// (Chapter 6, Basic Themes)
add_theme_support( 'nav-menus' );

// Add support for thumbnails
```

```
// (Chapter 6, Basic Themes)
add_theme_support( 'post-thumbnails' );

// Add support for backgrounds
// (Chapter 6, Basic Themes)
add_custom_background();

// Defining two widgets
// (Chapter 6, Basic Themes)
function my_widgets_init() {
        register_sidebar( array(
                'name' => 'First Widget Area',
                'id' => 'first-widget-area',
                'description' => __( 'The first widget area'),
                'before_widget' => '<li id="%1$s" class="widget-container %2$s">',
                'after_widget' => "</li>",
                'before_title' => '<h3 class="widget-title">',
                'after_title' => '</h3>',
        ) );
        register_sidebar( array(
                'name' => 'Second Widget Area',
                'id' => 'second-widget',
                'description' => __( 'The second widget area'),
                'before_widget' => '<li id="%1$s" class="widget-container %2$s">',
                'after_widget' => "</li>",
                'before_title' => '<h3 class="widget-title">',
                'after_title' => '</h3>',
        ) );
}

// Add the widget areas
add_action( 'init', 'my_widgets_init' );

// Enable shortcodes in widgets
// (Chapter 6, Basic Themes)
add_filter('the_excerpt', 'shortcode_unautop');
add_filter('the_excerpt', 'do_shortcode');

// Add an editorial comment shortcode
// (Chapter 10, Users and Roles)
// Usage: [ed]this is a note only editors can read.[/ed]
function editorial_note($content = null) {
    if (current_user_can('edit_pages') && is_single())
        return '<span class="private">'.$content.'</span>';
    else return '';
}
add_shortcode( 'ed', 'editorial_note' );

// Allow subscribers to view private posts and pages
// (Chapter 10, Users and Roles)
$PrivateRole = get_role('subscriber');
$PrivateRole -> add_cap('read_private_pages');
```

```php
$PrivateRole -> add_cap('read_private_posts');

// Change user contact fields
// (Chapter 10, Users and Roles)
function change_contactmethod( $contactmethods ) {
        // Add some fields
        $contactmethods['twitter'] = 'Twitter Name (no @)';
        $contactmethods['phone'] = 'Phone Number';
        $contactmethods['title'] = 'Title';
        // Remove AIM, Yahoo IM, Google Talk/Jabber
        unset($contactmethods['aim']);
        unset($contactmethods['yim']);
        unset($contactmethods['jabber']);
        // Make it go!
        return $contactmethods;
}
add_filter('user_contactmethods','change_contactmethod',10,1);

?>
```

■ ■ ■

Plugin Recipes

Unless you're creating a simple blog, the key to creating a robust WordPress site is choosing the right combination of plugins to accomplish your goals. Here are a few recipes for turning a WordPress installation into something more.

Wiki

The combination of Sidebar Login, Front End Editor, and Posthaste will allow users to register, edit, and create new posts without ever seeing the WordPress administration screens. In order to let new users publish posts and edit posts written by others, you'll need to either choose Editor as the default role for newly registered users, or choose Author or Contributor and use the Members plugin to adjust the role's editing capabilities. Revision History appends a list of the post revisions to the_content() in your theme. My Favorite Posts adds a watch list feature. Hackadelic SEO Table Of Contents generates the familiar wiki-style table of contents based on the post or page headings. For easier internal linking, try Simple Internal Links or RB Internal Links.

The built-in comments feature can serve as the Talk function. With a little help from the jQuery Tabs library (built in), you can show the content, history, and comments in separate areas, as shown in Figure C-1.

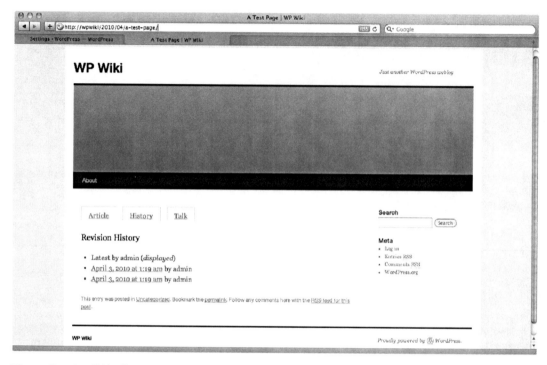

Figure C-1. A wiki built in WordPress

Document Sharing

For a committee or a club, finding a good way to share news and documents is always tricky. The Members Only plugin is ideal if your content should be visible only to registered users. Again, Sidebar Login is useful for letting people log in without dealing with the somewhat intimidating Dashboard. The List Child Attachments plugin (`code.google.com/p/list-child-attachments/`) will list any files uploaded to a post or page, without the user having to insert each one into the content individually. In other words, it works like a gallery, but for files other than images.

The Event Calendar or GigPress will be useful if your group needs to keep track of events. To let the group stay in touch by e-mail, Subscribe 2 and Subscribe to Comments will notify all users of new posts and new comments.

If your group needs to review documents, the Comment Author Checklist plugin prints a list of registered users and crosses people's names off the list once they've commented on a post. The Digress.it plugin (`digress.it/`) allows paragraph-level commenting, suitable for academic-style peer review.

Project Management

The CollabPress plugin builds basic project management, such as task assignments and due dates, into the dashboard screens (see Figure C-2). The plugin includes e-mail notifications for newly assigned tasks, and it places a widget on the Dashboard displaying recent activity.

Figure C-2. Creating a task in the CollabPress plugin

Newsroom

In addition to the Editorial Calendar and Edit Flow plugins described in Chapter 10, your newsroom will probably want to keep a close eye on your visitor statistics. In addition to Google Analyticator and the WordPress.com Stats plugins, use Google's free Feedburner service with the FeedSmith plugin to closely track your RSS readers. The service also provides an e-mail digest of your RSS feed, which might help if you need to reach people who aren't familiar with RSS. You might also try Revisionary, which lets authors submit changes to published posts for editorial review before the updates are published.

Twitter Archive

As described by Doug Bowman (`stopdesign.com/archive/2010/03/02/browsable-searchable-archive-of-tweets.html`), it's possible to use WordPress to create a long-term archive of your Twitter account. The TwitterTools plugin has an option to create a new post from each of your tweets. If you're new to Twitter, just set up the plugin and let it run. If you have an existing Twitter account with a long history, you'll need to import your old tweets into WordPress somehow. Bowman recommends the service from `tweetbackup.com`. Another service, TweetScan, lets you export a CSV file, which you could then import using the CSV Import plugin.

News Clipping Archive

Much like the Twitter archive, a news clipping archive in WordPress provides you with a searchable database of content that would otherwise be walled off in third-party sites. First, you'll have to create some news alert feeds using services like Google Alerts or Google Blog Search. You can then create the archive automatically from those feeds using FeedWordPress. However, if you find that the feeds return lots of false positives, you might want to curate your archive by hand instead. The PressThis bookmarklet, which you'll find on your Writing Settings screen, makes it easy to create new posts from stories you see on the web.

For better search results, be sure to include a brief excerpt of each article in addition to the title. Don't copy the entire thing, though, if the article is under copyright (which it almost certainly is).

If you're creating the archive for your business or organization, include the calendar widget in your sidebar. You'll probably have a few avid users who keep up with the archive daily. They'll appreciate being able to easily navigate the recent history when they miss a few days due to a trip or an illness.

Index

▨ D

■ I

i18n Function Block, 269
Identicons, 53
if_page function, 153
if_single function, 153
if_user_can function, 248
IIS, 15, 57
IIS web servers, 1
image.php, 149
images
    specifying a background image in a
        stylesheet, 132
    uploading a background image and setting its
        display options, 130
    using custom header and background
        images, 130
    wp_head function, 132
    See also media files
import tools
    Bulk Edit, 113
    changing internal links and media file paths,
        120
    creating a new user for the imported posts,
        108
    de Valk, Joost, 116
    downloading old versions of WordPress from
        the Release Archive, 116
    Edit Posts screen, 113
    exporting a blog before importing it, 107
    fixing errors in newly imported content, 120
    garbled or truncated text problems, 122
    handling database character set problems,
        122
    HTML Import plugin, 117
    Import panel, 105
    importing a blogroll from an OPML file, 106
    importing content from a WordPress.com
        blog, 107
    importing content from Drupal sites, 116
    importing content from other MySQL-based
        sites, 116
    importing HTML files, procedure for, 117
    importing Joomla or Mambo sites, procedure
        for, 113
    importing old media files, 108
    importing posts and comments from Blogger,
        110
    importing posts from an RSS feed, 106
    Khan, Azeem, 113
    list of available importers, 105
    making all site links root-relative, 121
    mapping authors to users in a new site, 108
    Norman, D'Arcy, 117
    precautions before importing content, 105
    running SQL queries through PHPMyAdmin,
        117
    Save Changes button, 113
    saving the XML file that contains your posts,
        107
    Screen Options, 113
    Set Authors button, 112
    Social Media Buzz website, 117
    tools for importing or converting categories
        and tags, 106
    updating the paths to linked files, 121
    uploading an XML (WXR) file for import, 107
    viewing all your imported posts, 113
    wp-config.php, 122
in* function, 152
in_category function, 154
in_the_loop conditional tag, 186
Incoming Links widget, 43
index.php, 3, 141
Install Themes tab, 26
insufficient caching, 289
internationalization, 266
is* function, 152
is_singular conditional tag, 249
is_tax function, 317

■ J

JavaScript
    adding scripts, 190
    adding scripts conditionally, 191
    adding sortable.js if the content contains a
        table, code listing, 191
    adding stylesheets other than style.css, 192
    adding the built-in jQuery and UI core
        libraries to a theme, 190
    enqueueing a script in the header, 191
    header.php, 190
    Prototype, 189
    <script> tag, 189
    Scriptaculous, 189
    <style> tag, 189
    SWFUpload, 189
    Thickbox, 189

Breinigsville, PA USA
23 September 2010

245880BV00005B/3/P